# IMAGINARY PEAKS

1
2
3
4

# IMAGINARY PEAKS

## THE RIESENSTEIN HOAX AND OTHER MOUNTAIN DREAMS

Keep dreaming!

KATIE IVES

MOUNTAINEERS BOOKS

**MOUNTAINEERS BOOKS** is dedicated to the exploration, preservation, and enjoyment of outdoor and wilderness areas.

1001 SW Klickitat Way, Suite 201, Seattle, WA 98134
800-553-4453, www.mountaineersbooks.org



Printed in Canada
Distributed in the United Kingdom by Cordee, www.cordee.co.uk

24 23 22 21 1 2 3 4 5

Copyeditor: Laura Lancaster
Design and layout: Jen Grable
Cover photograph: The "No Name Peak" map first appeared in *Summit* magazine, May 1960.
Frontispiece: Recreation of original "Riesenstein" route overlay by Jen Grable. Underlying Austin Post photo © Geophysical Institute, University of Alaska Fairbanks.

Library of Congress Cataloging-in-Publication data is on file for this title at https://lccn.loc.gov/2021018191 (print) and https://lccn.loc.gov/2021018192 (ebook).



Printed on 100% recycled and FSC-certified materials

ISBN (hardcover): 978-1-68051-541-1
ISBN (paperback): 978-1-59485-980-9
ISBN (ebook): 978-1-59485-981-6

FSC www.fsc.org MIX Paper from responsible sources FSC® C016245

*An independent nonprofit publisher since 1960*

FOR MY GRANDFATHER

ROBERT JAMES CALDWELL (1913–2015)

WHO HOPED THAT I WOULD ONE DAY WRITE A BOOK

# CONTENTS

# AUTHOR'S NOTE

"TO A LARGE EXTENT," AMERICAN geographer Roderick Peattie wrote in 1936, "a mountain is a mountain because of the part it plays in the popular imagination." While the term *imaginary* is part of the title of my book, its common definition doesn't capture the nuances of all the ways that mountains intersect with human minds. In addition to referring to nonexistent places, I've used the word more loosely, at times, to suggest layers of dreams that drape like second summits over actual formations of ice, stone, snow, and earth. In some cases, peaks considered to be fables by one group of people may be realities within other cultures, and I am not denying their existence.

Mountains reflect shifting cartographies of myth and meaning in regions and societies around the world. The more I researched, the more I realized how legends cling to the smallest knolls, and how invisible topographies of mirages, dreams, stories, and erasures underlie nearly every square of every map—their prominences arising even in areas where only lowlands are clearly visible. To tell a complete history of quests for imaginary, sacred, or mythic peaks—or of cartographic errors and exploration hoaxes—would be to retell the history of all geography and all humanity. Thus, to keep this book from swelling to dozens of volumes, while I've included some discussions of other traditions for comparison or contrast, I've focused on recounting a fraction of the stories that most likely influenced, consciously or unconsciously, the participants in the Riesenstein Hoax of 1962. In most instances, I selected examples of alpine legends because references to them appeared in my protagonists' recollections or because these tales had a direct or an indirect relevance to places and ideas that played a significant role in the history of this hoax.

This book does not, therefore, claim to be a thorough examination of the countless myths surrounding all real or unreal mountains. For more comprehensive accounts of legendary summits worldwide, there are many great sources, some of which can be found in my bibliography. For a broader introduction to the history of speculative cartography, I suggest readers turn to Edward Brooke-Hitching's *The Phantom Atlas: The Greatest Myths, Lies and Blunders on Maps*. For a detailed discussion of the evolution of hoaxes in the United States, I also recommend Kevin Young's brilliant account *Bunk: The Rise of Hoaxes, Humbug, Plagiarists, Phonies, Post-Facts, and Fake News*. And Ed Douglas's 2020 book, *Himalaya: A Human History* goes far more in depth into the origins and impacts of the story of Shangri-La than I have space to in this narrative.

Similarly, while I've included a few scenes from the past adventures of the protagonists as background for their involvement in the history—particularly Harvey Manning—I concentrated on experiences that related most clearly to the Riesenstein and other imaginary mountains. The full complexity of Manning's career as a writer and environmentalist, and his impact on the Northwest conservation movement, would make a worthy subject for another book by another author. So, too, would the lives of other figures who have only cameo appearances here.

By 2011, when I began studying the Riesenstein Hoax, several of the main people involved in the incident had died. I pieced together their experiences as best I could—based on interviews with their colleagues, family, and friends, as well as on their articles, books, letters, and other writings. There may be crucial scraps of paper tucked away in boxes that I missed or manuscripts lying in attics, file cabinets, or storage closets not yet found. Answers to lingering mysteries may await a future researcher.

Other participants were still living at the time of my work, and they devoted hours to sharing their stories with me. Some of these people—including Fred Beckey, Jean Crenshaw, Dee Molenaar, Helen Kilness, Austin Post, and George Whitmore—passed away before I finished the book. I am grateful to them for their assistance, and in their absence, I've tried to preserve their perspectives according to my notes, interview transcripts, personal memories, and archival research. Any errors in fact or interpretation are, of course, my own.

This book became, in many ways, a quarantine project. Portions of it had previously appeared in related articles that I'd written for *Alpinist* since 2011. I completed much of the final research and writing during an extended leave of absence from my job in 2020, while sheltering in place. As a result, I was unable to travel to some of the areas I'd hoped to see firsthand, and I depended on the generosity of librarians and colleagues to scan lengthy documents from archives that I couldn't visit in person. I also relied on climbers and their families who sent copies of copious letters, journals, and manuscripts and who agreed to long interviews by phone (see the acknowledgments at the end of the book). Prior to the global pandemic, in late summer 2019, I managed to retrace several of Harvey Manning's wanderings in the Olympic Mountains and the Cascade Range and to read through many of his manuscripts preserved in the Special Collections of the University of Washington Libraries and in The Mountaineers Archive. I attempted to follow his cadence of thought along marked and unmarked paths, through the dim green light of Northwest forests, across wildflower meadows and rocky summits, and over hundreds of typewritten and handwritten pages. I hope that a few echoes of his footfalls may be found in the pages of this book.

The North American scenes take place on traditional lands of Indigenous people, including, but not limited to, Massachusett, Abenaki, Natick, Ts'msyen, Núu-agha-tʉvʉ-pʉ̱, Lillooet, Diné, Mandan, Ĩyãȟé Nakoda, Blackfoot Confederacy, Tsuut'ina, Beaver, Cree, Ojibway, Secwépemc, Métis, Zuni, Nimiipuu, Stó:lō, Puyallup, Quinault, Skokomish, Duwamish, Suquamish, Nisqually, Snoqualmie, Chehalis, Cowlitz, Muckleshoot, S'Klallam, Snohomish, Stillaguamish, Upper Skagit, Sauk-Suiattle, Swinomish, Samish, Nooksack, Lummi, Nlaka'pamux, the Confederated Tribes of the Colville Reservation, Syilx Okanagan, Dena'ina, Upper Kuskokwim, Koyukon, Tanacross, Lower Tanana, Upper Tanana, Deg Hit'an, Alutiiq, Gwich'in, Iñupiat, Ahtna, and Inuit groups. Their stewardship and stories of mountains long predate any ascents, real or imagined, by nineteenth-, twentieth-, and twenty-first–century climbers featured here.

# A QUEST FOR THE RIESENSTEIN

IN JUNE 1962, READERS OF *Summit* magazine opened its pages to an intriguing photo of a seemingly unknown range. The mountains in the black-and-white image were unlike any that most American climbers had ever seen before. Sheer rock cliffs rose to intricate ridges and spires, stacked one above the other, thousands of feet high, like the ramparts of an extraterrestrial city.

White light poured through roiling clouds, flashing off patches of ice and snow and burnishing the rock to silver. Cracks splintered up flying buttresses of stone, hinting, to a climber's eye, of pathways to crenellated skylines. Glimpses of hanging glaciers and dark shadows suggested a landscape that was cold, remote, and stormy—a stark contrast to the sun-drenched Yosemite Valley where Californian climbers had begun to confront steep, giant walls only a few years before. Yet this unfamiliar range, with its aura of old, forgotten dreams, seemed just at the edge of the possible.

Despite the surreal appearance of the mountains, the photo caption located them in an accessible, though isolated, place: "The unclimbed summit of 'Rienenstein [*sic*],' approximately 8,100 feet, near Prince Rupert in British Columbia. It can be reached in two days by bushwhacking up the Klawatti River. Who will be the first to climb it?"

The picture was accompanied by an unattributed article about three intrepid Austrians—Machler, Bisserlich, and Kronofer—who thrashed through ancient forests as they followed the Nass River to its confluence with the Klawatti and then pressed on, ever deeper, into an unmapped wild. Atop a high col, the three men gazed at a vast glacier that flowed toward the Skeena River. Overhead, the fortress walls of the unfamiliar peaks must have blocked out the sky.

The narrator summarized their subsequent adventures in a short note. But the photo had already stirred readers' imaginations, and mountaineers were easily tempted to fill in gaps in the terse prose with their own daydreams. For their first climb (marked as route "4" on the photo), the Austrians scampered to the top of the nearest low peak, its small turrets half-hidden by the larger spires. From this summit, they would have stared, mesmerized and bewildered, at the views. Countless potential routes must have unfolded around them, a dense maze guarded by mysterious citadels of rock, ice, and snow.

Their next objective (route "3") was more ambitious: an attempt on what appeared to be the apex of the range. They crept into the shade of an immense, dark wall below an ice-capped tower. A hanging glacier loomed high above. Avalanches burst from its edges and exploded down the cliff. Afraid to venture farther, the Austrians turned back.

In search of a safer option, the trio teetered up a broken ridgeline toward the top of another dome (route "1"). Twice, they found the terrain too difficult to ascend with just their hands and feet, so they tugged on gear they'd jammed into fissures in the rock. At last, they attained the threshold where the white of the summit snows blurred into the white of the clouded sky.

Back down on the glacier, the emboldened group plotted another attempt on the crest of the tallest peak (route "2"). As the Austrians traversed a swath of pleated stone, clouds enveloped them. They huddled on a rocky perch for what was probably a miserable night of wind and snow, before deciding to retreat.

The blizzard must have lasted a long while, since the story picked up a month later when the Austrians crossed the avalanche hazard zone again to try to climb the ice-capped tower (route "3"). More clouds blew in as they reached a glistening rock face. About 150 to 200 feet high, this cliff seemed to be the last serious obstacle between the three men and the apex of the range. Bisserlich attempted to clamber over it, only to fall and rip out two of the pitons he'd pounded into a crack. Caught by the rope, he suffered only minor injuries. Discouraged, the climbers headed down for the final time while the sky darkened with storm.

It was the end of the expedition. The Austrians had ascended two of the smaller peaks, but failed to summit the highest, most coveted one. Nonetheless, they believed that someone could get up that last wall by drilling bolts into the rock. Traced across the photo, a series of white dotted lines, with wide spaces between them, showed that the Austrians' ascents and attempts had covered only a fragment of the possible pathways up this vertical labyrinth.

On another page, a sketched map included hatch marks that suggested the sharp summits, striped blobs that designated four unnamed glaciers, and arrows that indicated the Klawatti and Skeena Rivers. The words "Unexplored Area" were scrawled across the top left corner of the page. During a century when airplanes flew around the globe, these mysterious spires had somehow remained unnoticed—a blank on modern maps.

Savvy readers soon discerned that the strange name, "Riensenstein," must be a misspelling of *Riesenstein*, the German word for "giant stone," as it appeared, written out correctly, on the map. But where were these marvelous colossal rock walls?

Fred Beckey was among the many climbers who studied the *Summit* article carefully. An avid collector of first ascents, he seemed to have traveled—or so his fans supposed—to every group of peaks in North America. His name almost invariably turned up in stories of new climbs in the wildest places. Though he meticulously researched his own accounts of mountaineering history, Beckey himself was becoming half-myth in the minds of his fans: a larger-than-life figure said to roam North America on an endless road trip, speeding down highways and dirt roads in a pink Thunderbird and sending up clouds of dust. He allegedly carried a notorious "black book" with to-do lists of secret peaks. Several of his friends denied the book existed, but for those who believed, it was an encyclopedia of hidden, desirable places.

If there ever was a black book, however, the Riesenstein wasn't in it. As Beckey examined the *Summit* photo, he started to suspect something fishy. He didn't recall anything quite like it from his own trips to British Columbia. Such unusual peaks, he determined, were more likely to be found in less explored, icy regions of Alaska. For the moment, though, he put his curiosity aside. He was already busy plotting trips to legions of mountains.

Other readers of *Summit*, entranced by the Riesenstein, pored over Canadian maps in an effort to locate the range. Eventually, they all realized that no such peaks existed in British Columbia. Although the Nass and Skeena Rivers flowed through the province, "Klawatti" was the name of a glacier in northern Washington State—not a river. And "Riesenstein" was a cluster of boulders near the castle towers of Heidelberg, Germany. The entire article was a hoax!

In the 1966 issue of the *American Alpine Journal*, New York climbers Al DeMaria and Pete Geiser recalled: "Obviously, *Summit* had fallen victim to someone's sense of humor. Yet there were the pictures; palpable mountains—they must have some existence. But where? Chamonix? Africa? Asia? The moon? . . . The 'Riesenstein' appeared doomed to join the ranks of other mythical and fabulous regions like Shangri-La and the Seven Cities of Cíbola."

Today, we know who was behind the fake article. The word "Klawatti" was a sly clue—a piece of misplaced geography that hinted at the creators of the puzzle. The hoaxers were, in fact, mountaineers who lived in Washington. Austin Post, a photographer and glaciologist, had taken the original photo of the Riesenstein. A second glaciologist, Ed LaChapelle, well known for his avalanche research, had contributed to the plot. A brilliant and eccentric conservationist, Harvey Manning, the author of popular Northwest guidebooks and editor of the classic mountaineering textbook *Mountaineering: The Freedom of the Hills*, was the likely mastermind of the conspiracy. Harvey had a predilection—then known only to his friends—for coming up with elaborate pranks to fool other climbers.

For some mountaineers, who were determined to locate and climb the real mountains in the *Summit* photo, the hoax was the start of a cartographic treasure hunt. A few years later, two separate groups of American climbers had solved the mystery. Close studies of mountain photos and maps revealed that the true location of the Riesenstein peaks lay within a group of rock towers, called the Cathedral or Kichatna Spires, about seventy miles southwest of Denali in the Alaska Range. In 1965, one of these teams—made up of Al DeMaria, Pete Geiser, Claude Suhl, John Hudson, George Bloom, and Aaron Schneider—launched the first known climbing expedition to the area. As they reached the tops of three peaks there, the myth of the imaginary Riesenstein seemed, for a moment, to dissolve and the real mountaineering history of the Kichatnas to begin.

---

IN 2011, WHEN I FIRST READ ABOUT THE RIESENSTEIN HOAX IN ANDY Selters's history of North American climbing, *Ways to the Sky*, I was already mesmerized by imaginary spires. I'd grown up in Lincoln, Massachusetts, on the edge of a forest that stretched for miles through the cool shade of hemlock groves and the leaf-filtered light of maples and oaks, along the white crescent of sand that lined Flint's Pond. As a small child, I stared through my upstairs bedroom window, watching the treetops sway like cutout silhouettes of ancient ships sailing across the purpled evening sky. With a gust of wind, the masts of branches dipped low, revealing the darkness behind them. There was always that sense of mystery just beyond the old stone wall that bordered our lawn, a premonition of something unknown, hidden within the twilight and the leaves.

Back then, in the late 1980s, it was still common for children to slip like half-feral cats out the screen door whenever possible, reappearing only at mealtimes. By age nine, once I'd proven that I could walk to Flint's Pond and back without asking a grown-up for directions, my mother allowed me to roam the forest at will, alone or with my five-year-old sister in tow. We relied on an intuited sense of direction and on the arc of the sun and the moon to find our way. Quickly, we learned each twist of the worn paths within a few hours' walk, and we abandoned the trails for the spaces between them, jumping from tuffet to tuffet to cross swamps, untangling thorn bushes to venture along the pond's less visited shores. Often, we explored well into dusk, when the fringes of the wetlands faded into the sky and the shadows of trees spread far across the land, consuming streetlamps, highways, and houses.

All too soon, we'd visited nearly every corner of the forest. With each step, the mystery receded, leaving only the sunlight fading across dry oak leaves, the hollows behind low hills, the boundaries of roads reached too soon. I longed for something else, something *beyond*. I imagined it as a place that I had to find before I died—a lost, shining country on the other side of the mists that hid the far edges of the woods and fields. I had little idea of what existed there, but I was certain there would be mountains.

I'd been nine years old, on a family trip to the Cascade Range in Washington, when I first saw a patch of snow gleam across a summer hillside. In a realm where the regular course of seasons could unravel, anything appeared possible. The Paradise region seemed to match its name: the fairy-tale blues of harebells, the incandescent purples of lupine, and the pale dome of a giant mountain. While my father joined a guided climb of Mount Rainier, my mother, my sister, and I hiked on our own to get a closer look at Unicorn Peak, a destination I'd picked. Although I didn't glimpse any magical creatures near the base, the horn-like spire of the distant summit and the sparkling turquoise hues of a glacial stream promised all kinds of enchantment. My father returned from his ascent of Rainier with stories about an even more unearthly world of deep crevasses and thin air.

I felt keenly the lack of high places in my New England backyard. And so, perhaps, my unconscious mind conjured a giant peak into being, its invisible contours rising out of the swells of drumlins and other traces of vanished, ice age glaciers in the forest behind our house. In a recurring dream, I wandered deep into ever-expanding woods until the hillsides sharpened and I stood on the spine of a narrow ridge crest that arched into snow, seracs, and clouds.

That imaginary summit haunted me long after I left Massachusetts to climb real peaks and to become a mountaineering journalist. For decades, while I worked at a climbing magazine, *Alpinist*, I spent my waking hours immersed in visions of mountains: photos of icy golden spires in Patagonia, stories of maze-like hanging glaciers in the Karakoram, weekend ventures along the silvered gneiss ridges and suncupped snowfields of the Teton Range, winter rambles up narrow gullies of glasslike ice and frozen turf in the Appalachians. None of these summits appeared as vivid as the one I saw in my dreams. Night after night in my sleep, I explored its limitless topography, at times returning to familiar-looking landmarks. A golden sandstone wall glowed in a chasm between two hills. Pinnacles of gnarled granite twisted above alpine tundra and evergreen forests. A white tower emerged from a glacier streaked with black rocks and mirror pools. The azure of endless, unreachably distant ranges spread before me like the pages of an atlas drawn to the scale of another planet.

I could relate to the sense of yearning that led people to seek the Riesenstein. But as I searched for more information about the hoax, I found, to my surprise, that the story seemed largely forgotten outside of the Pacific Northwest. For the most part, its memory lingered as a curious anecdote in scattered paragraphs of old alpine journals and climbing history books, and in the occasional recollections of aging mountaineers. Of the original three hoaxers, all except Austin Post had died. When I reached out to him in August 2011, he wrote back that he was pleased to hear the Riesenstein Hoax was "still alive and well." His own health was fading, though, and he sent only brief responses to my inquiries for an article in *Alpinist*. A year after I'd published my initial summary of the hoax, I had many more questions, but Austin had died.

I couldn't help feeling that the riddle of the Riesenstein hadn't been fully solved, that there were more pieces of its story left to unfold. I was captivated by the fairy-tale aspect of the quest—the chance to climb the spires had to be earned. A similar mystery couldn't last that long anymore, I thought. Each year, as Andy Selters pointed out to me, photos of once-obscure peaks are mass-reproduced in catalogues and media. And yet, I knew that our perceptions of what we call *the known* are partly composed of projected fantasies. Blanks remain in the peripheries of most route lines that climbers sketch, as if their ascents took place in a historical and topographic void. Only a fraction of the multiple human visions of a place ever get recorded. Many guidebooks perpetuate an imperial legacy by erasing Indigenous histories, by imposing new names and claims to ownership, and by depicting features primarily chosen to facilitate the colonialization of vertical terrain. There are other ways to conceive of cartography, I believed, ones that are more qualitative, creative, and fluid, ones that convey different dreams, voices, and values. In an age when the internet is flooded with information on how to get from point A to point B, we could use a few more maps for wandering, formed of hints and riddles, of stories and images, that expand rather than shrink our vision of the wild.

And thus, I too joined the quest for the imaginary peaks of Riesenstein, belatedly, decades after the real summits had been found and climbed. The Riesenstein, I soon realized, was only one range among countless nonexistent mountains that have appeared for centuries: ghosts of legendary peaks eliminated from modern maps, implausibly high summits that turned out to be much lower than cartographers once believed, invisible outlines of sacred towers that transcend any ordinary notions of geography, and the ideal spire that persists in many climbers' minds, the one that glows ever farther in the distance, reflecting a vague longing that no attained summit ever fulfills.

In *The Phantom Atlas*, British author Edward Brooke-Hitching mused on how such an immense number of mythic landscapes came to be. There were phantom landforms left over from the early days of classical and medieval cartography, when dragons stalked the edges of sea charts and mapmakers drew outlines of unseen countries to match religious beliefs and philosophical speculations. There were second- or third-hand travelers' tales transcribed into rippling shorelines and towering ranges. There were icy coastal peaks glimpsed from ships that proved to be mirages. There were real places mapped in wildly incorrect locations because of imprecise navigational tools. There were mistakes or fantasies marked on one map and then copied onto others for generations. There were mapmakers, enraged by such plagiarism, who created intentionally false places—sometimes known as "trap streets"—so they could identify people who replicated their work. There were explorers and artists who invented landmarks to name after wealthy patrons or beloved spouses. There were seventeenth- and eighteenth-century writers who fabricated opulent utopias, not always clearly marked as fiction. There were mountainous islands that actually existed, only to vanish as a result of volcanic eruptions. And there were hoaxers who reported discoveries of fanciful realms to win glory for themselves, to hoodwink would-be settlers and investors, or to satisfy enigmatic longings of their own.

The Riesenstein's purported existence in British Columbia—and the Kichatna Spires' real presence in Alaska—formed part of a larger history of imaginary mountains that once extended all across North America. During the late nineteenth century, Thomas Wentworth Higginson (best known as an editor of Emily Dickinson's poetry) collected stories of cartographic errors and fables. In *Tales of the Enchanted Islands of the Atlantic*, he criticized other American historians for their neglect of mythological landscapes. These legends were an inherent part of exploration history, he claimed: "Every visitor had to cross the sea to reach [America], and the sea has always been, by the mystery of its horizon, the fury of its storms, and the variableness of the atmosphere above it, the foreordained land of romance."

Like Higginson, I think such tales deserve more attention. Dreams of fantastical riches and earthly paradises lured European seekers first to the shores of North and South America and then far into the interior—often contributing to the dispossession of the continents' original residents. While stories of claimed discoveries of real places dominate Western history books, many of these tales contain their own pernicious falsehood: the notion that such long-inhabited lands were ever *terra incognita*. This beguiling, yet dangerous, phrase for "unknown land" hints at empty spaces, pale and luminous as ice, where anything might be imagined or drawn. *Terra miscognita*, as Pacific Northwest historian Coll Thrush suggests, would be a far more accurate term in most cases, evoking the failures of explorers to acknowledge the realities of the traces, paths, and homes of local residents. Conversely, accounts of mythic landscapes in all cultures can suggest deeper truths: reflections of communal and individual desires, and vast geographies of human minds. The creation of imaginary mountains can also be a means of resistance, a way to mock the follies and hubris of climbers who envision themselves as conquerors of nature. Through these settings, modern cartographers can envision alternative ways to approach nature and reclaim dreams concealed by colonialist maps. By exploring how fantasies have shaped and misshaped human visions of geography, we might see the world more honestly as it was, as it is, and as it could become.

One of the Riesenstein hoaxers, Harvey Manning, looked to spiders as a model of exploration because, he explained, "they would not be seeking to capture the world in color slides but to web its pieces together in unity." The more I researched the origins and impacts of the Riesenstein, the more I became interested in what the people who were drawn, knowingly or unknowingly, into the hoax had in common. During and after their adventures, each of their lives seemed to replicate similar patterns, recalling ancient, interlacing fantasies, at times scarcely visible, like beads of dew lit by sunlight and quivering on a spider's web.

---

IN *THE MYTH OF SHANGRI-LA*, GEOGRAPHER PETER BISHOP DESCRIBES fictitious peaks as part of "an archaeology of imaginative landscapes." To start to understand them, you first have to find your way inside. "Sometimes their presence is revealed only by a single clue, such as a word or a phrase," he observed, "but these details are doorways." Of the three men behind the Riesenstein Hoax, Harvey Manning had left the largest number of manuscripts on both actual and nonexistent ranges—enough to fill more than 125 boxes in the archives of the University of Washington Libraries Special Collections. And as I read through stacks of Harvey's published and unpublished stories, among hundreds of place names, one real location seemed particularly promising as an entry into his imaginary worlds: Marmot Pass.

During a Boy Scout trip to the Olympic Mountains of Washington, at age twelve or thirteen, Harvey hiked alone up meadows that glimmered ever higher until they vanished into a rose-hued sky. Soon, he'd reached a state beyond exhaustion. He felt as if he were floating to the top of the col. A sign read MARMOT PASS, 6,000 FEET. Before him, the earth dropped into darkness. Silhouettes of coal-black mountains smoldered against the last flare of light. Memories of daydreams from adventure books rose in his mind: the tangled rainforests of the Amazon, rumpled ice sheets of the North Pole, hints of lost realms beyond distant ranges. But this vision was something more. The reflections of the sunset seemed to pierce his bare skin to his soul.

Years later, as an adult, Harvey tried again and again to put this experience into words. In one attempt, he wrote: "Suddenly it came to me that out there in those black peaks under the purple and red and orange and yellow sky, there were no roads at all. . . . There was no sound except the river, way down below in the night. There was no wind, everything was as still as in a painting, and me too. The flowers and rocks and grass had the colors of the sky. Night was coming up from the valley. I felt like somebody not me, some character in a fairy tale, under some kind of spell."

Harvey wasn't the first to fall under that spell. It was composed of fantasies that existed for centuries. Their afterimages still hover across twilit mountains: strange forms that glow and shift like the slides of a magic lantern. I'd experienced something similar at age twelve, during a summer camp trip in the Rocky Mountains of Colorado. Like Harvey, I'd wandered off by myself across a deep meadow. In the sunset, the tall grass turned into translucent threads of spun gold. Alpenglow shone pink along a skyline of distant peaks. Shadows of ponderosa groves enfolded me. All at once, I thought I knew the purpose of my life. I wanted to remain in that state of awe and wonder always, though I had no idea how to do so, or what that moment actually meant.

Marmot Pass was only one of many "clues" to the archaeology of Harvey's fictitious ranges. He'd read voraciously since childhood, and he planted clever literary allusions throughout his stories. Turning through the pages of his manuscripts, I felt as if I were unfolding sections of a treasure map. References to well-known mythic regions emerged like survey towers, points of orientation for re-creating charts of imaginary worlds: Shangri-La, the Mountains of the Moon, Xanadu. Some names were for places that Harvey had invented, such as No Name Peak, Mount Hornblower, Peak X, and Crazy Creek Crags. Many others recalled real areas befogged by histories of cartographic errors, exploration hoaxes, or dubious folklore.

There were additional geographies to consider as well, ones that persisted in the collective memories of would-be Riesenstein climbers, long-held fantasies that made them vulnerable to the allure of a fake range, such as the Seven Cities of Cíbola or Tolkien's Middle-earth. And there were even older tales of the Earthly Paradise, of Meru and of other sacred peaks lodged within the conscious and unconscious longings of many mountaineers. To understand the legacy of the Riesenstein, I realized, would require another kind of imaginary journey, through layers of snowdrifts and myths, from the distant past to the future. I'd need to go far into infinite countries of dreams that belonged not just to one man in the Pacific Northwest, but to numerous people around the world.

# PART I

# ARCHAEOLOGIES OF IMAGINARY PEAKS

It lingers yet in imagination and fragment of dream, the abode where mountains finally reach their greatest height. What is this inner need we humans have for the mountain seen from within? In cultures around the world, there are tales of mythical mountains assuming far more grandeur than any found on map or chart. . . . Yet [the] coordinates are those of the spirit alone, plotted by a cartography Ptolemy never knew.

—Belden C. Lane, *Landscapes of the Sacred*

CHAPTER 1

# *On* the Earth, but Not *of* the Earth

IT MIGHT SEEM ASTONISHING TO modern readers that a group of climbers could pass off a fake range as a real one as late as the 1960s. From their own reading of mountain literature, however, the Riesenstein hoaxers would have known just how easy it would be. The history of exploration has long been—and still is—formed partly by myths, errors, and fabrications. Illusory places continue to be un-discovered even during our present millennium. In 2012, scientists aboard the Australian ship RV *Southern Surveyor* sailed into a remote part of the South Pacific northwest of New Caledonia. When they noticed that several authoritative sources, including Google Earth, indicated a landform ahead of them, they were surprised. Their hydrographic charts and depth soundings showed nothing there. Gliding past this purported "Sandy Island" at night, geoscientist Maria Seton saw only the darkness of an empty sea and the brilliance of undimmed stars. Various forms of this phantom island had existed on maps for centuries. In 1774, Captain James Cook sketched it as a long, delicate squiggle. In 1876, the crew of the whaling ship *Velocity* moved it farther east, depicting it as "a line of sandy islets . . . along the meridian 159°57' E., between lat. 19°7' S., and 19°20' S." Nautical charts stopped including Sandy Island after the French Naval Hydrographic and Oceanographic Service reported no sign of it during a 1979 aerial reconnaissance. But the landform reemerged on digital maps, which derived some of their information from older cartographies. It took the 2012 report of *Southern Surveyor* to remove it once and for all.

In our Information Age, many of us have grown accustomed to illusions of technological omniscience. It's easy to forget that mapmaking is still an act of metaphor, turning complex, multidimensional places into flattened, simplified, and conventional symbols. As cartographic historian J. B. Harley wrote in *The New Nature of Maps*, "far from holding up a simple mirror of nature . . . maps redescribe the world . . . in terms of relations of power and of cultural practices, preferences and priorities. What we read on a map is as much related to an invisible social world and to ideology as it is to phenomena seen and measured in the landscape." From its earliest days, human depictions of geography have developed along a shifting threshold between the physical and the speculative, reflecting the influence of legends, approximations, and subjective choices.

Maps of imaginary peaks existed for millennia around the boundaries of cartographers' familiar worlds. A Babylonian clay tablet, more than 2,600 years old, hints at voyages, undertaken or dreamed, through real and mythic alpine regions. Known areas of Babylon, Susa, Bit Yakin, Habban, Urartu, Der, and Assyria appear within a ring that indicates the ocean. An unnamed summit lies at the top. Beyond it, triangles symbolize unknown outer lands, such as one region where "the Sun is hidden and nothing can be seen" or another one "beyond the flight of birds."

*The Guideways Through Mountains and Seas*—compiled by Chinese writers mainly between the fourth century BC and the first century AD—is one of the first comprehensive guidebooks to fantastical ranges, listing hundreds of peaks with magical flora and fauna. Among them, Shaking Mountain, speckled with cinnamon and jade, contains the confusion-mulberry, a glowing, black-veined plant that heals mental confusion in anyone who wears a piece of it. Mount Winding-Center is home to a unicorn-like creature with a black tail and sharp claws who rips apart tigers and leopards for food. The ear-rat roams through the ruddy haze of the Cinnabar-Smoke Mountain. Shaped like a rat, with the head of a rabbit and the body of a deer, it howls like a dog and uses its tail like a wing. This beast also provides immunity against poison.

Similar chimerical ranges jutted above distant oceans in the dreams of ancient Greeks. To the far North, the colossal summit of Saevo sparkled in the light of a never-setting sun, past islands where people had hooves for feet or ears that draped across their bodies like soft robes. Around 360 BC, in Plato's *Dialogues*, the Greek philosopher Socrates depicted a shining red citadel that rose from the island of Atlantis, surrounded by peaks "celebrated for their number and size and beauty." For many years, he said, local inhabitants lived virtuous and idyllic lives, until they became greedy and power-hungry, and the island sank beneath the waves. Many scholars think that Atlantis was never meant to be an actual place. As historian Murat Cem Mengüç notes, such tales represent an early form of "paradoxography," an allegorical story about a remote, imaginary country that offers an alternative vision of human societies. Nonetheless, spectral outlines of Atlantis and other lost continents have reemerged many times in exploration history, sought after by adventurers who continue to speculate that these places might once have been real.

During the fourth century BC, Greek explorer Pytheas allegedly reached one of the imagined countries, Thule, another realm of twenty-four–hour light, "six days' sail north from Britain and near the Frozen Sea." In his *Natural History*, completed around 77 AD, Roman philosopher Pliny the Elder called it the "most remote" of any land. Geographers and historians still argue over whether the account of Pytheas's voyage was a hoax or whether Thule was an identifiable region somewhere in Scandinavia or the Arctic, real lands of the midnight sun. Like the legend of Atlantis, the symbolism of Thule has endured, refracting over centuries to reflect various fears and desires, at times horrifying or idyllic, an icy blank glittering just beyond the reach of mapmakers, an emblem of some ultimate mystery. A real mountain in Alaska now bears the name of "Ultima Thule Peak," a testament to the ongoing influence of such legends on climbers' fantasies.

Born in Alexandria around the year 100 AD, Claudius Ptolemy set himself the task of collecting as much information as he could for his influential *Geographia*, a pastiche of speculation and reports by earlier mapmakers, writers, astronomers, and sailors. Here, too, imaginary peaks crept in. Among them glimmered the Mountains of the Moon, named after the reflections of light on high snows and believed to be the source of the Nile. Other mythic landforms included magnetic islands that could rip metal nails from passing ships, and realms where people had tails like satyrs. In response to the proliferating tales of countries of "huge beasts, cruel men and strange ways of living" among the geographies of their era, a second-century Assyrian satirist, Lucian of Samosata, composed his *True History*—a self-admitted fake voyage to the moon and onward to the morning star, across a giant web of spiders' silk. "That I might not be the only one excluded from the privileges of poetic license, not having had any adventures of significance," he declared, "I took to lying."

But Ptolemy also sought more scientific approaches to mapmaking, relying on geometry to render a three-dimensional Earth on a flat page. Subsequent cartographers refined this method of "map projection" as they tried to improve their portrayals of mountains' vertical relief. In 1154, Moroccan geographer al-Idrīsī drew on some of Ptolemy's information while he worked on a now-vanished map, forged from silver, that provided one of the most comprehensive early portrayals of swaths of Europe, Africa, and Asia. Throughout other, still-preserved maps, al-Idrīsī's mountains lie scattered like delicate seed pods. As historian Ernesto Capello has observed, their multicolored hues seem to prefigure the cartographic symbols of future centuries.

In much of medieval Europe, however, Ptolemy's influence became largely dormant, and other types of maps rose to prominence. One kind, known as *mappa mundi*, depicted a Christian view of the world. Drawings of landforms appeared vague and stylized as medieval cartographers emphasized the significance of places in biblical history rather than their physical locations. Mountains, frequently sketched as simple triangles, represented the settings of important events, such as Mount Sinai, where God gave Moses the Ten Commandments, or the Garden of Eden, where Adam and Eve dwelled before the Fall. Geographic prominences also served an allegorical role, as the fifth-century bishop Saint Eucherius explained: "The mountains are the church of the lord and of the apostles, or of the saints, a strength from on high."

Since sea voyages in the Middle Ages required precise knowledge of coastlines and ports, nautical charts began incorporating more nuances of the fringes of the Mediterranean, the Black Sea, and the shores of the Atlantic from Europe to North Africa, including some coastal peaks. Depictions of the interiors of European countries often remained less detailed or realistic. As long as they stayed on main roads, wayfarers and pilgrims could depend on simple lists of destinations and estimated travel times, stopping to ask for information from local residents along the way. Throughout literature and folklore, spaces between frequented tracks still appeared as vast wildwoods, rumored to be full of bandits, monsters, and wolves.

In an essay from the 2018 anthology *The Writer's Map: An Atlas of Imaginary Lands*, novelist David Mitchell recalled, "As a navigational tool, the Mappa Mundi would clearly be a dead loss. As a map of the medieval mind, however, it has few peers. I wonder if that isn't the point about maps of fictitious places, too? They are maps of minds. You lose yourself in them and find if not factual truth, then other kinds. . . . You meet yourself in them. . . . Fictitious maps give form to a thing—the imagination—that has no form."

---

AS THEY CREATED THE RIESENSTEIN, THE HOAXERS WOULD HAVE known that, on one level, alpine geographies are innately fictitious. Decades later, in *Mountains of the Mind*, British writer Robert Macfarlane would famously declare that all peaks were "*imagined* into existence," forged from a merging of topographic forms and human fantasies. But mountaineers have always sensed how reveries accumulate along the flanks of real peaks, like crystals of falling snow, coating the landscape with drifting layers of symbols, continually melting and freezing into new, translucent shapes. Physical summits also seep into the geographies of our unconscious, where their contours elicit longings we might not otherwise have felt. Some regions of my own dream peak are patchworks of places I've been: a shiver of grasslands from eastern Mongolia, a murk of hemlocks from behind my childhood home, a cloud-slashed upper ice world in the North Cascades. For many climbers, at times both unexpected and ecstatic, boundaries between outer and inner worlds seem to dissolve. And for a moment, there's no separation between an intake of breath and the dazzle of starlit snow, between the curve of a hand and a fissure of stone.

Surprisingly few researchers have ever agreed on how high, steep, and autonomous a real landform must be to earn the title of *mountain*. Impressions of altitude and prominence vary according to climates and cultures. A rocky Appalachian summit of about 5,000 feet, carpeted with windswept alpine tundra, receives the rarely disputed prefix of "Mount." A rugged, forested mound of almost 10,000 feet, partly terraced with farms, is merely one of the "Middle Hills" of Nepal. In the introduction to *Mountains of the World*, modern geographers Jack D. Ives, Bruno Messerli, and Ernst Spiess compared the search for a single definition to the quest for a chimera, a mythical creature composed of a lion's head, a goat's body, and a snake's tail, the kind of monster that lurked on the edges of old maps. They recommended using only the common terms for each region so as not to continue a "time-consuming debate with no satisfactory result." In 2003, SUNY–Buffalo professors Barry Smith and David M. Mark took the question a step farther with a provocatively titled article, "Do Mountains Exist?" Just as there are no clear boundaries between the end of a valley and the beginning of a peak, they wrote, "the category *mountain* is not distinguished in bona fide fashion from neighboring categories such as *hill*, *ridge*, *butte*, *plateau*, *plain*, and so on." While they didn't doubt the existence of physical molecules that make up a form called "Mount Everest," they argued that the essential idea of a mountain remains an illusion, merely a projection of habits of language.

In 1936, American geographer Roderick Peattie offered one of the most poetic and emotionally true definitions of mountains: "They should enter into the imagination of the people who live within their shadows." Though standardizing "such intangibles" is impossible, he added, and the power they hold over our minds may change with time. Maps are full of archaic "mounts" that can seem more or less nonexistent today, sometimes mere ripples of elevation, scarcely distinguishable from surrounding hills or plains. Swiss geographers Bernard Debarbieux and Gilles Rudaz recount the story of the Montagne de Reims in France, a gentle swell of green just 938 feet above sea level, its dark band of summit forest like the shadow of another world. Local people named this escarpment a "mountain" long ago, though its apex appears lost within a broad, nearly flat skyline, some 650 feet higher than the rooftops of the steepled town. "Although that Mountain of Reims may have been a mountain in the eyes of the city's residents, it is not so for specialists in the natural sciences," Debarbieux and Rudaz explain. "To be precise, it is no longer so."

---

FOR HUNDREDS OF YEARS, THE ELEVATION OF PEAKS ELUDED EXACT quantification. Religious traditions have long depicted summits as piercing the very heavens. Early mapmakers recorded unearthly altitudes around the world. As late as the seventeenth century, German geographer Bernhardus Varenius believed that Pico del Teide in the Canary Islands soared more than 38,800 feet above the waves.

While physical mountains remain challenging to delineate, imaginary ones evade clear designations altogether. Even the word *imaginary* is an inadequate one—for what is a fantasy to one individual or group or time can be an accepted reality to another. The term *mythic* has contradictory meanings. It can allude to legends that are purely fictitious or unverifiable. It can refer to traditional lore that has a long-standing cultural existence and reflects allegorical, psychological, or literal truths. It can also describe stories that appear extraordinary but are grounded in physical experiences.

As we climb higher, we enter landscapes that defy our expectations of the earth. Trees shrivel like snakeskin, their branches twisted and polished silver by gusts. Rare alpine flowers sparkle, bright as gems, from stone crevices. Snowfall and wind sculpt giant curls of cornices. Blizzards whirl above hot summer valleys. Ghostly illusions and hallucinations drift across thin air. The sense of closeness to the sky and the sudden expansion of the horizon can feel like a revelation. In *Topophilia* ("love of place"), American geographer Yi-Fu Tuan explained that the very topography of summits inherently attracts legends: "remote, difficult to approach, dangerous, and unassimilable to the workaday needs of man."

Spiritual geographies merge encounters with terrestrial places and visions of transcendent lands beyond ordinary measurements of space or time. As Tuan wrote, "People in widely different parts of the world regarded the mountain as the place where sky and earth met . . . where the human spirit could pass from one cosmic level to another." In the Sumerian and Babylonian *Epic of Gilgamesh*, one of the first written adventure stories, a hero embarks on a quest for the secret of eternal life by entering a doorway into a peak named Mashu, "which daily guards the rising and setting of the Sun, / above which only the dome of the heavens reaches, / and whose flank reaches as far as the Netherworld below." On the other side of a dark tunnel, he blinks before the jewel-bright trees of the Garden of the Gods.

Mahameru or Meru, a sacred mountain in Hindu, Buddhist, and Jain religions, rises from the center of the universe and forms the axis of the cosmos. In one story, the peak is shaped like a tree, spreading its roots into the underworld and lifting its branches to the heavens. Its slopes glisten with gold and gems. According to the fifth-century Buddhist scholar Vasubandhu, seven mountain walls and seven oceans trace concentric rings around Meru. The outermost sea contains islands of continents where humans live. Many people think that Mount Kailash, a real sacred peak in Tibet, is the same mountain as the Meru of the myths. A tributary of the holy Ganga River is said to cascade from the heavens to the top of Meru, where it branches into four streams. Since a source of the terrestrial Ganga springs from the Gangotri Glacier in the Indian Garhwal Himalaya, others associate the legendary Meru with a nearby physical peak of the same name. By the twentieth century, a particularly sharp ridge on this mapped Meru had become a coveted prize for international climbers who named it "the Shark's Fin." In 2011, when an American team finally scaled its crystal-like facets, numerous journalists conflated the two Meru mountains. Meera Baindur, an Indian philosopher, asked:

> *Is this geographical Meru—the one that appears in climbing tales and most recently in a movie—the same as the mountain of myth? Perhaps it is, perhaps it is not. There is a basic difference between the Meru plotted on a Himalayan map and the Mahameru that forms a ladder to the heavens. If you approach the mountain as merely a part of the physical landscape—as a summit to be vanquished—you can never reach Mahameru. If you look at the mountain from the perspective of a believer and if you perceive it as Mahameru, you can reach it, but you also know that you can never conquer it. Therein lies the mystery.*

In European traditions, Eden was also the source of four rivers. Often, it appeared as a walled garden atop an improbably high mountain in Asia or the Middle East. A giant waterfall cascaded nearby in a din of bright water. Historian Alessandro Scafi has described the quest to pinpoint this place on a terrestrial map as both contradictory and obsessive: "Throughout history paradise has appeared everywhere in a variety of secular and religious guises, always thought of as 'elsewhere' and 'out of time.' . . . Mapping the Garden of Eden presented the ultimate cartographical paradox: how to map a place that was *on* earth but not *of* earth." Fourth-century monk Saint Ephrem imagined this Earthly Paradise as a colossal peak that encircled all lands and seas, luminous like an aureole around the moon. Its elevation was so great that the Flood of the Old Testament only lapped gently against its foothills, even as it drowned the rest of the world.

---

SHARDS OF A LOST ANCIENT HIGHLAND, SCOURED AWAY WHILE FROZEN floods of glaciers receded, the otherworldly citadels of the Riesenstein recall places beyond the reach of human feet and memory. Yet if summits evoke the idea of proximity to the heavens, inevitably people will want to scale them. During the fourth century, a woman known as Egeria clambered up the rocky slopes of Mount Sinai, following a strain of longing that drew her to this desert peak and to other sacred places, thousands of miles from her home somewhere within the borders of modern-day France and Spain. Around her, cliffs and towers rose in furrowed waves of stone. The cadence of her footfalls blended with the prayers of local monks who served as guides. "These mountains are ascended with infinite toil," she wrote to her friends, "for you cannot go up gently by a spiral track, as we say snail-shell wise, but you climb straight up the whole way, as if up a wall." On the summit, she marveled at the distant glint of the Red Sea and the storied lands of Scriptures that unrolled before her like a map of dreams. Peaks that once appeared immensely high had dwindled to small bumps. "All so much below us as to be scarcely credible," she observed. At last, she decided, she had "fulfilled all the desire with which we had hastened to ascend."

Scholars debate which real mountain was the biblical summit, but Egeria likely climbed a 7,497-foot peak now known as Jebel Musa in the Sinai Peninsula of Egypt. In photos, the steep red granite shimmers rose-gold through dusk-lit haze. Although many climbers today may not have heard her story, a seventh-century Spanish monk named Valerius once extolled Egeria in terms that could describe a prototypical mountaineering hero: "Nothing could hold her back, whether it was the labor of travelling the whole world, the perils of seas and rivers, the dread crags and fearsome mountains." He attributed Egeria's achievements to "God's help," but also to "her own unconquerable bravery" and "iron strength." Twenty-first–century historians Jaś Elsner and Joan-Pau Rubiés describe the motivation behind Egeria's pilgrimages as an archetypical one that lingers in modern literature: the yearning for a geographic quest that might generate a sense of physical connection with the divine, a "purely mythic and always unachievable paradigm located in our historical memory, by contrast with which all human travelling—whatever its achievements and successes—can never transcend the abysm of futility."

In some religions, the holy nature of a mountain made its summit off-limits to early human mountaineers. Throughout much of the Himalaya, traders and pilgrims crossed glaciated passes. Visionaries searched for hidden doorways in mountain walls to enter secret paradises, known as *beyul*. But they left the apexes of most big, snowy peaks untouched. The holy summit of Mount Kailash, a bright half-moon shape above the pale turquoise of Lake Manasarovar, remains forbidden. Although pilgrims for centuries have circumambulated the rocky slopes of its base, the only tale of an ascent took place in 1093 when a ray of light lifted the Buddhist teacher Milarepa to the top.

Across other parts of the world, however, traces of ascents date back thousands of years. Many summits in the American West contain stone rings and enclosures built by Indigenous people who often climbed for religious reasons. Japanese monks, known as *yamabushi*, have scrambled up steep, craggy peaks as part of their spiritual practices since the sixth century. Among them, Banryū, who lived from 1786 to 1840, described a vision of the Buddha of Infinite Life and Light emerging from a rainbow of mist above the silvery, gnarled stone of Mount Yarigatake. In the ninth century, the Chinese poet Bai Juyi depicted his ascent of Incense Burner Peak as a means to encounter "the limits of sight and hearing" and to "know the vastness of the universe."

---

AROUND 1165, COPIES OF A MYSTERIOUS LETTER ADDRESSED TO THE Byzantine emperor began disseminating across Europe. Its author claimed to be "Prester John," a Nestorian Christian priest-king who ruled over a vast eastern empire that included the summit of Eden and other miraculous peaks. Near the Earthly Paradise, a spring gushed forth from "Mount Olympy" that prevented the onset of illness and old age. Earthquakes split hillsides to reveal an underground river of precious stones. The ground shook with the thunder of centaurs' hooves and giants' feet. Phoenixes burst into flame.

To make the letter even more appealing, Prester John suggested he could help Crusaders fight Muslim nations for the Holy Land. Over the following centuries, popes and European kings sent emissaries in search of this powerful sovereign. When they failed to find Prester John anywhere in Asia, cartographers moved his imaginary kingdom to other regions of the world, where he continued to rule for hundreds of years, serene and unperturbed, as if impervious to particularities of place or the passage of time. In 1573, the Flemish cartographer Abraham Ortelius published a map that transported Prester John's country to Ethiopia. Near its center rises Mount Amara, sometimes associated with a real summit, Amba Geshen. The Mountains of the Moon crenellate the lower end.

The dream of finding Prester John's empire didn't fade out until the seventeenth century. Fragments of its peaks endure in fantasies. In John Milton's *Paradise Lost*, the mountain of "Amara" is compared to Eden, which appears as "a Rock / Of Alabaster, pil'd up to the Clouds, / Conspicuous farr, winding with one ascent / Accessible from Earth, one entrance high; / The rest was craggie cliff, that overhung / Still as it rose, impossible to climbe." Within the walled, fragrant garden of Xanadu, in Coleridge's poem "Kubla Khan" (inspired partly by Marco Polo's *Travels*), an Abyssinian maid sings of Mount Abora, another incarnation of Mount Amara.

There was an insidious side to the way such myths shaped history, one that would haunt the Western history of imaginary peaks for centuries to come. As the Italian philosopher Umberto Eco argued, the allure of this "Force of Falsity" encouraged Europeans to explore and then to colonize distant lands. Somewhere, an unknown scribe, with a lavish imagination and a talent for forgery, had designed the seemingly irresistible realm of Prester John to sway the actions of real monarchs or to indulge in mischief making. "The problem is not so much its origin," Eco wrote in *Serendipities: Language and Lunacy*, "as its reception. The geographical fantasy gradually generated a political project . . . an alibi for the expansion of the Christian world toward Africa and Asia."

---

EUROPEANS, OF COURSE, WEREN'T THE ONLY ONES WHO DREAMED OF venturing to faraway ranges in search of wealth or wonders. From countries around the world, explorers, missionaries, traders, pilgrims, and emissaries traveled extraordinary distances over land and water. Fourteenth-century Moroccan writer and Muslim pilgrim Ibn Battuta journeyed more than 75,000 miles in his lifetime, seeking to expand his knowledge and follow his faith. As he crossed the high mountains of the Hindu Kush, he and his companions laid felt cloth on snow slopes so their camels could climb without sinking into drifts. Sailing over the China Seas, Ibn Battuta saw what looked like a flying mountain, only to learn from the crew that it was a *rukh*, a gigantic mythical bird of prey. What they glimpsed might have been a kind of mirage, now often called a *fata morgana*, which occurs when light refracts through a thermal inversion to create eerie projections of distant hilly shores that seem to float in the air. Similar illusions caused cartographers to include imaginary peaks, unintentionally, on maps well into the twentieth century.

By comparison with Battuta, Venetian traveler Marco Polo's estimated 15,000 miles of travel seems almost paltry, though his *Book of Marvels of the World*, which first appeared around 1300, cast a spell over Western audiences that persists today. In the province of Karazhan (now Yunnan), under the rule of Mongolian emperor Kublai Khan, Polo claimed that mountains were strewn with golden talus and teeming with giant serpents that could devour men in a single gulp. If you were clever enough to trap one of the creatures, their gallbladders could cure rabies.

Travel literature flourished from the rich seedbed of such memoirs, an often-indeterminate blend of direct experience, collected hearsay, local and foreign traditions, and vivid imaginations. Real and phantasmal places appeared next to one another in the same cartographies. Sea monsters wriggled in pale-blue waters inked across the Atlantic. Noah's Ark teetered atop a giant mountain in Armenia ("where snow is so constant that none can ascend," Polo affirmed).

None of these stories offered verifiable firsthand explorations of the mountain of Eden. Even Sir John Mandeville in his popular (and likely fabricated) fourteenth-century *Travels*—which reported tales of a waterfall so big its rapids deafened listeners and a summit so high it nearly scraped the moon—admitted he hadn't actually been there: "It is far beyond. . . . And also I was not worthy." Geographers began shifting the location of the Earthly Paradise to parts of continents that seekers hadn't yet visited, atop the mythic Mountains of the Moon or along high peaks of the unseen *Terra Australis Incognita*.

In 1498, as Christopher Columbus sailed into the Gulf of Paria during his third voyage of exploration, the pole star appeared to rotate unexpectedly in the sky. He thought his ship was rising toward an elevation point so great that the planet itself must be shaped like a pear. This must be the summit of Eden, he insisted, though he could never reach it (and no one else could, he warned, "save by the will of God"). But as the pace of Western exploration quickened, the belief that the Earthly Paradise still existed in a hidden terrestrial place transformed into the idea that it had disappeared into lost time. Some theologians argued that the original peak had been destroyed in the Flood; all that could be found on Earth, if anything, was the place where it had vanished. Others imagined it as an inner state that disappeared with the loss of innocence.

Sixteenth-century Swiss naturalist Conrad Gessner extolled the pleasures of wandering and climbing in the real Alps, instead, where the marvelous "spectacles" of a metaphorical Eden might be found: multitudes of unusual flowers, ramparts of unbreachable rocks, pinnacles above the clouds. Yet the absence of a literal Earthly Paradise haunted explorers' maps and dreams for many more years—a void that merged with different stories of "lost worlds," such as the tales of Atlantis and Thule. Other imaginary mountains crept in to fill the gaps of vanished mythic highlands. To explain why compasses point north, European cartographers imagined a giant, black, magnetic rock at the North Pole, an island mountain known as the Rupes Nigra. In a 1577 letter, Flemish mapmaker Gerardus Mercator described reading a lost book by a fourteenth-century monk in which the peak appears as "black and glistening," its apex reaching into the clouds and its base surrounded by a whirlpool. Mercator's 1595 polar map displays the dark, craggy monolith like an island mountain at the center of four rivers that flow toward walls of encircling peaks.

In Islamic cartographies, the great peak at the North Pole was occasionally identified as Mount Qāf. Persian geographer Hamd Allāh al-Mustawfī al-Qazwīnī described it as a range that ringed the entire earth and rose to a summit just a fathom short of the heavens. According to various traditions, Mount Qāf was made wholly of emerald, azure, or green chrysolite, and its reflections gave the sky its color. It might take five hundred years to reach the summit and two thousand years to circumnavigate the base. To some, ascents could represent a metaphor for the journey of the spiritual life or a passage across the boundary between known and unknown worlds.

Over time, Mount Qāf became connected with Kirghiz stories of the Köyqap peaks in the Tianshan. During the early 1900s, when a German mountaineer, Gottfried Merzbacher, arrived to explore the range, a local resident told him that "very high mountains" still existed beyond a narrow valley, "so long that nobody could get to its end." Unable to find a way through the twisting gorge of cliff walls and swift waters, Merzbacher turned back, full of regret that thick mist had prevented him from even seeing the distant peaks. After centuries of quests, the desire for an infinite mountain remained undimmed.

CHAPTER 2

# A Golden Age of Imaginary Voyages

SINCE THE NINETEENTH CENTURY, MANY Western writers have described the 1336 ascent of the real Mont Ventoux by the Italian poet Francesco Petrarch as the start of modern recreational European climbing, the first account of "mountaineering for mountaineering's sake." This claim can be misleading: it discounts previous climbs by narrowing the definition of the pursuit to require a particular motivation. It also assumes that earlier ascensionists didn't occasionally find some pleasure in the act of scrambling up cliffs or reaching summits. Enthusiastic mountain pilgrims such as Egeria predated Petrarch by hundreds of years. Early alpine guides, known as *marrons*, led travelers over snowy passes while wearing iron-spiked boots and carrying long poles to probe for crevasses. Chamois hunters and crystal prospectors crept along high, narrow ledges. Rulers ordered ascents of peaks to get a bird's-eye view of conquerable lands or to satisfy their curiosity. Roman historian Aelius Spartianus described how the emperor Hadrian made the ascent of a nearly 11,000-foot volcano, Mount Etna, in Sicily, to contemplate "the sunrise which has many colors, they say, like a rainbow." And as far back as the ninth century, climbers repeatedly tried to summit 11,608-foot Rochemelon, believed (erroneously) to be the highest mountain in the Alps and to contain a hidden treasure. According to legends, an irate spirit defended its apex with blasts of smoky fog and volleys of loose rocks. (The objective hazards, at least, sound real, though the supernatural cause might be in doubt.) Yet in retrospect, Petrarch's ascent of Mont Ventoux might represent a different mountaineering benchmark: an origin myth of Western climbing history that underscores the potential fallacies of taking some claimed "firsts" too literally.

Petrarch himself didn't claim any utter originality. In a letter to his spiritual advisor Dionisio da Borgo San Sepolcro, Petrarch explained that he'd been reading Livy's *History of Rome* when he came across an account of King Philip of Macedon's climb of Mount Haemus. According to Livy, Philip believed that he'd be able to see as far as the Adriatic Sea, the Hister (Danube) River, the Alps, and the Black Sea from the summit, an expansive vista that would help him plan military strategies. But as Philip's expedition trekked higher up the mountain, they entered a shadowy realm of interweaving branches and wafting mist. Livy expressed his doubts about their subsequent report: "After their descent they said nothing to contradict the popular belief [about the summit vista]; more, I suspect, to prevent the futility of their march from becoming a subject of ridicule than because the widely separated seas and mountains and rivers could really be seen from one spot."

Fascinated by the story, Petrarch decided to attempt the summit that loomed above his childhood home. Although Mont Ventoux is only 6,263 feet high, its pale limestone summit flashes in the sunlight like a long drift of snow, far above the lavender fields of Provence (now part of France). "My only motive was the wish to see what so great an elevation had to offer," he wrote. Accompanied by his brother and two servants, he struggled up an "almost inaccessible mass of stony soil." A local shepherd warned them that he'd already climbed the mountain and derived nothing "except fatigue and regret, and clothes and body torn by the rocks and briars." When they insisted on continuing, the shepherd indicated a faint path. Growing weary, Petrarch sought easier ways to the top, while the rest of the group strode up the most direct route. Again and again, Petrarch realized his detours were taking him farther from the summit. Eventually, he sat down to think. "What thou has repeatedly experienced today in the ascent," he admonished himself, "happens to thee, as to many, in the journey toward the blessed life." His desire to find a less steep trail represented his attraction to "low and worldly pleasures," while the commitment to the direct route symbolized a willingness to follow the difficult path to God.

When, at last, Petrarch joined his companions on the apex, the distant snows of the Alps seemed magnified in the clear, bright air. He thought of his mentor Dionisio in Italy, on the other side of the range, and he opened his copy of Saint Augustine's *Confessions*, Dionisio's gift to him, at random. "And men go about to wonder at the heights of the mountains," Petrarch read out loud, "and the mighty waves of the sea, and the wide sweep of rivers, and the circuit of the ocean, and the revolution of the stars, but themselves they consider not." Petrarch felt ashamed. He'd let himself become absorbed by the finite wonders of the earth, instead of concentrating on the infinite grandeur of the soul. "Then, in truth, I was satisfied that I had seen enough of the mountain," he declared, "I turned my inward eye upon myself."

Philosophy professor Unn Falkeid suggests that Petrarch's allusion to Philip of Macedon's controversial climb might represent a clue: an allusion to ultimate failure. Was Petrarch suggesting that the idea of climbing a mountain to become closer to the divine is inherently flawed, a misplacement of an internal pilgrimage onto the outside world? Or was he hinting that not everything might be as it seemed in his own account? Although many climbers and armchair mountaineers take Petrarch's claims literally, historians debate whether his climb happened at all. The sequence of scenes fits the structure of allegory too well to seem entirely natural. Even if Petrarch did plod his way to the summit of Mont Ventoux, he may have altered portions of the story to suit his themes—perhaps to please his reader, who was after all, a monk concerned about the state of Petrarch's soul.

Still, if Petrarch didn't climb the peak, the aim of his tale might not have been, precisely, to deceive. As alpine historian Peter Hansen muses, perhaps Petrarch, like Harvey Manning, wanted to convey a message, relying on "poetic license or the artistic imagination, in which something 'true' seems best conveyed through something 'made up.'" While the Mont Ventoux of Petrarch's tale may contain fictitious elements, the most important summit, it seems, was the one within his mind.

---

SUMMIT MAGAZINE READERS MAY HAVE ALSO BEEN PRIMED TO ACCEPT the fictionalized cartography of the Riesenstein because of the fantastical elements that have long lingered in alpine maps, as if reflecting the changing, evanescent qualities of mountain dreams. Even as cartographers began to depict the lowlands near their homes more accurately, the real shapes of mountains escaped them. "Ever since the very beginnings of cartography," Library of Congress cartographer John Hessler observes, "the problem of the vertical has been a central frustration for mapmakers trying to replicate a three-dimensional earth on a flat plane." While Ptolemy had devised ways to project a round earth on two-dimensional pieces of paper, he'd offered few solutions for charting the nuances of peaks. In one map, published with a fifteenth-century edition of his *Geographia*, an artist rendered the ridgelines of the Alps as streaked blobs. Separated from the rest of the land, they hint at not-quite-mappable realms, still "*on* the Earth, but not *of* the Earth," as Alessandro Scafi described the Eden of old.

As far back as the days of ancient Greece, geographers tried to estimate elevations mathematically through triangulation, measuring angles of a line drawn to an apex from other known points along a baseline. Small errors could result in wildly inaccurate numbers, and refractions of light could create mirages of taller summits. The development of barometers in the mid-seventeenth century seemed to promise a simpler and more reliable form of measurement: as the altitude increased and the air pressure diminished, a column of mercury sank down a glass tube. Although the device was both heavy and fragile, eager geographers could carry it on treks to the tops of hills.

The early barometers, too, had their drawbacks: fluctuations in air pressure could arise from changing weather patterns and skew the results. Still, by combining barometric readings with those of increasingly sophisticated triangulation methods, mapmakers began to cast ever larger and more intricate webs of estimated heights and distances across the ranges. Alongside attempts to calculate more precise elevations, quests for unearthly experiences persisted, at times performed by the same people. In the early 1700s, while Swiss naturalist Johann Jakob Scheuchzer took barometric readings to gauge elevations in the Alps, he also jotted notes for a meticulous taxonomy of dragons believed to exist in the upper regions, some "soft and full of poisoned blood," some "with and without wings," and some with the face of a cat.

If dragons still seemed possible on the high peaks of Western Europe, it was partly because the actual topography of those mountains appeared as largely blank or hazy spaces on eighteenth-century maps. During the 1740s, while the Cassini family carried out their generations-long cartographic expeditions across France, prior depictions of the Alps still showed an empty expanse near the village of Chamonix, with "La Mont Maudite" (an older name for the Massif of Mont Blanc) marked in the wrong spot. Even the final Cassini maps offered only vague indications of individual peaks, relying on an artistic blend of lines and shading to generate an illusion of three-dimensional space. At its worst, map historian John Noble Wilford wrote, such hatchwork made summits look like "hairy caterpillars." At its most refined, the technique provided merely "an impression" of summits that surveyors had not yet climbed. Other maps showed the radiating crests of mountains as they might have appeared if cartographers could have seen them from high above—perhaps clinging to the spiny backs of winged dragons—long before airplanes made true aerial views possible.

As ranges drew farther away from geographers' own horizons, images of peaks became condensed into mere symbols or else took on increasingly surreal forms. Since the time of ancient Greece, European mapmakers had envisioned an undiscovered southernmost continent as an ultimate *terra incognita*. By 1570, when Flemish cartographer Abraham Ortelius published his famous atlas, *Theatrum Orbis Terrarum* ("The Theater of the World"), the place he called *Terra Australis Nondum Cognita* ("The Not-Yet-Known Southern Land") took up nearly a fourth of the globe. It sprawled across an immense white space on his map, its borders tinged with green, its outline as jagged as a colossal, inverted mountain range at the bottom of the page.

Gradually, while sailors ventured farther south, the boundaries of the imagined landmass shrank, giving way to the verdant islands of the South Pacific and to the ever-colder waters and icy archipelagos beyond them. But there would be no recorded sightings of the real Antarctica until the nineteenth century. In the meantime, fragments of old and new legends still floated toward the unseen shores of the southernmost continent, accumulating like the wreckage of fallen empires. Some geographers and mapmakers continued to believe that this *Terra Australis Incognita* might be a kind of hidden, terrestrial paradise of fertile valleys and untold heights.

French author Denis Vairasse d'Allais drew on a few of the wildest rumors to create his 1675 novel *The History of the Sevarites or Sevarambi*. His narrator, Captain Siden, supposedly entrusted the manuscript to a friend who published it after his death. Various East India Company members allegedly confirmed certain details—or so the friend claimed. In his account, Siden explained that he was motivated to travel by all the wondrous stories he'd consumed of faraway places. As he sailed from Texel Island in The Netherlands toward the distant shores of Batavia, he noted (as if so much reading had made him somewhat blasé), "It is true, we saw several Sea Monsters, flying Fishes, new Constellations, &c. But because those things are usual, that they have been described by others, and have for many years lost the grace of Novelties, I purposely omit them." Gales drove the ship off course. By the time the skies cleared, they were no longer able to orient themselves by the unfamiliar stars.

A gust blew them southward into the shallows of an unmapped coast. In search of a "Paradise on Earth," they crossed a range of high mountains on the backs of unicorns. "As tame as our Horses," Siden observed, "they seemed to me far stronger and more swift, and so sure footed, that though we climbed over Rocks and Mountains, there was none of them seen so much as to stumble or fall." A giant cascade fell down the sides of an icy peak called Sporakas, splashing off ledges and creating "a pleasant Musick." At the summit, they spent the night in a diamond palace, where ice towers had hardened into crystal walls. Local inhabitants explained to Siden that the innermost part of their country was, in fact, a second Eden, moved there from Asia after the Flood.

At the time, some readers believed the novel was a true story about an actual range. During the seventeenth and eighteenth centuries, the genre of "imaginary voyages" surged just as published reports of European explorers began to overtake them. As humanities professor Paul Longley Arthur explained in *Virtual Voyages*, "It is as though [writers] were aware that this point in history provided a final, fleeting and rapidly diminishing opportunity for imaginative revelry."

Authors had plenty of motivation to blur the line between reality and illusion. Accustomed to depictions of magical creatures in phantasmagoric lands, people expected to be entertained with marvels. Fiction writers supplied them in droves: two of the best known examples are the diminutive Lilliputians of Jonathan Swift's *Gulliver's Travels* (which some readers initially mistook for nonfiction) and the eagle-back voyages of Rudolf Erich Raspe's notorious Baron Munchausen (an actual nobleman with the same name became so incensed at the tall tales he tried to sue the author). Once an account appeared in bound pages, with a preface vouching for its veracity, it simply looked like a genuine travelogue.

Even real adventurers knew that reports of riches and curiosities, exaggerated or wholly invented, could help secure backing for future trips. For editors who tried to compile accurate information, fact-checking reports of eighteenth-century explorers (genuine or fake) was nearly impossible. French philosopher Denis Diderot, whose *Encyclopédie* attempted to catalogue all the knowledge of the era, distrusted many of his contemporary sources for distant lands. "One must have a long sojourn in order to understand the most common phenomena with even a small degree of accuracy," he wrote. "The traveler who takes notes on his writing tablets as the wheels [of a carriage] are spinning is quite aware that what he composes [are] lies."

"To err and to be errant," as historian Neil Safier summarizes this phenomenon, "were thus seen as two sides of the same coin." The connection between wandering and erring in European literature had existed for centuries, related to the idea that people lived on Earth in a state of physical and spiritual roaming ever since the original exile from Eden. *Errance*, a word that has lingered from Old French, could signify the act of drifting away from the truth, of wandering lost or in exile, or of roving without a fixed goal. Yet it could also recall the quests of knights errant in search of miraculous objects such as the Holy Grail, or it could evoke the pilgrimage of every human life to return to paradise. Long after the original religious connotations faded, explorers and writers still dreamed of finding a lost and radiant place, "that light beyond the horizon," as Alessandro Scafi termed it, "the brightness that went before and that is to come."

When eighteenth-century writers tried to imagine better worlds on Earth, their visions often reflected emerging ideals of getting back to nature and away from the artifices of civilization. But many utopian fantasies helped spread the same empires their authors sought to escape. The very word *utopia*, coined by Thomas More in 1516 to describe an imaginary South Atlantic island society, comes from the Greek words for "no place," though it also sounds like *eutopia*, from the Greek for "good place." Before a place could become a "no place," however, its real Indigenous history had to be erased.

In 1749, the French cartographer Jean Baptiste Bourguignon d'Anville removed most of the imaginary mountains from his map of Africa, replacing neat rows of shaded, triangular mounds that once symbolized reputed peaks with empty, flat spaces. To him, a blank on a map signified a place where no Europeans had been. "Can a faithful historian, who finds a vacancy or interruption in any series of events, supply it by his own imagination, even though he might do it with probability?" he asked. In the process, he cleared away vast regions of projected Western myths. And yet, as English literature professor Siobhan Carroll notes, the disappearance created another illusion: "A visual *terra nullius*, a 'no person's land' invitingly open for colonial appropriation." Thousands of years of local knowledge, habitation, and rights lay buried beneath those expanses of white paper, like great cities beneath an apocalypse of snow.

CHAPTER 3

# Killing and Preserving Dragons

SOMETIMES, REAL MOUNTAINS WENT UP in smoke. Mount Tambora, whose name in the Bima language of Sumbawa means "an invitation to disappear," was one such peak. More than 450 volcanoes loom along the Ring of Fire that curls like a giant dragon's spine around the basin of the Pacific Ocean, its long tail pressing against the Sunda Arc of Indonesia. Once about 14,100 feet high, the entire summit cone of Tambora vanished during the eruptions of 1815, leaving only a cratered relic more than 4,700 feet shorter. Blizzards of ash dimmed the sun for months. Clouds of floating debris cast a chilly twilight as far away as the Alps. In the aftermath, 1816 became known as the Year Without a Summer. Amid the eerie, unseasonal darkness, gothic imaginations flourished.

That July, two British writers, Mary Wollstonecraft Godwin and her future husband, Percy Bysshe Shelley, rode mules up winding, snow-laden trails below Mont Blanc. Beyond the murky, splintered light of pine groves, Godwin looked out upon the Mer de Glace, a giant glacier that seethed like a roiling current transformed into ice. Later, in her science fiction novel *Frankenstein*, she drew on her memory of that day, as she imagined her monster leaping across the crevasses with "superhuman speed" past "glittering" domes and granite spires that appear like "the habitations of another race of beings."

Shelley's own poem "Mont Blanc" depicts the real summit as a seemingly infinite massif, at once shadowy and glistening. Its immense waterfalls, lightning bolts, and starlit snows flash like fragments of some "remoter world," seen only in a dream. Shattered pinnacles of ice arise from an apocalyptic "city of death." Blue crystal walls topple toward the valleys, ripping up trees. Images of storm, ruin, and chaos, which disturbed earlier travelers to the Alps, appealed to the young couple and to other early nineteenth-century visitors. Irish philosopher Edmund Burke had declared in his 1757 study, *A Philosophical Enquiry into the Origin of Our Ideas of the Sublime and Beautiful*: "The passion caused by the great and sublime in *nature*, when those causes operate most powerfully, is astonishment; and astonishment is that state of the soul, in which all its motions are suspended, with some degree of horror." To writers and philosophers inspired by him, mountains produced sensations of something so vast and awe-inspiring that it overwhelmed human perception and language. The very terror that the uncontrollable forces of a glacier could inflict became—when viewed from a reasonably safe distance—a means to experience what Burke called "the strongest emotion which the mind is capable of feeling."

Around the same time that early Romantic poets and authors were extolling the unquantifiable, the accuracy of barometers and other instruments was improving. Scientists carried a battery of heavy equipment to high points in the Alps and elsewhere: telescope-equipped theodolites for triangulation across greater distances (at times with crosshairs made of spider silk), cyanometers to measure the blueness of the sky, hygrometers for humidity, diaphonometers for the clarity of the air, and more. All their frenetically recorded numbers failed to capture the elusive and essential qualities of the mountains. Far from diminishing a sense of wonder, Prussian naturalist Alexander von Humboldt insisted, science enhanced it. Unpacking his instruments on the summits of South American volcanoes, he stared upward into the endless reaches of space, imagining clouds of nebulae crystallizing into innumerable stars. He turned his gaze downward into the steam-veiled abyss of the craters, and the tips of colossal stalagmites emerged, black and shimmering, like peaks of the underworld, their bases somewhere invisibly far below. He was awestruck by how many worlds remained undiscovered, still beyond the reach of body or mind. This is the "strange paradox" of high peaks, as University of London professor Veronica della Dora has observed: "They are spatially localized and finite, yet they stretch toward the infinite, the eternal, the ungraspable." The result, della Dora explains, is an ongoing conflict between the idea that mountains can be reduced to measurable data and the belief that they represent something ethereal and without bounds.

In his influential 1871 book, *The Playground of Europe*, Victorian mountaineer Leslie Stephen claimed, "The history of mountaineering is, to a great extent, the history of the process by which men have gradually conquered the phantoms of their own imagination." *Killing dragons* is a phrase sometimes used to describe mountaineering. For many alpinists, however, the experience of climbing evoked nostalgia for what the bygone creatures represented. "Fairies and elves, and other symbols by which people once interpreted to themselves the awe and wonder produced by natural scenery, have died too thoroughly even for poetical purposes," Stephen wrote. "How much will go with them? and how far will the same process applied in other directions destroy the beauty and the romance of our daily lives?" As historian Michael Reidy points out, Stephen was writing during an age when the rise of Darwinism and agnosticism shook the foundations of faith and myth. To him, and others since his time, encounters with the "sublime" offered a pathway to a kind of secular mysticism. Even those who rejected traditional religious doctrines could still feel ecstatic moments of union, timelessness, and transcendence in the mountains through an alchemy of physical exertion and intense focus, an awareness of risk and sense of awe, and contact with a wondrous natural world.

But the dragons in their literal form—and the supernatural beliefs they'd come to symbolize—proved less easy to slay than Stephen might have thought. Although visions of fire-breathing monsters dissipated before the daylit smoke of cog railways, the old magic held sway at night and in isolated corners. During the early twentieth century, British climber Geoffrey Winthrop Young described how the ragged edges of crevasses still looked like dragons' teeth in the moonlight. Gurgling rivulets, grinding ice, and falling shards crescendoed into strange atonal music. "It is a ghostly clamour," he recalled in *On High Hills*, "that night-shouting of glaciers, sufficient to account for the superstition that a spirit-life haunts their white dead spaces." Within those blank expanses, as rays of moon flickered in and out of silhouetted rock spires, phantoms of imaginary summits drifted in the air. "Unreal peaks and glaciers were projected out of darkness into a half-dreamworld about me, shifting as I walked," he wrote. "I was certain I could see the silvered shapes of mountain and glacier-fall floating spectrally across and even through the forms of more solid shadow."

Even well-known mountains preserved regions of mystery. Since the mid-nineteenth century, more familiar forms of contour lines and intervals had been spreading across maps of alpine ranges in billowing, concentric rings. The steepest places, cartographer John Hessler observes, "squeeze the contours on the paper together so tightly that one might very well think that nothing happens there. But it is these parts of the earth that appear to climbers in their dreams and nightmares. Within that blank, mountaineering produces its particular geography, dramas and stories." By the 1860s, climbers had started to create their own specialized maps of vertical terrain—currently referred to as "topos"—with sketches of features and lines of routes. Nevertheless, because of the sheer quantity and intricacy of cliff faces, arêtes, gullies, and buttresses, many vertical landscapes will never be charted in detail, even after their summits have been reached and their ranges mapped.

---

DESPITE JEAN BAPTISTE BOURGUIGNON D'ANVILLE'S EFFORTS TO ERASE imaginary ranges, myths crowded back into the blanks he'd left behind. "Ideas lose their form when they decay, yet do not necessarily lose their place in the mentality of an age," modern British author Francis Spufford concluded, after exploring the longevity of sublime ice worlds in English fantasies. "They turn to imaginative compost."

Phantom islands of the Atlantic, full of wonders, treasures, and mountains, were sprinkled throughout old stories, creating fertile ground for alleged new sightings. In *De Imagine Mundi*, twelfth-century European geographer Honorius of Autun had composed one of the most haunting descriptions: "There is a certain island of the Ocean called Perdita, and it excels all the lands of the earth in the beauty and fertility of all things. Found once by chance, it was later sought again and not found, whence it is called Perdita." For centuries, sailors reported visions of hillsides, crags, and towers of similar enchanted islands emerging and vanishing in the sea mists like lighthouse beacons in storms. Some mariners even claimed to have landed on their shores.

One element that contributed to myths about lost or imaginary landforms was the difficulty of knowing precisely where ships had traveled. While early navigators could determine latitudes based on the position of the sun and stars, longitudinal measurements required the knowledge of the exact time in two distant places: in the spot where the explorer currently was and at a predetermined prime meridian. No one could figure out how to obtain this information accurately at sea until the late eighteenth century, after the English clockmaker John Harrison perfected his intricate chronometer. In the meantime, mistakes, at times disastrous, abounded. On a foggy night in 1707, British warships crashed into the real, but invisible, Scilly Isles. As many as two thousand sailors died. Other seafarers recorded "new" mountainous islets in the wrong places. Some found that shorelines marked on maps had disappeared when they tried to repeat predecessors' itineraries. Often, the real coasts turned out to be different than the ones that previous travelers had described.

Even before they built permanent settlements and forts along the coasts of North and South America, Europeans tried to colonize islands and continents with their dreams, constructing spectral "outposts in the homelands of others," as Darran Anderson, a British historian of imaginary places, explains. The citadels and marvels of these unreal countries seemed to beckon from beyond the waves. The dangerous side of such fantasies, once symbolized by the Prester John hoax, continued to swell. In his essay, "From Pilgrimage to Crusade," twentieth-century Trappist monk Thomas Merton recalled the legacy of imaginary medieval realms: "Centuries of ardent, unconscious desire for the Lost Island had established [in the minds of European explorers] a kind of right to paradise once it was found.... Somehow it has been forgotten that a paradise that can be conquered and acquired by force is not paradise at all."

Within legends of storied lands that Europeans hoped to conquer, images of precious stones and metals sparked and faded—inside the borders of fabled kingdoms, beneath the surface of high mountains, or amid the shadows of deep woods. In 1492, when Christopher Columbus set out on his first voyage across the Atlantic, he'd hoped to resupply his ships at the seven golden cities of a fabulous Atlantic island known as Antilla, supposedly founded by seven eighth-century Catholic bishops who fled Moorish rule. Though ship after ship had failed to find it, a tale lingered of fifteenth-century Portuguese sailors who, blown there by a storm, discovered residents who spoke their language. They brought back sand that glittered with gold, but when Prince Henry the Navigator commanded them to obtain more, the mariners vanished. Flemish explorer Eustache de la Fosse claimed that one of the Antilla bishops, "knowing the art of necromancy," cast a spell over the place so that it would remain invisible until all of Spain became Catholic. As ships passed by the invisible island, he explained, flocks of birds rose into the air like puffs of magic smoke.

Columbus never encountered the gilded cities during his own voyages, though the name "Antilles" became associated with islands he visited in the Caribbean, blending with other tales, such as the Nahua stories of the Seven

Caves of Aztlán, the origin place of seven Indigenous tribes. Despite Columbus's inability to locate the mythic realm of Antilla, explorers kept pursuing golden wraiths that receded westward like the gleam of sunset along ever-farther horizons. In 1538, Viceroy Antonio de Mendoza ordered Friar Marcos de Niza to investigate rumors of seven rich towns past the northern border of New Spain. An enslaved Black explorer known as Esteban became the friar's guide. Esteban had already spent eight years wandering the region and learning the local Native languages after he and other sailors had been shipwrecked along the Gulf Coast of what is now the United States. He soon left the other expedition members to scout ahead, and a series of couriers brought back news about him to the friar. First, they reported his discovery of a place named Cíbola, where turquoise stones adorned the sides of grand multistoried buildings. Later, messengers announced that Esteban had been killed. (Since his body was never found, a few optimistic authors have speculated that Esteban seized the opportunity to escape from the Spanish.) Afterward, reports spread of vast quantities of gold and silver there. In 1540, the friar guided a conquistador's army to the region. They found no turquoise or golden metropolises, only the sheen of the desert sun on the adobe walls of seven Zuni pueblos.

By the nineteenth century, storytellers had blended the account of the real expedition to Cíbola with the quest for the seven gilded cities. Perhaps, as historians Richard and Shirley Flint suggest, the "gold fever" then rampant in the US spread its flush back through the years, tinting the old tales. Perhaps the seven pueblos reminded writers of the seven cities of the Antilla myth. However it happened, the "Seven Cities of Cíbola" became another byword for magical and impossible lands where, as climbers Al DeMaria and Pete Geiser later wrote, the Riesenstein, too, seemed fated to dwell.

As if scattered by wind, the golden phantoms also strayed over the mountains of the Andes. A sixteenth-century Spanish account described the ritual of a wealthy Muisca king who covered himself with gilt dust and then washed it off in a lake. While European adventurers continued to search the high country, the legend of the gilded king metamorphosed again into a hidden golden city: El Dorado. Since the days of Spanish conquistadors, this myth has taken so many different forms that it is no longer attached to any single geographic place. Over time, it has transformed into an allegory of feverish greed or otherworldly longing, of quests to plunder remote ranges for personal gain or to find some elusive object of desire. Many seekers died during their attempts to find El Dorado, and even more Indigenous people perished at the hands of its would-be conquerors. In Edgar Allan Poe's 1849 poem "Eldorado," a knight spends a lifetime looking for the fabled city. When he has grown old and weary, he meets a "pilgrim shadow," who informs him that all searchers must ride "Over the Mountains / Of the Moon, / Down the Valley of the Shadow." Poe seemed to be alluding at once to another fabled range and to the realm of death itself.

In a classic 1974 work of American geography, *Passage through the Garden*, John Logan Allen described how a similar "geography of desire" crept across the future United States. Inside aspiring settlers' imaginations, the North American continent morphed into "the Garden of the World," a place of balmy weather and fertile land. When they arrived, however, many colonists encountered what seemed to them a "wilderness" of long winters, thick woods, marshlands, or rocky soils. A second Eden, they decided, would have to be created there by clearing more forests, planting their own crops, and driving away the original inhabitants.

For hundreds of years, other explorers looked for a "Northwest Passage," a navigable sea route from Europe, past (or through) North America, and on to the riches of Asia. While they found only dead ends, land barriers, snowy mountains, and giant icebergs, the dream refracted into dozens of mythic places, ranging from wide, cross-continental rivers to ice-free Arctic waterways. US diplomat Benjamin Franklin desired the passage so much that he entreated American sailors not to interfere with British Captain James Cook's search for it, despite the ongoing Revolutionary War. Even the fictional Baron Munchausen contemplated joining the quest as he flew on the back of an eagle over Baffin Bay, only to give up after crashing into a frosted cloud and landing on a mountain of ice.

As these invisible waterways flowed through the imaginations of mapmakers, their currents picked up the flotsam and jetsam of other rumors and legends, bearing fragmentary images of fabulous ranges back to the dreams of city dwellers. Some of those peaks proved to be more or less real, albeit different from anyone's initial hopes. When seventeenth-century missionary Father Louis Hennepin returned from a reconnaissance of the Missouri River, he reported tales of a gigantic mountain at the source of several waterways. From its summit, he'd heard, "one might see the Sea, and now and then some great Ships." The story of this peak burgeoned into accounts of actual summits, known as "Mountains of Bright Stones," "the Glittering Mountains," the "Shining Mountains," or the "Rocky Mountains." Early nineteenth-century French Canadian explorer Gabriel Franchère explained: "The first travellers called them the 'Glittering mountains,' on account of the infinite number of immense rock crystals, which, they say, cover their surface, and which, when they are not covered with snow, or in the bare places, reflect to an immense distance the rays of sun. The name Rocky mountains was given them, probably, by later travellers, in consequence of the enormous isolated rocks which they offer here and there to view."

In the 1977 history book *These Mountains Are Our Sacred Places*, Chief John Snow (Intebeja Mani) of the Nakoda Wesley First Nation, described another story about the name: "We knew every trail and mountain pass. . . . We had special ceremonies and religious areas. . . . In the olden days some of the neighbouring tribes called us the 'People of the Shining Mountains.' These mountains are our temples, our sanctuaries, and our resting places. They are a place of hope, a place of vision, a place of refuge."

During the early nineteenth century, non-Native explorers who still hoped for a convenient route across the continent to the Pacific Ocean and Asia—and who hadn't yet seen the range themselves—viewed the Rocky Mountains as a potential barrier. Peter Fidler, a British surveyor and cartographer for the Hudson's Bay Company, copied detailed maps and travel routes that members of various Indigenous tribes had described or sketched by memory on paper, earth, and snow. But the range soon metamorphosed into strange forms in English and American cartographies. Some US geographers dreamed that these peaks contained the source of rivers that ran in all four cardinal directions. If a traveler found the right spot, he could float to any sea he liked.

President Thomas Jefferson believed the Rockies would prove to be even easier to cross than the Blue Ridge Mountains, which rose in low, hazy waves of forests near his Virginia home. In 1803, he sent Meriwether Lewis and William Clark on an expedition to find a form of Northwest Passage, "the most direct and practicable water communication across this continent for the purpose of commerce." Lewis and Clark hoped to canoe along the Missouri, make a short and easy portage over the Rockies, and then find another big river that would carry their boats to the Pacific. As they headed west, the pair found themselves relying on more accurate geographic knowledge from

Native American guides and translators, including a Lemhi Shoshone woman, Sacagawea, who accompanied them on part of their journey. Mandan villagers and other Indigenous residents traced new maps for the team on the ground, sketched distances with charcoal sticks on animal skins, or molded sculptures of the high country out of river sand.

The real Rockies proved to have nothing in common with the misty bluish hills of Jefferson's imagination. On July 4, 1805, Lewis wrote in his journal: "I do not believe that the clouds . . . reach the summits of those lofty mountains. . . . I have thought it probable that these mountains might have derived their appellation of *shining Mountains*, from their glittering appearance when the sun shines in certain directions on the snow." There was no wide super-river that glimmered to the sea. A long and arduous journey to the Pacific and back lay ahead.

Despite the disillusionments of Lewis and Clark's accounts, the myth-making impulse remained. A pattern emerged that lasted well into the nineteenth century. Explorers would report the alleged sighting of a mountain landscape that offered gold or diamonds or a water route to Asia or a fabulously high summit. The peaks would appear on European maps, only to be removed by disappointed, baffled, or irate seekers.

In 1818, John Ross and his crew sailed from London to renew attempts to find the Northwest Passage. On the outskirts of the Arctic Archipelago, he sketched icebergs that rose like glossy mountains, their pinnacles taller than the masts of his ships. As they entered the inlet of Lancaster Sound (Tallurutiup Imanga), his sailors thought they might have discovered the route that would lead them safely through the labyrinth of ice and islands and on to Asia. Then on August 31, Ross announced that they'd reached a dead end. A barricade of peaks, he said, blocked off the waters to the west. He called them "Croker's Mountains," after the First Secretary of the Admiralty, and he ordered his sailors to turn back. On the map that appeared in his memoir, their summits swell like thunderheads.

There was only one problem: Ross's crewmates insisted the mountains weren't actually there. His lieutenant William Edward Parry, bewildered and frustrated, returned a year later and steered his ship directly through the purported range, as if its invisible walls had crumbled into the icy air. Parry named this waterway "Barrow Strait," after the Second Secretary of the Admiralty, John Barrow, the likely author of a scorching review of Ross's book. Ultimately,

Parry turned out to have found the start of a passage across the Arctic Archipelago. In later years, other voyagers—including the Irish explorer Robert McClure and the Norwegian Roald Amundsen—successfully traveled this way. But their ice-ridden, hazardous journeys hardly matched the imagined easy trade route of previous myths.

In *The Man Who Ate His Boots*, adventure writer Anthony Brandt noted that optical illusions, such as *fata morgana*, are common to polar regions. Perhaps Ross's poor eyesight was to blame, or else he confused a rolling fog with billows of mountains. "But Barrow may have put his finger on the problem in his review," Brandt concluded. "There occur," Barrow wrote, "unfortunate moments in the history of a man's life when he is himself unable to account for his actions." Such words might also apply to one of the most famous mountain mythmakers in the years ahead: David Douglas.

---

WITHIN A DECADE OF THE DISAPPEARANCE OF CROKER'S MOUNTAINS, more European climbers began to think of North American peaks as objects of desire rather than mere obstacles to cross. The idea of the *highest* summit in each region, or in the world, had become a prize to be won. For would-be peakbaggers, each newly reported revelation provided an enticement to climb, even when it was simply the latest in a long history of cartographic mistakes.

During the summer of 1824, a young Scottish botanist and mountaineer named David Douglas set out on a multiyear expedition to gather plant specimens along the Columbia River. In May 1827, as he followed the fur trade route over Athabasca Pass—on the border between the modern Canadian provinces of Alberta and British Columbia—Douglas decided to attempt one of the peaks that towered overhead. At first, he floundered in snowshoes through pine-shadowed drifts. As he stepped onto a firmer slope, he quickened his pace. Above 4,800 feet, the last specks of green vanished into a seemingly infinite universe of ice and stone. "The view from the summit," Douglas wrote in one account of his journey, "is of that cast too awful to afford pleasure." Mountains multiplied around him, each one stacked taller than the other. Icicles sparkled into rainbows along sheer cliffs. Douglas named the peak "Mount Brown," after a noted botanist. Just to the south, he recalled, there was a sharper-looking summit. Douglas called that one "Mount Hooker," after the professor who had first taught him how to collect plants.

In his original field notebook, Douglas wrote that the height from the base of Mount Brown to its summit, "may be about 5,500 feet." At some point after he returned to England, either Douglas or an editor rounded his estimate of the vertical relief to 6,000 feet and guessed that the base of the peaks was about 10,000 feet above sea level. Thus, in William Hooker's 1829 *Flora Boreali-Americana*, Mount Brown became listed as 16,000 feet and Mount Hooker as 15,700. For the next seventy-five years, the peaks appeared erroneously on maps as the highest summits in the Rockies.

By the 1880s, Canadian mountaineer Arthur P. Coleman was obsessed with Mount Hooker and Mount Brown. "A high mountain is always seductive," Coleman wrote in *The Canadian Rockies: New and Old Trails*. "But a mountain with a mystery is doubly so." It seemed odd to him that none of the *voyageurs* of the fur trade who trudged over Athabasca Pass had reported seeing two colossal mountains that rose like watchtowers in the wild. A railway surveyor, Walter Moberly, had mentioned climbing partway up Mount Brown in 1872, but he'd offered few details about the mountains he noticed from the pass: a "high conical peak" and an "amphitheatre" of northern summits, with "innumerable torrents dashing down the rocks, with the white foam like silver spray."

Coleman decided that he had to see the enigmatic peaks for himself. Finding them proved unexpectedly hard. The fur trade had dwindled in the region, and once well-trodden paths to Athabasca Pass had fallen into disuse. So in 1888, Coleman and a friend, Frank Stover, planned to take the train to the logging town of Beavermouth and then paddle along the Columbia River to look for an old portage route that led to the base of Mount Hooker. Though the Beavermouth stationmaster warned of impassable rapids, the two men began in a euphoric mood. "A great river was swiftly taking us out of man's disfigured world, where axe and fire had done their wicked work, into the mysterious world of mountains," Coleman declared. Then a low hum crescendoed into a roar, and the river boiled between gray, flaking cliffs. As they left the water and searched for a trail past the rapids, faint blazes of previous travelers emerged and vanished like foxfire, luring them into deep swamps and alder thickets.

In search of an easier route, the pair climbed a nearby peak. Below them, the river twisted like a blue line on an old map. Rapids shone against dun-colored crags and dark forest shadows. Coleman gazed north, where alpenglow lit a multitude of summits, and "a great pale mass, faint as a cloud, but with delicately exact outlines" seemed to lift above the rest. *Was this Mount Brown?* He noticed another big peak that could be Mount Hooker. "There stretched the promised land," he recounted, "but what lay between?"

After a desperate attempt to float the rapids in an improvised raft, Coleman and Stover turned back, not sure they'd even seen the right summits. In 1892, Coleman tried again, hiring Ĩyãħé Nakoda guides and following ancient trails. Once more, he failed to reach "the fabulous mountains" before autumn frost glinted across the forest. In 1893, Coleman set out on a third attempt. This time, during a chance encounter in the woods, Chief Jonas Goodstoney agreed to sketch the route to Athabasca Pass. When Coleman arrived there, he searched in all directions for the giant peaks. He found only "commonplace mountains." That such low summits "should masquerade for generations as the highest points in North America seems absurd," he declared.

But Mount Hooker and Mount Brown's mythic elevations didn't fade from other dreamers' fancies. In 1897, while climbing Mount Freshfield, British alpinist J. Norman Collie noticed "a very lofty mountain" about thirty miles away, as he recounted in an article for *The Geographical Journal.* When he looked at his map of the Canadian Rockies again, the only peaks drawn in that region were Mount Hooker and Mount Brown. Perhaps, he thought, this mystery summit was one of the two—and perhaps it was, in fact, as tall as Douglas had said. Lines from a Kipling poem came into Collie's mind: *Something hidden. Go and find it. Go and look behind the Ranges.*

In 1898, Collie traveled to the Canadian Rockies, determined to solve the mystery. From the top of Mount Athabasca, he examined innumerable mountains. One summit jutted like a giant, white chisel through the golden evening haze. A ring of dark cliffs encircled a similar, even higher peak. These might be the "lost mountains" of Hooker and Brown, he thought. Days later, he and his teammates trudged by lantern light through a maze of glowing icefalls toward the mysterious "chisel-shaped peak." As the sun's rays intensified across the glacier, the topography wavered like a series of silver mirages. The summit they thought might be Mount Brown vanished behind another mountain. The chisel-shaped peak withdrew into unattainable distance. After days of searching, the team couldn't find anything resembling Douglas's descriptions of Athabasca Pass and its surroundings. Based on his own travails, Collie eventually decided that Douglas could never have summited a giant snow-crusted mountain in a mere afternoon. Mount Brown, wherever it was, was probably only 9,000 feet tall.

In 1920, a Canadian Interprovincial Survey expedition tried to resolve some of the contradictory claims. In their report, they declared that Douglas's Mount Brown must be the 9,156-foot summit on the west side of Athabasca Pass. They struggled to find a "sharp" peak that matched his depiction of Mount Hooker. When they looked east, they noticed a conical snowy mountain about six miles away from Mount Brown—not straight above the pass and not to the south, as Douglas's writings implied. After measuring this other summit at 10,782 feet, they determined it must be Mount Hooker.

Mountaineering historian J. Monroe Thorington had grown up obsessed by legends of Mount Hooker and Mount Brown around the turn of the century, when their enormous ghostly forms still haunted geography textbooks. As a boy, he'd craned his neck to look at the metallic gargoyles and roof cornices in his hometown of Philadelphia. The tin and copper sculptured forms glinted above the streets like the crests of strange peaks. He tried to imagine something even higher: "the sky-soaring propensities of those far-away mountains," as he recalled in his climbing memoir, *The Glittering Mountains of Canada*. Later, he uncovered rumors of extraordinary ice-bound heights that predated Douglas's journey. One of the most puzzling anecdotes appeared in a letter from Columbia professor James Renwick to American folklore writer Washington Irving. According to Renwick's account, Simon McGillivray of the Northwest Company had told him in 1822 that he'd seen snow-coated peaks above Athabasca Pass that were almost as tall as Himalayan mountains. The surveyor on McGillivray's expedition, a man named Thompson, confirmed that he'd measured the summits using a barometer and triangulation methods and that one of them was around 25,000 feet high.

During the summer of 1924, when Thorington made his own trek to Athabasca Pass, he felt even more bewildered than previous myth-chasers had been. He hadn't expected to encounter gigantic mountains, but he'd thought that Mount Hooker and Mount Brown would, at least, be somewhat easy to identify. Instead, on the western side, he noticed not one, but several peaks about the same size and shape as Mount Brown, and he had trouble picking out the right mountain. Mount Hooker appeared even less obvious: from the pass he couldn't see the peak that the Interprovincial Survey had identified. Perhaps, he thought, Douglas's Mount Hooker was actually another mountain, now called

McGillivray's Rock, listed as only 8,041 feet high. Even then, Thorington felt uncertain: "[Douglas's] journal and the lay of the land simply do not agree."

On July 1, Thorington and his companions clambered to the top of the peak they concluded was Mount Brown, trudging sluggishly through heat-rippling air up a long crest of shale. Five hours later, they smoked pipes on the summit and gazed at unnamed mountains on their maps. Then they stumbled and glissaded back toward the glow of their campfire in the fading light. According to his journal, Douglas had also taken five hours for his solo climb. He, too, had slid down snowfields—in his case, by attaching his shoes together to create an improvised sledge. But Thorington believed that Douglas's ascent was too fast for an untrained mountaineer confronting the deeper drifts of May.

When Thorington announced that Douglas might not have summited Mount Brown, other climbing writers fiercely defended the early explorer. Douglas had made cartographic mistakes, they agreed, but they were certain that he'd reached the top of some mountain. Maybe, as twenty-first–century Canadian historians Zac Robinson and Stephen Slemon have suggested, Douglas's position in alpine lore had become too important to affix an asterisk: many considered him "the first mountaineer" in North America. It was a claim that ignored prior ascents of continental peaks by Indigenous people and by other white explorers. But it echoed the status that nineteenth-century historians had assigned to Petrarch. Even Thorington felt grateful for Douglas. The mystery of Mount Hooker and Mount Brown had become another origin myth, inspiring climbers to explore a sublime and wild region. "And none . . . returned insensitive to the glory of that mountain vastness," Thorington concluded.

Many years later, Canadian mountaineer Jerry Auld described a modern-day quest in his novel *Hooker & Brown*. From the summit of Mount Hooker, the narrator turns to look at Mount Brown. Rays of moonlight and floating ice crystals form an optical illusion: a ghost summit projected over the real peak, a giant spire of translucent ice-white and limestone-blue that seems to cleave the heavens. "This is the real Mount Brown. The highest," the narrator observes. "Untraceable on maps but far more important, like clouds, like love, like gravity." Of the mistaken cartographers, he muses, "They created a dream that wouldn't die because it was needed."

CHAPTER 4

# Mountains of Diamonds and New El Dorados

FOR AMERICAN CLIMBERS, THE RIESENSTEIN also appealed to a longstanding love for tall tales. Beneath the dominant canon of mountain literature runs an undercurrent of oral histories, campfire myths, and barstool talk that teems with eccentric characters, implausible-but-real (or not-so-real) scenarios, dramatic epics with resounding punchlines, and extravagant claims designed to trick (and infuriate or delight) gullible listeners. "Never let the truth get in the way of a good story" is a proverb sometimes attributed to modern climbing storyteller John Long, as well as to nineteenth-century humorist Mark Twain, whose accounts of wild exploits and adventures are often described as part of the foundation of American fiction.

In an email, Long assured me that the quotation (at least in his usage) has been generally taken out of context: "What I meant was not an invitation to bullshit and exaggerate, but rather to explore narrative modes beyond journalistic reporting. And once you go there, it's like what they say about love and war: nothing is absolutely true because you can't quantify experience." Still, the common misreading of Long's statement seems pertinent: many Americans have long latched on to the idea that backwoods legends can (and even should) be embellished to heighten the fun.

"Is there something particularly American about the hoax?" asks Kevin Young, a historian of "bunk." The nineteenth century, he observes, could be called "an age of imposture" in the United States. It was a time when a new newspaper, *The Sun*, grew its circulation exponentially by running a fake story about the discovery of bat-winged humans on the spires of the moon. Circus impresario P. T. Barnum defended and celebrated the art of "humbug" with dazzling spectacles and bizarre sideshows. Audiences delighted in well-crafted illusions and impossible tales that appealed to their desire for novelty and marvels as part of an emerging heritage of US colonial folklore.

As late-nineteenth–century surveyors filled in maps, myths flared and extinguished like bursts of flame. Disbanded Civil War soldiers roved the high country in search of opportunity. Ghost towns decayed after prospectors left depleted mines to chase the next fleeting promise of an El Dorado. In histories of this era of high-risk investments and unfettered imaginations, the word *speculation* recurs. Out West "stretched the land of enchantment and adventure," recalled Asbury Harpending (himself a notorious speculator) in his memoir, where restless youths might find themselves caught up in "various wanderings and strange experience."

Americans eagerly consumed legends of trappers, fur traders, and mountain men such as Jim Bridger, one of the most prolific creators of imaginary peaks. Several of his improbable-sounding mountains proved to be more or less real. "He could have shut his mouth, but he felt the need to bear witness to the wonders [of Western landscapes]," mused climbing novelist Jeff Long in an article for *Alpinist* 54, "That left him with no choice, really, than to become a fantabulist." Bridger recounted a story of a summit with an icy stream that ran hot at its base—now considered to be the Firehole River that flows through the basins of Yellowstone geysers, the temperatures of its smoky cobalt waters reaching as high as 86° Fahrenheit. The petrified forests described in another Bridger tale also exist, though the real-life versions lack the sagebrush branches of diamonds, rubies, and sapphires that he claimed to have seen. And some believe that the idea for Bridger's transparent Glass Mountain came from the Obsidian Cliff of Wyoming: walls of dark, shiny volcanic stone that flash with reflected sky and sun.

Bridger's most consequential fable proved to be that of an alpine wall encrusted with a diamond so gigantic that its light was visible fifty miles away. Like many powerful, though implausible, legends, this one was an amalgamation of older myths, each story adding another layer to the aura of possibility. As far back as 1642, when Darby Field and his Abenaki guides (unnamed in colonial records) reached the summit of Agiocochook (later called Mount Washington) and peeled chunks of translucent mica from the rocks, stories of gem-strewn mountains flourished. "They brought some stones which they supposed had been diamonds," Massachusetts governor John Winthrop wrote in his journal, "but they were most crystal." Over the ensuing years, rumors of a mountain of diamonds had drifted across maps. Sometimes it was a ruddy desert tower at the entrance to a fathomless canyon or a scree-covered mountain curved like the back of a whale.

Around 1870, mining men Philip Arnold and John Slack arrived in San Francisco to deposit uncut diamonds at a bank. While there, they mentioned casually that they'd found plentiful gems in a remote part of the West. "In those days of mad excitement," Harpending noted, the "incident was bound to leak." Such was the hoaxers' intention: they had been as careful about planting their fictitious story in the minds of susceptible listeners as they were about arranging second-rate stones on a Colorado mesa to look like signs of underground wealth. News of a "Diamond Mountain" blazed from the bank to investment offices, newspapers, campfires, and ships. To hide the location from all except those willing to pay, during his return trips to the site, Arnold got off the train at different stations and covered his horse's hooves with canvas to minimize traces of their passage. In June 1872, he led a party of potential investors and miners, Harpending included, along circuitous paths, scrambling over peak after peak. By the time they saw the rubies and diamonds sparkling in anthill mounds, they'd been bewildered and beguiled into belief.

While others searched on their own across snowy ranges and desert bluffs throughout the West, an article in the *Arizona Miner* decried "fairy tales of sapphire paved courts in ant hill cities . . . of diamonds in such quantities that would stagger Gulliver." One explorer who shared the paper's mix of skepticism and curiosity was Clarence King. As he and his colleagues of the Fortieth Parallel Survey calculated elapsed times between the arrival and departure of hopeful prospectors at various stations and guessed their trajectories, they realized that the mountain might lie within the boundaries of the survey's past explorations. If this extraordinary peak turned out to be real, King thought, its absence from their reports would call their competence into question. In late October 1872, King and two colleagues left Fort Bridger (named after none other than the fantabulist Jim, who had established it as a trading post around 1843). For days, they rode through frigid gusts toward the location they'd estimated the Diamond Mountain to be. A mark on a cottonwood tree appeared in a gulch below the mesa, then a scrap of paper with a miner's water claim. They dismounted to explore a slab of rust-colored sandstone with wind-numbed hands. A gem glittered in a crevice. Then another. Feverish despite the cold air, they plucked a hundred rubies and four diamonds by nightfall.

In the morning light, the clusters of crystals in earthen mounds seemed unnatural. One diamond lay perfectly balanced atop a rock spike. Gusts should have blown it off long ago. No gems appeared in the dirt- and sage-filled sandstone cracks, only those that seemed weeded by human hands. The juxtapositions of stones made no geologic sense, King concluded: "four distinct types of diamond, a few oriental rubies, garnets, spinels, sapphires, emeralds, and amethysts—*an association of minerals of impossible occurrence in nature.*"

King's role in debunking the hoax helped turn his memoir, *Mountaineering in the Sierra Nevada,* into a bestseller. Over time, King, too, would be accused of mythmaking. When a mountaineer disproved King's claim of the first recorded ascent of Mount Whitney (though King had noted the traces of previous climbers: a little pile of stones shaped like "an Indian arrow-shaft"), King said that a disorienting mist must have caused him to climb the wrong peak. Subsequent mountaineers found the actual rock and snow of his other routes less vertiginous than the hair-raising terrain of his tales. Twenty-first–century climber Daniel Arnold, who repeated some of King's ascents, mused, "It's as if King worried that his travels wouldn't seem adventurous enough, so he squeezed his thrilling moments for every last splash of drama, trying to give his reader the tales he thought they expected, in which men dangled over precipices clinging to bits of shrubbery and lives were saved by the lucky snatch of a shirt-sleeve. In King's version of the Sierra, it is hard to tell where the projecting shadows of story end and the real stone begins."

Despite King's un-discovery, conspiracy theories spread that the diamond peak was real, its actual location hidden by clandestine investors. The name "Diamond" proliferated across American maps—marking different places assumed to be the site of the original mesa, or else the locations where later tricksters had tried to re-create the hoax. In 1922, the legend reemerged in a horror story by F. Scott Fitzgerald, "The Diamond as Big as the Ritz," about a mountain formed of a single giant jewel, its facets hidden under a skin of earth and talus. A fictional Confederate family schemes to keep the peak off USGS maps, murders anyone who might give away the secret, chips off fragments to sell, and uses the proceeds to build a dystopia with the labor of enslaved Black people. In *American Silence*, history writer Zeese Papanikolas retold the legend of the Diamond Mountain as a grim allegory of Westward conquest: "The real mountain . . . is not made out of dirt and rock, not created by plate tectonics and local stress and erosion and time. The real mountain, the Diamond Mountain, has been made by desire. . . . The other side of the shining quest, of the mountains that Clarence King climbed and named . . . was something blank and terrible and empty." Myths of grandiose possibilities and deeds, Papanikolas argued, were delusory attempts to fill voids that early white explorers themselves had enabled: the loss of wild lands and the removal of Indigenous peoples from ancestral homes.

During the late nineteenth century, while Clarence King was debunking the mineral riches of the Diamond Mountain, John Muir, among the most influential mountaineering writers in US history, was promoting quests for spiritual treasures. In *Our National Parks*, Muir later wrote: "Thousands of tired, nerve-shaken, over-civilized people are beginning to find out that going to the mountains is going home; that wildness is a necessity; and that mountain parks and reservations are useful not only as fountains of timber and irrigating rivers, but as fountains of life."

Whereas settlers had once seen the "wilderness" as the opposite of Eden, for Muir it resembled the fabled "Fountain of Life," part of an iteration of enchanted paradises of old that could be found (at least metaphorically) in any untrammeled range. In Muir's writing, the monumental peaks, canyons, and forests of the United States appeared as a sanctuary for weary city dwellers to renew and purify themselves, to feel truly at home again. There, he explained in *The Mountains of California*, wanderers could imagine reading "a manuscript written by the hand of Nature alone." And yet, to create the illusion of this untouched, pristine ideal, he and other early white conservationists would often try to displace the history and presence of the people who have inhabited these lands since time immemorial.

As J. B. Harley proposed in *The New Nature of Maps*, there are many kinds of "silences" that can be discerned on maps. Among them are the unfilled spaces between traced lines of rivers, contours, and boundaries, like the gaps between musical notes. There are the mysteries that individuals decide to preserve for themselves, hidden ranges of mind and memory. There are the charts of regions that imperial governments once kept secret, concealing key trade and military routes from rivals. And finally, most hauntingly, there are the attempted suppressions of the heritages of Indigenous people—first with colonialist myths and imagined blanks projected onto maps, then with new boundaries drawn across conquered lands and new names imposed on ancient rivers, valleys, and peaks.

---

WHILE NINETEENTH-CENTURY MOUNTAINEERS WERE ABLE TO DISPROVE the myths of Mounts Hooker and Brown and the Diamond Mountain, other illusions, bolstered by multiple eyewitness accounts, seemed almost impossible to remove from atlases.

The Mountains of the Moon had grown to an astonishing size since Ptolemy's day. By 1805, they'd even acquired a phantom subrange, the Mountains of Kong. First sighted in 1796 by Scottish explorer Mungo Park from a hill near Bamako (in modern-day Mali), these additional summits completed a row of bumps on British maps that extended for thousands of miles all the way across West Africa. Distant glimpses of this immense bluish range reappeared in reports of subsequent visitors. British adventurer Richard Francis Burton recounted stories in which the mountains were covered in bands of crystal and a dusting of gold, with granite pinnacles that twisted like half-ruined gothic spires. Burton ignored the words of a local guide who explained that he'd never heard of such a place. After traveling to the region in 1888, French officer Louis-Gustave Binger tried to dispel the myth once and for all. "On the horizon, not even a ridge of hills!" he announced to the Geographical Society of Paris. "The Kong mountain chain . . . never existed except in the imaginations of a few poorly informed explorers."

Despite Binger's emphatic statement, Rand McNally's 1890 Africa map retained the summits, and the 1928 index of *The Oxford Advanced Atlas* recorded their coordinates as 8°40 N 5°0 W. According to geographers Thomas J. Bassett and Philip W. Porter, these mythic mountains were able to persist because of "the authoritative power of maps." Since the mid-seventeenth century, mapmakers had been instituting more rules, which led their readers to believe that cartography had become a reliable science. If the giant range was still on the maps, it simply had to exist. Any sign of hills, however small, must be the Mountains of Kong.

After Binger's report, the myth of the Mountains of the Moon unraveled and reformed. Today, some identify the range as the real Rwenzori

Mountains on the border of Uganda and the Democratic Republic of Congo. As high as 16,762 feet, their summits are streaked with the remnants of once-extensive glaciers that are now melting away, like legends themselves, into the ever-warming air. The name "Mountains of the Moon" wavers back and forth between geography and myth, between actual peaks and imagined ones, populating both travelogues and fantasy books. Such phantom regions never really go away, even when they no longer appear on maps. As Alastair Bonnett explained in *Unruly Places*, "When the world has been fully codified and collated . . . a sense of loss arises. . . . It is within this context that the unnamed and discarded places . . . take on a romantic aura. In a fully discovered world exploration does not stop; it just has to be reinvented. . . . Hidden geographies are the inverse of lost places; they hint at the possibility that the age of discovery is not quite over."

By the late nineteenth century, the world was both abruptly shrinking and accelerating. A year after the official demise of the Mountains of Kong, an intrepid American journalist named Nellie Bly set out from Hoboken, New Jersey, carrying only a small travel case and wearing a cash-stuffed bag around her neck. Relying on steamships and fast trains, as well as horses and donkeys, she circumnavigated the globe in seventy-two days—eight days faster than the character Phileas Fogg in Jules Verne's 1873 novel, *Around the World in Eighty Days*. Along the way, she sent wireless cables back to her newspaper, *The New York World*, bringing once-remote lands into the homes of her readers.

Reality, it seemed, was quickly catching up to the fantasies of Verne and other writers of adventure tales and science fiction. The development of airplanes allowed for a real bird's-eye view of vast tracts of terrain of which the early mapmakers could only dream. Pilots, like sailors of times past, encountered mirages above the clouds, snows, and seas—particularly in the polar regions—and they, too, inadvertently created phantom peaks. To many people, however, now that surveyors could gaze down on uncharted rainforests, convoluted massifs, and labyrinthine ice fields, the last geographic mysteries seemed on the cusp of being extinguished. "The twentieth [century]," recalled Scottish writer Malachy Tallack in *The Un-Discovered Islands*, "was largely a time of un-discovery."

From 1914 to 1918, the First World War brought the apocalyptic horrors of industrialized total warfare and mass-scale death to many regions of the globe. In the aftermath, some authors wrote of an irresolvable nostalgia for lost places that existed only in the dreaming or unconscious mind or in some unattainable realm in distant time or space. Published in 1932, *The Journey to the East*, by German Swiss novelist Hermann Hesse, depicted a League of pilgrims who reject all modern forms of travel and communication. Roaming in and out of different centuries, and across countries both real and mythic, they search for a kind of redemption. "Our goal was not only the East," the narrator explains, "it was the home and youth of the soul, it was everywhere and nowhere." For members of the League, these travels seemed like a means of transmuting a "war-shattered world" into a "Paradise."

As the old frontiers for mythmaking withdrew, fantasies drifted into ever higher and more inaccessible places. Each of these fabulous mountains had a fleeting existence, like the flash of twilight on a distant peak. When climbers approached their summits, they encountered only ordinary rock, ice, and snow. At last, for many, the displaced longings became detached from any mappable geography, dispersing like so many terrestrial paradises into realms of pure imagination. Near the beginning of James Hilton's 1933 novel, *Lost Horizon*, Hugh Conway stares out the window of a hijacked plane. Entranced by unclimbed mountaintops in the Karakoram, he feels "a glow of satisfaction that there were such places still left on earth, distant, inaccessible, as yet unhumanized." After the plane crashes in Tibet, he notices other unfamiliar mountains that might be "the less known heights of the Kuen-Lun," mountains sometimes believed to bridge the underworld and the heavens in Chinese mythology. Moonbeams reflect off an unfamiliar peak that gleams like a shaft of light. Its description evokes the kind of ideal mountain that has appeared in countless mountaineering stories, with similar wording, ever since: "It was an almost perfect cone of snow, simple in outline as if a child had drawn it, and impossible to classify as to size, height or nearness. It was so radiant, so serenely poised, that he wondered for a moment if it were real at all." After the pilot dies, Conway and the other passengers trek to a lamasery in the secret alpine valley of Shangri-La, below the unearthly peak. There, enclosed by high mountains, they discover a land of fertile fields and gold mines, and a utopian community where inhabitants live for abnormally long spans.

Hilton's book became a bestseller. As the geographer Peter Bishop later wrote, the landscape of Shangri-La seemed real partially because it arose from centuries of past travelers' dreams. Half-conscious memories and desires had accumulated and solidified like layers of winter snow transforming into the ice of a surging glacier. Many have described Shangri-La as an appropriation of the Buddhist concept of Shambhala, a mysterious mountain kingdom, which, as the Tibetan scholar Lobsang Yongdan observes, might be "a real land or a symbol of spiritual achievement." In *A Detailed Description of the Great World*, published in 1830, the Fourth Tsenpo Nomonhan had located Shambhala in far-off, unseen Europe.

For Europeans, Shangri-La could reflect their own ideas of Shambhala, refracted and altered through the writings of Western spiritualists, or else it could evoke the age-old longings for a lost mountainous Eden. It could conjure Orientalist notions about Tibet as an enchanted place. Or it could offer a readily consumable (though heavily distorted) version of Buddhist ideas of *beyul*, or hidden lands, a refuge from urbanized, materialistic society and from the horrors of world war. The ruler of Hilton's Shangri-La turns out to be a European priest, a kind of pacifist Prester John, and the popularity of the novel, like the earlier myth, also reveals something of the unseemly side of imaginary geographies. In a 2011 *Japanese Alpine News* article, "Alpine Paradise," the prolific explorer Tamotsu Nakamura recounted a twenty-first–century expedition to northwestern Yunnan, where Chinese developers had built a city named "Shangri-La," complete with "artificial Tibetan villages" for tourists. It was as if the actual Tibetan significance of the surrounding landscapes lay buried, in part, beneath the pages of Hilton's fantasy.

Again and again in post–World War I novels, characters seek out other gaps in the contours of maps, portals where they might slip into wonderlands and escape from factories, subdivisions, offices, pavement, and clocks. It was as if all you needed was to find the right clue, the right password, the right door. Like many children of the twentieth century, I, too, wriggled past thick wool coats to reach the backs of closets in friends' houses, only to be disappointed each time that my hands brushed against wooden walls and not the snow-laden pines of Narnia, the fantasy world behind the wardrobe in C. S. Lewis's novels. Like many climbers, when I first ventured up cliffs, I felt as though I'd briefly crossed a threshold into a transmuted world. A flare of autumn sun across shiny oak leaves, a dark-silver flake of mica, a spray of fragrant pine needles—all the familiar details of the New England woods seemed brighter viewed from partway up a cliff, my senses sharpened by the void under my feet. Sometimes, an afterglow of euphoria would last through the next day, suffusing even ordinary objects with a hazy radiance. All these vertical realms seemed like fleeting reflections of what I sought, but they were never the place itself.

In the 1934 novella *N*, Arthur Machen described his protagonist gazing out a window in the middle of contemporary London as streets and buildings dissolve to reveal meadows of "flowers such as only dreams can show," their petals luminous as dark amethysts and "beaten gold." When he rushes outside, the view has vanished like a mirage, but he is left with the feeling that he'd glimpsed the lost alpine paradise of Coleridge's poem "Kubla Khan." As another character explains, "Some have declared that it lies within our own choice to gaze continually upon a world of equal or even greater wonder and beauty. It is said by these that the experiments of the alchemists of the Dark Ages . . . are, in fact, related, not to the transmutation of metals, but to the transmutation of the entire Universe . . . to restore the delights of the primal Paradise; to enable men, if they will, to inhabit a world of joy and splendour. It is perhaps possible that there is such an experiment, and that there are some who have made it." Maybe, for some, it was partly a similar dream—of familiar places tearing open to reveal otherworlds—that made the Riesenstein Hoax so successful.

CHAPTER 5

# The Fall of Sanctuaries

REGARDLESS OF WHETHER OR NOT the *Summit* editors were aware the Riesenstein was a hoax when they published the unattributed article, they'd known exactly what they were doing when they added the words "Who will be the first to climb it?" to the photo caption. This was the perfect question to entice readers and to boost magazine sales, one that had echoed in climbers' minds for decades, resisting all efforts to demystify it. Many twentieth-century explorers weren't satisfied with simply reading about imaginary mountains. They wanted them to be real, and they wanted to get to their summits before anyone else did.

As climbers pursued rumors of cartographic enigmas, the idea of a summit taller than any known peak never entirely faded. Early surveyors had mistakenly designated various Himalayan peaks as the highest mountain in the world, including Nanda Devi, Kangchenjunga, and K2. Those errors were corrected in the 1850s after Indian mathematician Radhanath Sikdar and his colleagues at the Great Trigonometrical Survey finished calculating the elevation of "Peak XV," the mountain Tibetans call Chomolungma, at 29,000 feet, and the summit gained its superlative status on maps. Sikdar's British director, Andrew Waugh, recommended the peak be termed "Mount Everest" after the previous Surveyor General of India, much to the dismay of George Everest himself, who preferred the use of local names. Waugh also added two more feet to its estimated height for extra plausibility, giving it the more precise-looking number of 29,002. ("Wags noted that Waugh was the first person to put two feet on the top of Everest," *New Yorker* writer Ed Caesar later quipped.) But some mountaineers still hoped that an even bigger peak existed in a remote corner of the world.

In March 1930, American mountaineers Terris Moore and Allen Carpé lingered in The Explorers Club library in New York, transfixed by an intricately detailed map in *Trailing the Giant Panda*, a 1929 account by the brothers Kermit and Theodore Roosevelt Jr. of a hunting expedition along the border of China and Tibet. "Is there really any chance Mount Koonka could be *that* high?" Moore asked.

Carpé pointed toward a short, but beguiling paragraph: "The altitude of this mighty peak is unknown, but there are those who claim that it rises more than thirty thousand feet and is the highest in the world. A geologist from Chengtu [Chengdu] made a special expedition to establish Koonka's height, but after he had taken his observations, he refused for some entirely unaccountable reason to divulge them."

Minya Konka, as it's more commonly spelled today, Moore and Carpé soon learned, wasn't the only candidate for the true Roof of the World. Just a month prior, *National Geographic* had published an article by botanist Joseph Rock with an intriguing title: "Seeking the Mountains of Mystery: An Expedition on the China-Tibet Frontier to the Unexplored Amnyi Machen Range, One of Whose Peaks Rivals Everest." Rock was sure he'd reached 16,000 feet on his journey. The flash of snow at the apex of "Amnyi Machen" (or Amye Machen) appeared to be at least 12,000 feet higher. During an earlier trek, British Brigadier General George Pereira had reported a glimmer of uncertain height in the same region. According to Rock, Pereira informed him that the peak "when surveyed, might prove higher than Everest." (Cecil Pereira, the late brigadier general's brother, disputed this statement, which he attributed to an "optimistic reporter" who sprang upon the explorer while he was ill.)

A 1925 map in The Explorers Club library, based on Pereira's report, generated even more questions. The contour intervals implied that the broader massif of Amye Machen was only about 25,000 feet high, though no elevation number appeared on its actual summit point. And at the location where Moore and Carpé expected to see Minya Konka, they found contour lines that indicated nothing above 16,500 feet. Perhaps, they thought, clouds had hidden its summit when Pereira plodded by. A National Geographic Society cartographer told them that Rock had originally announced an elevation of 30,000 feet for Minya Konka. But since Rock had relied merely on guesswork, a simple aneroid barometer, and a pocket sighting compass, the editors refused to publish any estimate above 28,000 feet.

The only way to find out the real numbers, Moore determined, was to climb the peaks and remeasure them. He planned to start with Amye Machen. Although Carpé was tempted to come along, he decided to head to the Alaska Range, instead, with a grant to research cosmic rays. Jack Young, a Chinese American college student who had guided the Roosevelts on their hunting expedition, took his place. By January 1932, Moore and Young had arrived at a hotel in Shanghai, and they were lunching with their teammates when the blast wave of a bomb shook the walls. A battle had just broken out between China and Japan. Several of the climbers joined a volunteer force to patrol the American-controlled sector of the city. Young went to help the Chinese army. After the conflict lulled, four weary members still wanted to look for the world's highest summit: Moore, Young, Arthur B. Emmons, and Richard Burdsall. By then, they'd switched their objective to Minya Konka, which they'd come to believe was the most promising option.

After weeks of traveling by riverboat and bus, and trekking through misty foothills, they saw Minya Konka for the first time: cloud-white and unknowably high. "Here was one of the greatest mountain giants of our planet," Burdsall declared in the team's coauthored memoir, *Men Against the Clouds*. "No wonder its call had been powerful enough to summon us from so far." To local Tibetans, the peak was the abode of a deity, Dorjé Lodrö. A sunlit plume of spindrift seemed to extend its apex ever higher into the sky. "Climb it?" Emmons thought. "It seemed almost a desecration even to attempt such a thing." When Burdsall and Moore reached the top of Minya Konya, the elevation proved to be more than 4,000 feet lower than that of Everest. Nonetheless, the rest of the world sank so far below them they might have been gazing at the earth from outer space. Large snowy mountains shrank to tiny puffs of white against the gold-brown swath of the Tibetan Plateau. The horizon formed an indigo ring, uninterrupted by any view of higher peaks.

In the wake of their expedition, rumors continued to build about Amye Machen, which Moore and Carpé had identified as the other contender for the world's highest peak. For more than a decade afterward, reports by pilots still hinted that it might be above 30,000 feet. To Moore, however, the next best hope for a mountain taller than Everest lay in the mysterious interior of Antarctica. There, tales of unseen ranges, subterranean summits, and uncanny light effects lent themselves to bizarre fantasies, such as H. P. Lovecraft's infamous Mountains of Madness, where a lost extraterrestrial civilization lurked beneath the ice.

During the 1940s, US explorers Richard Byrd and Paul Siple reported sighting a cone-shaped mountain that soared higher than their plane. The peak became known as Mount Vinson. Yet in 1959, when Scottish mountaineer John Pirrit and his teammates lumbered into the area on snow tractors to verify its existence, they found no sign of the mountain. Another high summit, Mount Nimitz, was also missing. The original discoverers of these nonexistent mountains had likely mistaken clouds and mirages for actual rock, ice, and snow.

The designation of "Vinson" eventually moved to a 16,046-foot summit in the Sentinel Range, the continent's true highest point. While surveyors kept correcting elevation errors of other Antarctic peaks well into the twenty-first century, by the culmination of the multinational expeditions of the 1957–1958 International Geophysical Year, one fact seemed clear: among the many unclimbed summits that corrugated the southernmost continent, no greater elevations than that of Everest existed. In 1957, Russia launched Sputnik, the first artificial satellite. Soon after, US scientists began the research that led to the creation of GPS and the spread of satellite mapping—technologies that would generate a sense of cartographic omniscience even greater than airplane photos could achieve.

Decades later, as Moore looked back on the long history of quests for the "highest mountain in the world," he thought of new interpretations. The tallest peak could be the one that pokes out farthest from the surface of the earth when viewed from space (Chimborazo in the Andes). Or it could be the one that has the highest vertical relief from its terrestrial base to its summit (Denali in the Alaska Range) or from the ocean floor (Mauna Kea in Hawaii). Moore recalled a story told by his departed friend Allen Carpé, who had vanished into the depths of the Muldrow Glacier during his 1932 Alaskan expedition, leaving behind only the faint trace of ski tracks that faded into snow and shadow. During the eighteenth century, as Carpé recounted, while carrying out experiments near Chimborazo, French geophysicist Pierre Bouguer realized that the topography beneath his observation points, as well as the altitude of where he stood, affected the measured value of gravity. It was as though high peaks really did create their own world.

"So relax," Moore's wife, Katrina, told him. "There *is* no highest mountain on earth." *Was the quest over?* Moore wondered. He remembered standing outside the Minya Konka base camp under a sky that trembled with stars. The upper regions of the peak seemed suddenly close by, like a blazing white *fata morgana* in the clear night air. "In the presence of this vision," Moore wrote, "ellipsoids of reference, Bouguer's Anomaly, centrifugal force from the unfelt thousand-mile-an-hour spin of the earth's rotation, all seem to vanish into unimportance: there before us rises our reality."

---

THE REAL OBJECTS OF MYTHOLOGICAL QUESTS DON'T ALWAYS FARE well. The story of Nanda Devi, also once believed to be the world's highest mountain, has long been a powerful warning of the potential consequences of certain desires for enchanted massifs. A 25,643-foot peak in the Garhwal Himalaya of India, its opalescent summit tower is encircled by steep mountains that form a seemingly insurmountable barrier. At the center of this ring is the Inner Sanctuary, where lush meadows and green firs provide a refuge for rare plants, snow leopards, and blue sheep. From the 1880s to the 1930s, expedition after expedition had tried to enter this hidden basin without success. The only feasible passage was through the Rishi Gorge, a narrow, maze-like ravine where meltwater cascaded from glaciers toward the holy Ganga. For local Hindu people, who took their herds to pastures in the gorge, Nanda Devi was the abode of a goddess. For Western visitors, the place recalled the alpine paradise of ancient legends. British travel writer Hugh Thomson later described it in *Nanda Devi: A Journey to the Last Sanctuary* as "a secluded sanctuary 'girdled round' with walls and towers," like the Xanadu of Coleridge's Kubla Khan, the fabled kingdom of Prester John, or even the mountaintop realm of Eden itself.

On May 28, 1934, a group of British and Sherpa explorers—Eric Shipton, Bill Tilman, Ang Tharkay, Kusang Namgir, and Pasang Bhotia—established a campsite near the meeting point of two rivers, the Rishi Ganga and the Rhamini. This was as close as any foreign team had managed to get to the Inner Sanctuary. The five men sent their local porters home and began to look for a way through walled corridors of winding ledges, slick grassy slopes, abrupt cliffs, wild rapids, and frequent dead ends. At one point, a gigantic shield of dark stone seemed to block the way entirely, rising straight out of the waters toward the sky. Shipton called it "Pisgah," after a mountain in the Old Testament, "for we felt that if we could climb it we would have access to the 'Promised Land' beyond."

After days of struggling to make any progress, they divided into two groups and searched for a feasible route on both sides of the gorge: Tilman and Tharkay on the south side and Shipton and Bhotia on the north. "We tried places which were obviously quite ridiculous," Shipton wrote in his memoir *Nanda Devi*, "just as one searches under the teapot or in the coalscuttle for a lost fountain pen when one has exhausted every likely place." That evening, Shipton and Bhotia sat in a cave behind a curtain of soft rain to wait for their companions. The gray air had darkened to charcoal when they finally heard Tharkay's triumphant voice above the din of the whitewater. He and Tilman had just found the "last frail link" in a series of unexpected fissures in the rock that led to the Inner Sanctuary.

The following evening, the team camped amid meadows of wild rhubarb. As the skies cleared, the sunset transformed Nanda Devi into a gilded tower that floated above the earth. During the days ahead, they explored the basin, meandering across soft green grass that lapped against rock-studded glaciers. Hidden spires of ice emerged on the other side of rock walls. Blue sheep gazed unafraid at human passersby. Shipton recalled the ecstasy of the experience: "My most blissful dream as a child was to be in some such valley, free to wander where I liked, and discover for myself some hitherto unrevealed glory of Nature. Now the reality was no less wonderful than that half-forgotten dream; and of how many childish fancies can that be said, in this age of disillusionment?" But he couldn't remain there forever. When the group's departure drew near, Shipton stared, transfixed, into the twilight that drifted through the darkening clouds and wind-brushed meadows, feeling an ineluctable loss.

Two years later, while Shipton was participating in an attempt on Mount Everest, Tilman and British climber Noel Odell completed the first ascent of Nanda Devi. When they stood on the top of the mountain, only the sharp white summit of nearby 23,360-foot Trisul emerged above a gloom of clouds. Hamlet's words upon seeing his father's ghost passed through Tilman's mind: "Thoughts beyond the reaches of our souls." A snow pigeon flew by, its pale form glowing against cold, ashen cliffs, reminding Tilman of the spirit of the mountain.

Far below, in base camp, one of the Sherpa staff members, Kitar, had been ill with dysentery for weeks. Despite requests from the other Sherpa workers, Tilman hadn't agreed to evacuate him. Now, while Tilman was away making his summit push, Kitar had died. In a later interview with Jonathan Neale, author of *Tigers of the Snow*, two of Kitar's companions, Pasang Phutar and Ang Tsering, blamed Tilman for the loss. The Pindar River had also flooded, drowning forty villagers and many animals. An Indian journalist suggested the disaster was a result of the trespass into the goddess's sanctuary.

Shipton never returned to climb Nanda Devi. Instead, he wandered through other scarcely mapped regions. "Lost civilisations beyond the ranges exist only in the imaginations of romantic novelists," he admitted, but "the detailed exploration of the world is very far from complete." Nearly four decades later, in *That Untravelled World*, Shipton looked back on a lifetime spent pursuing the "vague dream worlds of strange lands" found in the adventure books he'd read as a boy, from the snowy mountains that bloomed in lilac hues on evening horizons to the arid ranges that shivered gold along mirage-drenched deserts. With each step he took, his dream worlds receded farther, toward a vanishing point he could never reach. "The springs of enchantment lie within ourselves," he finally concluded. "They arise from our sense of wonder, that most precious of gifts, the birthright of every child. Lose it and life becomes flat and colorless; keep it and [quoting Alfred Lord Tennyson] . . . *all experience is an arch wherethro' / Gleams that untravell'd world, whose margin fades / For ever and for ever when I move.*"

Shipton's biographer Jim Perrin believes this longing for a magic place arises from early memories that form "a lost landscape of experience," an inner paradise of wonder. A child's mind can transmute a neighboring farmer's field into a vast tundra, a patch of weeds into a trackless rainforest—a power of imagination that, for many, fades as they reach adulthood. Climbers might experience its return in brief moments of euphoria that seem outside of time, as if they are once more seeing the world as they first encountered it, when everything seemed marvelous and new.

In the history of exploration, however, such dreams can exact a cost. "If the [Inner] Sanctuary seemed an Eden in the fantasies of early Western travelers," American climber Pete Takeda wrote in *Alpinist*, "it's hard not to imagine a certain inevitability to its beleaguered status." The popularity of Nanda Devi with international visitors resulted in "an environmental disaster," Indian mountaineer Harish Kapadia recalls. Trekkers, climbers, and expedition workers cut trees and burned juniper bushes for campfires. Endangered plants slipped away under eroding hillsides or vanished into smugglers' packs. Blue sheep and snow leopards fled. Garbage accumulated. During the mid-1960s, covert expeditions sponsored by the CIA and the Indian Intelligence Bureau put plutonium-powered sensors on Nanda Devi and nearby Nanda Kot to spy on Chinese nuclear tests north of the range. One of the sensors disappeared, perhaps swept away by an avalanche. Its radioactive core is likely still buried under the ice that is the source of the holy Ganga. "A powerful symbol," Takeda concluded, "of the dangers of human choices."

In 1982, to prevent further damage, the Indian government forbade most visitors from entering the Inner Sanctuary. Eighteen years later, Hugh Thomson took part in one of the few research expeditions allowed into the area after the closure. Within the ring of white peaks, he felt as if he'd entered a "secret garden." Snow leopard prints dotted the ground again. A herd of blue sheep seemed astounded to see trekkers. Thomson recalled the trash-choked streams of earlier decades. He thought of the memorials for those who died on climbing expeditions, so many of them local workers. He remembered the sounds of "ancestral voices prophesying war" that troubled Xanadu. Before leaving, Thomson buried an edition of *Paradise Lost* under a pile of stones, like a warning to future visitors. "Implicit in the idea of entering a sanctuary," he observed, "was the idea of its fall."

CHAPTER 6

# Revolts Against a Disenchanted World

INKED LINES OF SHADED PEAKS curl across a yellowed page with names that sound both ancient and familiar, though they don't belong entirely to any language spoken on Earth: *Hithaeglir*, the "Misty Mountains"; *Erebor*, the "Lonely Mountain." First published during the 1950s, the maps and stories of *The Lord of the Rings* trilogy became an imaginary refuge for generations of readers desperate to find some invulnerable place beyond the grim realities of their world. By the time J. R. R. Tolkien finished writing the books, he'd lived through two world wars. He'd fought in the first and watched his children leave home to fight in the second. Millions of people had died, cities had burned, trenches had furrowed the countryside, woodlands had been laid waste, and the first detonation of atomic bombs seemed like a precursor to global apocalypse. There appeared to be "only one thing triumphant," he'd written to his son Christopher, "the Machines."

As a young British soldier during the First World War, Tolkien had sketched out fragments of his elaborate fantasy worlds "in grimy canteens, at lectures in cold fog . . . or by candle light in bell-tents, even some down in dugouts under shell fire," as he later wrote. In contrast with the devastation, he recalled memories of a hiking trip in Switzerland, where the "eternal snow" of the Jungfrau seemed "etched . . . against eternal sunshine." Silberhorn, a satellite peak, "sharp against dark blue," recurred in his dreams, morphing into his fictional peak of "Silvertine." In his novels, the hobbit character Sam Gamgee notices starlight above a high alpine spire and imagines a world beyond terror and bloodshed: "Like a shaft, clear and cold, the thought pierced him that in the end the Shadow was only a small and passing thing: there was light and high beauty for ever beyond its reach."

"It seems to become fashionable soon after the great voyages had begun," Tolkien lamented in a 1947 essay, for people to consider the world "too narrow to hold both men and elves." The onslaught of "'rationalisation'... transformed the glamour of Elfland into mere finesse, and invisibility into a fragility that could hide in a cowslip." Tolkien believed that the realm of Faërie—and the sense of enchantment and possibility that it symbolized—could be expanded again through storytelling. Imaginary realms could remind readers of the unlimited potential of human creativity, offering visions of "Joy, beyond the walls of the world, poignant as grief." To those who derided the genre of fantasy as escapism, Tolkien responded, "Why should a man be scorned if, finding himself in prison, he tries to get out and go home?"

In *The Road to Middle-Earth,* literature professor Tom Shippey defined Tolkien's concept of "glamour" as "that shimmer of suggestion which never quite becomes clear sight, but always hints at something deeper, further on." It was something like this glamour that I'd felt as a small girl gazing at the mists that settled on the hayfields and cow pastures of my town and wishing for invisible highlands of snow. Harvey Manning, too, experienced it when, as a young boy, he looked out from Marmot Pass while mountains swelled into the gathering night. The novels of *The Lord of the Rings* trilogy were among Harvey's favorite books, and Tolkien's blend of fantasy and environmentalism may have inspired some of his own stories of unreal peaks. Tolkien's protagonists try to destroy the power of the Dark Lord Sauron whose industries of war have desolated the Mountains of Shadow. The ents fight to stop orcs from slashing and burning their ancient trees in the Forest of Fangorn. Even the ultimate victory over Sauron, however, feels too late. The elves sail west across the sea to the Undying Lands, taking their magic with them and leaving humans to long for something that draws ever farther away.

I'd read Tolkien's trilogy obsessively, more than a dozen times between elementary school and high school, and I remember the overwhelming sadness that washed over me whenever I put the books down and returned to ordinary life. I often brought the books along during my own early hiking trips in the White Mountains of New Hampshire. Images of Fangorn merged with the gnarled roots that crisscrossed the footpaths and the boreal woods that dimmed the sun. Constellations of *Diapensia lapponica*, white and yellow flowers that grow only in alpine zones, reminded me of elanors, the golden, star-shaped blossoms of the elven forest of Lothlórien, where the passage of time seems to slow to a near standstill. These low peaks, too, were a refuge for mountain flora, their summits like islands in the sky. Eventually, I realized, what I yearned for wasn't in the books. It was related to a feeling that I experienced in the cold air above tree line: a sense of inner stillness and emptiness; a glass-like clarity of being, as if the light passed unfiltered into me; a presentiment of the vastness glimmering beyond the edge of sight and mind.

In *Mountains of the Mind*, Robert Macfarlane suggested a desire for this kind of glamour might have influenced the British mountaineer George Mallory's early attempt on Everest, at least initially. To most climbers at the start of the 1920s, the mountain existed primarily in daydreams, a patchwork of reported, faraway glimpses or a set of vague contour lines on a map. On an early June morning in 1921, when Mallory first saw the real peak as a white tower in the distance, a "slight haze" veiled its snows, contributing "a touch of mystery and grandeur." In that moment, Macfarlane argued, Mallory didn't really want a clearer view; he wished it might somehow remain "a conspiracy of imagination and geology, a half-imagined, half-real hill." Three years later, when Mallory and his climbing partner Sandy Irvine vanished in the mists somewhere near the summit, they became part of that mystery in the minds of armchair mountaineers: two eternally young men, enveloped, as Macfarlane put it, "in a cloud of unknowing."

More than two decades later, as European countries recovered from World War II, national expeditions marched inexorably on the world's biggest mountains. Support staff ferried loads to dizzying altitudes. Amid the trampling of feet on worn-down paths and the flurries of telegrams sent to distant press offices, reveries dissolved into the dusty glaciers and broken scree of base camps, the shattered blocks and indigo chasms of icefalls, and finally the upper regions of sharp wind and thin air. In 1950, Annapurna became the first 8,000-meter summit to succumb. Three years later, climbers Tenzing Norgay and Edmund Hillary stood atop Everest. To Tenzing Norgay, who was born not far from the peak, this mountain was Chomolungma, the dwelling of the Goddess of Inexhaustible Giving, Miyolangsangma. Once a forbidden place, the summit felt welcoming to him; none of its sacredness was lost. "My mountain did not seem to me a lifeless thing of rock and ice, but warm and friendly and living," he recalled.

Back in England, however, newspapers celebrated the first ascent of Everest as a definitive conquest. The story splayed across front pages alongside articles about the crowning of Queen Elizabeth II. Although Hillary was a New Zealander and Tenzing Norgay had lived in Tibet, Nepal, and India (he later became an Indian citizen), the expedition had been organized by British climbers. Its success, as expedition reporter Jan Morris recalled in *Coronation Everest*, provided a symbol of resurgence for a country that was "emerging at last from the austerity which had plagued them since the second world war, but at the same time facing the loss of their great Empire, and the inevitable decline of their power in the world."

Still, the idea of mountains as metaphors for national dominion or imperialist nostalgia had long troubled some mid-twentieth–century fiction writers, even in Britain. In 1936, W. H. Auden and Christopher Isherwood published *The Ascent of F6*, a play about the first ascent of an imaginary peak. When their idealistic hero, Ransom (modeled after Mallory), perishes on the summit of F6, his death turns him into the perfect symbol for British statesmen and journalists to exploit for colonial ambitions and media profits. "He has died," one cynical newspaper reader declares, "to satisfy our smug suburban pride." Two decades later, British novelist Mary Stewart set her mystery *Wildfire at Midnight* during the days before and after the first ascent of the world's highest mountain. "I'd always imagined [Everest] as the last inviolate spot that arrogant man hadn't smeared himself over, sort of remote and white and unattainable," her heroine says. A serial killer overhears the heroine's words and vows to seek vengeance against climbers who want to "conquer" the wild and destroy its last sanctuaries.

The dream of "inviolate" heights lived on in literature. French author René Daumal's novel *Mount Analogue*, left unfinished at the time of his death and published in 1952, locates an even taller peak than Everest on a hidden island. Daumal, like the characters in his novel, longed for the old myths of a bridge to the heavens to be real. "*Its summit must be inaccessible*," he wrote, "*but its base accessible* to human beings as nature has made them. It must be *unique* and it must *exist geographically*. The door to the invisible must be visible." Like the phantom islands of the Atlantic, the "invisible continent" of his dream peak could only be reached by ship at certain times. In the case of Mount Analogue, this moment arrived at sunset, when the wind was just right and the light could unbend the "curvature of space" that sealed its realm off from the rest of the world. And like the seventeenth- and eighteenth-century writers of imaginary voyages, Daumal drew a hazy line between geography and myth. In a note to a literary critic, Daumal implied that the secret mountain actually existed in a spiritual, psychological, or physical sense: "My friends and I have, in reality, found the door."

*Mount Analogue* remains a cult classic among modern climbers. There's something intrinsically alluring about the notion that a shift in the sun's rays or a change in perspective can open a secret alpine realm, visible only to those seeking it—an *anomaly*, to use a term beloved by Daumal, that defies the theories of modern science and the authority of maps. The depiction of a real peak in Leigh Ortenburger and Renny Jackson's *Climber's Guide to the Teton Range* echoes Daumal's mesmeric ideas: "Overlooked for decades because it is usually not easily seen, Moxie Tower is readily visible from the valley given the correct lighting conditions. Even the map neglects this tower, as no closed contour is depicted on the Grand Teton quadrangle sheet." Lured by their words, some years ago, my friend Dylan and I hiked up Death Canyon to the rarely visited southeast corner of the spire. As we got closer and the angle of light changed, the broad tower emerged from what seemed like a solid canyon wall. It mattered little to me, afterward, that the actual climb consisted mainly of what mountaineers call *choss*, loose rocks that peeled away and clattered beneath our hands and feet. The vision of the tower itself remained in my mind, an anomaly hinting at the possibility that other unusual places were concealed in the intricate folds of hillsides and the tight contours of maps.

The acts of planting flags on giant summits and replacing mountains' local names can represent powerful images of conquest. But the landscapes of peaks can also symbolize nature's ability to overturn assumptions of dominion. The disorienting quality of their scale eludes cartography, while the hazards of their storms and their avalanches of rocks and snow unsettle notions of imposed order and control. In W. E. Bowman's *The Ascent of Rum Doodle*, a 1956 satirical novel, local porters are the ones who complete the ascent of the 40,000½-foot summit, "nature's last citadel against the conquering spirit of man." One expedition worker—called, appropriately, "Un Sung"—carries the British doctor Ridley Prone to the apex on his back. While the peak was imaginary, the portrayal of some of the inequities and absurdities of imperialist expeditions was all too apt. Several years later, Australian explorers gave the mountain's name to an actual Antarctic peak—though this real Rumdoodle Peak is only 2,871 feet above sea level.

In 1952, British novelist Daphne du Maurier envisioned an imaginary summit called Monte Verità, a kind of feminist Shangri-La where women vanish to join a secret utopia beyond the restrictions and depredations of an industrial world. Behind high mountain walls, the protagonist finds a place where "nothing once felt is lost." Like the characters of Hilton's *Lost Horizon*, these inhabitants look "ageless," but they also transcend binary notions of gender, appearing "neither male nor female." Although the name "Monte Verità" might have been inspired by an actual early twentieth-century hilltop commune in Ascona, Switzerland, du Maurier's narrator declares: "There are many mountain peaks in Europe, and countless numbers may bear the name of Monte Verità. . . . I prefer to give no precise locality to mine. In these days, after two world wars, no mountain seems inaccessible. . . . I have little doubt that today my Monte Verità has been plotted upon the map. . . . There may be resting camps near the summit . . . and the tourist [may be] lifted to the twin peaks by electric cable. Even so, I like to think there can be no final desecration, that at midnight, when the full moon rises, the mountain face is still inviolate, unchanged."

Other writers tried to free their minds from the iron framework of national borders and property boundaries that covered maps of the real world. A group of postwar French writers developed "psychogeography," a practice that involved *dérive*, "drifting," and *detournement*, "rerouting." They played various walking games, such as using the map of one city to navigate another (and thus allowing themselves to become lost). Along the way, they sought to escape predictable patterns of travel and perception, to ignore predetermined routes and delimitations, and to find a more intimate and natural sense of place.

As Austin Post, Ed LaChappelle, and Harvey Manning soon realized, if modern maps and guidebooks detract from their users' imaginations, you can always shift the peaks around, mix in a few errors and fables, and then see what happens to the people you fool.

# PART II

# ANSWERS STILL HIDDEN IN THE ICE

But it's the truth, even if it didn't happen.

—Ken Kesey, *One Flew Over the Cuckoo's Nest*

CHAPTER 7

# Recollections of Long-Vanished Uplands

BY THE EARLY 1960S, WHEN the Riesenstein emerged from the pages of *Summit*, centuries of dreams of imaginary peaks had burnished their granite walls, invisible forces as mighty as the glaciers that carved out the valleys and spires. There's a haunted feeling to the original hoax photo, suffused with the aura of old legends. Clouds billow above the summits like a higher phantom range. Shadows plunge like deep, wide chasms. As the narrator of *Monte Verità* said, "Nothing once felt is lost."

I'd begun my search with Austin Post, the photographer of the Riesenstein, but it was only after his death that I learned from his friends and family about the sheer extent of the cartographies that existed in his mind. If you gave him a blank piece of paper, his son Richard told me, Austin could sketch every detail of the Inside Passage from Puget Sound to Alaska by memory: each channel, island, peak, and shoreline ripple. His imagination was an infinite atlas of mysterious, frozen ranges.

For decades, Austin had flown in small planes across the western ranges of North America, taking hundreds of thousands of aerial photos of mountains and glaciers. He'd crouch near an open aircraft door or else remove a window to get an unobstructed view, using hand signals to communicate with his pilot while the cold wind roared by. At times, he asked a pilot to angle the plane between sharp peaks or to rise to altitudes where they shivered in the icy, thin air. Once, a pilot agreed to fly him into the depths of a crevasse as big as a canyon. "I can't recall a single close call," Austin insisted in an autobiographical essay. "There were anxious moments, true." Engulfed by clouds, one pilot accidently flew the aircraft between the masts of a ship. On another occasion, when the engine failed above the Wind River Range of Wyoming, the plane made an emergency landing on a just-paved fragment of an unfinished highway. But Austin wasn't a "daredevil," Richard explained to me. "He would calculate what needed to be done and the best way to avoid any unnecessary risks but still get the job done."

Austin's ability to take such care came from a lifetime of studying the intricacies of winds, storms, and mountains. Born in 1922, he grew up in Chelan, Washington, a small town in the rain shadow of the North Cascades. His parents, Asa and Beatrice Post, labored over a family apple ranch. Both were college graduates, and Beatrice channeled her creative impulses into designing an opulent flower garden: rows of dahlias and irises, a trellis draped with roses, ornamental pools that glimmered with goldfish. But the dust of the eastern Washington desert always crept back to the edges of their shaded lawn and their irrigated apple trees. The drought years and the Depression of the 1930s thwarted their efforts to make any profit off the fruit. From a young age, Austin and his sister, Phyllis, helped their parents with what he recalled as an existence of "unremitting toil," raising hundreds of chickens to help subsidize the ranch, pruning trees in winter while their toes numbed inside rubber boots, and thinning green apples in the summer while the dry heat seared the arid land.

In his memoir *Pyramid Mountain* (published after his death), Austin wrote, "You may wonder what events in my early childhood set the course for [my] intense desire for freedom and deliberate seeking of solitude. As in all persons' lives, traumatic things do happen." Stricken with polio at age two, and suffering from hay fever, he remained "sickly" well into his adolescence. He became a target for school bullies who beat him, at times severely. For the rest of his life, he felt a "near phobia" of large groups of people. As a boy, he fled his classmates whenever he could to explore the ridge crests far above Chelan, where the mountain air cooled with the hint of ice and the mossy forests filled with the green fragrance of a "different world." Carrying only matches and a tin pail full of bread, sausage, and canned food, he hiked and hitchhiked across the Cascades.

His father, Asa, was also a climber. In 1908, he'd bushwhacked through dense Northwest forests and scrambled up rocks and heather to the top of an isolated 7,060-foot peak. For a summit register, Asa and his companions penciled their names on a piece of paper, placed it in a tin can, and lodged it between the rocks of a cairn. Their feat was almost entirely forgotten. Decades later, Fred Beckey's influential *Cascade Alpine Guide* briefly mentioned their ascent in a section about the exploration of the adjacent, and slightly better known, Agnes Mountain. By 1991, only three other parties had added their names to the summit register of what has become known as Asa Peak. One of them, in 1947, included Austin himself. Above his signature, Austin wrote, "*39 years later Hello Dad!*"

In 1936, Asa had taken the young Austin and Phyllis on a hike up Pyramid Mountain, veering off the trail to scoop up debris from a half-melted cornice so his children could touch midsummer snow for the first time. "To me," Austin recounted, "the top of the mountain was heaven. . . . The lookout building . . . was as near Utopia as one could possibly get." Outside the windows, glaciers sprawled like giant white dragons across serrated peaks—an early glimpse of what would become Austin's lifelong love.

Back home, Austin and a neighbor's son built their own tower out of scrap wood (some stolen from a local ranch) on a nearby brushy knoll, where they daydreamed of becoming fire lookouts. When a local Forest Service ranger, Sim Beeson, chanced upon the structure, he was so impressed that he gave the boys a set of maps and fire reports. Austin began practicing in earnest for a career he saw as an escape from society. In the autumn of 1939, he got his chance. Wildfires bloomed all around Chelan, and short on crewmembers, Beeson recruited the promising teenager to serve as an emergency fire lookout on Horton Butte. Decades later, Austin recalled "the wonder of being in the wilderness amid so much beauty. And, BEING ALONE, away from people." After his solitary rambles, returning to school felt even harder. Austin made it to class less and less. Eventually, he dropped out for good. "I fondly imagined I'd become a recluse," he wrote, "a mystic contemplating the universe."

Beeson helped him get other lookout jobs, first on Cooper Mountain, and later, on his dream peak, Pyramid, where he could gaze from window to window at a kaleidoscope of contrasting landscapes: arid plains, snowy heights, dark forests, and row upon row of bristling rock spires. He didn't mind the hardships, the nights when it was so cold he had to curl up under the stove to sleep. Once, when he was still new to the work, he saw a moonrise so bright that he nearly mistook it for a fire. The electric storms that rattled his shelters created strange marvels: globes of blue flame that hovered in the clouded air; a larch tree split down the center by a lightning bolt, its slivers spreading in the shape of a gigantic flower. In the evenings, he'd light a lantern, and he'd watch as the lights of other lookouts twinkled like stars across the range, some perched on peaks so distant they never spoke even by radio. After years of loneliness, he felt part of a warm "fraternity" of hermits, each one far away in the dark, but close in spirit.

---

AUSTIN WOULD BE ABLE TO ENJOY THAT FEELING OF SANCTUARY FOR only a short time. In 1941, the United States entered World War II. Toward the autumn of 1942, realizing he would soon be drafted, Austin descended from the mountains and traveled to Seattle to enlist in the navy. Soon, he became a ship's carpenter on boats that sailed across the South Pacific. His sense of the wonders of nature and the horrors of civilization deepened as he witnessed the iridescent blues of lagoons, the blaze of stars, the thunder of the sea, the craters left by bombs, and the smoke of planes shot down nearby, their interiors filled with dying men. By 1946, his cousin and most of his scant childhood friends would be dead. Not long after the surrender of Japan, Austin received word from the Red Cross that his mother was terminally ill with cancer. It took weeks for him to obtain leave from a reluctant superior and then to sail back to Seattle, only to learn that she'd already been buried.

Discharged from the navy, Austin discovered that he couldn't return to live on Pyramid Mountain, his alpine home: the lookout system had been disbanded. For a time, adrift, he wandered from job to job in the Northwest ranges. While working as a carpenter aboard a US Coast and Geodetic Survey ship, he seized his first opportunities to hitch rides on small planes and take photos of Alaskan glaciers from the air. Slowly, the pieces of his future life were fitting together. During the summer of 1947, Austin was working as the leader of a Forest Service trail crew when a bedraggled stranger stumbled into their camp by the Stehekin River, his sunburned skin covered with raised welts from insect bites, thorns, and nettles. Larry Nielsen's climbing partners had all abandoned him. They were tired of toiling through rain-drenched underbrush, of teetering on the edge of crumbling precipices, and of sleeping on pointy rocks. Austin had no problem with any of those activities. He agreed to join Larry on an exploration of the spires near the peak named for his father, Asa. Afterward, he and Larry wrote letters to each other, plotting expeditions to

Alaska. Relying on military aerial photos, Austin sketched his first maps of uncharted ranges.

Larry was a chemist who shared Austin's passion for glaciers, and in 1953 he invited his friend to join the Juneau Icefield Research Project of the American Geographical Society in Southeast Alaska. While modern concepts of climate change hadn't yet spread throughout the scientific community, let alone to the mainstream public, postwar journalists and science fiction writers were already speculating about a future of ice-free Arctic ports that recalled fantasies of an open-water Northwest Passage. In a *Popular Science* article about the 1953 expedition, Gardner Soule asked, "Why are most of the world's glaciers shrinking?" Drilling for ice cores in search of the answer represented the next front in exploration, Soule declared. "Men in the past always have hurried to cross the crevasses as they tried to reach something like a mountaintop or the North Pole. Now men have learned that chasms contain secrets found nowhere else."

That summer, while working on the Lemon Creek Glacier, Austin fell ill with pneumonia. A storm blew in and no pilot could fly, so one of the scientists, Richard Hubley, trekked out to Juneau and back on foot to bring him penicillin. When Austin recovered, he credited Hubley with saving his life. The bond between them would shape much of Austin's existence. As Austin continued to work at remote northern field stations, he made other close friends within the community of glaciologists and bush pilots, though he still struggled with relationships. Early marriages to fellow adventurers fell apart. He seemed to find comfort in his imagination and in the wild. In a fiction story Austin wrote, a protagonist tried to explain, "Glaciers to me are a solace I can't find anywhere else. Don't ask me why. There is something so mysterious about the entrancing blue color of the glacier ice, the livingness of its perpetual motion, the wonders it chisels out of solid rock in its ageless flow."

In 1957, Austin accepted an invitation from Hubley to take part in the International Geophysical Year (IGY), a collaboration between scientists from sixty-seven countries that spanned both sides of the Cold War. In the *American Alpine Journal*, Hubley noted how bodies of ice were dwindling in regions that had been warming over the last few decades. There wasn't enough data yet, he thought, to draw global conclusions, but he hoped that IGY studies would begin to fill in those gaps.

Some of this research involved Austin, now an experienced fieldwork manager. He would lead a team of surveyors as they worked with the navy to create detailed maps from aerial imagery in Alaska—part of the largest glacier cartography project at the time. An IGY bush pilot took one of the doors off his plane so Austin could photograph the giant bodies of ice. Frame by frame, Austin learned how to capture images of such marvels as the mighty surge of the Muldrow and the hanging tendrils of the Polychrome Glaciers below the summit of Denali. During a break in the small settlement of Glennallen, Alaska, he called home to hear that his then-wife, Betty, had just given birth to their first son, Charles.

Meanwhile, Hubley flew out to a remote station in the Brooks Range with three other scientists. They intended to remain on the McCall Glacier for sixteen months, through the long winter's dark, to record shifts in its temperatures and to observe the transformation of snowdrifts into layers of ice. At first, the expedition appeared to be going well. A few weeks after they were dropped off on the glacier, Hubley and one of his colleagues, Robert W. Mason, climbed to the top of a peak encrusted with sculpted ice flutings. Hundreds of scarcely mapped Arctic mountains unrolled before them. Unseen clues to the world's past and future lay buried in the glacier below. But as the autumn nights grew longer, other shadows were spreading in Hubley's mind. On October 28, he walked out alone into the cold evening air. His body was found outstretched on the ice; his death was determined to be a suicide.

Desperate to do something for his friend, Austin resigned from his IGY job and flew to the McCall Glacier in February 1958 to try to complete part of Hubley's project. While he was there, Austin climbed some of the surrounding peaks with Mason and one of the other scientists, Charles M. Keeler. They called the most impressive mountain they scaled "Mount Hubley," a vast crest of granite, spackled with ice that sharpened to a rocky point. Austin gave the name "Richard Hubley" to his second son, born a year later. He spent the rest of his life pursuing absences and voids in the mountains: the contours of uncharted glaciers, the creation of unreal peaks, the gaps in the research Hubley left behind.

Austin dreamed of taking pictures of every alpine glacier in the western United States. He knew that, as a high school dropout, he might have trouble obtaining grant money, so he teamed up with prominent snow and ice researchers, including his future Riesenstein collaborator Ed LaChapelle. Soon, Austin was well on his way to becoming a highly respected, self-taught glaciologist and glacier photographer. His pictures, blending usefulness and art, appealed to scientists, climbers, and general audiences alike. There's a sense of both awe and intimacy to Austin's photos. In an aerial image of the Taku Glacier, near the place where he nearly lost his life to pneumonia, the nuances of frozen white facets and gray rock dust resemble the soft shading and fine lines of a charcoal drawing. Sunlight catches on innumerable tiny branches of evergreens at the periphery.

A wide range of patterns and chaos appear across Austin's body of work: glossy surfaces like crackled porcelain, striped bands of moraines as vibrant as sand paintings, glacial arches curved into gothic vaults. Ghostlike traces of receding ice appear in what was left behind: In the ashen hues of rubble and in the velvety shadows of regrown trees where glacial tongues disappeared over a century prior. In the dark towers of nunataks that rise like islands of rock in a sea of ice. In the horned silhouettes of spires and in the steep walls of cirques, sculpted by ancient glaciers as they drew back, so many years ago.

When Austin flew over the ranges of the Northwest and the Arctic in the 1960s, he looked down on numerous peaks that were only roughly surveyed, with no established routes to their summits. Blank patches still existed on published maps. Austin got in the habit of submitting names for glaciers left undesignated by previous surveyors. One elegant body of ice became "Klawatti," a term derived from a misspelling of the Chinook word *Kehloke* or *Kaloke* for "swan." The name would resurface in Austin's mind when he helped dream up an imaginary river near the Riesenstein. He'd seen plenty of options, by then, for a mystery range, though the Kichatna Spires would have been one of the most eye-catching. Bradford Washburn, the founding director of the Boston Museum of Science, had also noticed the peaks from the air. At the time, Washburn was already a legendary mountaineer and aerial photographer. His artistic black-and-white images of corniced ridgelines and fluted walls had inspired alpinists to seek out some of the wildest unclimbed peaks in Alaska. But Washburn hadn't bothered to take pictures of the Kichatnas, despite their surreal beauty. He was more drawn to big snowy mountains than to rock towers, and this region seemed too stormy to interest other climbers, he thought.

In 2011, when I emailed Austin to ask about his famous photograph of the Kichatnas—the one that got used for the Riesenstein Hoax—he responded as though bemused: "I take mountain photos? Glaciers, ma'am; mountains only incidentally. But it's hard to photograph glaciers in Alaska and not include a fine peak now and then." Yet the spires must have caught his attention when he saw them from his plane, if only as scoured rock formations that bore the marks of glaciers past. In the 1971 book *Glacier Ice*, coauthored with Ed LaChapelle, Austin included another photo of the peaks. Soft fog rolls like smoke over some of the utmost summits. Cloud shadows float across glacier and stone. Contour lines of sunstruck buttresses and dark fissures sweep in wild arcs. Light quickens and fades. The landscape seems alive, frozen for a mere instant in the midst of change, still full of the wonder of the photographer's initial view.

*Glacier Ice* was published about five years after Al DeMaria and Pete Geiser's *American Alpine Journal* article appeared to lay the mystery of the Riesenstein to rest. In the book, Austin and Ed used the real names of the peaks. "When ice has intensively eroded the massive granite, the arêtes stand to the sky in dizzying pinnacles and ridges that attract the more daring mountaineers," they explained. Rock spires, such as those of the Kichatnas, represent fragmentary relics of a "long-vanished upland" that once rose, dome-shaped, like the upper half of a colossal snow globe glittering beneath the northern lights.

Ed had also worked and climbed with Richard Hubley, and he and Austin dedicated *Glacier Ice* to their friend's memory, as well as to the late Bill Fairchild, a pilot who had taken Austin on many of his photo flights. Like Austin, Ed had found a childhood sanctuary within the ever-changing worlds of ice and snow. Born in 1926, he, too, had grown up within sight of the Cascades. During Ed's early childhood, his father worked as a logger and a union organizer, and the family moved from camp to camp in the foothills of Mount Rainier. Ed roamed the woods, picking berries and fishing with his parents. At age five, he'd also become ill with polio, and without any hope for a medical cure, a doctor suggested trying to keep his body as still as possible. So Ed lay in bed for a month while his mother read books to him. Eventually, he recovered enough to walk with a limp, but he pushed himself to train until his gait steadied. As a teenager, Ed got a summer job as a bellhop at Paradise Inn just below the great white crest of Mount Rainier. One day, he was standing on the porch of the staff dorm when the clouds drew back from the mountain and the sunset lit up the snow. To his future wife, Dolores, he later wrote, "I can still remember to this day as clear and simple as the note of a bell—this was the single biggest turning point in my life, when in a single blinding moment, I knew what I must do and where I must live with my life."

The memory of that moment propelled Ed into an intense, adventurous life. By the 1950s, he'd become a climber and a ski mountaineer, a World War II navy veteran, a graduate from the University of Puget Sound and the Swiss Federal Institute for Snow and Avalanche Research, a snow ranger with the Forest Service, a glaciologist with the American Geographical Society, a participant in the Juneau Icefield Research Project, the author of an important avalanche safety manual, the husband of Dolores (herself a groundbreaking skier, writer, and deep ecologist), and the father of their son, David.

Ed was soon recognized as one of the foremost experts on snow science in the country. For the 1960 first edition of *Mountaineering: The Freedom of the Hills*, he wrote "The Cycle of Snow" chapter, with the help of Richard Hubley's and Mark Meier's research. There, Ed described the snow line on high peaks as if it were the threshold to an otherworld: "When the climber leaves behind the rock crags and cliffs of lesser hills and ventures into the zone of perpetual snow, he passes from terrain of stable, known and reasonably predictable character to a region where change is the rule and where, as a consequence, his previous experience is often of little avail." He promised readers that they would find "a beauty foreign to lower peaks," landscapes of ice and snow forming and reforming in an endless array of new shapes, sculpted by wind, sun, and storm. There would be innumerable obstacles to surmount, dangers to confront, and puzzles to resolve.

Although Ed was known as a serious and meticulous scientist, he took an occasional delight in clever antics and practical jokes. When he was boy, Ed and his friends amused themselves by creating miniature explosives out of pill capsules, which got the attention of the Tacoma police. Later, when his son was still young and Ed was a snow ranger at Alta in Utah, he figured out a way to wire the resort's PA system to serve as a personal baby monitor. This way, Ed could head out on skis to check the snow conditions while David napped at the Upper Guard Station. Each time David woke and his cries reverberated across the mountain, Ed quickly skied back to his son. "Apparently," Ed's colleague Doug Fesler told me, the "system was so successful he used it several times." During the early 1960s, while directing a research station on Blue Glacier in Olympic National Park, Ed put his ingenuity to work improvising Fourth of July rockets out of fifty-five-gallon drums. As a child, David was obsessed with the magical animals in C. S. Lewis's *The Chronicles of Narnia*. "I was enjoying the fantasy of imagining such creatures in a distant place and land," David recalled. "My father decided to bring them closer to home." Ed asked one of his research assistants to put on a dragon costume made of cardboard and parachute cloth and to conceal himself with a fire extinguisher in a rocky nook. "I was led up the crevice on some pretext," David recounted. "As I climbed down ... I heard a bellow, saw rolling carbon dioxide smoke clouds coming towards me, and the dim shape of a dragon behind." Terrified, he fled.

---

AUSTIN AND HARVEY, EVEN MORE THAN ED, WERE KNOWN FOR THEIR offbeat humor. The Northwest climbing community was still relatively small in the 1960s, and such kindred spirits would have naturally become friends. Perhaps a prank became inevitable once the three men got together and realized the opportunities presented by so many little-known mountains. Perhaps the surreal appearance of the spires and other "long-vanished uplands" proved too alluring to their combined imaginations, evoking mythic landscapes of lost worlds.

Back in Washington State in 1961, Austin brought prints of his aerial photos to Ed's house to show him and Harvey. The three men amused themselves by laying the images on the living-room floor and pointing out potential routes on unfamiliar peaks. The spines of eerie rock towers caught their eyes. They realized it was possible that no climbers had ever seen the Kichatnas. Someone (likely Harvey) started drawing lines that indicated imaginary routes on one photo. The others joined him. "Some really terrific routes were inked in," Austin wrote to me in 2011. "Ed (or Harvey, I forget which), spoke in a voice of hushed reverence, 'Ah! The *Riesenstein*.' And thus the hoax was inspired."

The trio composed the story from the point of view of a Canadian writer who had allegedly spoken with the Austrian climbers. For extra plausibility, since a Washington address might have seemed suspect after Harvey's previous hoaxes, one of their friends mailed the article to *Summit* from Calgary, Alberta. Much to the three conspirators' amusement, as the editors condensed the article, they seemed to have accidently transcribed the name "Riesenstein" as "Riensenstein": a "factual" error introduced into an already fake article that added an extra layer of unreality.

Or was this "mistake," as other readers have suggested to me, a jest of the editors' own? The word *rien* in French means "nothing." *Sens* means "sense." Whether deliberately or not, the editors had changed the name to another made-up word that could describe the range as "nonsense."

When I asked Austin why he and his fellow pranksters created the Riesenstein, and whether the rumors were true that Fred Beckey was their main target, he responded simply, "Motive behind the hoax? Joke! Aimed at Fred? Rather, aimed at most anyone naive enough to fall for it." Beckey, of course, hadn't been naive enough, but plenty of others had. Some readers felt angry or baffled when they realized they'd been duped. Others delighted in the whimsy of the idea or identified with the spirit of the joke, interpreting its purpose in different ways: as a means to stir the imagination, to mock peakbaggers, or just to have fun. "I'd hazard a hoax is a hoax is a hoax most anytime," Austin continued. "How humorous depends on which party one is in, most likely."

When I spoke with some of Ed LaChapelle's colleagues and loved ones, none of them remembered the reasons for his involvement beyond, perhaps, his sense of humor. *The Ascent of Rum Doodle*, Rich Marriott said, was one of Ed's favorite books. But the more I learned about Harvey Manning, the more I was drawn into the complex landscapes of his imagination and the more I believed that the key to understanding the mysteries of the Riesenstein lay there. Harvey, his friends assured me, was always the instigator when any really elaborate mischief took place. Dale Cole, who participated in two of Harvey's earlier pranks, told me Harvey had designed multiple hoaxes, in addition to the Riesenstein, to convey messages about the direction he thought the mountaineering world was heading. To decipher these messages, I'd need to comprehend Harvey's inspirations, hopes, and fears.

CHAPTER 8

# Go and Look Behind the Ranges

SCRAPS OF OLD IMAGES THAT drifted from illuminated manuscripts and sepia-toned maps, tales that slipped from leather-bound volumes and ink-blurred magazine pages, chimeras that formed out of fragments of fairy tales and folklore and children's picture books—all fell through the centuries and settled into the mind of a daydreaming boy. When Harvey Manning first stood on Marmot Pass, he felt that he was on the verge of an enchanted world. He'd spend the rest of his life trying to find it again. "In that 1938 sunset atop the pass, the first sunset of my life, I *felt* were answers—answers to questions I didn't yet know enough to ask," he later wrote.

Harvey Hawthorne Manning was born in the Ballard neighborhood of Seattle in 1925 to Kathryn Hawthorne and Harvey Manning Sr., a couple who met at a summer bonfire on nearby Bainbridge Island when Harvey Sr. was in the navy. Kathryn had grown up fishing, hiking, and boating along the shores of Puget Sound, paddling around steamships and warships in her small canoe. As a boy in Lowell, Massachusetts, Harvey Sr. had fished in the Concord River and roamed the surrounding marshlands and forests. There, he and a friend turned a split rock into a secret camp and roasted apples and corn pilfered from local farmers over a fire. As an adult, Harvey Sr. left a bank job and, in search of adventure, motorcycled to Boston to become a sailor.

When Harvey was young, the family lived on Bainbridge for a while, within view of the jagged skyline of Seattle and the blue horizons of mountains. There's an unusual quality to the light around the islands of Puget Sound, as I learned from my own trip there many years later. A still and heavy glow fills the damp forests like mist and casts a pale sheen across the waters. It's the kind of place where silence seems to fall like snow, where a person might sleep long and dream deeply.

An only child, Harvey grew up immersed in imaginative realms. His Uncle Bill imparted the outdoor survival skills he'd learned from prospectors and trappers on their way to the Klondike during the gold rush of the late nineteenth century. Riding the ferry to and from Seattle, Harvey dreamed about sailing around the world. On clear days, the snowy dome of Mount Rainier (which Puyallup Tribal members call təqʷuʔbəd) rose like a second moon above the horizon. One Thanksgiving, the family went for a hike above Paradise Valley. Back in school, Harvey wrote a story about how they'd "climbed Rainier." It might have been his first hoax, though it wasn't a deliberate one. His teacher pointed out that they probably hadn't gone all the way to the 14,411-foot summit. "I was sore," Harvey recalled. "Later on I realized she was right, my folks were kidding me."

In 1932, during the Depression, the Manning family joined masses of workers migrating around the country in search of employment. By then, Harvey Sr. had left the navy, and he hoped his own father could help him get a job in Lowell. One night, after stopping to sleep in a Nebraska city park with other displaced people, Harvey's father caught a lightning bug. Holding out his hands, he gave his son his first view of the unfamiliar, magical glow.

That sense of marvels faded by the end of their journey. To a young boy accustomed to the green Pacific coast, New England was a dull-gray world of bleak mill towns, torrid summers, and winter ice storms. The family still struggled to get by, and during the long December nights, the walls of their poorly heated home seemed to constrict with tension. A damp chill seeped into Harvey's bedroom, so he slept like a polar explorer, bundled in a hat, jacket, and mittens and huddled beside a heated, felt-wrapped brick. When he walked to and from school, Harvey imagined he was the Arctic explorer Robert E. Peary crossing the "frozen wastes" as he tried to reach the North Pole.

In Lowell, however, the obstacles that Harvey faced weren't the jumbled ice ridges and hungry polar bears of the Far North, but the attacks of other children. Local bullies chased him, mocking his unfashionable long pants and his West Coast accent. One evening, a boy whom Harvey called the "Tormentor" shoved him off the sidewalk and into an icy pond. Whenever Harvey crept back up the shore, the Tormentor pushed him into the frigid water again. By the time Harvey escaped, shivering, his soaked clothes crackled with frost. A day later, feverish, Harvey lurked at the bottom of the school stairs, waiting for the bell to ring. When the Tormentor descended, Harvey punched him in the face. Soon afterward, Harvey's temperature spiked and he ended up in the hospital, where he lay delirious with nightmares of demons and flames. During the rest of his life, he would suffer from a deep-set terror of illness and death. For years, while returning home from school or asleep in his bed, he would imagine he was being pursued by knife-wielding assassins. The phantoms would vanish into the bushes each time he turned to look.

His Aunt Mildred and Uncle Les lived just south of Lowell, and on visits Harvey could escape his anxieties for hours while reading their collection of early *National Geographic* magazines. Within the pages, he recalled, "vast expanses on maps were marked 'unexplored' or 'unknown' or simply left blank white." Even during the 1930s, there were still high, remote places beyond the reach of any human feet. The top of Everest remained a blurry unknown. The only men who might have climbed it, George Mallory and Sandy Irvine, had disappeared near its mist-draped summit in 1924—just a year before Harvey was born.

In 1933, deeply homesick for Puget Sound, Harvey's parents decided to move back West. While there was little hope for work, at least the weather would be better, his mother said. From their new home in the northern outskirts of Seattle, Harvey could again visit his childhood paradises in the Cascades. At Huckleberry Creek, near Chinook Pass, the grown-ups fished by wading out into currents that flowed from the glaciers of Mount Rainer. Harvey and his cousins built castles out of river sand, launched small stick boats, and climbed the twisted roots of giant fallen trees until they were high above the ground. At night, the children waved burning marshmallow sticks like magic wands in the dark. Owls hooted above the murmur of the river. Stars blazed undimmed by city lights.

From another campsite by the North Fork of the Stillaguamish River, Harvey gazed up at Whitehorse Mountain, the first peak whose name he could remember learning. The mountain seemed alive, a "Being" in its own right, its distant white glaciers as rumpled as a horse's mane, its spires like giant ears pricked toward the sky. He kept looking, trying to see "the great animal prancing from summit to summit." He thought it was the "highest mountain in the world."

Though Harvey wasn't aware of conservation issues as a child, his beloved wild was already under threat. His father had found a job with Simpson Saws, selling hardware to the logging companies that were clear-cutting old-growth forests ever deeper into the backcountry. While Mount Rainier National Park had been established in 1899 and Olympic National Park in 1938, much of the Cascades remained largely unprotected. Hikers rarely visited the most isolated peaks. Despite the proximity of the range to Seattle and other cities, the labyrinths of ancient woods, steep-walled ravines, tendriled glaciers, and spiry mountains appeared almost mythological. In tale after tale, the dense underbrush of devil's club, vine maple, and slide alder seemed to come alive to fend off cartographers and climbers alike.

---

THOUSANDS OF YEARS BEFORE THE ARRIVAL OF WHITE EXPLORERS, Stó:lō people traveled widely across the Cascades, from the Fraser and Chilliwack Rivers of current British Columbia to the icy passes of turreted peaks in modern Washington State, gathering chert and huckleberries and hunting goats and bears along the way. In Stó:lō oral traditions, prominent peaks within the range were created by XeXà:ls ("Transformers"). These powerful beings arrived to change a formerly unpredictable and chaotic world into its current and recognizable form by turning some ancient people into rocks and mountains, landforms that remain sentient today.

Thiusoloc, a Stó:lō man, drew one of the oldest surviving maps of the Cascades. He'd guided topographer Henry Custer (known as Heinrich Küster in his birthplace of Switzerland) through the range during an 1859 survey to define the border between British Columbia and the recently established Washington Territory. "No where do the Mountain masses and Peaks present such strange, fantastic, dauntless, and startling outlines as here," Custer declared, though he described parts of their journey with foreboding words that are now legendary among Washington climbers:

> *Had it not been, for the bushes and small trees, which gave us an occasional point of appuy* [support], *we would have found it impracticable. As it was, it could only be overcome by the utmost caution on our part, by using our hands, arms, legs, and sticks freely in a multitude of novel positions. Once to have lost foot hold here, nothing would have been left to the unlucky climber but to resign himself to the inevitable fate of being dashed to pieces on the sharp and frightful rocks below.*

Thiusoloc charted some of the existing trails of Stó:lō people, sketching features according to a scale that reflected the time required to travel from place to place, rather than the geographic distances—practical for a range of dense woods and rain-slick ravines where (as Custer noted) journeys of even a few miles can stretch into multiple days. Custer praised Thiusoloc's cartography as "remarkable for its correctness and completeness." On his map, Indigenous names of summits still flourish in elegant script across the land.

Gradually, however, government mapmakers replaced the rich multitude of Coast Salish terms for many Cascade peaks with new, largely imported names chosen by non-Native explorers, while climbers focused on summiting prominent, snowy volcanoes: Mount Baker in 1868, Mount Rainier in 1870. Indigenous guides led their clients to the snow line or beyond, at times imparting mountaineering skills that had been acquired over thousands of years. In an 1870 journal entry, surveyor Daniel C. Linsley described learning how to glissade down steep slopes from Skagit people near Glacier Peak during a reconnaissance for the Northern Pacific Railroad.

Among many Coast Salish groups, tales abound of ancestors who took refuge on high summits of the Cascades and the Olympics during catastrophic floods. One Puyallup storyteller recalled a great-great grandfather who climbed təqʷuʔbəd (Mount Rainier) "in search of spirit power," relying on shards of elk horn to carve steps in the ice. He spent the night by a summit lake, where the mountain told him he would live to an advanced age and the waters would disappear after his death, a prediction that rang true many decades later. "White people have never seen the lake," affirmed the narrator. Clarence Pickernell of the Quinault Indian Nation described another lost place: a sacred valley deep in the Olympics that is walled by high peaks where a stream runs past wildflower meadows and vibrant evergreens.

In *High Worlds of the Mountain Climber*, Harvey later observed: "Often the climber entertains an exciting notion that perhaps he is the very first human being ever to visit this particular small part of the surface of the earth. And certainly there are still a good many dips and rises in the high country of the Northwest not described in any climbing guide or journal." Nonetheless, Harvey pointed out, Native hunters had long followed animals high up volcanic mountainsides. Early settlers, foresters, and cartographers had scrambled up summits to get better views of the surrounding land. Miners had pursued glints of riches, real or imaginary, on tall cliffs. "It gravels a man, as he hammers a piton into a crack during a daring lead, to suddenly spy a vein of quartz chipped by some prospector of sixty years ago," Harvey admitted. Still, he noted, summits of less accessible spires may have remained untrodden through the 1930s, "so well defended by valley jungles and alpine rock and ice that probably only the modern climber has been sufficiently unreasonable to make the effort."

When Harvey first arrived as a Boy Scout at Camp Parsons on the Olympic Peninsula in 1938, he hadn't yet given in to the allure of these hidden peaks. He was still planning to sign up for a boat trip along the Hood Canal—a way of practicing for his dream of sailing around the globe. He switched to the backpacking trip to Marmot Pass as soon as he read the words of the Kipling poem—the same lines that had echoed through the dreams of J. Norman Collie—scorched across a wooden sign in the mess hall:

Something hidden. Go and find it.
Go and look behind the Ranges—
Something lost behind the Ranges.
Lost and waiting for you. Go!

Past the road's end, giant firs, hemlocks, and cedars loomed on either side of the Quilcene Trail that led to Marmot Pass. Flashes of sunlight glanced off countless tints of green—moss, lichen, needles, leaves, ferns, and devil's club—like the facets of emeralds. The woods reminded Harvey of the groves of Huckleberry Creek, only much thicker and wilder. After hours of hiking, the troop emerged into the bright alpine light. Rocky bluffs rose like watchtowers above arid rockslides. A steep slope plunged below the trail toward the river's silver thread. The Boy Scout leader hadn't allowed them to bring water bottles, tents, or heavy warm clothes. Harvey sucked on a pebble to distract himself from his thirst as he stumbled, panting, to Camp Mystery, a small clearing by a tree-shaded stream. After dinner, he shivered in his cheap wool sleeping bag. High mountaintops still glowed with evening sun. Night pooled in the valleys.

Too cold to sleep, Harvey got up again and walked along the trail by himself to stay warm, pretending he was on a quest. "I discovered the Source of the Big Quilcene River," he recounted, "where it gushed from under a boulder, cold and sparkling and delicious." Even if it wasn't "the source of the Nile," he felt purified. Ahead, the meadows seemed both strange and recognizable, like fragments of familiar fairy tales and forgotten dreams. Flowers multiplied like stars.

He remained at the top of Marmot Pass until the sun disappeared and the western peaks turned black. One was named Mount Mystery. "I'd thought all the wilderness was in Africa and South America and places like that," he later wrote. "I didn't know there was any just 30 miles from our house." The edges of the mountains dissolved and grew until they became bigger than they were on any map. The forest stretched into a dark wildwood. The valley sunk into a fathomless chasm of shadows. The hues of crimson dusk and purple night seemed too vivid to be real. This was "the World-as-it-Should-Be," he thought, "the World-as-it-was-Promised-in-Storybooks."

By the time the group returned to Seattle, Harvey had lost interest in sailing. He wanted to become the first person to climb Mount Everest. "Actually, I hoped Mallory had got to the top and I'd find the proof up there," he explained. "But if he hadn't, it might as well be me." Reading Noel Odell's words in John Noel's *The Story of Everest*, Harvey imagined himself standing with the author above 25,000 feet, watching as the clouds cleared for a moment and the silhouetted figures of Mallory and Irvine flickered along the summit ridge. "They were going strong," Odell recalled. "It is quite possible and even likely that Mallory and Irvine reached the top and were overtaken by the night in the descent, exhausted and frozen to death." The unsolved mystery fascinated Harvey. "That's where I came in," he recounted. "Whatever happened after 1924 was unknown to the Seattle Public Library. For me in 1938, Everest was Mallory and Irvine 600 feet from the summit of the earth, going strong." Book by book, Harvey read the library's entire collection of exploration literature, dreaming about visiting real places such as Denali and the North and South Poles, as well as quasi-mythic ones, like the Mountains of the Moon.

Once a week, after his high school classes, Harvey took a streetcar to downtown Seattle and snuck up the staircases of tall buildings, sliding past office doors to stand on roofs and stare at the distant snows of Mount Rainier. Settlers once thought this peak was the tallest mountain on the planet, he remembered. Even now, its immense vertical relief and otherworldly ice made it seem, to Harvey, like a backyard Roof of the World, "the largest single-peak glacier system of the old 48 states," he wrote. Later, in one of his imaginative tales, he described a plot by Seattle mountaineers to pile stones, concrete, or cinders atop the apex of Rainier until it became the tallest summit in the Lower 48.

At Camp Parsons, Harvey heard stories about a twenty-two-year-old Eagle Scout, Delmar Fadden, who tried to climb Rainier alone in the winter of 1936, reportedly (or so the Parsons rumors went) to gain the attention of someone who might sponsor him on an Everest expedition. Searchers found Delmar's body at around 13,000 feet, frozen against the ice. One of his pockets contained a roll of film that proved he'd reached the summit of Rainier—the first known winter ascent of the Emmons Glacier route. To Harvey, it seemed like a local version of the Mallory legend. He copied down lines from a poem that Fadden had written in his journal: "If a dream / Meant anything to me / Would it seem / A bold reality? / If I knew / My hand of fate, / Would I do— / Or hesitate?"

As a teenager, Harvey began producing stacks of creative stories, full of allusions to medieval myths, eighteenth-century imaginary voyages, and twentieth-century fantasy novels. Already, he was trying to rewrite history. In "King of the Cannibal Island," Harvey presented what he called "my idea of what an adventure story should be." The protagonist, a US Marine, describes having second thoughts about conquering a mythic country: "And now the whites were attempting to steal their [the Indigenous people's] island, for theft it was, whatever the name." The Marine finally drives off his fellow Americans and declares that he "never cared much for imperialism anyway."

In 1942, Harvey composed an early hoax, although this one was obviously satirical, and he mailed it off to *The New Yorker*. Titled "The Truth About Shakespeare and Other Frauds," his pseudo-scholarly article addressed long-standing debates about whether someone other than Shakespeare wrote the great bard's plays. Harvey began: "For the better part of ninety-seven years I have devoted every waking hour to the searching out and making known of facts relative to the case. My full report is contained in my 10,567 page forthcoming book." After advancing various absurdist theories, he concluded with glee: "Anne Boleyn wrote the plays, and that is why Henry VIII cut off her head . . . and after her death blamed them on William Shakespeare. . . . Those interested in a complete discussion of my numerous discoveries, along with a full size map of the world and ten simple cures for colds, may obtain copies from me for thirty seven cents plus tax, which is exactly what any reputable scrap paper dealer will give you for them." Harvey saved the magazine's form rejection letter, one of the first in a large collection of similar slips.

Other early Harvey stories describe quests for ideal peaks. In one unfinished draft, a group of climbers set off on a journey to find the "mysterious goal toward which our lives since high school had been pointed." At last, the narrator declares, "This mountain range of all ranges, the most beautiful and most rarely visited, was now before us. . . . We slept supperless in a weird fantasy that night, but with a hunger of the soul, which had afflicted us for years, at least partly satisfied." The characters fall asleep as if spellbound, without pitching their tents. When they awake, drenched from a rainstorm, they feel the foreboding of an approaching "nightmare," and they sense that their search will be "wasted."

In a poem, Harvey depicted an imaginary mountain as "a peaceful, secret home." The summit is "high," "barren," "rocky," "forbidding, grand, with mystery." A snowfield shines on its shoulder. Delicate blossoms create an impression of "Utopian order" and a "fairyland of splendor." Throughout his writings and his wanderings as an adult, Harvey would return to similar landscapes in the mountains of Washington. In one particular alpine basin in the Cascades, he encountered wildflowers, barren summits, a bright snowfield, and a shadowed, mysterious peak. When he first started writing guidebooks, he would include oblique allusions to this place. Later, he would try to keep it secret.

All through high school, Harvey kept hiking in the mountains with the Boy Scouts and with friends. He used an old-fashioned alpenstock (an iron-tipped wooden staff popular before the spread of ice axes) to climb his first glacier and slid down in a billow of snow. On another excursion, as he scrambled through a gap between the evocatively named Mount Deception and Mount Mystery, he felt as if he'd entered one of the Shangri-La scenes in the 1937 movie version of *Lost Horizon*. At the foot of Mystery Glacier, a buttress towered above a moat-like lake. Streams of meltwater sparkled through wildflowers and lush meadows, converging into a waterfall that poured from the basin toward the shadows of dark woods. Higher up, a hillock of alpine tundra and stunted trees appeared like a miniature garden.

"One might still build a castle there," he daydreamed. "One might still, with a band of comrades, stand off the world. Even one might still save a princess from ogres—for despite all I still believe in a nut-brown maid, a damsel with a dulcimer, a Deirdre in a Land of Youth. As I believe I might still be self-forgiven and become a prince again if I go on pilgrimage: 'The hooly blissful martir for to seke, / That hem hath holpen what they were seeke.'" Here, Harvey could picture himself seeking "a vision of the Grail." Long-lost, mythic places still seemed nearby: the imaginary realm of Xanadu, where the "damsel with the dulcimer" sang of Mount Abora; the Land of Youth (Tír na nÓg) of Irish legends, a country where no one ages; and the marvels of "strange strondes" and "sondry londes" described by Chaucer in *The Canterbury Tales.*

During a Boy Scout trip to Lillian Glacier in the Olympic Mountains, Harvey woke to the quickening beat of raindrops on his sleeping bag—the start of a storm that turned into an icy gale. Before long, water soaked through his layers of cotton clothing. The trailhead was about twenty-five miles away. Waves of fog swept across the mountains as he and the other Scouts fled. At the top of Lost Ridge, gusts blasted rain and snow horizontally against them until their legs turned blue with cold. Harvey paused to rest, and the memory of Marmot Pass engulfed him again. As terrifying as the storm was, it was also wondrous, part of some transcendent force he couldn't define. If he could survive his own epic, he concluded, "It wasn't so ridiculous to think about Rainier and the Mountains of the Moon and Everest."

Not long afterward, an intense pain developed in his hip and spread to other parts of his legs. A doctor told Harvey to stay out of the backcountry for a year—a pronouncement that made him feel as though he'd been exiled from heaven. Still longing for the wild, he hobbled around the small groves and overgrown roads closer to home. His friend Arild showed him how to trespass onto an expanse of private land called Hidden Lake. Only a short distance from downtown Seattle, the old-growth forest had its own particular, ancient fragrance. There was even a ravine filled with giant ferns and devil's club, and a stream that glimmered over glossy rocks, like a miniature version of a remote Cascades valley.

One day, Harvey ventured into a part of Hidden Lake he called the "White Space on my map," floundering through nets of tree branches and thorns as he pursued daydreams of long-vanished ice age glaciers. "I had a fantasy of stumbling into a secret basin, a miniature Deception Basin," he wrote. "That was scientifically impossible. . . . But struggling and sweating through the White Space I could imagine . . . that I was at the foot of peaks I couldn't quite see." For hours, he thrashed up and down brush-choked hills and gullies. Somehow, he thought, the small woodlands must have expanded again into a vast, archaic wild. Then he stumbled back onto a broad trail. He recognized where he was—only about a dozen paces from where he'd started his hike. Disoriented by the dense vegetation, he'd been turning around in circles and loops. His bewilderment and imagination had worked like magic to scramble time and space.

During his senior year in high school, Harvey came across the term *mystical experience*. He knew right away what it meant to him: Marmot Pass. At Hidden Lake, where the trees were just as big as those along the Quilcene Trail, he tried to re-create a similar sensation: "I'd lie on my back in the breezes of a waterfall and soak up the coolness of the forest floor, breathe smells of trees and bushes, listen to birds near and far, and fix my gaze straight up through the trees to the sky. I sent the simplest message possible. Put in words it would have been: 'I am here. Are You?'"

CHAPTER 9

# The Ticking of Doomsday Clocks

BY 1942, WHEN HARVEY HAD recovered enough from the pain in his hip and legs to return to the mountains, the United States had entered World War II. There were blackouts and air-raid drills, along with the rumble of military trucks on the roads and antiaircraft guns in city parks. The carefully built worlds of Harvey's boyhood dreams seemed about to shatter. He and Arild cut school on weekdays to hike and worked on weekends to buy gas for road trips in Harvey's rattly 1930 Model A. As they wallowed around the snow-drifted shores of an alpine lake, they saw that avalanche debris had crushed some of the bushes. Invisible slides fell through a white fog of snow and clouds, roaring like the sounds of distant bombs. "We burst out laughing," Manning recalled. While their friends were still stuck in a classroom, he and Arild were "here, cool and calm and sane, in a void loud with death."

Arild soon left to serve in the navy. Since Harvey was too young for the draft, he enrolled at the University of Washington, where he again fell ill. This time, a doctor told him, the problem lay in his heart. Although Harvey was thus officially disqualified from military service, he thought he could die at any moment. He stumbled out of the health center to the circular pond at the heart of campus. From there, on clear days, Mount Rainier shines in the distance, but on that evening it was hidden behind clouds. Drops of rain beat the surface of the water like the noise of a broken pendulum, striking back and forth erratically. For the rest of his life, Harvey would be haunted by the sound of clocks, echoed in the rhythm of his boots on a mountainside and the pulse of his heart. He was "always waiting for the 'tick' with no answering 'tock.'"

He tried to distract himself from his fear by writing, dreaming, drinking, and hiking. One morning, in a university library in Parrington Hall, Harvey was obsessively rereading Percy Bysshe Shelley's elegy, "Adonais," about the death of John Keats at twenty-five. Light and shadow blinked through the windows above the bookshelves. Outside, the gusts of a departing storm blew scraps of white clouds through green trees. Glimpses of blue dazzled. Verses streamed through Harvey's mind: "He is made one with Nature: there is heard / His voice in all her music." The wind seemed to lift him through the fading library walls, past the rustling leaves, and into the clouds. "I am borne darkly, fearfully, afar; / Whilst, burning through the inmost veil of Heaven, / The soul of Adonais, like a star, / Beacons from the abode where the Eternal are." Harvey put the book down and walked across campus. The lawns stretched on and on, extending like a vast alpine meadow toward a vanishing point in the sky. Once more, the sky seemed tinged with the afterglow of the dusk above Marmot Pass. A sense of uncertain promise seemed to linger in the air: the possibility of some transformative power in the heights.

The roof of Parrington Hall turned out to be a good place for a solitary aspiring mountaineer to practice. Harvey relied on the friction generated by the soles of his feet and the palms of his hands to scramble up the steeply sloped shingles. From the top of a ventilator shaft, he watched the sunrise light up Mount Rainier. Along the horizons to the west and east, the peaks of the Olympics and the Cascades were still in shadows, waiting, trembling on the verge of the miraculous. In a few hours, whenever he could escape from school, his car would take him away from the city to mountainsides where mists drifted through ancient trees and dewdrops glittered like diamonds. Alone in the hills after dark, he felt his worst nightmares dissolve: "The fears proper to the place were the old ones, the natural ones."

His alpine idylls were interrupted by reminders of the ongoing war. Mountain warfare troops marched by him in the hills. A pair of skywatchers peered out the windows of a Cascades lookout cabin, poised to warn of potential enemy planes. Japanese American classmates were sent to internment camps. In the summer of 1945, Harvey read "the breath-stopping August headline announcing man had created hell on Earth," the news that American forces had dropped atomic bombs on Hiroshima and Nagasaki. It seemed to Harvey that the remnants of his country's idealism began to perish in the mushroom clouds.

During the aftermath of World War II, as Cold War tensions heightened between the US and the Soviet Union and the nuclear arms race took off, defense industries in the Seattle area boomed. In 1943, the government had evicted residents of Hanford in the eastern half of the state to create a plutonium production center, which grew to include nine reactors. Modern society appeared to be ticking closer to apocalypse. He'd have to search for signs of inspiration elsewhere, Harvey decided, in the visions he experienced in the mountains and in the worlds he created in his mind.

After he finished his BA in English in 1945, Harvey thought of getting a PhD, but he decided to take time off first. While working at a lumber mill, he learned that the old-growth forest at Hidden Lake had been logged, its sanctuary turned into a ruddy gash of stumps and mud—a "home" to which he could never return. With the war's end, however, Arild came back to Washington, ready for more alpine misadventures. During one ill-conceived glissade that turned into a headlong fall, Harvey somersaulted through clouds of snow. After hundreds of feet, he stopped sensing movement or sound, apart from the musical notes of unseen water. Just as he pictured himself merging into the universe, he came to a halt. "Life—abundant, exuberant, transcendent—that's what Marmot Pass was all about, and Deception Basin, and even at the worst of the blow, Lost Ridge," he declared.

Harvey also explored the backstreets of Seattle, encountering pockets of lost wild time amid the walls of old shanties and ruined mills. He met aged men and women in the Northlake neighborhood who told stories of nineteenth-century quests for gold, deep within the Alaska Range and the Washington Cascades. In 1889, the prospector Joseph Pearsall had scrambled to a ridge crest on Hubbart Peak, where he caught sight of a strange, luminous mountain beyond the high walls of a canyon. Sparkles of reddish gold and silvery gray coated the flanks of the peak, hinting at veins of precious minerals. "Boys, the world is ours!" one of Pearsall's friends later exclaimed when he viewed the same gleaming mountainsides. But the difficulties of extracting silver, gold, and lead from this isolated region proved greater than any of its riches. After years of fighting mudslides, floods, and heavy winter snows, the miners gave up and followed other gold-rush dreams to the Far North. Only a ghost town remained of the mines of Monte Cristo, its legend rusting alongside its old buildings. "There'd been wilderness then," Harvey realized, "a vast wilderness of which I'd known a tiny remnant at Hidden Lake. . . . If I lived to their age, what memories would I have of 1946?

Looking back from the 21st century, what transformations would I see in the city? And in the wilderness, now pushed far up mountain valleys?"

One day, as he headed down University Way to meet his friend Bob at a tavern, Harvey bumped into Betty Lorraine Williams, a fellow English major. "Or better say," Harvey wrote, "she ran into (literally) me." Betty had taken time off school to recover from eye surgery, and she was still having problems with her depth perception. Harvey invited her to join them for a drink. At the tavern, Betty tried to smoke a cigarette, but she set her eyebrow alight instead. To Harvey, she seemed reassuringly unthreatening, "an amusing kid sister." But when he and Bob started talking about epics in the mountains, Betty contributed her own tale about getting benighted with a friend in a rain-swept forest, shivering over a meal of raw potatoes after their fire wouldn't start.

"Was she as artless as she seemed?" Harvey wondered. Betty brought the friend from her alpine ordeal to a subsequent night of drinking. "Monie *climbs* mountains!" Betty said, and she laughed as the boys stared. Harvey had, up until then, more or less only hiked up mountains. And here was a twenty-something woman, Monie Long, a budding mathematician who had summited all the peaks he'd heard of in the Cascades, along with many more he hadn't. "Worst of all," he recalled, Monie "had climbed Rainier—often."

When Bob asked Monie why she climbed mountains, she responded with an offhand rendition of Mallory's famous words about Everest: "Because it is there." Then she recited two lines of grandiose verse from a Swiss guide, Andreas Maurer. Perhaps, as Monie eyed her male listeners through her coke-bottle glasses, she infused Maurer's words with an edge of sarcasm: "Men can go where the clouds can go / But they must be *sturdy* men!"

On the West Coast, local alpine clubs, such as the Sierra Club in California and The Mountaineers in Washington, promoted a relatively inclusive culture, and women participated in greater numbers than in many other parts of the country. Some of them, like Betty and Monie, found that climbing offered more scope for self-liberation than the rest of society. Betty had initially gone to Reed College in Portland, Oregon, where she'd rebelled against her conservative upbringing by briefly becoming a Communist (of the Trotskyite variety) and (even more "scandalous") by swimming alone with male classmates. Despairing, Betty's mother pulled her out of Reed. A year later, Betty transferred to the University of Washington, where she met Monie. "Somehow," her son, Paul, later wrote, "she found the Mountaineers, a place where her mother would never find her, and the mountains became her symbol of freedom and happiness." To improve their climbing skills, Betty and Monie anchored one end of a rope to the frame of a bed, and then took turns belaying each other outside the window and onto the walls of their shared Seattle apartment.

Intimidated at first, Harvey only agreed to join Monie and Betty on hiking trips. By autumn, however, he'd begun to trust Monie's leadership and he realized he could follow her to "a rich lode of alpine lore." That October, she promised something "a bit more interesting" for Harvey, Betty, and Bob. She'd take them up a climbing route on Cruiser Peak, a slender rock spire in the Olympics, with some "exposure," she said.

"That's the climbers' euphemism for 'one false step and you go screaming through space and splatter your brains on a rockside,'" Harvey thought. Robust nylon ropes were not yet commercially available. For Monie's less resilient manila rope, the old adage of "The leader must not fall" remained terrifyingly true.

"A cheap thrill," Monie assured Harvey. "Good for laughs."

Icy gusts buffeted the four friends at the top of a col. Monie said they'd been moving too slowly to reach the true apex that day, so she'd guide them to a false summit instead. With the rope coiled and slung over her shoulder, she scurried up a narrow slab of stone until she vanished into the winds. Bob rushed after her. Behind them, Harvey felt as if he were crawling up a roof into the sky. "The knobby basalt was easier than the slick shingles of Parrington Hall. . . . But this roof was high, way high . . . and below me everywhere was air and I'd no gin in my blood. Wind wailed by ears, deafening, unsettling. I needed one hand to hang onto my hat, the other to hang onto my glasses. No hands for hanging onto Earth. The next gust would hurl me into the void." Terrified, he turned back and huddled with Betty in a sheltered nook. Later, he realized that was the moment he and Betty fell in love.

That autumn, Betty started her senior year. Harvey tried to focus on graduate school classes at the university and on his work as a teaching assistant. But as he paged through the piles of bluebook exams he had to grade, he couldn't stop daydreaming about mountains. He knew that, if he proved lucky enough to get a tenure-track position, he might have to leave the Cascades for some desolate flatland college town. After he and Betty spent a particularly idyllic day of scrambling around mossy boulders by a snowmelt creek, Harvey gave up on academia—and on trying to find a secure job at all.

But he still had to make a living. Surviving by shoplifting, he mused (with his typical sense of humor), could only go on for so long before he got caught. "What does an English major do if he doesn't professorize?" he wondered. "What does he know? Words. Who in Seattle buys words?" No one wanted his, it seemed. After his applications to various media outlets were rejected, Harvey went to work at a warehouse. When he got in trouble for reading on the job, he found employment in the University of Washington chemistry stockroom. He and Betty rented an apartment in a ramshackle house near University Way—although Harvey couldn't officially move in until he produced a marriage license to prove to the landlady that they weren't living in sin.

Soon after the legal matters were taken care of and the landlady was appeased, the Mannings set off for their honeymoon—another climbing trip in the Cascades with Monie as their stalwart guide. The couple had chosen Monte Cristo, one of the false El Dorados that Harvey continued to find fascinating. Relics of rusted mining equipment appeared in the mists. Alders and firs were growing back, consuming the remnants of the lost town. From here, as mountaineering historian Lowell Skoog recounts, nineteenth-century prospectors had made nocturnal winter ascents, racing up mountainsides with alpenstocks, snowshoes, and hatchets, to stake their mining claims as soon as midnight struck, at the very beginning of a new year. Monie, Betty, and Harvey kicked steps up a nearby slope in a more leisurely fashion to the crest of Silvertip Peak. For a moment, while the sun flashed through dark clouds and lit the snows, Harvey imagined himself in "Mallory's world." Then he gazed down to Silver Creek: only gashes of clearcuts and piles of debris remained where he and Arild had once wandered past old-growth trees. Solely above tree line, it seemed, could a paradise be secure.

When Harvey's Model A sputtered out, he purchased a used car with a V-8 engine, capable of bumping along at forty-two miles an hour instead of twenty-eight. Although he missed the rambling pace of his old vehicle, the new car enabled more frequent trips to the mountains. Climbing had become his escape hatch from the conventional life that was closing in on him and Betty. Monie sensed his restlessness and suggested they return to complete the ascent of Cruiser Peak before the first winter storms. At the base of the summit tower, past his previous high point, the stone turned as hard and glossy as congealed lava. Harvey couldn't discern any edges or ripples where a climber could even pause to rest. There were no cracks to place a piton. If Monie slipped while leading, the sharp rocks below her might cut the rope that connected them. Harvey might watch her tumble to the valley, unable to stop her fall.

Monie told him not to worry. Soon, she disappeared around a corner, her progress indicated only by the slow movement of the fragile manila strands through his fingers. The rope stopped for fifteen minutes. Harvey lit a cigarette with one hand while he held on tightly with the other. "Bad spot . . . hang on," Monie's voice wobbled from somewhere above. The rope quivered and slid upward again. Harvey smelled something burning: he'd been so focused on grasping the rope that he'd singed himself with the cigarette. At last, Monie called out that she was safe at an anchor. Harvey felt dizzy at the sight of what she'd just climbed. The slant of rock shimmered like glass, reflecting the greenish tints of distant trees. As he wriggled upward, his legs trembled and his tennis shoes skittered off the volcanic stone. Finally, the surface became more corrugated, and he scampered to the top.

"The rope from above was my faith, my prayer, my church," Harvey declared in rapture, but the experience convinced Monie that he needed to take more responsibility for his own safety. At the start of the next summer season, in 1948, she told the Mannings they had to sign up for a climbing course with The Mountaineers. Despite his dislike of large groups, Harvey conceded.

Their first trips weren't too auspicious. During one course, other climbers knocked off a large rock that whizzed through the air, almost striking Harvey and Betty. On another outing, while Betty practiced glissading, students above her began tumbling uncontrollably in a mass of falling bodies, sharp metal gear, and sloughing snow. A flying ice axe struck Betty's side. By the time Harvey and the others caught up to her, she was lying in a patch of blood, the only person injured. Evacuated to a Seattle hospital, Betty recovered, and though the near-disaster stirred forebodings in their minds, the couple remained drawn to the mountains. As his skills grew and he met more local climbers, Harvey realized how little published information about the North Cascades existed. Scattered across the maps, topographic names beckoned like signals from imaginary countries: *Inspiration Glacier, Phantom, Deception, Mystery*. Others, such as *Azurite* and *Ruby*, reflected fleeting dreams of riches. Near the top of 8,868-foot Eldorado, Harvey watched mysterious summits emerge through gaps in the mist like visions from storybooks. His trip leader didn't know what to call some of the local mountains. "Neither did the map," Harvey observed.

CHAPTER 10

# The Ascent of the Peak Formerly Known as North Star

DURING HIS RAMBLES IN THE Cascades, Harvey continued to keep an eye out for unusual peaks. The distant white speck of Glacier Peak flashed like a star from the north, its summit half-hidden by a nebula of other snowy mountains. "Entirely overlooked by school geography books and Chambers of Commerce," he exulted. "A secret volcano known only to initiates." Through his work in the university stockroom, Harvey had met chemical engineers Kermit Bengtson and Dick Widrig, and in July 1948, they'd invited him to join a six-man team to establish a new route on the southwest shoulder of the secluded mountain. At 10,525 feet, the summit elevation was greater than that of any peak Harvey had climbed before. He'd long been afraid that high altitudes might jar the rhythm of his heart, but as they scurried up and down the icy slopes, pursued by dark storm clouds, his pulse ticked on, steady and safe.

Back in Seattle, Harvey went to sit by the campus pond where he'd once imagined hearing a premonition of his death in the raindrops that pounded the waters. This day, the sky was clear and Rainier appeared vast beyond measurement or thought, like the translucent orb of another planet hovering above the city streets. "Whereas hiking stretches out time," Harvey mused, "climbing shatters the temporal prison altogether." Since he'd started exploring the mountains, each year of his life had seemed ten times as long. It was as if a secret of eternal life actually existed in the heights—just as it did in the old legends—or else an illusion that you might die trying to find.

To Harvey, Rainier had become "The Mountain," an archetype, more than any specific geographic place on Earth. Later that month, when he finally slogged his way up its glaciated slopes with a Mountaineers group, the beat of his heart remained steady, but the ordinary world unspun. As he neared the summit, he recalled "a sudden unEarthly loftiness, as if The Mountain . . . has broken away from roots in hidden lowlands and is adrift in infinity."

What could be next? He'd probably never go on the kind of Himalayan or Arctic expedition that he'd dreamed about as a child. He had neither the money nor the vacation time. Sponsorship seemed unlikely. Still, there were ways to re-create the experience of classic adventures and mythic tales closer to home, with a little imagination. In 1949, when Fred Beckey's *Climber's Guide to the Cascade and Olympic Mountains of Washington* became available, some unknowns had been lost, yet new mysteries emerged. Harvey noticed the description of a strange-sounding mountain in the North Cascades called Bonanza, one that Beckey hadn't had a chance to climb yet. A glaciated mass of "flaring ridges" and "fringing summits," it looked like a "huge granitic spider," as Beckey later wrote in *Challenge of the North Cascades*.

Harvey turned to a *Mazama* article to read about its first ascent. The author Curtis Ijames described the summit in the kind of tantalizing style that Harvey later used in his own stories of imaginary peaks: "Bonanza, the greatest peak of the Chelan Range, has long occupied the uncertain position of being Washington's mystery mountain." In June 1937, Ijames had approached the peak with a team from Portland on "a journey through trackless country seldom seen by man," he boasted. After enduring a furious blizzard, stomping up an ice slope studded with avalanche debris, chopping a passage through a giant cornice, reaching an impassable chasm, and backtracking to try another route, the Portland climbers nearly got buried by a series of snowslides. "A real thrill!" he declared. Only three of the original five members continued all the way to the top. "Another milestone in the conquest of the North Cascades," concluded the author.

In his own analysis of the *Mazama* article, Harvey sounded bemused, though intrigued, by Ijames's enthusiastic prose. Near the top, Harvey observed, the Portland team seemed to have encountered "such an obstacle as Mallory and Irvine faced 600 feet from Everest's summit. The *Mazama* author shuddered in print at the memory of the hundred-foot wall of flawless rock." Such difficulties were at odds with local rumors that Bonanza was an easy mountain to climb. But, Ijames explained, these discrepancies appeared to arise from a cartographic error in 1904, when the USGS switched its name with that of a lower peak once called North Star Mountain. Compared to the 8,096-foot peak previously known as Bonanza, the new Bonanza (formerly known as North Star) appeared far more daunting. At 9,511 feet, it was the highest non-volcanic peak in Washington.

In May 1950, with some trepidation, Harvey joined several friends on an attempt to make the second ascent of the new Bonanza. When they arrived at the base, fresh drifts had turned the glaciers to a "Himalayan white." At 8,000 feet, a sheen of wispy clouds blurred the sun: more snow was on its way. They retreated to the nearby community of Holden Village, where they asked local residents about the mountain. An engineer told them of someone who'd already completed a second ascent. Perhaps, Harvey thought, his group could at least make the third ascent. One of Harvey's climbing partners wrote a letter to the engineer's acquaintance, who replied that Bonanza was "nowhere near as bad as those Portland folks make out"—though he added that his young climbing partner had tumbled into a crevasse there, landed on an ice axe, and died.

Maybe the author of the *Mazama* article wasn't that experienced a climber, Harvey speculated. Perhaps Ijames had exaggerated the difficulties, and Bonanza's reputation as a mere scramble—even if it was based on the other mountain—wasn't that far off.

That June, Harvey and his friends hiked back into a world of burgeoning summer to try again. Forests of larches and aspens quivered with hints of green. Streaks of blue glowed across a melting glacial lake. To their surprise, they found an easy passage that avoided a barricade of frozen cliffs, and they continued over blocky stone steps to the summit ridge of Bonanza. Atop a final bump, Harvey glanced around him in confusion: the huge wall of the Portlanders' report was still nowhere in sight. It was only early afternoon, and there was no more mountain left.

The summit register contained something else unexpected: at least fifteen other parties had preceded them. "Who were all those others?" Harvey wondered. "One of them, presumably a non-fishing teetotaling bachelor with no other entertainment handy had climbed repeatedly, by several routes, sometimes alone, setting speed records and breaking them." With self-deprecating irony, Harvey concluded: "Ours was only the second 'mainstream' (non-Holden) ascent. We had rescued the giant from obscurity, would see to due honors in Seattle, where it mattered."

Perhaps the cartographic error that turned North Star into Bonanza inspired Harvey's future hoaxes. A careless or clever geographer, he must have realized, could change the name of a peak and move it from one place to another on a map. A mischief-minded writer could deliberately confuse locations and histories to make a mountain seem more daunting than it really was. A prankster could lure would-be peakbaggers, especially those who desired to set a record, and then abruptly disappoint them. A satirist could make a point about the hubris of visiting climbers by revealing the disparities between their perception of a route and that of local residents. Even the misadventures of a hapless "team from Portland" could suggest amusing future possibilities.

---

THE ENIGMAS AND ILLUSIONS OF BONANZA SPURRED HARVEY TO LOOK deeper into other mountain legends. In his fantasies, he roamed ever farther north, where he could imagine his way into the plots of classic stories, within "dreaming distance of the Pole." Harvey recalled tales of hardy prospectors stumbling through boreal forests and muskeg swamps during the Alaska and Yukon gold rushes. He pored over accounts of wooden ships crushed in a frozen Arctic Ocean and hot-air balloonists who crashed trying to fly to the North Pole. According to one of Harvey's unpublished memoirs, "Mount Everest and Me," a friend claimed that he'd seen gold-flecked sand on a rock island in the midst of an icecap, during an expedition to an unnamed location. He invited Harvey to make a return trip with him to claim the treasure. Briefly, Harvey felt tempted by the idea, before remembering he lacked the means for such a remote, unlikely quest. "He never told a simple, dull truth when an invention was more entertaining," Harvey admitted about his friend. "I preferred to believe everything."

Still, voyagers who fell prey to hoaxes or delusions interested Harvey the most. There was the American explorer Frederick Cook, infamous for his disputed claim to have been the first to summit Denali in 1906. Or the British Royal Navy officer Sir John Franklin, who unwittingly led his men to an icy doom while searching for the fabled Northwest Passage. Harvey's favorite book in this genre was Vilhjalmur Stefansson's *Unsolved Mysteries of the Arctic*, "wherein he pretty much solves the mysteries," Harvey noted, "including how and why Franklin's people starved to death in an area the natives of the region considered their richest hunting ground."

Since Alaska was too distant and expensive, Harvey made mini-expeditions across the Canadian border, venturing into the periphery of his dreams. Atop Mount Athabasca in the Rockies of Alberta, he looked inside the summit register—a wine bottle filled with pieces of paper—to find the signature of Noel Odell. One of the first ascensionists was J. Norman Collie, who had sought the mysteries of Mount Hooker and Mount Brown. On Mount Sir Donald, in British Columbia's Selkirks, Harvey stared out at numerous unsummited peaks whose names he didn't know—a "reservoir of wildness to slake the thirst of generations." And from the Niuts, isolated peaks deep in the Coast Mountains, he looked toward a region that still bewildered mapmakers, who described it merely as having "extensive icefields."

Back in Washington, Harvey joined a January 1951 expedition to Mount Olympus. As his team stomped through rain-crusted snow toward the peak, he felt he was no longer in "the same space-time as Seattle." The "*true* pole of remoteness," Harvey mused, "has to be somewhere in winter." In the Olympics and Cascades, winter storms buried roads under dozens of feet of drifts, avalanches shook the mountainsides like earthquakes, and gusts screamed between frosted spires. Few people, then, were attempting ascents of remote Washington peaks during the coldest and darkest months of the year. In the long alpine dusk below Olympus, everything turned deep azure, from the cliffs glittering with rime to the swiftly flowing clouds. "Even the wind felt blue," Harvey noticed. Although the peaks had been climbed before, no one had yet trampled all those newly formed crystals of ice. His sense of awe swelled as a cold gale tore through their camp. By the time he and his partners had retreated through waist-high drifts to escape days of storm, Harvey felt he had survived a partial reenactment of British explorer Robert Falcon Scott's ill-fated expedition to the South Pole.

Around the same time, Harvey's interest in reaching actual summits was gradually waning. Like most longtime mountaineers, he confronted the rising death toll of friends. During an unroped ascent of Mount St. Helens in 1949, when Harvey tumbled into a crevasse, his outspread arms had caught hold of its edges and he'd dragged himself out. In 1952, the snow gave way on the same glacier, and a student named Art Jessett plunged into a chasm. Art, too, had been unroped, but he continued falling for more than seventy feet. By the time rescuers got to him, he was dead. That same year, another local climber, Dick Berge, was scrambling down brush-choked cliffs on the north face of Mount Baring when he plummeted into a hidden abyss. Harvey had been to the same place, and he could picture all too easily how the fatal accident happened. His own close calls were accumulating. During a solitary ascent of Castle Peak in the Pasayten Wilderness of the North Cascades, he'd felt a foothold shift and then snap off. As he clung to the rock with his hands, a void opened below him like a window into boundless mist.

Harvey's responsibilities were also growing. In addition to starting a family with Betty, he'd agreed to become the Climbing Committee chairman of The Mountaineers, and he'd finally taken a steady white-collar job, working in advertising at the *Seattle Post-Intelligencer*, one of the city's major newspapers. In the spring of 1952, Harvey and Betty bought a house and three acres on Cougar Mountain, a rolling hill above the town of Issaquah, fifteen miles from Seattle. Though only 1,598 feet above sea level at its highest point, Cougar Mountain bristled with dark forests of mossy trees—a refuge of wildness on the outskirts of developed lands.

On August 10, Harvey sat in a meadow outside their new house, daydreaming as he traced the distant blue skyline of peaks. Thunderheads bulged along the horizon like a second ridge crest, white and gleaming against a clear blue sky. The summits of the clouds must be three times higher than any earthly mountain, he calculated. Lost in wonder, he didn't realize how ominous they were. Just then, two of his younger climbing friends, University of Washington students Paul Brikoff and Robert Grant, were headed for the summit of Mount Stuart, a ragged peak in the central part of the Cascade Range. Harvey had turned down their invitation to join them so he could stay home with Betty, who was pregnant with their first child. Later, he learned that by the time Paul and Robert reached the top, lightning already flashed across surrounding mountaintops. As Paul put the summit register back in the metal container, the first of several bolts hit them.

The next day, Harvey joined the rescue team that found Paul lying dead on the summit. Robert, still alive, had collapsed by a creek where he'd managed to drag himself, and they evacuated him, slowly and painfully, on the back of a burro. Cam Beckwith, a member of the search party, told Harvey, "I've got to get the hell out of this country. I don't want my sons growing up looking at mountains." Harvey recalled Paul's own words to him during a recent alpine trip, when they'd worried about getting swept down cliffs by avalanches: "I don't care how brave anybody thinks I am. All I want is to come home alive from every peak I ever climb."

Harvey started to experience a strange vertigo during his ascents, as if the mountains kept turning on their sides. A crimson flower growing from an arête seemed to keel over when he glanced at it. A wall appeared to be shoving him backward into the void. His perspective on the purpose of wildland travel was also shifting, from climbing mountains to experiencing the landscape as a whole. "A climber must achieve the summit to extract the full goodness from a peak," he'd once thought. "In the last several years," he now realized, "I had learned (re-learned) to extract the goodness from below." It was what lay beneath the summits that made the Cascades unique: The juxtaposition of deep-green woods with shining glacial ice. The lush wildflowers, waterfalls, and snowfields. The sense of isolation, created not only by distance, but also by the slowness of moving through densely woven trees.

CHAPTER 11

# Private Mountains Free of Public Logic

BY THE MID-1950S, HARVEY REALIZED that much of the "goodness" of the old-growth woods in the Olympics and Cascades was in danger of vanishing. Logging had accelerated during World War II with the invention of the chain saw. Timber companies cut giant swaths across mountain valleys, like Tolkien's orcs tearing down ancient trees in Fangorn, creating "wastes of stump and bramble." In a 1960 letter to a local conservationist, Harvey described a "diabolical" Forest Service map of planned logging roads into Olympic National Park that threatened to extend almost to Camp Mystery, below Marmot Pass: "They have wiped out the scenes of my mountain childhood. They are busy now wiping out the scenes of my mountain maturity."

The rapid destruction of Pacific Northwest forests was part of a larger transformation of the American landscape. As journalist James Howard Kunstler later wrote, a "Geography of Nowhere" was consuming vast expanses of former countryside across the United States. Parking lots, superhighways, and suburban sprawl oozed like the lava of a giant, erupting volcano, destroying acres of lush meadows, farmland, and woods, and leaving desolations of pavement in its wake. A sense of disorientation sprung from endless iterations of the same fast-food restaurants, chain stores, and motels, and from wastelands of shopping plazas, strip malls, tract homes, and office parks. Main streets gave way to noisy traffic-jammed roads with little or no space for pedestrians to roam. "Why did America build a reality of terrible places from which people longed to escape?" Kunstler asked.

"Junkspace," Dutch architect Rem Koolhaas mused after moving to the United States, "is authorless, yet surprisingly authoritarian." Atop his Cougar

Mountain home, Harvey watched a sea of urban lights wash across the landscape, from the shores of Lake Washington to the satellite city of Bellevue, and finally to Issaquah. Coast to coast, city life seemed more and more dystopian as officials of the Canwell Committee and the House Un-American Activities Committee pursued hundreds of people accused of socialist leanings. In 1949, after refusing to testify before the Canwell Committee, Harvey's beloved philosophy professor and climbing partner Herbert Phillips had been fired for alleged Communism and forced to leave academia permanently. When Betty was a student, she'd been briefly involved in American Youth for Democracy, one of the organizations the US attorney general now listed as "subversive." In his memoirs, Harvey wrote of FBI agents in neatly pressed suits and ties who visited Cougar Mountain to ask intrusive questions. Staring at the freeway to Seattle, Harvey imagined drivers crashing into each other as a new form of bleak escapist sport: "A person angry at the society that condemns him/her to waste his/her life manufacturing poison, selling garbage, ticky-tackying Eden, building jets, or writing manuals on how to launch an ICBM [intercontinental ballistic missile], may score enough on the drive to work to keep him/her cheerful all morning."

---

AS GRAY TENDRILS OF ROADS AND HIGHWAYS STRETCHED ACROSS THE country, distances also seemed to contract. The blue and white horizons of mountains suddenly appeared much closer to the growing cities and suburbs of Washington State. From 1940 to 1960, the state's population rose by 63 percent. And with the surging economy of the postwar decades, more people could afford cars and fuel for weekend trips. REI, founded in Seattle in 1938 as a small gear-purchasing co-op, began its growth into a nationwide chain. New equipment, initially developed for the military during World War II, helped popularize mountaineering. Nylon ropes made falling safer. Warmer clothing offered better protection from storms like the one that struck Harvey and the other cotton-clad Scouts on Lost Ridge. The diminishment of backcountry suffering, Harvey later realized, carried a cost: "If wilderness could speak, it would protest bulldozers and chain saws and motorcycles—but also feet, feet, feet."

During the 1950s, however, Harvey still viewed logging as the greatest threat to the forests, so he began to use his writing skills to try to enlist this new generation of eager hikers, backpackers, and mountaineers in the fight to protect wildlands. In 1955, he became the head of the subcommittee formed to update The Mountaineers' how-to manual, which eventually became the classic instruction book, *Mountaineering: The Freedom of the Hills*. Although numerous writers contributed to the text, Harvey's editorial vision played a key role in the final result, imbued with flashes of quirky humor and an ethos of respect for the natural world.

Two years later, Harvey and Betty joined the newly formed North Cascades Conservation Council. The board members, who soon became their allies and friends, included some of the most influential West Coast conservationists of the mid-twentieth century, such as Patrick Goldsworthy, a key figure in the movement to create a North Cascades national park; his fellow leader Polly Dyer, an indefatigable cofounder of the Pacific Northwest chapter of the Sierra Club; and David Brower, the first executive director of the Sierra Club. Brower was also a prolific mountaineer who had recently relinquished bagging summits in favor of saving trees, just as Harvey was contemplating doing. In 1939, Brower had been part of the first recorded ascent of Shiprock (Tsé Bit'a'í), a desert monadnock in the Navajo Nation. Formed of volcanic rock, the peak rises out of the earth like the giant bird that once bore the ancestors of Navajo/Diné people on its back. High above the plains, Brower and his partners drilled a bolt below an expanse of overhanging stone, where they felt as if they were "walking on air." Today, climbing is forbidden within the boundaries of the Navajo Nation. Diné mountaineer Len Necefer observes that marks left by past climbers on sacred rock formations appear "to my relatives . . . just as distasteful as those of someone pounding pitons into the Western Wall in Jerusalem." Brower, too, came to regret the bolts, which he perceived as symbols of greater environmental damage to come.

During World War II, Brower served with the Tenth Mountain Division. While stationed in the Alps, he saw how war had devastated the landscape—but also how the tourism industry extended its networks of pavement and iron far up the peaks. Trails had become roads. Stone farmhouses and mountain huts had given way to big hotels and power plants. "Improve it and exploit it. Keep adding the comforts that each preceding addition has brought people to demand," he wrote in "How to Kill a Wilderness," a satirical list of "steps" published in the August 1945 *Sierra Club Bulletin* that likely inspired some of Harvey's future literary efforts. By 1956, Brower had largely given up climbing to devote himself to conservation, though he continued to scale mountains in his dreams at night.

Many of the mountains that glowed brightest in Harvey's mind likewise belonged to his memory and imagination. He began working as a textbook salesman, and as he traveled from hotel to hotel, town to town, he became afraid that he'd die far from the Cascades, a "lost spirit never able to find its way home." When he found time to go hiking, he stared at dawn-lit glacier snows as if he could imprint them on a photographic plate inside his mind: "Eyes opened and closed throughout the day, letting in the peaks—Magic, Mixup, Triplets, Johannesburg, Sahale, Forbidden, Eldorado. On the inside, these mingled with peaks from other places and other years in the Cascades and Olympics and Canadian Rockies and Selkirks, and with the peaks of a certain strange range known only in a recurring dream, private mountains free of public logic, ever in a state of becoming."

With his friends and family, Harvey worked out the details of his own "private mountains." Heidi Brooks, daughter of Dick and Grace Brooks, recalled that her parents and the Mannings were part of "a merry band" of hiking and climbing partners who amused themselves around campfires by designing elaborate pranks to embarrass anti-conservationists, outdoor industry profiteers, and egotistical climbers. "Most of the [plots] never came to fruition," Heidi said, but some of the ideas emerged in Harvey's climbing hoaxes.

Although they were still relatively young, a core group of Harvey's friends—Dick Brooks, Ted Beck, and Pat Goldsworthy—called themselves the Elderly Birdwatchers Hiking and Griping Society. ("We grew into the name," Dick later joked.) "Birdwatchers" alluded to an editorial by a *Seattle Times* writer who criticized conservationists as mere "mountain climbers and birdwatchers." Harvey also started to use "the Irate Birdwatcher" as a pen name for many of his more over-the-top editorials in *The Wild Cascades*, the North Cascades Conservation Council publication that he and Betty began editing in 1961. On one occasion, the Irate Birdwatcher suggested organizing an elephant stampede ("a much more organic sport") as a protest against the flights of helicopters in the range. ("A final caution," he noted, "please keep . . . mice on leash.") Various friends joined in the fun, composing fake letters to the editor in response to Irate's rants. Ed LaChapelle even contributed an article about hydroelectric companies researching how to melt glaciers to power their plants—published under the title "The Plot That is Not."

The Mannings' home on Cougar Mountain became a gathering place for local climbers to sample Harvey's home-brewed beer and to philosophize late into the evenings. When they needed to stretch their legs, they'd clamber up the piton-studded rocks of the Mannings' fireplace to the beams of the A-frame house, where they sat and sang and talked some more. One of Harvey's friends, Lyn Cole, worked with him on *Mountaineering: The Freedom of the Hills*. Her husband, Dale, a future professor at the University of Washington's College of Forest Resources, became another one of Harvey's closest companions and fellow hoaxers. During a spring night of drinking in 1958, Dale wandered out onto the hillsides, where he gazed up at the stars until he passed out. When he woke up the next morning, Lyn and Betty were nowhere to be seen, and the Manning car was missing. A few hours later, the two women returned. "Guess what, Dale?" they said to him. "You've got a new place." Lyn had purchased a shack and six acres of land, close to the former Newcastle coal mines, so the two families could be near each other. Harvey made a sign for their abode: COLES CARRIED TO NEWCASTLE.

For these two families, Cougar Mountain was, in many ways, their own imaginary country. The Mannings planted a sequoia tree from a seedling they'd brought back from one of their backcountry trips. Betty created a flower garden to resemble an alpine meadow. "What wonders awaited?" Harvey asked himself, as he stumbled about the nearby woods and small ravines, pushing through thickets of sword ferns and salmonberries, pondering the Spanish quest for the Seven Cities of Cíbola or recalling the ideas of the notorious tall-tale narrator Jim Bridger: "I was not lost. . . . I knew where I was every minute, it was the rest of the world I wasn't sure about." On a map of the property that Harvey drew for visitors, one section is marked "Dragons."

As they grew up, the four Manning children—Claudia, Paul, Becky, and Penny—explored the surrounding woods, just as their parents did. After she reached school age, Claudia noticed how different her dad seemed from other local fathers, many of whom had upscale office jobs. Harvey was "a grizzly kind of guy who would not wear a suit very often," she told me. "He didn't like the newfangled things. Zippers would break and he would just use big old safety pins." In the mountains, however, "he made everything magical," taking them to "little paradises" of meadows with alpine streams, where they scrambled up boulders and gave them new names. At campsites, they listened to Harvey tell ghost stories while the fog rolled around high summits and the unearthly music of Betty's recorder wafted through the air. As they hiked deeper into the backcountry, Betty told stories about Tolkien's hobbits traveling across the Misty Mountains. "It was never about getting to the place," Claudia recalled. "It was always about the experience. The slower you go, the more you see. If you want to walk slower, you'll see a beautiful flower."

But the Mannings couldn't forget the rest of the world. At the height of the Cold War, the military installed a missile system on Cougar Mountain as a defense against a potential Russian attack. And with four children to support and limited income, Harvey and Betty struggled to pay bills and to fund the family's escapes into the Cascades and Olympics. During the years ahead, Betty went back to school to get a master's degree in library science, and she helped support the family as an editor and a librarian. Harvey picked up various writing and editing jobs for the University of Washington and other regional employers. At one point, despite his opposition to nuclear warfare, he resorted to working on technical manuals for the defense industry. He composed most of his own stories in the loft late at night, where the sound of his typing often pounded like heavy rain until dawn.

Since high school, he'd completed multiple adventure novels. As rejection letters from New York publishing houses piled up, Harvey despaired of ever succeeding as a fiction writer. Over and over, prominent editors had praised his writing talent, asked to see more work, and then decided his manuscripts were too "fanciful" or "undisciplined" for their needs. Discouraged, Harvey focused his imagination on creating humorous, but pointed, satires to dramatize the opposing sides of environmental battles and to educate readers about the high stakes. He found more luck getting these stories published in conservation and climbing journals. Often, his tales included imaginary peaks, such as "Mount Hornblower," first climbed "by Lewis and Clark while lost in the fog," where a small band of conservationists fought to stop the developers of "Damp City" (a.k.a. Seattle) from carving up the peak to sell its pumice.

Harvey also started experimenting with the idea of passing off fake climbing stories as true. Many of his tales from that era obscured boundaries between fact and fiction. In a 1960 article for *The Mountaineer* (the annual of The Mountaineers organization) entitled "Things to Climb When Mountains Aren't Worth It," Harvey included the dubious story of a strange call he received while serving as Climbing Committee chairman: a man purportedly told him about the discovery of wire gold (a rare form of thread-like crystals) in a cave on "Peak X." The original prospector, the man explained, hauled out so much treasure he'd perished from exhaustion. Harvey's "informant" now hoped some climbers could help him find other deposits on less accessible parts of the mountain. "It'll take ropes to get to them caves," the man said. Harvey allegedly set out with a large expedition to summit Peak X and extract its gold, only to be driven back by blasts of storms. He explained that he'd misplaced the phone number of his informant (which meant, presumably, no one could fact-check his story), but that the suspiciously named "Brewing and Goldfinding corporation of Issaquah and Las Vegas" was continuing the search.

The rest of the article discussed eccentric but real objectives, though Harvey's gleeful, mock-heroic style occasionally veered into tall tales. One such pursuit ("at least as old as Petrarch," he assured his readers) was the art of "blobbing," or climbing miniature pinnacles. Harvey's in-depth history of diminutive Washington mountains included claimed first ascents of Herpicide Spire and Rattlesnake Ledge, two actual "blobs" near Snoqualmie Pass. As a follow-up, a flurry of seemingly bellicose letters appeared between Harvey and a reader called Marian Arlin—the name of a real Seattle mountaineer who may have been convinced by Harvey to participate in a fake debate. Marian accused Harvey of the typical arrogance of visitors who claimed first ascents of peaks that local residents had long climbed, and she included a photo of herself and others atop Rattlesnake.

Harvey's tongue-in-cheek reply cut to the core of the absurd but widespread belief that what makes someone a "real climber" includes "proper" gear, media attention, and membership in a certain demographic: "Please recognize that there is an important distinction between a 'mountaineering first ascent' and 'first people on top.' . . . I rather doubt you carried ice axes and ropes and Ten Essentials. We *did*, you know, and it makes a difference. The first people on top of that peak probably were Indians, but it's not the same thing at all. You won't find any Indians listed in the *Climbers' Guide*. Basically, it's a matter of having a journal to climb for. If you haven't got a journal it doesn't mean much, history-wise."

In his next published letter to Marian, Harvey admitted to fabricating parts of his original article: "I don't mind confessing that my chosen role is to test the ability of later historians by deliberately passing on and amplifying every vague rumor, tall story, and fantastic fabrication that comes my way. The cause of TRUTH can only be served by putting historians on their mettle. Though my range of action is far more limited than that of H. L. Mencken, I do believe that in my small way I've carried on the tradition of his famous Bathtub Hoax."

Harvey was referring to American journalist H. L. Mencken's wholly fictitious history of the invention of the bathtub, published in 1917, and teeming with fabricated accounts of dismayed authorities trying to ban its use. The writer later explained that he'd simply meant to provide some comic relief during the horrors of World War I. Despite his repeated disavowals, the fake story became entrenched in many of his readers' minds as straightforward, unquestionable "truth." In follow-up articles, Mencken described the success of the Bathtub Hoax as a cautionary tale: "What begins as a guess—or perhaps, not infrequently, as a downright and deliberate lie—ends up as fact and is embalmed in the history books." He concluded that, for many people, fictitious narratives may be more appealing than factual ones. "What ails the truth," he wrote, "is that it is mainly uncomfortable and often dull." Fabricated news could be filled with grand conflicts between heroes and villains with far more satisfying endings than the frequently messy and disappointing conclusions to real events. What people most desired, it seemed, was folklore, particularly if its content matched what they already wanted to hear.

When I read Mencken's account of the Bathtub Hoax, it was easy to picture Harvey taking careful notes for his own future plans. As a "later historian," I realized, I was one of the people Harvey was planning to test with his stories and hoaxes. Each time I sat down to write about him, I began imagining Harvey as a wild-haired, rumpled man sitting in a corner of my office and quietly laughing at my words.

CHAPTER 12

# The Ascent of No Name Peak

TO UNDERSTAND HARVEY AND HIS hoaxes, Dale Cole told me, people needed to understand the burgeoning outdoors industry at the cusp of the 1960s:

*We saw the climbing culture itself change. New manufacturers moved into the scene and they were selling their materials for prices that we thought were cruel and high. There was another breed of climber [who] took climbing far more seriously. Not that we didn't do serious climbing. But it wasn't a question of bragging about it in an arrogant way.*

*Well, Harvey was particularly put out by this kind of climber. Especially their accounts of accomplishments in climbing journals and magazines . . . depictions that made [an ascent] more of an ego trip than a climbing trip. As you well know, climbing dates and climbing facts and bragging rights and exaggerations come up in articles submitted to climbing magazines and misrepresent what's really there. Harvey himself said, facts and fiction read the very same way in print.*

On August 1, 1959, Harvey wrote to his friend Ted Beck, detailing plans for his first (known) prank on the gear industry:

*Incidentally, I'll be calling on you shortly to take a proper part in the Great Hoax. While down at the [REI] Coop in June I picked up a copy of Summit Magazine, and the thing irritated me—especially all the pseudo-scholarly crap about sleeping bag research. So I wrote a long, circumstantial letter to the editor describing a research project being carried on by the Cougar Mountaineers, of which I, H. Hawthorne*

*Manning, am president. . . . Dale Cole is going to follow-up with some correct and further research, as Chairman of the Sleeping System Committee.*

*Ideally we hope dullards from all over the country are taken in, and start criticizing the "System." We can then answer them—having the tremendous advantage that we can invent all the necessary research and statistics while they will be dependent on fact. . . .*

*Actually, this is proposed merely as a test. . . . The experience should prove useful for a later hoax—unplanned—involving the American Alpine Club—Maybe we could discover a new climbing area in the Cascades, the Crazy Creek Crags. Crazy Creek is the third tributary on the left of the Blank River (this has to be a real river). We would need a real climbing party, like Becky Manning, and Cole. . . .*

*. . . Stand ready to take action. But keep it quiet, since only about 4 people are in on the thing. It's a very promising lead. Might in the long run be possible to destroy the whole sport of climbing. . . .*

*Yours for mutual self-destruction,*
*Doctor Jekyll*
*and*
*Mister Hyde*

While drinking homebrew, Dale and Harvey sketched out fake designs for a high-tech sleeping bag as a parody of modern gear: a tube inserted into an army surplus mask would conduct a sleeping person's breath into a container and through a calcium-oxide filter. This chamber would, in theory, convert the moist air into heat, which another tube would then carry to "what had been determined (by Cougar Mountaineers in their research laboratories) to be the body's temperature-control centers: the hands, the feet, and the small of the back," Harvey explained. Layers of tightly woven wool would further insulate those vulnerable areas. Climbers and hikers could assemble the system at home at little expense, apart from the calcium oxide, which, the Cougar Mountaineers lamented, was generally produced only for "missile research." But, they assured their readers, they were seeking a more accessible substitute for the chemical compound.

"The next day, when we'd sobered up a bit, Harvey decided we should submit this," Dale said. Dick Brooks, a chemical engineer, added just enough of an aura of scientific research to make the hoax appear legitimate to lay readers. *Summit* printed it. One of the main targets of the hoax, Gerry

Cunningham, had founded a Colorado-based climbing equipment company in 1946, which he'd named after himself. "Gerry Cunningham was as energetic and ingenious a builder of backpacking gear as there was," Harvey later recounted, "and he frequently and generously shared his frontiering with readers of *Summit*."

Gerry Cunningham seemed to fall for the prank immediately. For the following issue of *Summit*, he composed a lengthy letter to the editor attempting to debunk the "Sleeping System," with detailed analyses of various forms of heat loss. Given a chance to respond by the *Summit* editors, Harvey hinted that the gear manufacturer might be wasting his energy: "The *Gerry* reputation speaks for itself. . . . It was highly flattering for you to devote so much time to considering our work. But, I scarcely think we have progressed to the point where we can merit your attention." As a cautionary note, Harvey claimed that he'd seared his own lungs by accidently breathing in calcium oxide during one test.

In another letter to Ted, Harvey privately exulted over Cunningham's reply: "GOOD GAWD!!! . . . I got a letter from Gerry Cunningham—which will be printed in the next SUMMIT. Please don't waste a minute—write SUMMIT immediately. . . . You must have a letter in no later than October—GO GO GO!" He proposed a few suggestions for Ted's follow-up letter:

*(1) Present an alternative weird-type system*
*(2) By a weerd* [sic] *coincidence, you've been working on a very similar scheme—your experiences and methods*
*(3) You think we are insane. (But don't bust up our invented statistics too thoroughly—Gerry is already trying to do that.)*
*(4) You think we are inspired—you have followed our instructions and built a system and you think it's promising*
*(5) Or what?*

Harvey continued in a subsequent note to Ted:

*I wrote 4 [letters] myself. . . . One was from a Professor of Chemistry at Willamette University in Salem, Oregon. Another was an illiterate scrawl from "Tall Tom, the Old Toutle River Trapper," sent to White Salmon, Washington for re-mailing. Another from a research physicist in Manhattan, another from an "over-aged Boy Scout" in New Jersey.*

In the next issue of *Summit*, "John R. Stevens," the so-called Willamette professor of chemistry, produced a vehement defense of the system, complete with a formula for the chemical reaction and a suggestion to replace the calcium oxide with anhydrous calcium chloride. "Tall Tom" shared his endorsement as a crusty "Old Trapper" from the days before "fancy sleeping bags." Since Harvey was then working as a traveling textbook salesman, he posted the fake letters from various stops along his routes, while Dale worked on his follow-up report as "Chairman" of the Sleeping System to submit to *Summit.*

In a private note to Harvey, Ted (another chemical engineer) quipped about the science behind their hoax: "You would have a nuclear explosion if you were able to grind [calcium oxide] to that size. That would destroy Cougar MT and part of Seattle, which might be a good idea." Dale's subsequent *Summit* article blamed the hazardous dimensions of the calcium-oxide particles and the alleged lung-burning incident on the "gross errors" of the Cougar Mountaineers president. Dale also took issue with Cunningham's reliance on convective heat loss numbers that, Dale claimed, must have been "derived from studies of a naked man. In the Northwest we find clothing a necessity. (By law if not by weather alone.)"

Heidi Brooks recalled that her father, Dick, "convulsed in laughter" when he noticed one of his colleagues had tried to work out the math of the system to the "subatomic level." The tactics of Harvey and his friends worked, she realized, "setting people up so that their own egos would take them down." The fabricated letters gave rise to earnest missives from backpackers unaware of the conspiracy. The hoax was becoming part of real history. And for some people, it might have stayed that way, even after Harvey described the Sleeping System as a "joke" by the "Cougar Mountaineers" in his 1972 manual, *Backpacking One Step at a Time*. Few climbers beyond their circle of acquaintances may have realized the identity of the chief prankster until Dale recounted the story in Harvey's obituary. "We certainly never let on," Dale told me decades later, still delighted at their creation.

After several months, however, the *Summit* editors had decided enough was enough and stopped publishing letters about the Sleeping System. "Damn!" Harvey complained to Ted. "Well, next trip. . . . Up the Revolution."

---

EVEN BEFORE THE SLEEPING SYSTEM LETTERS COMPLETELY SPUTTERED out, Dale and Harvey were again plotting around a campfire in the North

Cascades. Before them, the swirled white-and-gray stone of the east face of Southeast Mox Peak rose like a surreal castle tower. It was hard to imagine that anyone could climb its steep and twisted walls, concealed behind thick forests and snarled brush, deep in a region few mountaineers visited.

The ubiquitous Fred Beckey had been on the summit, of course. Back in 1941, when Beckey made the twenty-three-mile approach with his brother, Helmy, the peak wasn't even on his maps. Beckey thought it looked "spectral," like a set of "phantom spires," surrounded by black clouds and serpentine mists. "A climber's dream, waiting to be made real, to be conquered," he recalled. "What was the force that impelled me?" It was one of the rare moments that he seemed on the verge of questioning his own ambitions. "Something complex and indefinable, the attraction of uncertainty," he mused. Even after he'd climbed the crumbling stone of its airy northwest face, the peak still seemed like a shadowy nightmare. During the descent, a giant rock broke loose and nearly crushed him. He never forgot the noise of its exploding shards like a bomb blast, or his sense of helpless fear.

While the sun set behind Southeast Mox, Harvey began to rant about the climbing world again. The postwar generation fixated too much on self-promotional first ascents, he told Dale. Climbers were losing their respect for the environment and forgetting "the real value of the wild" as they competed over dwindling unknowns. Some journal articles, he continued, appeared so full of hype that written geographies no longer matched physical ones. With that thought, an idea stirred in Harvey's mind. "And before I knew it," Dale recalled, "Harvey was talking about this imaginary climb going up Mox."

Back on Cougar Mountain, Harvey and Dale transformed Southeast Mox into "No Name Peak." They would play a prank on "competitive peakbaggers," Dale explained, "by sending them looking for things that weren't there." First, Dale drew dotted lines on a photo of its east face, showing the attempted ascents of a fictitious party. Then the pair altered a map, moving the mountain a few miles away from its real location to the headwaters of No Name Creek. Finally, Harvey fabricated a story about its "discovery," purportedly written by a climber named "Paul Williams" (the name of his non-climbing father-in-law).

The imaginary tale began with an enticing proclamation about hidden, unclimbed spires in the Pacific Northwest: "The famous North Cascade jungles tend to discourage climbers from exploring the smaller peaks unless there is a good trail leading to them—and there aren't many good trails in the North Cascades." According to Paul Williams, a small group of firefighters had trekked into the Arctic Creek area during the summer of 1957. Once they'd extinguished a wildfire, a member of the team named Arthur Short clambered up a nearby ridge to look around. "When he returned home to Portland that fall," Paul recounted, "he told us he had seen one of the most fantastic cliffs in the Cascades. We found this hard to believe, never having heard or read that there were any interesting peaks in that area."

For two years, Arthur kept talking about the immense wall he'd seen. Eventually, he persuaded Paul and two other friends—James "Jim" Millegan and John "Jack" Patrick—to follow him into the woods. At Ross Lake, they boarded a small outboard vessel. "The huge waves made it impossible to land at No Name Creek since at this point there is no shore at all, only cliffs and steep forests," Paul wrote. They continued to a small inlet near Arctic Creek, where they managed to scramble ashore.

For hours, they stumbled along the hillsides and through a box canyon to No Name Creek. When they finally arrived, they had to excavate a burrow in the thickets to create a place to sleep. "Next day we wasted time finding a stream crossing to reach a trail the map showed on the south bank," Paul continued. "We then wasted more time trying to follow the trail. Like most trails in this area it was built by the CCC [Civilian Conservation Corps] sometime around 1935 and hasn't been touched since." Unable to find their way through curtains of rain, they camped again. In the morning, clouds hung low over the mountaintops. As the group parted tangles of fog-soaked branches and heavy brush, glimmers of avalanche debris and rock cliffs hinted at an alpine world above.

When the mists lifted a day later, the landscape didn't match the position where they thought they were on the map. Instead of heading up the valley that led to No Name Lake, they'd gotten disoriented by the rain and fog, and they'd followed a tributary. By getting lost, however, they'd stumbled upon the right place. "All the way through the wet brush we had been giving Art a bad time about his fantastic 'No Name Peak,' but now that we saw it we agreed . . . it has what is certainly one of the longest and most difficult faces in North Cascades. . . . It was easy enough to understand why climbers have been unaware of this face, for to see it one must either be in the valley of No Name Creek or on the No Name-Arctic Creek divide."

Thick, dark clouds hid the sun while the four men searched for a way to approach the mysterious summit. They plodded up a long glacier toward a notch to the west, taking two detours onto bands of rock to avoid the deep, icy holes of bergschrunds. Cold gusts whirled as they clung to rain-slick stone. Another murk of fog closed in around them.

When they arrived at the col, Paul and Jack looked in vain for easier routes on the south side of the tower. Art and Jim headed up the cliff directly above them. After several hundred feet of scrambling, they stood atop a pinnacle below the apex. Mists obscured the upper reaches. Below them, a gap opened, too intimidating to cross. They returned to the col, "thoroughly bedraggled." On the way back to their base camp, Jack and Paul investigated another gully that might bypass the gap beneath the pinnacle. "In our opinion," Paul declared, "the patches of snow and the wet slabs and waterfalls make this an undesirable route."

The next morning, they tried the 3,000-foot main wall that led straight to the summit. "The lower half of the face is steep," Paul observed, "but the rock is strong solid gneiss and is so well-banded many pitches that look impossible turn out to be staircases. Also there are quite a few handy ledges that allow easy traverses." The group reached a high point below a bulge where the east face reared up—too daunting for them to go farther. Nonetheless, Paul claimed to find solid rock, fissured with cracks for pitons. "Although we did not conquer No Name Peak," he concluded, "we are sure that the Great Wall of No Name Peak will eventually be ranked as one of the finest and most difficult climbs in the North Cascades."

Harvey and Dale tried to submit the article to the *American Alpine Journal*, whose editor, Ad Carter, apparently took their story seriously. In a letter to "Mr. Williams," Carter expressed his regret that the report had missed the print deadline: "It certainly looks as if you have found a very interesting peak. It may be that next year you will have the good fortune to return and climb it to the top. . . . If you do, or if you make any other new climbs in the course of next summer, please let me know the details earlier in the year."

Next, Harvey and Dale sent the article to *Summit* ("our old reliable," Dale called it), where the feature appeared in May 1960 with the altered map and the photo that showed the routes of the imaginary attempts. The editors contributed an enticing caption strikingly similar to the one they later added to the Riesenstein article: "Who will be the first to climb this 3000-foot 'great wall' of No Name Peak in the northern cascade [*sic*] region of Washington?"

When the real Paul Williams—likely somewhat baffled—let his son-in-law know that he'd received a three-year subscription as payment for a feature he hadn't written, Harvey wrote back:

> *The mountain is not missing. It's just misplaced. If there is any correspondence on the subject you can send it to me, if you like, for answering.*
>
> *—Or if someone in Portland should call asking for route information, just say it was your son who wrote the article, and he has since moved. To: Los Angeles Cougar Mountain? We do hope a few parties attempt No Name Peak.*

Had the editors of *Summit* really been fooled twice, first by the Sleeping System hoax and then by No Name Peak? Or did they have an inkling of what Harvey was up to? Could it be that they even appreciated the joke? In a letter to Ted, Harvey speculated:

> *It takes all my energy keeping SUMMIT going. Did you catch the June issue? We were thinking SUMMIT had a sense of humor and finally caught on about the Sleeping System. Then old Gerry Cunningham (who obviously has been brooding for months) rises up and slaps me down.*
>
> *—Then Dee Molenaar puts No Name Peak in the right location. Damn it! Bill Long is a traitor. Just as we had Fred Beckey all set to bust up No Name Creek, too.*

A month after the publication of the "No Name Peak" article, Cascades climber Dee Molenaar (an artist who worked with Harvey on illustrations for *Mountaineering: The Freedom of the Hills*) had written an earnest letter to *Summit* explaining the current name and actual whereabouts of Mox Peaks (or "Twin Spires" as the summits were also called). The editors printed his missive as a follow-up feature: "Letter Questions Location of 'No Name' Peak.'" Dee included two photographs by glaciologist Bill Long (the alleged "traitor" in Harvey's letter to Ted). One was taken from a similar vantage point as the photo Harvey and Dale used in their hoax. The other image, from the top of Glacier Peak II (now known as Mount Spickard), featured the southeast and northwest summits of Mox Peaks in the context of the surrounding landscape, with Mount Fury, Mount Challenger, and Whatcom Peak inked in. A map displayed the difference between the geographic position of Mox Peaks and the "Supposed Location of 'No Name Pk.'"

Dee noted that there was, indeed, no reported ascent of the east face of Southeast Mox—the "great wall" showcased in the hoax. But he pointed out that Fred and Helmy Beckey had reached the top of the mountain from the west side in 1941. As if trying to make sense of what seemed to be a bizarre cartographic error, Dee concluded: "It is difficult to understand how Williams' party could have become so geographically disoriented. . . . Cloud cover and poor visibility during the approach and climb to the col between the two spires may account for their not being able to spot other well-known nearby peaks. . . . However, their approach up Ross Lake to Arctic Creek is puzzling. Is it possible that they actually continued up the lake to above Little Beaver Creek, then worked their way back to Little Beaver Creek and up Perry Creek?"

Perhaps many climbers fell for the story of No Name Peak because it sounded like the kind of folklore they wanted to be true: a courageous struggle by a group of friends in the wild toward a mysterious mountain that still awaited its first ascent. Like the Bathtub Hoax, the No Name Peak story slipped into a few histories of the North Cascades as a mistake-filled, but seemingly genuine account of an actual misadventure. Some climbers even ascribed the feats of "Paul Williams" to an active local climber of the same name, merging their accomplishments into those of a single protagonist.

The sophisticated conspiracy behind No Name Peak served as good practice for Harvey's next practical joke, one that would be even more ambitious. "He went from one peak—didn't he?" Dale mused, "to a whole range."

CHAPTER 13

# The Door in the Cliff

AS FAR BACK AS THE Victorian era, climbers have relied on journals of record to document what takes place above the clouds. Inevitably, events morph as they are turned into stories. Old errors become enshrined in books and perpetuated for centuries. Contrasting accounts by different participants remain irreconcilable. Distortions arise from shifting memories, altitude-addled brains, and subjective viewpoints. Uncertainties linger amid the chaos of a whiteout blizzard, a dark night, or swirling fog. Longings create their own realities. In one legendary anecdote, a mountaineer announced that he'd reached the top of the world's second-highest peak, only to admit, later, that he must have merely imagined the summit as he climbed in a state of hypoxic delirium. Such confessions are rare. In most cases of disputed ascents, as climbing writer Greg Child once said, "It's not like the murder mystery where you finally find the killer—in the end, there's no smoking gun. You don't have proof of the truth."

During the 1950s, it was harder for magazine staff to fact-check accounts of first ascents than it is today. There was no Google Earth, no readily available online photos of remote places. Although Indigenous trails and stories criss-crossed North America—as did a patchwork of government maps—printed cartographies of remote ranges retained some errors and gaps. Certain regions of the continent were still *terra incognita* to non-Native mountaineers. The deep forests of the Pacific Northwest hid isolated summits from their eyes, requiring days of arduous bushwhacking to approach. Entire Alaskan ranges remained unscouted by climbers, though they could already dream about the mysteries between waving contour lines.

Mountaineering communities were much more scattered and disconnected from each other than they are now. News and rumors disseminated slowly and often remained incomplete, fragments spread by word of mouth or reported in regional bulletins and annual alpine club journals. The only source of information about the first ascent of a lesser known peak or the topographic details of its upper regions might be the people who claimed to have climbed it.

Founded in 1955, *Summit* was the first monthly climbing magazine in the United States, and its influence remained paramount until the 1970s. When I visited its old office in October 2014, one of the retired editors, Jean Crenshaw, told me she'd often had to depend on her instincts to decide whether a writer was telling the truth. While she and co-editor Helen Kilness had struggled to verify the reports they received during the decades before our current Information Age, they'd also relied on that lack of connectedness to conceal facts about themselves. Concerned that no one would buy the magazine if readers knew it was run by women, they'd hidden their gender on the masthead, listing themselves as "J. M. Crenshaw" and "H. V. J. Kilness." Later, Jean switched to using "Jene M. Crenshaw" in print (which sounded more like a man's name to her than "Jean" did). They published letters to the editor that addressed them as "Dear Sirs," without correcting the writers' assumptions. By the time their secret was out, the magazine was well established. "It was a man's world," Jean said. "I didn't resent it. It was just the facts of life. The less people knew about us, the easier it was to work. We had to do our own thing. We kept to ourselves. We had to."

The cabin where they lived and worked for much of the year was on a mountainside above Big Bear Lake in California, reachable only by long, winding roads. Stark light fell around the oak leaves, pinecones, and needles as I gazed at the surroundings. Low peaks rose across the valley, pale green and sunbaked white. The distant lake narrowed to an iridescent blue band. The small, brown-shingled building perched atop a granite crag, its sides merging with giant boulders. To train, Jean explained to me, the editors and their guests traversed around the outside walls of the house, clinging to the rocks and bricks, trying not to let their feet touch the ground. Other boulders clustered in alcoves nearby, offering rounded cracks and sloping holds that were perfect for practicing all kinds of movements—a natural sculpture garden of stone. It was the kind of place where a climber might dream of living.

The previous owner had designed each architectural detail according to his eccentric imagination, creating toy-size model dwellings nestled high in the rocks and constructing a little bridge over a small pool. For the front door of the main building, Helen and Jean had hired the magazine's main cartoonist, Sheridan Anderson, to paint a sign with the image of a piton and the words SUMMIT HOUSE.

When I stepped over the threshold, I felt as if I'd passed through a cliff face into the cool quiet interior of a peak. A blue waterfall glistened within a diorama of a mountainside. Beneath the floor was a catacomb-like basement, formed by a natural cave of wedged boulders, with stairs cut into the rock itself. Jean and Helen had created a darkroom inside a nook partly jackhammered out of the surrounding stone. There, they set up their printing press and stitched together the early issues.

Although other female editors had served at North American club publications such as *The Canadian Alpine Journal* and *The Mugelnoos*, Helen and Jean had launched *Summit* at a time when women had largely faded to the background of mountaineering stories in the US. Wartime posters of heroines working in offices and factories disappeared during the late 1940s, replaced by gleaming advertisements that showcased suburban housewives consuming new kitchen and beauty products. Women's magazines alternated between publishing scattered stories about female career achievements and promoting a vision of domestic bliss so perfect it was unattainable for real families.

Some men who felt stifled by the conventions of 1950s society could find an outlet by pursuing adventures in the mountains. Women who sought similar forms of escape sometimes had trouble finding a place in the growing counterculture of climbing, where their presence wasn't always welcomed. As American historian Ruth Rosen explained in *The World Split Open*, "For young men determined to avoid the world of their fathers, freedom meant cutting loose from women and children." Alongside the rise of postwar technology, Yosemite climber Joe Fitschen recalled, big-wall climbing became "quite violent . . . with the bashing of pitons and the struggling over overhangs." For many, "it just didn't seem to be the kind of thing young women should be doing." Examples of strong female lead climbers, such as Bonnie Prudden, who established dozens of new routes in the Shawangunks of New York between 1946 and 1955, or Jan Conn, who made hundreds of first ascents across America, remained fairly rare. Irene Beardsley (who later took part in the first American ascent of Annapurna) met a number of talented, active women when she joined the Stanford Alpine Club in Palo Alto, California, in the early 1950s. But she didn't start leading, herself, for several years. "I think I positively enjoyed the freedom to be different," she recalled. "At the same time, I was quite shy. I did feel I was defying norms." With few clear paths to follow, female adventurers of the era often had to create their own.

"Everything was a challenge, and I was out to meet it," Jean told me. "I've never been frightened in my life. I can't even remember what it's like to be frightened." After the death of her father, an electrician, Jean's mother struggled to raise her and her brothers in Huntington Park, California. Like many of her high school classmates, Jean enlisted during World War II. While stationed in Georgia with the US Coast Guard, she met fellow radio operator Helen—a quiet woman who had grown up on a South Dakota farm. At the end of the war, the two friends pooled their small savings, bought a motorcycle, taught themselves to drive it, and set off across the country together.

Jean learned to climb with the Sierra Club on large, coed trips to the hills that provided a relatively friendly environment for female members. The idea of *Summit* came from her passion for the mountains and from her desire, after years of working for a Masonic publication, to have a magazine of her own. "Once we got started," she said, "the stories came to us." Many now-legendary climbing writers published their earliest articles in *Summit*, experimenting with new styles and ideas. Royal Robbins, who served as *Summit*'s rock climbing editor from 1964 to 1974, helped usher in the age of clean climbing. Cartoonist Sheridan Anderson poked fun at the grand protagonists of the Golden Age of Yosemite climbing. Jean and Helen presented groundbreaking first ascents and ordinary excursions on an equal level, as if all that mattered was a love of mountains for their own sake—the ability, as contributor Rick Sylvester wrote, "to take pleasure from the experiencing, not just the experience."

In 1956, a reader penned an infamous letter that began, "Sir: I find a regrettable tendency in your magazine to refer to mountaineering as a career equally adaptable to both men and women." Outraged responses flooded the letters section over the next several issues (which perhaps was the publishers' intent) defending women's right to climb—including a note from Elizabeth Knowlton, who had accompanied a 1932 attempt on 26,657-foot Nanga Parbat. A year later, Jan and Herb Conn's article "We Work in Our Spare Time" explained the principles of dirtbaggery for couples: "It's a simple matter of mathematics—two people working six months a year are just as good as one person working twelve months to support two people."

Between *Summit* deadlines, Jean and Helen went on climbing trips in an old pickup with a small trailer. After dark, they'd turn off some back road, extinguish the headlights, and continue by moonlight or starlight until they found a hidden place to sleep. They preferred scrambling up unfrequented peaks, and they kept no record of their ascents. During one of their last big Sierra Club excursions, the trip leader had asked them to take a novice along on a route. At the top of a pitch, Jean told the man to stay to one side while she belayed Helen up, but he kept shifting back and forth, knocking rocks loose. A big stone thundered down, and for a moment, Jean thought Helen was dead. At last, Helen shouted up, "I'm all right." Jean recalled that "those were the happiest words I heard in my life."

After that day, they mostly climbed by themselves. "It was safer that way," Jean explained. "We knew what we were capable of." They trusted each other more than anyone else. "People would often try to play tricks on you," Jean said of her days as an editor, when I asked her about the Riesenstein. "People liked to do that to us." And then she laughed, with a glint in her eye, at once mischievous and mysterious. "That's the sort of thing I would do to someone else."

CHAPTER 14

# The Land of Beyond

EVER SINCE I SAW THAT sly expression on Jean's face in 2014, I've wondered if she'd known the Riesenstein was a hoax when she published the original story in 1962. Had she gone along with the practical joke out of sheer amusement? To get readers riled up and sell more magazines? Or to watch the ensuing scramble to find the real peaks? If she had, it didn't surprise me that she'd said nothing about her complicity over the decades or that she'd allowed other climbers, mostly men, to think she was gullible. A skilled mechanic, Jean used to approach male drivers whose cars had broken down in the mountains, ask them what was wrong in her charming voice, and then enjoy their shock while she swiftly fixed their machines. Silent humor, she told me, was a means of coping with sexism: "That's your reward. You can laugh in your head, but not out loud."

If, on the other hand, Jean and Helen had fallen for the prank, they weren't the only ones—climbers across the United States did as well. "Like any good joke," mountaineering historian Andy Selters explained in an email to me, "timing was critical. Because Half Dome and El Cap had been climbed, [the Riesenstein] could then seem a logical, but mythical step, a Yosemite in a faraway pristine land with unlimited potential for challenge and expansion."

If the hoax had been published even a few years before 1962, *Summit* readers might have simply fantasized about the peaks of the Riesenstein, never imagining themselves capable of scaling such long, steep, storm-blasted rock walls. But the article came out in the midst of the Golden Age of Yosemite climbing. In 1957, Royal Robbins, Jerry Gallwas, and Mike Sherrick had made the first ascent of the Regular Northwest Face of Half Dome, a sheer, monolithic cliff more than 2,000 feet high. "We feared the enormity of the wall,"

Robbins recalled in his memoir *Fail Falling*. "We dreaded having to reach so deeply within ourselves and maybe find ourselves lacking."

In 1958, Warren Harding, Wayne Merry, and George Whitmore became the first to complete the Nose on El Capitan, a granite prow that sweeps in a lunate arc for nearly 3,000 feet up a cliff face. It was a feat that once seemed impossible, even in climbers' dreams. Other routes soon multiplied across daunting big walls throughout Yosemite. A year after *Summit* printed the Riesenstein Hoax, one of the leading figures of the Golden Age, Yvon Chouinard, published his manifesto, "Modern Yosemite Climbing," in the *American Alpine Journal*. "The future of Yosemite climbing lies not in Yosemite, but in using the new techniques in the great granite ranges of the world," he declared. "The Coast Ranges, the Logan Mountains, the innumerable ranges of Alaska, the Andes, the Baltoro Himalaya all have walls which defy the imagination.... A new generation of super-alpinists ... will venture forth ... to do the most esthetic and difficult walls on the face of the earth."

Heidi Brooks remembers listening to Harvey and his friends laugh about how climbers were responding to their hoax. In those days, she explains, "[There was] a race to see who could get the most first ascents. That just drove Harvey and everybody else in his group nuts because it was such a pretentious bullshit thing." When a well-known mountaineer announced that the Riesenstein was next on his tick list, the joke seemed complete.

Like other imaginary peaks, the Riesenstein flourished because it reflected the longings of its audience. For ambitious American climbers, the fake routes marked on the *Summit* photo corresponded to half-conscious reveries they'd just become bold enough to try to pursue. The real ranges in Chouinard's manifesto also included granite cliffs and spires that soared above glaciers. There, alpinists would face not only the sustained, technical challenges of climbing vast rock walls, but also the high-mountain hazards of storms and cold, ice and snow—just as in the Riesenstein.

That the Riesenstein might exist in the isolated Coast Mountains of British Columbia seemed feasible to many readers, at least initially. In *High Worlds of the Mountain Climber*, a few years prior, Harvey himself had observed that there were still a lot of unclimbed peaks north of the US border. "Canada," he joked, has enough "mountains to use, mountains to waste and mountains to export if practical."

Like prospectors of the gold rush days, many US climbers were eager to get to a seemingly untapped resource before anyone else. As Mike Graber recounted in his history of the Kichatnas for the 1980 *Ascent*, "enthusiastic American mountaineers began planning expeditions [to the Riesenstein] and flooding the Canadian government map office in Ottawa with requests for topographical maps and aerial photos." Fred Beckey wasn't fooled for a moment. "It was immediately obvious this was a hoax, to me anyway," he recalled in an email in 2011. Fred had explored the Coast Mountains since 1942 when he and Helmy made the second ascent of Mount Waddington (Xwox in the local Tŝilhqot'in language), once known as "Mystery Mountain," a 13,186-foot peak hidden beyond a mass of chaotic forests and crevassed glaciers. But even without drawing on his personal knowledge of the geography of British Columbia, Beckey spotted the clues the hoaxers had planted, including the resemblance between the name of one of the imaginary Austrian climbers, Kronofer, and a climbing-shoe brand.

Nonetheless, Beckey admitted, he wasn't sure of the actual peaks' location at the time. He hadn't come across anything exactly like them during his endless peregrinations across North American ranges. "The photos were obviously real," he wrote to me. "I did not know about the Kichatnas . . . but suspected [the Riesenstein was] in Alaska [in] some place that Washburn had not seen." Maybe it was something about the combination of roiling clouds, crevassed glaciers, and snow-crusted walls that gave Beckey the idea. There weren't a lot of mountaineers who could have guessed correctly, he added. "There was still so much left [unknown in the 1960s]. Only a few had the energy, time and money and wilderness zeal to go after such remote places."

Canadian climber Glenn Woodsworth was also sure the Riesenstein was a hoax when it was first published, but he appreciated its cleverness. Back then, printed maps of the Coast Mountains still recalled the old sepia cartographies of much earlier days. In one 1959 map, which Glenn later sent me, Mount Waddington, the highest peak of the range, is surrounded by blank patches, the color of ocher, broken only by the tentative lines of rivers, a few dots of elevation points, occasional eruptions of contour lines, and the enticing admonition of "RELIEF DATA INCOMPLETE."

In 1962, as Glenn carefully examined aerial pictures of the Skeena region, he didn't discern any mountain faces that appeared steep and long enough to be the grand walls of the Riesenstein. Local pilots assured Glenn that they hadn't flown over anything like the mountains that appeared in *Summit*. Climber and cartographer Neal Carter had photographed the same area from the apex of the nearby Seven Sisters Peaks on a clear day in 1941. He told Glenn that he hadn't seen any giant rock towers either.

During the early 1960s, Glenn's friend Dick Culbert was working on a guidebook to the Coast Mountains, and he, too, hadn't come across any record of big spires. To complete his guidebook, however, Dick still had to visit the region in person. "We both knew that the alpine journals—the records of recreational mountaineers—were only part of the story of those mountains," Glenn explained. "Their history was also in the memories of prospectors, loggers, trappers, bush-rats, misfits, First Nations, and others who lived in and near the mountains and occasionally climbed them."

Members of the Ts'mysen tribes had long charted their unceded lands between the Nass and Skeena Rivers with footpaths, canoe routes, and stories. In an oral history recorded by Ts'mysen chief William Beynon, a local Gitksan shaman, Isaac Tens, had described a vision of flying in a canoe toward a great, sheer mountain. As he got closer, its summit split into two sentient peaks who spoke to each other in a language that sounded like the ringing of bells.

Now, spurred by a flurry of letters asking him about the imaginary spires of the Riesenstein, Dick invited Glenn to join him on a reconnaissance trip in the winter of 1963. To save money, they got a ride from their home city of Vancouver to Squamish and then began hopping trains. When Glenn hoisted his backpack onto the top of a flatcar and jumped aboard after it, he tried not to remember how a similar leap had left his hero W. H. Davies, Welsh author of *The Autobiography of a Super-Tramp*, with a wooden leg. As the train went around a bend in the dark, Glenn noticed sparks flying off the metal of its wheels "like a line of fireflies twinkling along the track."

From the town of Terrace, southeast of the alleged site of the Riesenstein, they hitchhiked and walked up back roads in search of longtime residents who lived in cabins and might have stories to share. A Swiss Canadian prospector, Joe Felber, told them about wandering across rugged ridgelines, climbing several nearby mountains and attempting 9,052-foot Howson Peak, the tallest real summit in the area, during the 1920s. Howson Peak wasn't as technical as the imaginary spires (though it turned out to be dozens of feet higher). Still, its particular combination of isolation, obscurity, rock, and ice was enough to keep many people away, and it has at least one thing in common with the real Kichatnas, as Glenn later realized. "It is a magnet for foul, beastly weather," he told me.

About five miles from Terrace, at a Copper City cabin, Glenn and Dick met Arthur Clore, a Black explorer who left Virginia around 1910 to seek a place where "his abilities and steadiness were more important than the colour of his skin." Arthur had prospected along the entirety of many local rivers, including one that now bears his name. He kept a porcelain tea set in his cabin, but when he headed into the woods, he traveled light and lived off the land. "With his rifle and a bit of fishing line," Glenn recalled, "he could usually find something to put in the pot. To my surprise, he went without a tent or even a tarp, but he knew where to find rain-free shelter under large boulders and trees."

Although Glenn and Dick didn't find the Riesenstein on their trip, they sensed how a wide array of meanings can accumulate around a wild range. For years afterward, Glenn returned to the area to study the geology of the Coast Mountains, to have tea with Arthur, and to explore some of the real and mythic peaks. From a high point on a clear day, he could see the spaces where the Riesenstein peaks were supposed to be—part of an invisible cartography of other imaginary mountains. One of the formations in this region Glenn called "pseudo spires." From a distance, they looked like big towers. Up close, they turned out to be mere buttresses that merged into hillsides.

There were also the stories of nonexistent or quasi-fictitious peaks that he and Dick collected as they aimed to clear up old errors and to amuse their readers. Dick's published guidebooks later included intriguing statements about other mountains farther south, such as: "The 7500-ft Nahatlatch Needle, located by some maps N of Nahatlatch Lks., does not exist." Back in 1957, he'd gone looking for Nahatlatch Needle near a river of the same name in the Lillooet Ranges of the Coast Mountains. He scrambled ever higher up a ridge until he reached the exact spot where the peak appeared on the map—only there was no prominent summit there. Today, the name "Nahatlatch Needle" marks a small bump in the long crest that leads to the apex of Tachewana Peak. The higher, more dramatic spire that once appeared on a 1923 Department of Interior map has dissolved into climbers' daydreams.

Dick dedicated his 1965 guidebook to "the 'land of beyond'—its explorers, its dreamers, and its victims." The quotation came from a Robert Service poem that describes a realm "at the gates of the day," which lures adventurers ever deeper and higher. In the middle of the night, climbers might arrive on a summit, believing that they've reached their goal—only to realize that the "land of beyond" glimmers still farther away, like a dream vision lit up by the stars. "Thank God!" the narrator concludes, for the existence of an unreachable place: "A vision to seek, a beckoning peak."

Dick was aware of the potentially severe consequences of such dreams. In 2009, Glenn published a collection of Dick's poetry, *The Coast Mountains Trilogy*. One poem, "A Mountain," recounts the first ascent of an unnamed, sentient peak: "A citadel of finest granite / Smooth as glass and steeped in storm." After four climbers scale its ramparts, men and machines churn roads into the mountainsides and demolish the forests. Slopes erode and collapse. Glaciers wilt. Another poem, "The Ballad of the Border Survey," tells the tale of an enigmatic summit named Matsaac. Dick told Glenn that he'd seen the name on an old map, but Glenn could never locate the map or the mountain. Neither could Fred Beckey, after Glenn requested his help. When Glenn asked Dick about Matsaac again, Dick could no longer remember where the peak was, and he said he might have invented it. In his 1965 guidebook, Dick tried to designate another peak near the US-Canada border as "Matsaac," but the name didn't stick. Today, it's known as Mount Custer.

The Matsaac in the poem remains, "misty and waiting," in the North Cascades, somewhere "out beyond" Hozomeen Mountain: "Across the dark moat of the dim, deathless Skagit, / A tall twisted country, alive and aloof. / A great phantom network of mist-tangled ridges." Closer up, Matsaac appears like part of a supernatural realm. "The peak of cloud no wind could change / Soared from a land of crumpled ice / Into a world its own." Men who set out to climb this mountain suffer from mysterious misfortunes, as if cursed for their desires. "The unknown will haunt them, allure them, addict them," Dick wrote.

"Nobody was totally clear as to which parts of the poem were based on fact and which were fiction," Glenn recalled. In addition to solving some of the cartographic mysteries in the Coast Mountains, Dick, who died in 2017, left behind at least one of his own. Looking back on Matsaac and the Riesenstein, Glenn realized that the lure of imaginary places—the persistent longing for unseen lands beyond the horizon—might lie at the heart of mountaineering. "You never know what's on the other side except when you can make it up," he said.

---

WHILE CLIMBERS FROM THE LOWER 48 SEARCHED FOR THE RIESENSTEIN on Canadian maps, Indigenous people had long been aware of Alaskan peaks that fit the description of the imaginary spires. For thousands of years, they paddled along the braided currents of glacial rivers, hunted wild sheep, caribou, and bears across the foothills, and trekked over vast expanses of ice and high passes in the mountains. They created summer trails that wove through dense thickets and winter tracks that vanished and reappeared across the snows. They made their own cartographies of tales and songs. Miska Deaphon, a storyteller from the upper Kuskokwim region, recalled tales of Dzi » yehwt'ana (Hill-People) who lived inside a mountain west of the spires and who helped those who left gifts at its doorway. Dena'ina Dene (Athabascan) residents gave the name "K'its'atnu" to the river that flows near the peaks of the fictitious Riesenstein. And they called the real mountains K'its'atnu Dghelaya.

To Europeans, the entire expanse of land that came to be known as Alaska had remained a mostly imaginary place for centuries, a lost corner at the upper edges of maps. Rumors, errors, and hoaxes flourished there long before the invention of the Riesenstein. In eighteenth-century cartographies, Alaska oozed like a giant white amoeba that mutated as generations of mapmakers blended facts and myths. Some cartographers drew it erroneously as a giant island with shorelines that wriggled into emptiness. Others depicted a fragmentary coastline, its largely blank interior speckled with high peaks. In the spring of 1794, British explorer George Vancouver jotted grumpy notes in his journal about an inlet that Captain James Cook mistook for a river: "Had the great and first discoverer of it, whose name it bears, dedicated one more day to its further examination, he would have spared the theoretical navigators, who have followed him in their closets, the task of ingeniously ascribing to this arm of the ocean a channel, through which a north-west passage . . . might ultimately be discovered." Vancouver added that he hoped his own meticulous remapping of the area would finally put the absurd myth of the Northwest Passage to rest. More than a century later, it was through Cook Inlet—known to Dena'ina people as Tikahtnu—that the Kichatna Spires first came to the attention of white American explorers.

When the United States bought the Alaska territory from Russia in 1867 (without consulting Indigenous people, who hadn't ceded their lands), members of Congress and the media alike denounced the purchase of a frozen wasteland or "polar bear garden." Decades afterward, non-Native explorers had still mapped only fragments of its vast interior, mainly near the coastlines and major rivers. Then the discovery of gold in southern Alaska increased the demand for geographic information. In the spring of 1898, US geologist Josiah Edward Spurr and his companions set out with cedar canoes from Tyonek (Tubughnenq'), a Dena'ina village on the shore of Cook Inlet. They intended to chart a course up the Susitna River, to cross the divide to the Kuskokwim River, and then to float downstream toward the Bering Sea, while surveying mineral resources along the way. "Nearly all of this region was entirely unknown," Spurr insisted in his expedition report, "never before having been explored by white men."

Before his expedition, Spurr had woven together a hazy speculative cartography, formed of scraps of information from previous travelers and vague reports that traders told him they'd heard from Alaska Natives, possibly Dena'ina people of the Susitnuht'ana and Tubughna bands, who went on regular hunting trips in the K'its'atnu region. During the 1830s, Russian Alutiiq explorer Andrei Glazunov had ventured up the Kuskokwim, and he'd reported seeing a giant ice mountain in the distance. He referred to it as "Tenada," a Deg Hit'an Dene (Athabascan) name for the peak that Koyukon Dene people termed "Deenaalee" (the "High One"), later rendered as "Denali." On a Russian map based on Glazunov's report, fuzzy hachures radiate around Tenada like the body of a giant "hairy caterpillar," indicating a series of summits between the Kuskokwim and Susitna Rivers. Subsequent explorers charted more pieces of terrain along those two waterways, but large gaps remained in printed geographies. By the 1880s, the surrounding arc of peaks—Deghi:lo:yi in the Lower Tanana language—became known as the "Alaska Range" to American surveyors who hadn't yet tried to trek across the mountain chain. In 1896, US prospector William Dickey gave the highest summit a new name, "McKinley," after the soon-to-be successful presidential candidate of the time. On his own map, Dickey sketched what he called a "GREAT RANGE VERY RUGGED AND HIGH" to its south.

Spurr likely had misty notions about these big mountains, but he also believed in a swath of "low, flat country," where he could rely on a "string of lakes" to paddle from one headwater to the next. From a fork in the Susitna, Spurr and his companions headed up the Yentna River, averaging about four or five miles a day, yanking on branches to haul themselves and their canoes upstream. Dena'ina hunters glided by in moose-skin boats, floating downstream on their way back to their villages. Many of them paused to sketch maps for Spurr of the land ahead, including some troubling pictures of labyrinthine highlands.

By early June, the distant slopes of Denali had billowed into the sky like a mass of bluish-white clouds. River currents swelled with melting snow. Floodwaters sliced at the shores, and trees crashed into the rapids. Spurr and his companions kept going up a tributary that he called the "Skwentna," an Anglicization of a Dena'ina name, *Shqitnu*, which might roughly translate to "sloping ridge river." Inside its web of narrow channels, shallow water snarled around collapsed trees. When a battered canoe leaked, the group tore strips of canvas from provision sacks and used spruce resin to glue the cloth in place. Each time a boat overturned, they lost crucial supplies.

By late June, Spurr fully admitted that the "low, flat country" between the Susitna and the Kuskokwim didn't exist. They would have to find a pass through the ramparts of high peaks ahead. Although they had little food left, Spurr was determined to continue, by himself if need be. His companions agreed to follow him. They could always chew on tree bark while they starved, one of them said. On July 10, after they'd spent weeks searching for a navigable gap in the range, Spurr left his long-suffering teammates behind to stagger up a hillside alone. At the top, the sketches of the Dena'ina hunters finally aligned with the panorama of peaks and valleys. Spurr returned to camp, elated, with the news: he'd found a pass through the range. Many more miles still stretched ahead before the end of their journey, but they would survive.

Slowly and wearily, Spurr and the others ferried gear through dense alder and over broken rock to the place he called "Portage Pass." There, they seemed to enter an unearthly world. Butterflies arose in a glittering mist. The fragrance of wildflowers filled the air like wafting magic. Fireweed burst pink against stone cliffs. White and yellow crowberry shone alongside the snows. Spurr, who loved composing poetry, carefully noted each wonder. The clouds had tattered, and from the apex of the pass, as he wrote in his *Log of the Kuskokwim*, he contemplated "magnificent precipitous bare mountains, set with many spires and columns . . . gray, awe-inspiring, like vast Gothic cathedrals . . . but 1,000 times more vast and elaborate, with glaciers for roofs." In general, he tried to use Indigenous names in his report, but he hadn't heard of these peaks before. He thought of the term "Cathedral Mountain," which later morphed into "Cathedral Spires," for a cluster of rock towers to the south, eventually known as the Kichatnas.

A year later, when Lieutenant Joseph Herron headed toward the same region, he understood the Alaska Range to be "a mass of enormous peaks and glaciers about seventy miles wide, extending across Alaska and constituting the chief barrier to the interior." Nonetheless, he hoped to find an overland route from Cook Inlet through the mountains to the goldfields of Cape Nome and the Klondike without crossing the border into Canada. In June 1899, with three soldiers, two horsepackers, and fifteen horses, Herron took a steamboat to Susitna Station. From there, two Alaska Native men (possibly Dena'ina Susitnuht'ana), whom Herron referred to as Stepan and Slinkta, agreed to guide him up the Kichatna River, to a gap that led to the other side of the range. Herron's team brought more than three thousand pounds of gear (including six hundred pounds of bacon) to sustain them for over one thousand miles of wild terrain, which he, too, claimed in his expedition report was largely "hitherto unknown and unexplored" (except by the Indigenous people whose geographical knowledge would prove essential for his team).

Day after day, members of his expedition cut paths for the horses through thick forests, placed logs where the ground might sink beneath the animals' hooves, and built bridges over streams. The use of pack animals had drawbacks, Herron noted: "The transportation stampeded back on the trail at every opportunity, raced through the woods, knocked off packs, plunged into mud holes, bogged down." By July 10, the Dena'ina guides informed Herron that the horses couldn't make it over the steep pass. Herron insisted on trying. That same day, a pack animal stumbled, rolled over one of the horsepackers, and tumbled with him down a bluff. To their teammates' likely surprise, they both survived. Stepan and Slinkta urged the expedition to turn back. A week later, the rapids of the Kichatna River swept a soldier away, dashing him against boulders. Stepan pulled him out. It seemed only a matter of time before someone died. When they reached the break in the hills, which Herron called "Simpson Pass," they could see the Cathedral Spires. Herron added names of his own to three of the visible peaks: Gurney, Augustin, and Lewis. As mountaineering author David Roberts later observed in his 1968 chronicle of the Kichatnas (published in *Summit* a few years after the Riesenstein Hoax was revealed), any justifications for Herron's choices appear to have been lost to history: "To Herron's survival we owe some of the worst names in the Alaska Range. . . . It was his habit to sprinkle the scenery with names of politicians and personal friends from his own (no doubt beloved) state of Ohio."

Six days after Simpson Pass, Slinkta and Stepan abandoned the journey. Maybe the guides decided they'd had enough of herding white soldiers over the mountains, chopping paths and hunting for them, rescuing them from drowning, observing their dangerously ineffective attempts to shoot bears, and trying to convince them to go home. Perhaps the guides were also concerned that the expedition was entering the traditional land of another Dene group, the Upper Kuskokwim people. Left to their own devices, the remaining team members floundered. Soon, the grass withered in the evening frost of early autumn. The horses became unable to graze, and Herron abandoned them. As the men trudged through archways of snow-bowed trees, wet clumps dropped onto their heads and snowdrifts soaked their feet. Their provisions were nearly gone, and they lacked adequate gear for the approaching winter. Both Herron and one of his fellow soldiers limped on sprained ankles. "The outlook," Herron noted, "was becoming annoying."

In September, during a hunting trip, Chief Seseui of the Telida band of Upper Kuskokwim people was butchering a bear he'd shot when he found bacon in its stomach. He guessed that the animal must have stolen food from a party of lost white men. Retracing the bear's path, he tracked down the famished expedition members, offered them some of his own provisions, and brought them to his village. Herron and his team camped there for two months while they waited for the snow to firm up so travel would become easier again. Villagers sewed warm clothing for the group and gave them fur hats, moccasins, and snowshoes. On December 11, with the help of local guides, Herron's expedition reached a new military post at the confluence of the Tanana and Yukon Rivers, the goal of their journey. "This report," Herron declared, "represents the earnest efforts of a small party in unknown regions against extraordinary obstacles, deserted by guides, caught by winter, deprived of transportation, and hampered by scarcity of food."

A modern-day reader might sum up the story otherwise: a group of white soldiers set out to gather information that might lay the groundwork for colonization. They found themselves hopelessly underprepared for the challenges of the backcountry, left their depleted horses to starve, and were saved from nearly certain death by the aid of Alaska Native residents—the same people whose traditional rights white settlers wanted to displace. Decades afterward, Carl Seseui, the chief's son, told anthropologist Raymond L. Collins that he'd never forgotten how much assistance his father had given to Herron's expedition "and how little he received in return."

On his map, Herron sketched Gurney, Augustin, and Lewis Peaks with delicate hatch marks, as ornate as the patterns on a seashell. The sinuous lines of two bodies of ice, which he called the "Fleischmann" and "Caldwell" Glaciers, flow past the summits. Rivers and marshlands extend outward like the veins of leaves. He added the name "Foraker" to another big mountain near Denali, thus replacing the original Koyukon Dene name, Sołt'aanh ("Woman") with the name of an Ohio senator. The long dotted line of an "Indian winter trail" runs alongside parts of his own itinerary. "In exploring my route," Herron admitted, "I found that there already existed throughout its length winter sled trails cut out, blazed, and in regular use by the Indians and coinciding with or paralleling my trail throughout. . . . These trails represent the result of a knowledge of the country accumulated during many generations." To Herron, these paths seemed like possible locations for future roads and railroads. Readers of his epic account were less optimistic, and the search for a route to the goldfields shifted elsewhere.

The next wave of explorers through the region were drawn to the tallest peak on the continent, and they showed no discernable interest in the obscure granite towers called Gurney, Lewis, and Augustin, or in the group of peaks that had come to be known as the Cathedral (and later the Kichatna) Spires. Within a few years, as if conjured into being by their quest, a new imaginary mountain would take shape in the wilds of Alaska. In 1906, American mountaineer Frederick Cook would claim that he'd stood on the summit of Denali, and he would publish a series of photos as alleged evidence. His critics would develop another term for the prominence he reached: "Fake Peak." Over time, amplified by decades of debate, the controversy would become so immense that it would cast its shadow across all other phantom peaks in the northern ranges, including the Riesenstein.

CHAPTER 15

# The Ascent of Fake Peak

PERHAPS IT AROSE FROM DEEP longings for adventure and escape, colliding in a man's mind like tectonic plates and creating an eruption of dreams: visions of heroes cutting thousands of steps to create a grand staircase of ice; fantasies of white cornices and misted summits glowing above a land of frost and gold. Perhaps it materialized out of the optical illusions and ice crystals that filled the Northern air with strange lights and hues. Or else it combined with the incalculable layers of memories and myths that folded and overlapped in the Alaska Range, pushing its slopes ever higher toward the sky. However it emerged, the invisible summit that became Fake Peak soared for thousands of feet above a small nondescript rock outcrop, while its base slid miles across the glaciers to the geographic point of Denali.

Born in 1865, Frederick Cook was, as one biographer, Robert M. Bryce, later put it, "a true romantic," at least in some regards. Like others of his era, Cook fantasized about quests for realms beyond "the life-sapping conditions of modern city life" and "the maddening pace of this material age," as he wrote in his memoirs. His prose sometimes resembles an overwrought version of Harvey Manning's, without the sharp edge of self-deprecating satire. Growing up, Cook had also been vulnerable to bullying. And he'd sought refuge by exploring the wooded hills and caves near his childhood home in Hortonville, New York, where he felt a "yearning for something that was vague and undefined."

He had more reasons than most dreamers do for wanting a way out of reality. His father had passed away when Cook was four years old, leaving the family impoverished, and his early memories were full of relentless struggle and, at times, scant food. From age twelve on, Cook worked while going to school. Later, while a medical student at Columbia University, he woke at 1:00 a.m. each day to deliver milk before his classes started at 9:00. In 1890, just as Cook was about to graduate, his first child died several hours after birth. His wife, Libby, succumbed soon afterward. Depressed and adrift, the young doctor lost himself in adventure books, imagining uncharted regions of Africa and the Arctic. A year later, he picked up a newspaper and read that Robert E. Peary was planning an expedition to map the northernmost parts of Greenland. "It was as if a door to a prison cell had opened. I felt the first indomitable, commanding call of the Northland," Cook recalled.

The turn of the century was a time when distant visions of the Far North flashed like *fata morgana* across the minds of American city dwellers. During the early 1900s, British Canadian poet Robert Service would further spread unearthly images of high-latitude lands, where a wanderer might search "the Vastness for a something . . . lost" amid "big mountains heaved to heaven" and "the map's void spaces." American novelist Jack London would pen his popular gold rush saga *The Call of the Wild*. Tales of actual polar explorers already enthralled commuters packed into trains on their way to the dull routines of factories and offices. Newspaper publishers realized that sponsoring expeditions in exchange for exclusive coverage led to big profits. The resulting stories—heavily edited, ghostwritten, or sensationalized—tended to avoid banal or complex realities in favor of more marketable epics of indomitable heroes traversing magnificent worlds of ice. Over time, the relationship between publicity and future funding put even more pressure on adventurers to achieve (or concoct) success.

Cook wrote to Peary and offered to serve as a doctor on his 1891 expedition. When their ship struck floating ice, a tiller swung against Peary's leg and fractured two bones. In his account of the journey, Peary praised Cook's ability to heal him, to tend to the rest of the crew, and to remain calm throughout the crisis. Cook, in turn, extolled Peary's "sublime courage." Their mutual esteem gave way to rivalry as Cook began his own attempts to reach both the North Pole and what he called "the Alpine North Pole"—the apex of Denali. In 1903, accompanied by Native guides (probably Dena'ina Susitnuht'ana), whom he referred to as Stephen and Evan, and carrying the incomplete maps of prior expeditions, Cook left Tyonek with four other companions to try to climb what he called "perhaps the most inaccessible of all the great mountains of the world."

Cook wasn't exaggerating the difficulties of attaining Denali's summit. A previous explorer, Alfred Brooks, had suggested that climbers should attempt the mountain from the north side. Merely to reach that aspect of Denali from Tyonek, however, they would have to traverse hundreds of miles of swift rivers, tangled forests, and boggy tundra, crossing some of the same terrain where Spurr's and Herron's teams had nearly perished. Once there, they'd need to ascend about 18,000 feet of vertical relief from the surrounding glaciers toward the frigid, windswept 20,310-foot summit. As Cook and his teammates trudged with their pack horses toward Simpson Pass, gaps in the mists revealed tempting views of distant lower spires, but there was no time to waste.

Beyond the crest, after scouting various options, they headed for the northern flanks of Denali. To their surprise, they passed the abandoned campsite of another mountaineering party. A rusted tin can was still full of salt, the very thing they'd craved since their horses had devoured their own supply. They later found out the can had been left earlier that same year by Alaskan Judge James Wickersham and his teammates, who turned back at the start of a steep wall that soared for about 14,000 feet to the north summit. Cook's expedition hadn't brought enough mountaineering axes for everyone, so while they teetered their way up the frozen slopes of a lofty northwest buttress, one climber had to lean on a wooden tent pole. They gave up their attempt as the precipices multiplied, after reaching a high point of roughly 10,000 to 11,000 feet above sea level and spending a night perched in an aerie chopped into a cliff of sheer blue ice.

Once they'd descended the mountain, Cook's party continued northeast into unfamiliar regions where waves of snowy peaks crested above vast seas of glaciers. "And it is all unmapped, undiscovered, bleak and shriveled under the breath of autumn," one member, newspaper journalist Robert Dunn, declared. By the end of the trip, they'd traveled a thousand miles and circumnavigated the entire Denali massif. On the map that Dunn sketched of their journey, the Indian trail of Herron's map has vanished, as have the Cathedral Spires, leaving only a blank space between the Fleishmann and Caldwell Glaciers. Perhaps the Kichatnas seemed too insignificant compared to the continent's highest mountain, or their sheer walls simply too inconceivable.

Three years later, Cook returned to try to reach the summit of Denali again. This time, in addition to horsepacker Edward Barrill and several others, Cook was joined—fatefully as events would prove—by two mountaineers who would become his future critics, Belmore Browne and Herschel Parker. Cook intended to find a different way over the divide to attempt the peak from the southwest. And so they squandered days near the upper forks of the Yentna, searching for a pass that their pack horses could manage. When at last they turned farther south toward distant foothills, the expedition lost even more time flailing through streams and swamps. After chancing upon a new settlement of gold prospectors at Sunflower Creek, they hired a Dena'ina guide they called "Susitna Pete" (Tsel Ch'a'ilk'elen), and they made their way to the headwaters of the Tokositna River and the start of the ice. By then, Browne realized failure was inevitable: "Between us and the mountain was a tangled, chaotic mass of rugged mountains and glaciers. The night air was already beginning to have the tang that presaged the coming of frost, and we knew that with the coming of frost our horses would die."

The team soon began the long retreat to Tyonek. Once there, in late August, Cook announced that he wanted to examine another approach to Denali with Barrill. In the meantime, he asked Browne to go hunting up the Matanuska River so they could send wildlife specimens to a museum. Cook promised Browne that he wouldn't attempt the summit without him.

Upon his return from this second foray, however, Cook announced that he and Barrill had continued to the top of Denali, and they'd attained the summit on September 16. Already, hints of possible fiction had emerged like tightly packed leaves poised to unfold. Cook and Barrill hadn't been gone long enough to trek all the way to the mountain and to climb it. Browne later asserted that when he spoke with Barrill alone, the horsepacker offered an ambiguous reply: "I can tell you all about the big peaks just south of the mountain, but if you want to know about Mount McKinley go and ask Cook."

Many people initially believed Cook's version of the story, though the prose in his climbing descriptions could sometimes be hard to follow. Nineteenth- and early twentieth-century exploration accounts are replete with ornate descriptions of ice-sculpted wonderlands and shimmering northern lights. Yet when Cook began to describe the upper portions of Denali in his book *To the Top of the Continent*, the sheer excess of his metaphors became striking. The written topography morphs continually in shape and hue. "It is a region of pulseless eternity where the spirits with the clouds fall to the earth in weeping sadness," Cook wrote in one section. In another, he compared the peak to a "geography of heaven" attainable on Earth. This was the language of the old imaginary voyages, and a reader might almost expect to see Denis Vairasse d'Allais's pack train of unicorns trotting by. Perhaps, when Cook declared, "This supra-cloud world is a land of fantasy, of strange other-world illusions," he was, in fact, revealing an emotional truth: his Denali was merely a dream summit of his own creation. One *Alpine Journal* reviewer described the difficulty of discerning any specifics of the actual ascent beneath the jumbles of ethereal phrases: "The author alleges that his subject 'strains the English Dictionary.' He has accordingly done his best to enlarge that volume . . . words are put to what may seem . . . strange uses. For instance . . . the Alpine rope is a 'life-line,' an avalanche a 'reducing train.' Even the 'foot hills' are 'sky piercing' and loftier summits are alternately 'heaven-scraped' and 'sky-scraping.'"

In 1909, Cook emerged from the Arctic after another expedition to declare that he and two Inughuit companions, Aapilak and Ittukusuk, had reached the North Pole on April 21, 1908—about a year before Peary claimed to have arrived there with the help of Black American explorer Matthew Henson and Inughuit teammates Ukujaaq, Uutaaq, Iggiannguaq, and Sigluk. Many critics have disputed Cook's and Peary's stories, in part because neither man could ever offer conclusive proof. Peary reported seemingly implausible speeds of travel, as well as an itinerary based on unreliable compass readings and dead reckoning. Cook published a hazy, florid account of his achievement of the long-coveted objective. Images of mirages seem to float like colorful gossamer across the pages. According to two Arctic travelers, Knud Rasmussen and Paul Rainey, Cook's Inughuit companions later said they didn't think they'd actually reached the North Pole.

In October 1909, Barrill signed an official affidavit that Cook's Denali claim, at least, was fraudulent. Cook agreed to answer questions about the climb at an Explorers Club meeting in November, but he never appeared. Meanwhile, a group of local miners made plans to summit the mountain themselves and prove that Cook had lied. In the spring of 1910, members of their Sourdough expedition climbed, unroped, for thousands of feet. They used a coal shovel, pike poles, and "ice-irons" (as they called their nine-pointed crampons) to move over sheer ice and deep snow. As provisions for their final dash to the lower north summit, they packed little more than a bag of doughnuts and thermoses of hot chocolate. Two members planted a spruce pole as a sign of their arrival. But when they returned to tell the tale, they found their own stories doubted. For men with no mountaineering experience, they'd made an astoundingly rapid ascent, and one of their teammates had inflated their feat by claiming they'd reached the higher south summit as well.

Later that year, Belmore Browne and Herschel Parker set out with six companions to make another attempt on Denali—and to search for the location of "Fake Peak," where they believed Cook had taken his purported summit picture. "Our mountain detective work was based on the fact that no man can lie topographically," Browne wrote. "We knew that if we could find one of the peaks shown in his photographs we could trace him peak by peak, and snowfield by snowfield, to within a foot of the spot where he exposed his negatives." Recalling the horrific suffering of the horses on past expeditions, Browne decided that his teammates should carry supplies on their own backs. After lurching up snag-filled rivers in a kerosene-powered boat, they ferried loads across thirty-seven miles of underbrush, swamp, moraine, and slush to the Ruth Glacier (unwilling to use Cook's 1903 name for the place, Browne referred to it as the "big glacier").

Within the crystalline silences of a northern dusk, Browne forgot the pain of a sprained ankle and the eighty-pound weight of his pack. A jagged line of peaks above a tributary glacier fit the contours of those in Cook's photos. Ice surged against rock cliffs and broke into frozen waves. Their tracks vanished into a quiet blue ether that stretched endlessly before and behind them. Browne recited poetry to create a beat to snowshoe by.

Soon, he discovered another piece of the puzzle: above a col, there was a cliff that resembled the precipice below the top of Fake Peak. As Browne and Parker climbed toward the saddle, the contours of the landscape continued to align. Nonetheless, Browne felt bewildered. Cook had described the cliff face as 8,000 feet high, but the one that Browne saw seemed only a few hundred feet higher than the glacier, its altitude about 5,300 feet. Its summit was merely a small stone outcrop. Just below the top, Parker, who was in front, paused to knock down a little cornice. Then Browne heard his voice ring out. "We've got it!"

Browne's group took their own pictures for evidence. In one image, Parker is photographing Browne, who is photographing expedition member Herman L. Tucker atop Fake Peak, who is re-creating Barrill's pose on the "summit" of Denali. Silhouetted against the sky, Tucker looks like an iconic image of a mountaineer holding a flag. The exposed cliff edge near his feet and the fin-shaped snow ridge beyond him generate a dramatic effect—as if this were a parody of some major ascent heralded in bombastic fashion in newspapers around the world.

For a moment, however, as Browne rested on the sun-warmed stone, he forgot about the hoax he'd come to unravel. Cook's "heaven-scraped granite" had turned out to be a mere knoll. Yet Fake Peak's surroundings were captivating. Bright sunlight set the glacier aflame. Sharp ridges jutted out like cathedral ruins. Nearly twenty miles away, the real Denali dazzled his eyes. It was, he recalled, "a picture of such sublime beauty that our powers of appreciation seemed benumbed." A bluish mist lit other enigmatic peaks along the horizons. Far away, he thought he saw "green meadows and hunting grounds as yet untouched by man." Although he'd banished the illusion of Cook's summit, another delusion took its place: the idea that no human being had ever wandered in those distant valleys.

Browne's own attempt on Denali stalled before the steep maze of ice walls, cliffs, and crevasses along its southern buttress. A rival team also failed to summit Denali that season: a group from the Mazamas (an Oregon-based club) led by Claude E. Rusk, who hoped to clear Cook's name by climbing his alleged route to the top of the continent. By the end of his trip, Rusk, too, became convinced that Cook had lied: the discrepancies between Rusk's own experience of the mountain and the descriptions in Cook's account appeared too great. The loss of his belief in a former hero left Rusk with a sense of melancholy. Even without an act of imagination, the high peaks of Alaska seemed too grand to be real. In a subsequent report, Rusk retold Cook's story as an allegory of a paradise lost and a Biblical temptation:

> *Since the morning of Creation solitude reigned, through countless centuries, over the stupendous panorama at the head of the Ruth Glacier. Then came two human atoms to marvel for a few hours at the wondrous sight. . . . That one trip alone—when with a single companion [Cook] . . . penetrated the wild, crag-guarded region near the foot of Mt. McKinley—should have made him famous. But the Devil took him onto an exceeding high mount and showed him the glories of the icy alpine world and—the Doctor fell.*

The story of Fake Peak wasn't over. In another twist, some of Cook's supporters insisted Browne had faked his own evidence that the Denali summit photo was a hoax. One of them, photographer Ernest Rost, even claimed that Browne had painted over the views from the top of Fake Peak himself, doctoring the photo to make it look like Cook's image. Another Cook advocate, Edwin Balch, traced the topographic contours of Browne's Fake Peak and Cook's alleged Denali summit pictures, placing one outline on top of the other to indicate small variations.

In 1956, hoping to put the fifty-year-old controversy to rest, Bradford Washburn went on his own expedition to Fake Peak. He waited until late summer to get conditions similar to those in Cook's photo, without the heavy snowdrifts that had impeded Browne's efforts to capture an entirely identical view. Browne, Washburn determined, had taken his picture just a few feet away from the right place. The stone knobs and fissures visible in all the images—Cook's, Browne's, and his own—matched each other "as precisely as in a fingerprint," Washburn observed in his *American Alpine Journal* report. Yet the angle of his photo was slightly off. Fake Peak had thawed and shrunk over the decades, he realized. Some of its fragile stone had toppled. No lichen grew on the lower two thirds of the outcrop, as if a blanket of snow had melted off the rock. "It would be impossible for us to have done any better than we had in duplicating Cook's 'summit picture,'" Washburn determined, "as the point from which he took it was at least forty feet up in the air in August 1956! . . . A substantial part of the right skyline is gone forever (and what still remains is going fast)." Fake Peak itself was becoming a phantom.

A year later, the future *American Alpine Journal* editor Ad Carter trekked to Fake Peak with his wife Ann, their son, and other companions, carrying fifty feet of aluminum piping. When they arrived where the previous photographers had stood, they assembled the pieces of metal into a single long pole. One member of the expedition, Roddie Dane, climbed the wobbling shaft, only to find it wasn't high enough to re-create the Denali "summit" photo. Around ten more feet of ice and snow had vanished since the previous year, leaving shards of gray rubble and dust-stained snow. Carter's team cached their aluminum piping, in case other "topographic detectives" wanted to try to raise the mast to its proper height. "They had better hurry," Carter noted, "as the famous little 'Fake Peak' is fast disintegrating, and it will not be long before its countenance of 1906 will have completely and irretrievably crumbled away."

---

HARVEY MANNING PONDERED THE RIVALRY OF PEARY AND COOK AGAIN and again in his writings. Parts of the story overlapped with his own childhood. As a boy, Harvey had mowed the lawn of a neighbor, Joe Quigley, a famous prospector, who showed him a sample of Alaskan wire gold and told him a story about sitting in a bar in Fairbanks with other miners when the

Sourdoughs hatched their plan to prove Cook wrong. When Harvey's uncle asked Joe why he didn't join them, Joe responded, "Wasn't drunk enough."

In many ways, Harvey's hoaxes were the opposite of Cook's. Instead of claiming a false record, Harvey's imaginary climbers told stories in which they failed to reach their ultimate goals. They tempted their readers to try to make the first ascents themselves. These narratives fit Harvey's aim of pointing out the absurdity and inappropriateness of climbing mountains for personal glory in the first place. Yet Harvey also wondered why so many people believed Peary's word instead of Cook's, when it was possible that both men might be hoaxers. "The 1906 Cook climb is not accepted because the Establishment (Peary-National Geographic Society-U.S. Navy-Brad Washburn) ganged up on Outsider Cook," Harvey decided.

There was much about Cook's life to make him a sympathetic character in Harvey's mind. Like Harvey, Cook had struggled to find a place for himself in a world of adventurers from more privileged backgrounds. Both men's writings, true or false, testify to an opulent imagination and a keen ability to create detailed fantasy worlds. By the 1960s, as biographer Robert M. Bryce has pointed out, Cook had become a kind of "antiestablishment" hero (or antihero) in the minds of readers skeptical of all authorities. Cook's own words, taken out of context, could provide an attractive defense for future hoaxers: "The world has important use for dreamers, even if they fail."

Over the decades after Cook's tale, Denali seemed to transform from the otherworldly mountain of his writings into a commercial playground. "What made Denali not merely a super-Blanc but a whole other species," Harvey wrote in "Mount Everest and Me," "was the sledging over the snows to the start of the climb and the fording of thawed-out and meltwater-raging rivers on the way back. The airplane cut it down to size, a wilderness grizzly shrunk to a playroom teddy." Whether or not Cook summited, the landscapes of his epic adventures were vanishing into thin air as surely as the snows of Fake Peak. Harvey could only gaze backward in time through books at a lost world that receded ever farther from his grasp—except, that is, when he re-created it by doctoring the maps.

Other aspects of Cook and Peary's rivalry fascinated Harvey as well. The North Pole was a kind of ultra-imaginary place, as Bryce has observed, "a point with no dimensions . . . where every direction is south." Time seems unhinged by twenty-four-hour summer light. The very idea of claiming a specific point on this terrain is meaningless. Nothing permanent exists within its shifting heaps and ridges of ice. There are no landmarks and no summits, as Harvey noted with bemusement, just an immense, disorienting lowland, reflecting the sun like a giant, broken mirror. "From the earliest days of poleward voyages to the present," Cook himself had written, "every book of narratives is prefaced with illusion and ends in delusion."

Peary had his own history with imaginary Arctic mountains. In the spring of 1906, after an earlier failed attempt to reach the North Pole, Peary sledged toward an unmapped region of the Canadian Arctic. His hope was to give some purpose to all the intense effort of his expedition—and to justify his sponsors' expense. Heading ever westward, he and his Inughuit teammates, Ulloriaq and Iggiannguaq, pursued distant pale hills that wavered in the cold, bright air. When they arrived at Cape Thomas Hubbard (which Peary named after one of his backers), they clambered up one of the summits. From there, Peary reported, he peered through field glasses at the misty, white mountain-tops of another faraway shore. "My heart leaped the intervening miles of ice as I looked longingly at this land," Peary wrote in *Nearest the Pole*, "and in fancy I trod its shores and climbed its summits." But summer was approaching, and fissures were already appearing in the frozen sea. It was time to head home. Peary called the vision "Crocker Land," the name of another patron. He claimed it was about 130 miles away.

To Peary's readers, his report of an immense unknown territory recalled rumors of mythic lands that dated back to Atlantis and Thule. Sixteenth-century maps had once depicted a *Terra Septemtrionalis Incognita* (an "Unknown Northern Land") to balance out the *Terra Australis Incognita* to the south. Twentieth-century geographers still speculated about the possibility of an entire "lost continent" somewhere in the Arctic. In a 1904 *National Geographic* article, geodesist Rollin A. Harris had even argued that the trajectories of ships trapped in drifting pack ice suggested the branching of currents around a giant landmass.

In 1913, an ardent Peary supporter, Donald Baxter MacMillan, organized an expedition to prove the existence of Crocker Land. A *New York Tribune* headline heralded his "Hope to Solve the Earth's Final Puzzle." At a press conference, as MacMillan described what he longed to find, his words recalled the marvels that once sprouted along the edges of ancient maps: "Its boundaries and extent can only be guessed at, but I am certain that strange animals will be found there, and I hope to discover a new race of men." On April 21, 1914, after dogsledding across hundreds of miles of ice, MacMillan wrote that he was certain he could see the dreamed-of mountains in the distance. One of his Inughuit guides, Piugaattoq, told him he was simply looking at mist. MacMillan refused to believe him. For two more spring days, the men crept farther across the cracked ridges and jade-like shards of the frozen sea with another guide, Ittukusuk, and a navy ensign, Fitzhugh Green. Soon, dark chasms of open water would snake around them as the surface thawed. Finally, MacMillan had to admit that Piugaattoq was right. In *Four Years in the White North*, MacMillan recalled: "The day was exceptionally clear, not a cloud or trace of mist; if land could be seen, now was our time. Yes, there it was!. . . . Our powerful glasses . . . brought out more clearly the dark background in contrast with the white, the whole resembling hills, valleys and snow-capped peaks. . . . Our judgment, then as now, is that this was a mirage or loom of the sea ice."

The myth of Crocker Land had fatal consequences for one of the Inughuit men who helped debunk it. After they turned back, MacMillan sent Green and Piugaattoq to survey another unmapped area southwest along the coast. The two men sledded on through gale-force winds until a whiteout trapped them in a snow cave. Left outside, Green's dogs suffocated under the weight of the swiftly falling blizzard; Piugaattoq's dogs survived. Green later claimed that he shot his guide because he was scared that Piugaattoq would abandon him and take their supplies. (Analysis of the evidence by subsequent historians, such as David Welky, indicates that Piugaattoq was actually trying to help Green get home alive.) When Green returned alone, he confessed his act to MacMillan, but he never faced trial for the murder. Expedition doctor Harrison Hunt, who considered Piugaattoq a friend, later asked in disgust in his own memoir whether "the ideals of the expedition to which I had pledged myself were not also a mirage, a will-o'-the-wisp?"

In the November 26, 1914, edition of the *Star Tribune*, Peary declared that if Crocker Land truly didn't exist, it wasn't because it was a deliberate hoax. Instead, he wrote, he must have made the same error so many other polar explorers had made, mistaking an optical illusion for reality. Since then, however, Arctic historians have found a clue that Peary might have consciously invented the peaks. Unlike Peary's subsequent book, his diary makes no reference to the entrancing white mountains of Crocker Land. On June 24, 1906, Peary had written simply "no land visible."

EVENTUALLY, THE MYSTERIES SURROUNDING EARTHLY PEAKS AND DISTANT geographic points leave the realm of utter imagination, and once-inaccessible summits become tangible places to human visitors. On June 7, 1913, a young man named Walter Harper, the son of an Irish American prospector and a Koyukon Dene woman, finally stood at the highest point of North America. Gusts roared across the clear, icy sky as his companions—Harry Karstens, Robert Tatum, and the Episcopal Archdeacon of the Yukon, Hudson Stuck—plodded toward him up the trail he'd broken. Instead of the "frosted granite" Cook claimed to see on the summit, they'd encountered heaps of snow. Certain that Frederick Cook had lied about reaching the top, Stuck was glad that theirs would be the first confirmed ascent of the mountain. He was also pleased that Harper, an Alaska Native, was the first person to reach the apex. Stuck would use his report of Harper's accomplishment to advocate for the placement of "Denali" on official maps instead of "Mount McKinley," though it would take more than a century for the US government to agree to restore the name derived from the Koyukon Dene word "Deenaalee."

On their way to the top, Harper helped resolve another mystery. Some people still didn't believe that any of the Sourdoughs had attained the lower north summit of the mountain. But Harper had glimpsed the silhouette of their spruce pole against the sky and recorded it in his expedition journal. "It had been there for three years," he marveled.

The apex of Denali was no longer an unknown place. Yet as the sunlight sparkled across the six-hundred-mile crescent of the Alaska Range, it illuminated seemingly innumerable peaks. Most of these summits were still unclimbed—and scarcely dreamed of by mountaineers of the day. Many would remain in that obscurity for decades more.

CHAPTER 16

# The Search for a Transcendent Quest

THE KICHATNA SPIRES WEREN'T COMPLETELY ignored as the twentieth century progressed. Hunters continued to glance toward their walls when they passed by them to the south. Pilots caught sight of their summits as they flew overhead. And when the air was crystalline, their tiny, sharply cut forms could even be glimpsed from the top floor of a tall Anchorage building, more than a hundred miles away. But few American climbers were aware of the spires' existence or their potential when Harvey and his friends published the Riesenstein Hoax in *Summit*. And from 1962 to 1965, mountaineers from across the country struggled to solve the riddle of where the photographer had actually been when he snapped the picture of those enigmatic peaks.

At the time, one of the largest collections of aerial images of untrodden Alaskan and northern Canadian mountains lay in a secluded closet annex at the Boston Museum of Science. The director Bradford Washburn had gotten in the habit of keeping his photos there, atlases of dream peaks carefully organized into albums, arranged by date and stacked along bookshelves. Then in his fifties, Washburn liked to share images of the most beautiful unclimbed routes with younger climbers to encourage them to explore.

Since 1964, one of his protégés, Harvard student David Roberts, had been making regular visits to the annex to peruse the pictures and pick out his next climb. In January 1965, David wasn't looking for the Riesenstein, but simply for an objective appealing enough to persuade his estranged mountaineering partner, Don Jensen, to go on an expedition with him again. During the previous summer, the two classmates had made an ambitious attempt on the immense, unclimbed east ridge of Mount Deborah in Alaska (another route that David had seen in Washburn's photos). The trip had turned into a forty-two–day ordeal of gale-blown drifts, depleted rations, escalating quarrels, and long, tent-bound silences. After they'd given up and begun staggering out of the wild, Don plummeted twice into unseen crevasses. During the second fall, a wound sliced all the way through his cheek. By the time they returned home, their friendship appeared to be over. Don, who had never felt comfortable in the elitist atmosphere of Harvard, dropped out, returned to his home state of California, got a construction job, and spent as much time as he could in the Palisades Range of the Sierra. There, he immersed himself in the hidden corners of its sun-dazzled granite spires.

Now that months had passed since the ill-fated expedition, David missed the intensity of their partnership. Perhaps the right climb could reignite the sense of invincibility they felt when they were together, a "kindred passion [that] seemed to transform the act of inching our way up a mountain wall into a transcendent quest," as he recalled in *Limits of the Known*. During the winter of 1964–1965, they'd started writing letters to each other again and speculating about future expeditions. Glancing at photos of the unclimbed West Face of Mount Huntington, a 12,240-foot peak in the Alaska Range, David noticed a ridge that twisted like a serpent across an old map. Using a method that Don had showed him, he stared, cross-eyed, at two photos of the face until they blurred together into one image, and the whole architecture of cornices and walls seemed to rise into three dimensions like an unearthly fortress, beautiful but terrifying. Feeling intimidated, David turned to topographic maps to look for other options in some of the lesser known regions of the Alaska Range. A mysterious cluster of peaks jutted southwest of Denali. None of the summits were above 9,000 feet. But the density of the contour lines hinted at steep walls thousands of feet high. A half-forgotten image from *Summit* magazine reemerged in his mind: these must be the Riesenstein.

David later asked Washburn why there were no pictures of the Kichatna Spires in his collection, since he'd taken aerial images of so many other unusual mountains. "They call that area the asshole of the Alaska Range," Washburn replied.

Decades afterward, in an email to me, David mused: "It took me a minute to realize that he was alluding to the weather, not the quality of the peaks. But think how different the history would have been if Brad had photographed the Kichatnas. . . . Climbers would have headed there pronto. And the Riesenstein hoax would never have come to pass."

On May 12, 1965, David wrote to Don, detailing an ambitious plan to climb the West Face of Mount Huntington and then continue on to the Kichatnas:

> *At first I was put off by the fact that three of the peaks (though not the highest) are named. I thought it probably implied climbing in them, and thus since we hadn't heard any stir, not outstanding climbing. Only today I finally traced their naming to Lieutenant Joseph Herron's 1899 expedition, the first in the area, who only saw these three peaks through a gap in the foothills from Simpson Pass.*
>
> *This area is completely untouched. I've read everything written about it (not much anywhere). . . . I think if mountaineers weren't so lazy and had heard of this area, they'd be fighting each other to get there first.*

Maps, photos, and imagination could only tell the climbers so much about the real mountains. They had no way of determining the quality of the rock other than to go there. The remoteness of the peaks posed a challenge in itself, especially for college students who couldn't afford to hire a bush plane to taxi them from one distant glacier to another. After discussing various approaches, David suggested flying to the Tokositna Glacier below Mount Huntington, summiting that peak, and then trekking from there to an airdrop of additional supplies near the Kichatnas. Along the way, they'd have to ford several dangerous rivers and pass six glaciers (four of which David believed to be unexplored) for a total distance of seventy miles. (Decades later, David commented to me, "We not only would never have made it—we'd have been lucky to survive.")

Another idea was to hike back to Talkeetna after climbing Mount Huntington, ride the train to Anchorage, and find a pilot to take them from there to Rainy Pass. They'd still have to haul loads across twenty-five miles or more of brush, river, and glacier to the Kichatnas. As an inducement, David wrote to Don, "[The area] has totally escaped notice since [Frederick Cook's expedition in] 1903. . . . At worst, we can at least name all the peaks." In a follow-up note, he reminded Don that some other climbers were rumored to be eyeing a trip to the same place: "I hope these Snyders are true duffers. I can't see from the map a single one of the central peaks that looks like an easy climb by any route."

Don was clearly interested in the possibilities. In the margins of David's letter, he'd scrawled "UNTOUCHED" in enthusiastic all caps. There was much about the otherworldly spires of the Riesenstein that could appeal to him. Don had felt drawn to exploration ever since his childhood trips to the High Sierra, where he'd scrambled on rocks with his older brother, Lin. On one trip, still a toddler, Don had wandered off on his own. When he returned to his terrified family, he appeared entirely at ease, as if he were incapable of getting lost in a place that seemed like home. Since age thirteen, as he later wrote, he'd been aware of "the magical power of the mountains" over his imagination.

To mitigate the tensions that strained their two-man Mount Deborah attempt, David and Don invited other Harvard Mountaineering Club members: Matt Hale, who had become one of David's frequent climbing partners, and Ed Bernd, an exuberant sophomore who was familiar with the sheer rock cliffs and icy winter summits of the Northeast, but who had never climbed a big peak before. They'd start with the daunting West Face of Mount Huntington before potentially continuing to the Kichatnas. The legendary bush pilot Don Sheldon agreed to fly them from Talkeetna, Alaska, to the Tokositna Glacier. On the long drive from Massachusetts, the team detoured to stop at Ed's parents' house near Philadelphia. For decades afterward, David would remember the drawn-out pause in the living room before Ed's parents hugged their son good-bye, while the scent of new rain and azalea blossoms wafted from the dark night outside.

In late July, after weeks of storms, the four young men neared the top of the West Face of Huntington. Summer was dimming around them. Shadows thickened into phantasmagoric shades. From the summit of Huntington, they could see the site of David and Don's past misery, Mount Deborah, which had shrunk to a small, faint point more than one hundred miles away. "This makes up for a lot," David said to Don. They stood for around forty minutes in near silence, thinking about all that had transpired. On the forty-fourth pitch of the West Face, with only a single piton hammered in for aid, Don had moved free and unprotected up steep, airy rock, imagining himself borne along by a mysterious power he compared to Beethoven's Ninth Symphony. It was as if the world had taken on a new dimension and he'd arrived, for a moment, in a place released from gravity, surrounded by a glimpse of what he called "paradise."

That moment of euphoria soon vanished as they began the arduous journey back to base camp. Many hours later, while David and Ed descended into the twilight, ahead of the others, a rappel setup failed. Ed fell, without a word, to his death. That instant would reemerge in David's writing again and again, at once brief and unending: a grating noise, the flash of a spark, and then a figure of a man falling and gradually disappearing into the lower dark, until all sight and sound went out.

They never found Ed's body. There was no longer any question, if there ever really had been, of continuing on a lengthy and uncertain expedition to the Kichatnas. After the surviving team members gathered at base camp, they stamped out the signal for Don Sheldon to pick them up—the start of a journey back to a world where they would have to share unspeakable news.

---

IN THE MEANTIME, ANOTHER TEAM HAD ALREADY BEGUN EXPLORING a few of the summits of the Riesenstein: members of a group that would become famous (and infamous) as the "Vulgarians."

As many readers of climbing history know, the term *Vulgarians* isn't an insult. It was, and remains, the preferred designation of a particular set of New York climbers. One of them was Claude Suhl (or "Clawed Sool," as he referred to himself), who later described the origins of their cohort on the website The Vulgarian Chronicles:

> *The Vulgarians were ULTRA-ALL-INCLUSIVE!!! Our stated and enacted mission was to provide a safe haven for all and any Fraternity (or Sorority) rejects in particular—although one could also be welcome if one had such affiliations... for example successful lawyer [Jim] McCarthy of Princeton—but McCarthy publicly rejected membership in a Princeton eating club because a good friend of his who was Jewish was denied membership. . . .*
>
> *so we had nerdiest geeks. . . .*
>
> *we had grade school dropouts—*
>
> *a person who earned his PhD in math from MIT before he was 21. . . .*
>
> *Too many eternal dirt bags to count. . . . Army veterans . . . Army drop-outs . . . communist sympathizers, civil rights activists, anti-Vietnam war protesters who after burning all their draft cards tried to lead a brigade to burn down a draft board. . . .*
>
> *The Vulgarians were and still are Egalitarians [I hope]—egalitarians with dirt bag roots [or dirt bag wannabe rub off patina] and a grubby grumpy edge who had a lot of fun.*

In many ways, the Vulgarians were the perfect protagonists for a Harvey Manning story. Like the creators of the Riesenstein, they had their own traditions of wild pranks, and they formed their own elaborate countercultural world. Many early Vulgarians were members of the City College of New York Outdoor Club. During the late 1950s, they began frequenting the steep quartz conglomerate crags of the Shawangunks, about ninety miles from New York City. Art Gran, a frequent Gunks climber, became their climbing mentor.

Back then, a staunchly conservative approach prevailed at the local cliffs, enforced by the Appalachian Mountain Club. The AMC determined which members were qualified to go first up a particular climb and set up an anchor to belay those who followed. There were precise regulations governing when these leaders could progress to the next level of difficulty in their choice of routes. Vulgarians disdained such rules, and their revolts against "Appies" (as they called AMC members) became legendary: naked ascents of Gunks routes, an impromptu car race around nearby roads (the "Vulgarian Grand Prix"), clever evasions of security guards and state police during illicit climbs of local water towers, and the tipping over of a car they believed belonged to an Appie. On a particularly notorious evening, a Vulgarian stood on the roof of a nearby restaurant-bar and urinated on their rivals while they walked out the door.

In retrospect, these Vulgarian rebellions seem like early ripples of the youth movements that would soon surge across the nation. Participants shared a distrust of top-down leadership, a dislike of any form of ironclad hierarchy or institutional control, and a preference for personal freedom and individual creativity. "The key word . . . which cannot be applied to the Vulgarians is organization," reads the history on The Vulgarian Chronicles. "The Vulgarians never were and never will be an organization of any sort, serious or not." To older, disaffected writers such as Harvey, the 1950s had represented an age of social rigidity, corporate dominance, and conservatism. The Riesenstein Hoax, in its own way, had taken aim at political boundaries (moving a range from the US to Canada) and at rampant consumerism and stodgy grandiosity (mocking the acquisitive, self-aggrandizing attitudes of first ascensionists). With his imaginative approach to mapmaking, Harvey had tried to overturn the notion that preponderant, restrictive visions of the world were all that was possible. While he'd targeted the prank at peakbaggers, he might not have anticipated that a younger generation of climbers would not only get the joke, but would respond to it so eagerly.

"The hoax was definitely in the spirit of the times," Vulgarian climber Pete Geiser told me when I reached out to him in 2011. "There was kind of a class warfare of a sort, where the early dominance of mountaineering by the wealthy was rapidly breaking down as climbing began to be done by more working-class folks [like the Vulgarians]. . . . It seemed to us that a lot of the climbing journals had these stories about climbs in exotic places, seemingly out of reach of us hoi polloi, where for all we knew they could have made the whole thing up with a few selected photos. So we were very much in tune. . . . But hoax or not, the mountains were real!"

In their letters, David Roberts and Don Jensen had worried that the "Snyders" might get to the Kichatnas first, a probable reference to the mountaineering couple Aaron and Ruth Schneider, who climbed with the Vulgarians. (Aaron told me that he might have mentioned his own Kichatna plans to Don when they met at Lake Tahoe. In one note to David, Don had written somewhat cryptically, "It is much within the realm of possibility that this friend of Ruth & Erin Snyder is planning his 'secret expedition' to the same area.") The misspelling of the Schneider's name seems almost symbolic. Beat poet Gary Snyder was a student of Zen Buddhism, and he described climbing and hiking as a means to break free of ego and to reconnect with wild nature in the mountains and the mind. His friend Jack Kerouac transformed him into "Japhy Ryder," a character in a 1958 mountaintop novel, *The Dharma Bums*, set partly at a fire lookout on Desolation Peak in the North Cascades. In one scene, Ryder delivers a speech that became a manifesto for their generation: "See the whole thing is a world full of rucksack wanderers, Dharma Bums refusing to subscribe to the general demand that they consume production and therefore have to work for the privilege of consuming. . . . I see a vision of a great rucksack revolution . . . of young Americans wandering around with rucksacks, going up to the mountains to pray . . . all of 'em Zen Lunatics who . . . by strange unexpected acts keep giving visions of eternal freedom to everybody."

"Kerouac was certainly a major inspiration," Claude Suhl told me. The first of the Suhls to be born in the US, Claude came from a family of Jewish immigrants who had fled Eastern Europe and Nazi Germany during the late 1930s. His father, who started out working in Manhattan's fur district, longed to become a professor—a dream he eventually achieved after many years of night school. Claude's father and stepmother became students at CCNY around the same time that Claude did, and they introduced him to a wide range of "Bohemian anti-establishment artists" and "political renegades." As he studied the French philosopher Jean-Paul Sartre, Claude's father explored how "the imaginary . . . can be a vehicle to a heightened awareness of reality." Claude himself experimented with creative writing, invented words and wild puns, composing long riffs on personal philosophies at once cosmic and very earthy (even the simplest emails he later sent to me are chaotic works of art). Sentence fragments scattered across a page reflected a world that appeared on the verge of bursting around him, as if the unknowns of the present and the future blazed in the gaps.

"The whole era was just wild with life, just pulsating," mountain guide and philosopher Jack Turner, a friend of the Vulgarians, recalled. "So many people felt that we'd run into a dead end. They wanted to escape." Claude and his climbing partners attended the readings of Beat writers in New York City and listened to Thelonious Monk and other avant-garde jazz musicians at the original Five Spot Café. They joined early civil rights actions and later anti–Vietnam War protests, came up with complicated schemes to avoid getting drafted, and welcomed anyone who wanted to take part in their ascents or capers. Writer and prankster Ken Kesey (an honorary "Vulgarian fellow traveler") and his followers painted a school bus in swirling, psychedelic hues and then rode it cross-country, holding acid parties along the way, seeking to disrupt the banalities of 1950s mindsets and to experience altered states of perception. ("To hell with facts! We need stories," asserts a Kesey quotation on The Vulgarian Chronicles. "But it's the truth, even if it didn't happen," states another.) One Vulgarian described trying LSD on the Olympic Peninsula and feeling as if the essence of the forests and tidal pools, the sunset and moonrise, unveiled itself in unmitigated, terrifying wonder. "There's a thin line between a religious experience and a psychiatric episode," he warned me. "You talk about seeing God. Well, you only want to do that once." Another Vulgarian told me that he was in Washington, DC, during the autumn of 1967 when Beat poet Allen Ginsberg and other activists performed rituals and chants to try to make the Pentagon building rise into the air. "They levitated the Pentagon. I saw it happen," this Vulgarian said. Then he paused. "But it might have been more what I was smoking."

Roman Laba (who described himself as an aspiring Vulgarian) recalled how the group descended upon Jackson, Wyoming, like "chattering magpies," alternately fascinating and horrifying local climbers. At the time, ski mountaineer

Bill Briggs still held his Teton Tea Parties at a campground below the jagged silhouettes of the Teton Range. Named for a special mix of tea, spices, and wine ("It was really terrible," Aaron Schneider admitted), these evenings of tipsy outdoor folk music seemed too genteel by the Vulgarians' standards. So they did their best to liven up the excessive solemnity with obscene songs and improvised instruments, such as the infamous "Vulgaraphone" (a twenty-foot water pipe molded into a tuba-like shape), which they filled with gasoline and set on fire to create what Claude called a "FLAMING KAZOO!!"

Despite their antics, Vulgarians were making first ascents in the Gunks on increasingly hard rock routes using "only pitons and lousy footwear," as local guidebook writer Dick Williams remembers. Some of them inevitably dreamed of higher and more distant cliffs. The remote Northern ranges were still an icy, white blank on the edges of many American climbers' imaginations and, like a fantasy world, the peaks had a powerful draw. The Vulgarians and others of their generation were as passionate about Tolkien as Harvey Manning was. In an introduction to a 1973 edition of *The Lord of the Rings*, fantasy writer Peter S. Beagle explained: "The Sixties were no fouler a decade than the Fifties—they merely reaped the Fifties' foul harvest—but they were the years when millions of people grew aware that the industrial society had become paradoxically unlivable, incalculably immoral, and ultimately deadly. . . . The Sixties were the time when the word *progress* lost its ancient holiness, and *escape* stopped being comically obscene . . . lovers of Middle-earth want to go there."

Pete Geiser spent his childhood scrambling up the schist walls along Manhattan's Riverside Drive, feeling a longing for stone that he couldn't put into words. Pictures of peaks with year-round snow hinted at a magical realm just beyond his reach. In the summer of 1959, at age nineteen, he joined a Vulgarian trip to the Bugaboos in British Columbia, "a climbing Shangri-La," as he later called it. The peaks resembled the photos he'd later see of the Riesenstein. Back then, before the modern roads, the Bugaboos were much harder to reach. After a wild drive up a crumbling dirt track, Pete's group carried hundred-plus-pound loads along game trails and across stretches of broken moraine and scrub cedar. When the granite spires emerged out of the mist, they appeared dizzyingly tall. "I began to sense that they were almost alive," Pete recalled. "I had the feeling like I wanted to throw myself into this mystery." The ever-roving Fred Beckey showed up at their campsite, like a dirtbag antihero, inviting Pete and fellow Vulgarian Roman Sadowy to join his attempt on the West

Face of Bugaboo Spire. They reached the top just as dusk enveloped them and the peaks vanished into the falling snow. Beckey started descending a steep, frozen gully that ended in a cliff. None of them had ice axes, and they were no longer roped together. "Fred romped down first, braced himself across the gully, turned to us, and said, 'Don't worry, if you slip, I'll catch you,'" Pete recalled. "And you know, I was sure he would."

Years later, Pete wrote a poem about the Bugaboos that, he told me, "best describes how I felt about the inchoate hidden place that I had longed to visit since I was a boy."

We left the fragment of a town.
Across the broad graveled bed of the river,
Into the gloom of the forested hills,
Following the narrow twist of a road,
Time lengthening its slow pace.
The thickness of the trees gradually thinning.
The road struggled its way upwards, higher and deeper
Into mystery. . . .

They came as in a dream.
Dream mountains.
Fragments suspended above the valley,
Above the deserted track,
In a land where reality's chain seemed stretched to breaking
Across the late day's sky. . . .

Larger and larger,
Growing in the misty unreal, until a final bend
Ripped our questions from us
And the dream of stone towers
Became our consciousness.

"We felt enlarged [in the mountains]," Aaron Schneider told me. "It was risky, but the payoff was enormous. It could become an addiction. For a lot of people, I think it did." Aaron was captivated by the story of the quest for the Inner Sanctuary of Nanda Devi. In Alaska, he'd encountered other rarely climbed ranges where even the approach was a struggle. Bush pilots who could fly to such high, remote places seemed like protagonists in old adventure tales. In 1960, when Aaron's friend Helga Bading became severely ill on Denali, Don Sheldon had managed to pick her up from roughly 14,300 feet, setting a new record for a high-altitude landing in a Super Cub plane. That same day, helicopter pilot Link Luckett had fetched another incapacitated climber from 17,000 feet on Denali after removing everything possible from his aircraft to lighten it—down to the starter battery. *Life* magazine heralded the two men as heroes.

At the time, Aaron felt disillusioned with his job in atomic submarine manufacturing and "all the public delusion that was going on to make people feel comfortable with the possibilities of nuclear war," he recalled. Climbing provided a respite from his anxieties about the future, a way to force himself to be in the present moment. "It was an antidote to a lot of things," he told me, "to a world that you mistrusted, basically." During a road trip out West in 1961, he met Ruth Ann Morris, who was performing mock stagecoach robberies for tourists in Jackson, Wyoming. A year later, they married. Aaron left the defense industry for good and became a science and math teacher, spending his vacations in the mountains with Ruth and their friends. He delighted in the subversive humor of the Riesenstein Hoax, which reminded him of *The Ascent of Rum Doodle*, a popular book among Vulgarians. He was also intrigued by the mystery of the real spires in the *Summit* photo, though they looked higher and more serious than any peak he'd scaled before.

Aaron had firsthand knowledge of the hazards of climbing in isolated alpine ranges. In 1964, he, Ruth, and two others had attempted Mount Marcus Baker, a 13,176-foot peak in the Chugach Mountains of Alaska. Through the fog of a whiteout, they could see shadows of giant seracs that had snapped off a ridge during a recent massive earthquake and tumbled to rest on the glacier. Ruth was breaking trail for the team through waist-deep drifts when she fell about twenty-five feet into a hidden crevasse. She landed on a bulge of ice and injured her leg. Without any means to call for a rescue, the others dragged her down the glacier on an improvised sled. The next morning, a plane glinted in the distance. Quickly, they stomped out a call for help in the snow. As the pilot flew overhead, he shouted out the window that help was on its way. Some time later, a rescue helicopter hovered above them, its buzz like the beating wings of a giant insect. "I learned about thinking clearly when things go wrong in remote scenarios," Aaron told me.

Despite the risks, the youngest of the Vulgarians, John Hudson, was eager to explore Alaska. "He had a strong will, the soul of an elf, the beatific gaze of a mystic," his friend Jack Turner recalled. John had started climbing at the Gunks in 1960, when he was about fourteen. He had little spending money, and when the soles of his boots started flapping off, he tied them back on with shoelaces. "You know, there's a lot of things you want," he explained to Aaron, "but you don't really need them." John's thick red hair swept low over his forehead, and a disarming smile lit up his freckled face. Older climbers thought of him as a precocious little brother. "Everyone understood that he was very talented right away," Jim McCarthy, who often climbed with the Vulgarians, told me. According to Jim, John was the first Gunks climber to figure out how to perform a "heel hook"—a move that involves latching a hold (often above your waist) with your heel, enabling you to use your leg like a third arm to help pull yourself up. John could make such contorted moves appear fluid, effortless. During the summers, he accompanied Vulgarians on their wanderings out West, where he learned from some of the top climbers of the day, including Yvon Chouinard, who taught him the art of climbing alpine rock walls. In 1961 in the Wind Rivers with Art Gran, John and Chouinard made the first ascent of Steeple, a granite pyramid mirrored in a sky-blue lake, surrounded by wildflowers. That same year, John and Beckey became the first to stand atop Lost Temple Spire, which rises across a nearby chasm. This semidetached tower appears invisible from certain vantage points, blending into the burnished monolith of East Temple Peak. Decades later, during my own trip to climb Steeple, I kept turning to gaze at Lost Temple Spire, and I felt dizzy merely thinking about it. I couldn't conceive of scaling something so implausible and surreal.

While John seemed like an "elf," Al DeMaria reminded one of their friends of the dwarf character Gimli in *The Lord of the Rings*—a tough, pragmatic warrior. Other climbers described Al as quiet and subdued on the surface, attributes that concealed a quirky humor and an intense pursuit of whatever caught his interest. When he first saw the *Summit* article a year or so after it was published, Al had trouble believing such dramatic towers existed in North America. "The Alps have walls like that," he thought, remembering the stories of legendary European climbers Walter Bonatti and Hermann Buhl. Art Gran explained to Al that the story was definitely fabricated and the peak was probably somewhere in Europe. "But surely walls that beautiful would have been climbed before," Al imagined, "unless they were somewhere really remote."

Once the Vulgarians realized the *Summit* article was a hoax and the picture of the mountains could be from "anywhere in the world," Pete recalled, the search for the real peaks seemed like "a hopeless quest." But Al remained curious. The map in the article reminded him of stories of the Stikine region in British Columbia. Al knew that Beckey had climbed in the Stikine and that he had a habit of keeping magnificent untouched peaks a secret, saving the possibility of first ascents for himself. So Al sent away for photos of the area. Jagged spires appeared in those images; yet nothing matched the Riesenstein.

In those days, Al had never visited an unclimbed mountain range. The cliffs at the Gunks, where he'd done most of his climbing, are at most 230 feet high—though their sheer walls and jutting roofs rise above the treetops with an airy shimmer that can seem almost alpine. The walls in the *Summit* photo looked much, much bigger, and they were clearly somewhere cold and distant. "If a picture like the Riesenstein had appeared before it was common for people to climb rock routes in the mountains," he recalled, "it might not have attracted much attention." But he felt drawn to the images of vast stone, "more than old mountaineers who would have preferred snow and ice."

Perhaps it was inevitable that Al's inquisitive friend Brownell Bergen, who had a strong interest in mountain photography, would solve the mystery of the Riesenstein. Brownell was married to Jeanne Bergen, the secretary of the American Alpine Club, and the two of them were living in a remodeled firehouse that served as the organization's headquarters in New York City. On the second floor, a library contained thousands of books and maps of peaks around the world. It wasn't there, however, that Brownell found the real location of the *Summit* photo, despite what many people later assumed.

One of Brownell's friends was a fellow at the American Geographical Society (AGS), and at some point after the hoax was published (he no longer remembers exactly when), Brownell happened to visit the imposing AGS headquarters on the corner of West 156$^{th}$ Street and Broadway, with its stone façade of Grecian columns and engraved names of explorers such as Columbus and Marco Polo. There, his friend showed him a stack of shoeboxes filled with Austin Post's pictures. Impressed by the granite peaks, Brownell examined each image carefully. He wasn't thinking about the Riesenstein Hoax at the time. But one picture of rock walls looked strangely familiar. "There was the exact photo of the giant stone, the Riesenstein," he concluded. "The exact photo that [Post] had published in *Summit*. Bang, there it was."

Brownell unfolded a topographic map of Alaska and looked southwest of Denali. On a USGS chart, the peaks of the Kichatnas appear like the perfect object for a magic quest: steep contours press into tight, dark lines between bands of white glaciers that radiate like the long arms of a snow crystal or a starfish or an *X*-marks-the-spot. A modern climber might well wonder why the summits had been neglected for so long. But Brownell's decision to share the real identity of the Riesenstein with the Vulgarians could seem, at first, surprising: It was his car they'd flipped over in 1960 (having mistaken the vehicle for someone else's). After learning that one of the men responsible was partway up a Gunks route, Brownell had walked around to the top of the cliff to lie in wait. As the climber got closer, Brownell said, "What's the story?" The man denied his involvement. "Are you in a position to argue with me?" Brownell asked. At that, the climber—who still had some eight to ten feet of rock between him and the top—confessed. Later, he sent Brownell a check to help cover the damage. Brownell forgave the car-tippers, and he passed on the information about the Kichatnas to several members of the community, including Al DeMaria, who made plans for a June 1965 expedition with Claude Suhl, Aaron Schneider, Pete Geiser, John Hudson, and another Vulgarian, George Bloom. "It sometimes happens in life," Al and Pete mused in the 1966 *American Alpine Journal*, "that a practical joke leads to practical results."

Pete recalled their sense of excitement:

> *We did feel like the best mountains in the Lower 48 were sort of done. I don't think we had any illusions about Alaska being limitless; by the 60s it was pretty clear to us that nothing on the planet was limitless. That said, it was pretty close. . . .*
>
> *Various Vulgarians, myself included, spent a fair amount of time with Yvon Chouinard, partying, doing occasional casual climbs, swapping lies, etc. We were all in a sort of subliminal agreement that the "mountains" was where it was at. . . . The best peaks were the ones that could only be climbed by technically demanding routes. So when the "Riesenstein" showed up, it was a dream realized.*

As they got ready to leave, their friend Jim McCarthy shook his head. "They were completely unprepared," he recalled. "The Vulgarians were good climbers and they were visionaries, but they had no idea what it was like to climb walls in harsh conditions."

CHAPTER 17

# Imagination Is No Match for Reality

ON JUNE 18, 1965, Al, Pete, and Claude crammed bags and mattresses into the back of a VW Microbus and left New York City for Alaska. They drove twenty-four hours a day, taking turns to sleep and look out the window. In Minneapolis, they stopped to pick up George Bloom. A physiology graduate student at the University of Minnesota, George was a fun-loving climber who shared their appreciation for practical jokes and who had an unflappable stoicism—a quality, Pete observed, that would prove essential to the trip.

John and Aaron had taken a separate car from Lake Tahoe to Dawson Creek, British Columbia, at the southern end of the Alaska Highway, which was not yet completely paved. There, the group met up and continued north, driving on gravel for more than a thousand miles. "Getting to Talkeetna itself seemed like penetrating the last remnants of a lost continent," Pete remembered. Icy air drifted toward them from distant glaciers. Chance visions appeared like signs from another world. One morning, Pete woke to see the body of a nighthawk stuck like a ship's figurehead to the front of the bus. Staring at the vast expanses on either side of the bus, Claude fixed his gaze on "minute encroachments that occasionally speckle the road." There was a lone gas station that served coffee with dried milk, and a dust cloud that churned like an inverted tornado until its smoke enshrouded them in temporary darkness. The eerie ruin of a large bus emerged through the fog. Claude dreamed that they were driving off the map and outside of time, pulled by the cosmos toward a place where they could find everything they wanted to know. "This treasure hunt is real," he thought.

In Talkeetna at last, they boarded Don Sheldon's bush plane for the Kichatnas. "He was more expensive than anyone else," Aaron recalled, "but we hired him because we knew that he had a reputation for flying in the most adverse conditions." Concerned about their safety, Sheldon gave the Vulgarians a radio in case they needed to contact him. It came with a long dipole antenna, which extended in opposite directions. To call Sheldon, they would attach the ends to ice axes and string the wires across the snow.

The Vulgarians had picked out a route on a spire that would come to be known as North Triple Peak—a blend of rock, snow, and ice that resembled their previous climbs in the Bugaboos. But Sheldon couldn't see a place to land amid the broken ice near their desired spot. So he dropped them off on a different glacier on the other side of a sheer ridgeline.

To Claude, Sheldon's plane seemed to vanish like a "silver gnat" into the sky. "It's the first time I've ever heard silence come down with a crash," Pete thought. Before them, a bewildering labyrinth of leaning spires and prickling ridges twisted in various directions. Within a few square miles, there were more than forty summits between 7,000 and nearly 9,000 feet. Pale amber and ash-colored granite faces swept high into the air between flying buttresses, long arcs of cracks and couloirs, strange nooks of sudden chasms, stone windows, and caves. Glaciers emanated from the center of the range in rays of white, separated by sharp rock spines. Gusts of wind groaned like discordant, gothic music.

"As usually occurs, imagination is no match for reality, especially when you're essentially dropped into it by the closest thing to teleportation," Pete remembered. To Aaron, the radiating stone crests looked like the giant "fingers of an outspread hand . . . [with] peaks as knuckles." The spires reminded Claude of photos of the golden towers of Patagonia, slathered in rime and buffeted by gusts, "the ultimate expression then known of the perfection in climbing," he told me. Then he added with one of his characteristically inventive verbs: "They were also loathed in wet snow."

Even some of the easiest rock routes appeared as challenging as the giant cliffs of Yosemite. But here, instead of reflecting back the warm California sunshine, the stone was buffeted by blizzards, sleet, and rain generated by powerful storms in the Bering Sea and the Gulf of Alaska. In the *American Alpine Journal*, Pete and Al recalled that "the immensity of the walls . . . suddenly took on the proportions of an absurd joke. Climb? These walls? Plastered with snow and icy couloirs, rising two to three thousand feet above the glacier, the summits seemed the epitome of inaccessibility."

They still hoped to trek to their original objective. First, for a "warm-up," Pete, Al, and John chose what appeared to be the least challenging nearby summit. While snowflakes whirled through the air, they spent half a day thrashing up a long snow slope, its icy crystals clumped like wet down feathers, to the top of the 7,270-foot mountain. For the next ten days, they attempted col after col as they searched for a way over a sharp crest to the cirque where they'd initially planned to climb. In the end, they clambered up about 1,500 feet of steep snow to reach the lowest saddle. When they peered down the other side, they saw a chaos of loose rocks. Baked by the sun, a gully seemed on the verge of collapsing. Nonetheless, they decided to have a look. As they rappelled over the edge, a clatter of falling stones cut one rope. In horror, they called the place "Gashlycrumb Col" after a book by Edward Gorey that illustrates the deaths of twenty-six children, one for each letter of the alphabet.

Soft rain fell, gradually soaking their clothes. During the retreat back over the col to their tents, whenever they stopped to belay, they hugged each other to stave off hypothermia. (George was "a big bear of a guy," Aaron remembered. "Definitely an advantage" for keeping the group warm.) No one wanted to repeat the harrowing journey up and down Gashlycrumb Col to ferry loads and set up a new camp. They realized that they were essentially trapped in the spot where Sheldon's plane had dropped them off. They named the glacier of their original base camp "Cool Sac" (for cul-de-sac), and they resigned themselves to exploring only the mountains directly above it until Sheldon returned to pick them up again.

Accustomed to the Bugaboos, they'd been expecting to find rivulets for drinking water, but the glacier was frozen solid, and they hadn't brought enough stove fuel to thaw snow or ice for a week. George came up with the idea of creating what he called a "water mine." An air mattress, placed atop a mound of snow that they'd carefully sculpted to catch the sunlight, could funnel melting water into six-gallon milk bags. It had all the homespun ingenuity of Harvey's Sleeping System, and it actually worked.

During their efforts to escape the Cool Sac, the group had glimpsed three snow-crusted towers that ended in sharp points above burnished granite walls. A host of smaller peaks crenellated the rim of the unattainable cirque. Nothing about any of these formations appeared accessible. One 8,985-foot summit loomed above all the others like a silver citadel, glorious and unattainable. In the *American Alpine Journal*, Pete and Al later declared it "the prize of the range . . . from a mountaineering as well as aesthetic viewpoint . . . one of the outstanding peaks of North America." (Here, one might almost imagine a Harvey Manning character interjecting, "Who will be the first to climb it?" and cackling.)

The Vulgarians drew their own map, inventing names that played on words or that hinted at private meanings. One peak they called "After You" so, as Claude explained, "I can truthfully say that I named a mountain After You—no need to thank me." Since the unreachable walls were "the ultimate expression" of their aspirations, they designated another summit "ASpire." At the head of the Cool Sac Glacier, Claude said, "there was a Spire . . . that seemed, under certain light conditions, to have a hole in it. Proof—one day with blue sky as a backdrop, a little cloud came right through the hole—so 'TranSpire' is that peak's name!" For other mountains, they chose "Kotzebue Complex" after an Alaskan town that Claude saw on a map and found appealing and the "Spyder," which, like the "Spider," a well-known feature on the Eiger North Face, consisted of "a spideriferous manifestation of tapering tendrils of snow and ice couloirs evanescing from a central snow/ice field mass," Claude recalled. "Sartre Couloir" derived from Claude's (and his father's) obsession with the French philosopher. "We obviously thought it had No Exit," Claude joked to me, referring to the title of one of Sartre's plays.

Maybe something of Sartre's sense of existential absurdity applied to their adventure. After groveling up a snow-streaked gully to the top of the roughly 7,900-foot Kotzebue (known today as Sunrise Spire), Claude, Al, and George realized just how narrow the ridge crests were—like serrated blades of stone. It was yet another unusual aspect that would increase the difficulty of traveling from cirque to cirque. And when John, Pete, and Aaron made an attempt on the 7,785-foot mountain they called Vulgarian Peak, they also encountered an unpleasant surprise. "We ran into snow conditions we had no experience with," Pete recounted. "The snow looked solid but it had zero strength. As soon as you stepped into it, it collapsed. It was like stepping into air. You sank up to your crotch and would just start to slide." Frightened, they turned back.

Several days later, the morning sky turned an unexpected blue—one of only a few clear days in the expedition. John and Pete started up the 8,250-foot Spyder, where they were delighted to find firm, cleanly faceted stone, with plenty of fissures to place gear for protection. "It was the best rock either John or I had ever climbed on," Pete said, "and for me at least remains so to this day." That pleasure quickly faded. When they initially looked up at the route from the Cool Sac Glacier, they believed that they'd just be climbing rock, so they hadn't brought any crampons. Now, they found themselves at the edge of a slick ice slope above a big cliff. Pete sat on a boulder to belay while John swung his axe again and again to cut shallow steps that they could teeter up in their boots. Dark clouds boiled overhead. Across the glaciers, the faraway dome of Denali vanished piece by piece into the gloom. Pete eyed the precipice below them and shuddered: if John slipped, there was no anchor to prevent them both from falling into the void.

Meanwhile, Al, Aaron, and George were in the midst of their own attempt on Vulgarian Peak, which they'd begun the day before. Mist enfolded them as they fumbled along the final snowy ridge toward the summit. Unable to see through the whiteout, and increasingly worried about the location of a large but invisible cornice, they decided to wait for daybreak. That night, they huddled in the open. The next morning, they crept upward again, only to be caught in the tempest. By the time they retreated to base camp, Claude was grappling to keep the tents from blowing away in hurricane-force gusts.

John and Pete turned back somewhere near the summit of the Spyder as the storm clouds finished consuming Denali and rushed toward them. They skittered down the small steps they'd nicked into the smooth pane of ice. The cliff plunged directly below them again. "It was like climbing the roof of a house," Pete remembered, "a *very* slippery, steep roof." They touched down on the glacier just as the winds and sleet flattened base camp. After repitching and securing the tents, they tried to sleep. Late that night, Pete awoke to "an enormous low organ note that filled the valley," he said. "It wasn't loud; it just seemed to fill all space. The only thing that I can attribute that sound to was that the headwall of the cirque had a narrow, giant, elliptical hole in it and a shift of the wind was playing it."

Gusts tore rough grains of snow from the glacier and flung them at the tent walls. For a day and a half, the six men scarcely ventured outside. Waves of rain, snow, and fog washed over them. On rare occasions, the glow of dusk shone through the clouds before disappearing again. During a relative lull, John and Pete found a way up Vulgarian Peak that avoided the worst of the hoar snow. As they traversed through damp, heavy drifts, above fracture lines where old avalanches had the split the slope, they felt relieved that dense clouds and soft rain hid the abyss below.

The sun wouldn't appear again for nearly eight days. Aaron decided to leave early. Any major ascents seemed unlikely in this weather. He knew that his wife, Ruth, was heading into the Wind River Range with her father, and he wanted to join them. On the day that Sheldon came to take him out, the aircraft darted through a small window in the clouds. During the journey back to Talkeetna, they landed on a glacier partway up the South Buttress of Denali so Sheldon could drop off supplies for another expedition. The plane's skis sank a foot into the snow. Three Denali climbers had to use all their strength to push the aircraft forward until it got enough momentum to take off again. The skis glided over the rim of the hanging glacier and, for a moment, Aaron recalled, the plane seemed to be falling into nothingness before it began "thrumming" upward "into the crystalline air." He could tell that his virtuoso pilot was enjoying himself.

As they gained altitude, Aaron looked at the fuel gauges: both indicated *Empty*. "So, Don," he asked, "how much fuel do we actually still have?"

"None," said Sheldon. He stared back at Aaron in silence as if assessing his reaction. Aaron laughed, guessing that Sheldon was just enjoying scaring him.

Sheldon took one more detour to fly over Mount Huntington to check on David Roberts and his teammates. The Harvard students waved at Sheldon's aircraft as it passed by. Their figures seemed tiny against the vastness of the peak—all of them, including Ed Bernd, still hopeful and alive.

"So, did you climb your mountain?" Sheldon asked Aaron.

"No," Aaron said.

"It's terrible to fail, isn't it?"

Outside the window, the light on the mountains dimmed. Vast glaciers extended like a desert, cold and bare. Another storm was coming. They arrived in Talkeetna (as Sheldon later told Aaron) with just one minute's worth of fuel left.

As Aaron spent days hitchhiking south, away from the Kichatna Spires, the dusks grew longer and finally turned into full summer nights. At a Wyoming post office, he picked up a letter from Ruth explaining where to find her and her father in the mountains near Shadow Lake. It was another kind of treasure map, one he followed eagerly as he bushwhacked along riverbanks and through open woods, back to the woman he loved.

For the rest of the Kichatnas expedition, Aaron's teammates were mostly stuck in their tents while falling snow blurred the mountains and the air into an almost uniform white. At last, another window of blue sky opened and the gnat-like silver plane reappeared in the sky. On the flight out, the Vulgarians took a last look at the Riesenstein before the mountains dissolved into the mists. Once more, the peaks became invisible and imaginary. Only flashes of memory remained. In some ways, their real adventure had resembled the fictitious Austrian expedition of the Riesenstein Hoax. Although the Vulgarians attained three minor summits, they hadn't managed to climb any of the giant walls in the *Summit* photo. Still, they'd experienced moments that lingered with an afterglow of magic: strange towers that rose like visions from dreams; a glacier so intensely solitary that their metallic-red cooler seemed incongruous against its vast white snows; unexpected animal tracks that looked like those of a mountain lion; and the jewel-like form of an insect, lying as if lifeless on the ice. "I picked it up in wonder," Claude remembered. "As my hand warmed the bee, it came back to life and soon flew away."

Today, Pete calls the entire experience "a harsh but indirect lesson . . . to always be humble in the face of Nature. . . . I felt like I'd been there, but the mountains were unperturbed. They were just *there*, and we could sort of live in their *thereness* for a while. That was it. Then we'd have to go." The longing remained.

From Haines Junction, Alaska, Pete and John hitchhiked to the coast, rode a ferry, and hopped a freight train to meet up with Art Gran in Jasper, Alberta, near the border of British Columbia. The trio wrestled with the sharp-spined leaves of slide alder as they bushwhacked to the unclimbed east face of Mount Chephren. By the time they dragged themselves onto a final shelf of stone at the summit, they'd climbed for 5,200 feet amid cascades of falling rocks and ice shards. Yet they'd failed to set the altimeter before they began the ascent, and the instrument indicated that the apex was some 800 feet higher from where they stood—as if a phantom mountain hovered above them, still bewitching and unattainable, in the late July air.

After returning to New York City, Claude continued his own road trip to South Carolina, where he and his then-wife, Joy Hornung, joined a drive to help register Black voters. The mythic appeal of the Riesenstein dimmed against the ongoing realities of the civil rights struggle.

Most of the Vulgarian names for summits in Kichatna Spires never made it onto official maps. The editor of the *American Alpine Journal*, Ad Carter, removed their terms from the trip report he published—perhaps he thought the names lacked dignity or maybe he was worried they represented coded references to Vulgarian obscenities. Instead, Carter designated a number for each mountain that corresponded to its elevation.

Back in California, when Jean Crenshaw and Helen Kilness assembled the October 1966 *Summit* issue, they also included Al and Pete's account of the Kichatna Spires expedition with numbers for peaks instead of names. In the "Know Your Mountains" section, Jean and Helen reprinted the original Riesenstein Hoax photo and its dotted route lines. Below the image, now correctly captioned, they wrote: "This picture of these spectacular mountains was published in the June 1962 issue of SUMMIT and mislabeled 'Riesenstein Peaks' by a practical jokester who claimed they were located near Prince Rupert in British Columbia."

CHAPTER 18

# The Secret Passage

DAVID ROBERTS WAS RELIEVED TO learn that the Vulgarians had climbed so little in the Kichatnas. Still mourning the death of Ed Bernd, he'd enrolled as a graduate student at the University of Denver in the summer of 1965. He'd exchanged a few half-hearted letters with Don Jensen about the spires, but the intensity of their shared dreams had faded. They never went on an expedition together again.

That autumn, David immersed himself in literature classes. Absorbed by the imaginary voyages of eighteenth-century travelers, he marveled at how easily readers could be fooled by the most extravagant tales. "The credulous bishop who voiced his doubts about *Gulliver's Travels* only because he could not find its countries on his map of the world became the laughingstock of London," he recalled. Years later, he returned to these stories when he wrote a history of fraudulent claims, *Great Exploration Hoaxes*.

But in 1966, he was still focused on trying to capture the real experience of Mount Huntington. Overcome by the need to communicate "the wonder and agony," David scrawled a draft on notebook paper in a mere nine days, typed the story up, made a few minor revisions, and mailed it off to a New York publisher. To his astonishment, his manuscript, *The Mountain of My Fear*, was accepted. It became the first of more than thirty books he would write.

In one chapter, David regretted the vanishing of imaginary places and the enchantment of exploration:

> *As long as men had been confined to the earth's surface, there was still the allure of hidden places; there were still "Shangri-La's" and "Golden West's" in their minds, at least. But the airplane ended that; it proved that the world looks pretty much the same all over; big places and cold places exist, of course, but the pattern is the same:*

> *there are only seas and deserts, jungles and forests, plains and mountains, swamps and icecaps. . . .*
>
> *The summits one may now visit before anyone else look remarkably like other parts of their mountains. The air is the same as, if a little thinner than, that at the bottom; the snow there would melt in one's hand to the same dreary water that flows from its foot. No ladder leads into the sky, and to try to get higher would be as futile for the climber as it was for Icarus.*

For the summer of 1966, however, as if unable to relinquish his dreams of *terra incognita* in Alaska, David accepted a job teaching composition and literature at the Elmendorf Air Force Base in Anchorage, where his girlfriend (and future wife), Sharon Morris, would join him. Before their departure, David sat in a bar listening to Art Davidson, a climber, rave about the state. "His monologue," David recounted in his memoir *On the Ridge Between Life and Death*, "[was] an extended paean to the tundra wastes, the dancing northern lights, the gleaming limitless ranges. . . . I listened, stupefied and fascinated, as the poetry awakened my own dormant love."

Art broke off his description to invite David to the Kichatnas. David, startled, replied that he would be working until August. Art countered that they could go in September. And with an overpowering impulse, David agreed.

In Anchorage, on cloudless summer evenings, David, Sharon, and Art took the elevator to the top-floor bar of the Westward Hotel to watch the dark, faraway towers of the Kichatnas emerge from the backlight of dusk. Art and David still didn't have a complete sense of what they'd find there, only scraps of information, pieced together from the Vulgarians' report, one or two aerial photos, and some elevation points and squiggles marked on topographic maps.

One night, Dave Johnston, a climber who had just returned from working as a field assistant in the St. Elias Mountains, showed up at David and Sharon's rented shack by chance, brought by a mutual acquaintance on a visit. Decades later, Dave still remembered his excitement about their plans for the Kichatnas. "I thought it was pretty darn neat," he told me over the phone. "Even in those days when you had satellite, airplanes, it just seemed amazing that there could still be a place that looked so inviting that was off the radar." He'd eagerly accepted an invitation to join the expedition.

On September 2, bush pilot Eric Barnes flew Art, David, and Dave to the Kichatnas along with three other companions: climber Peter Meisler, filmmaker Jerry Bernass, and Harvard Mountaineering Club alum Rick Millikan. The Vulgarians' article had drawn attention to Peak 8985, the highest point in the range. Al DeMaria and Pete Geiser's words echoed with the kind of resounding declaration that made the original Riesenstein story so successful: "We all considered this mountain—from a mountaineering as well as esthetic viewpoint—to be one of the outstanding peaks of North America." Art and David's team decided to call this superlative mountain "Kichatna Spire."

The 1966 group knew how to avoid some of the Vulgarians' mistakes, such as landing on the hemmed-in "Cool Sac" glacier or the "Cul-de-Sac" as it came to be known. They also understood, as David wrote in their *American Alpine Journal* report, that they were on the cusp of a new form of alpinism: "The Cathedral Spires have not long attracted mountaineers, partly because almost no one knew about them, and partly because they require a style of mountaineering that is only now coming into being: that of difficult technical climbing on expeditionary mountains."

Even so, their first view of Kichatna Spire awed them. "It was beyond our imagination," Art recalled. "We just stood on the glacier and looked at this incredible wall, and we howled." The dark, ice-crusted monolith rose for thousands of feet like a giant's fortress. In the *American Alpine Journal*, David marveled: "No other area combines heavy glaciation, remoteness, and bad weather with such an abundance of vertical walls, pinnacles, and obelisks. Nowhere else had any of us seen such remarkable sights as huge ceilings interrupting knife-edged ridges, mushroom-shaped towers of rock, or rime ice coating overhanging walls."

Rays of autumn light passed between the spires and brushed their base camp for only a few hours each day before fading into the murky air. Within a couple of weeks, even that hint of warmth vanished. They called the place the "Shadows Glacier." They had to trek over a mile away from the shade of the high walls to find fleeting patches of sun to dry out storm-soaked down sleeping bags. When Jerry's movie camera failed, he busied himself enlarging their base-camp igloo until he and the others had turned it into a small palace of ice.

Closer up, the lower section of the Kichatna Spire appeared insurmountable: Rivulets of snow slid down a steep wall, spackled with patches of ice. The stone looked polished and nearly blank apart from a hairline crack that vanished after a few hundred feet. In an aerial photo, however, they'd noticed a gully concealed within the mountain's folds. On September 4, David watched Dave, Rick, and Peter head up the rift and disappear into shadows and mist. Several hours later, the trio descended to base camp with good news: the corridor of snow and ice continued to a col 2,300 feet below the top. They named it the "Secret Passage."

For days, expedition members took turns fixing ropes as they slowly made their way above the col. A thick plumage of rime and frost adhered to the sunless walls. When they looked behind them, the snow-lit summits of some of the best-known peaks in the Alaska Range wavered like mirages across vast glaciers. Even familiar contours looked faraway and dreamlike.

Between bouts of work on the Kichatna Spire route, they took breaks to explore several of the lower mountains nearby. On September 7, Rick and David climbed ice-tendriled rock to the top of a 7,300-foot summit they called "Vertex Peak." Four days later, a blizzard inundated their base camp. For the next twelve days, only a few clearings appeared in the sky. Expedition members tried various means of distracting themselves, including a game of "golf" that Rick and David played with ice axes and a film canister. The pilot managed to fly through a brief gap in the clouds to pick up Jerry.

During other lulls, Pete and Dave stomped through drifts to the top of an unnamed 6,500-foot peak. Team members scurried up the Secret Passage to take down a tent at 7,100 feet, so that the wind couldn't tear the fabric apart. As David and Rick slogged up a snowy 6,900-foot mountain, the slope fractured and they were swept up in a current of debris. "I remember distinctly . . . the sense of being totally out of control and of the whole mountain moving," Rick told me. "But it didn't seem to be burying me. I was just sitting on [the avalanche] and riding it out." After 350 feet, the slide came to a stop. The pair were stunned, though not seriously hurt.

David had already felt fearful for his partners whenever they were out of sight. His unease grew in the aftermath of the avalanche. In his diary, he wrote, "I am not sure always if the risk is worth it. . . . Perhaps I have only in the last year found other things that mean (or that could eventually mean) as much, possibly more, than climbing does to me." He thought of Ed's body, lost somewhere in the masses of ice and snow below Mount Huntington. He thought of Sharon, waiting for him to return. Each time his team ventured up the Secret Passage, David imagined another slide rushing down the 1,600-foot couloir and burying them all.

Day after day, snow fell across the mountains, piling higher around the base-camp igloo. On September 21, Art and Rick went back up the Secret Passage to reestablish the camp at 7,100 feet, where they would wait to see if a break in the storm permitted a summit attempt. Watching them go, David felt an irresistible sense of relief that, this time, he wasn't headed into the icy upper world. A sharp regret also pierced through his mind. Perhaps he already knew that the image of that lost spire would remain imprinted, lifelong, in his memory.

"One way or another we would make do with what the gods of the mountains gave us," Rick recalled thinking as he and Art got ready to sleep at their old camp that night. The next day, mist still hung over their path. The snow seemed poised to slide at the mere touch of sunlight or a too-heavy footfall. They placed their boots cautiously, packing down the drifts and pounding a piton into rock whenever they could.

By four in the afternoon, they decided to return to a narrow ledge to bivouac in the failing light. The clouds finally lifted. Dusk glowed like phosphorescence across the mountain walls. As they huddled on their tiny platform to cook, one of the men bumped against the stove and the gas separator fell over the edge. They listened to the tinkling sound of metal bouncing against the rock until it vanished into the silent void. To melt a little snow to drink, Rick took the aluminum wrapper from a stick of chewing gum and improvised a flimsy replacement for the missing part.

They awoke the next morning to an irresistibly clear sky. "I remember being almost disappointed that we were going to have to climb this thing," Rick told me, "because it was scary." Art was spellbound by the beauty of the light. "There were a lot of little quartz crystals in the granite," he remembered. "They just lit up and sparkled, and as the sun rose a little more, the reflection would come at a different angle. Some of the sparkles would fade. Others would pick up. Every step we took . . . we didn't know what we were going to find. Really, we didn't know until the last couple hundred feet, the last little step, if we'd be able to make the summit. . . . Of course we wanted to. But even if we hadn't, if we had been stuck by that ice edge and snow ridge . . . the whole thing was exquisite and magical."

After they passed their footprints from the day before, Art and Rick climbed over a thin sheet of snow and rime that crumpled beneath their weight, exposing rock so rotten that their crampons stuck in it. Then they crept along a crest of soft cornices with thousands of feet of air on either side. Right before the summit, a large block poked out from the ridge. For a moment, Art thought they were stuck. Aware that any fall could be fatal, he picked his way over the steep, loose stone and snow. Finally, they stood on the apex of the Kichatnas. Before them, the snow flutings of Mount Augustin shone for thousands of feet. Dim granite walls hinted at unknown possibilities on other peaks. But the sun was on the brink of setting, and the autumn sky now glinted like cold glass. They descended into the rising dark.

Art and Rick flashed a light to indicate they were safely back at their bivouac ledge. To David, who was watching from far below, the signal seemed "like a bright star." That perfect summit day proved to be the last moment of crystalline weather. In the morning, David, Pete, and Dave climbed up the Secret Passage through drifting clouds to assist their friends. While David accompanied Art and Rick down to base camp, Pete and Dave lingered to remove the team's fixed ropes and pitons. That night, David waited, sleepless, for the two to return as stars faded into the gloom of another approaching blizzard. Near midnight, the small light of a headlamp glimmered through the mist. When Pete and Dave arrived, they explained that a rappel rope had gotten stuck and they'd had to abandon it.

During their last few days at the Shadows Glacier base camp, the group hoped to climb the sharp-walled tower that the Vulgarians called "the Spyder" (now known as "The Citadel"), which rose between them and the Cul-de-Sac Glacier. But when no second lull appeared in the storms, they confined themselves to smaller objectives. Dave and David finished slogging to the top of the 6,900-foot mountain, and they named it "Avalanche Peak," for the slide that had struck David and Rick there during their earlier attempt. With Rick, they also climbed a nearby "rock prong" to a 6,500-foot summit.

Once the pilot showed up to collect some of their gear, the five men began a forty-five-mile circuit of the range, an old-fashioned adventure "in the spirit of Shipton and Tilman," as David described it. After trudging over the Shadows Glacier, they intended to cross the snout of the Cul-de-Sac Glacier and traverse the full length of the Tatina and Monolith Glaciers (which they named). They would continue to Rainy Pass Lodge, where a plane could pick them up. Untracked expanses of ice and snow unrolled beneath their feet like blank spaces on a giant map. Peak after peak surged in a staggering array. Wintry gusts crashed against rime-crusted walls. In the fading October light, the icy towers resembled the architecture of an underworld metropolis. Beyond the Shadows Glacier, the group clambered over the glittering schist of a rocky pass and down soft drifts. The next day, the flat light on the snow erased the landscape. Invisible in the vast white, an avalanche rumbled.

Past the edge of the Cul-de-Sac Glacier, two lakes, not yet frozen, glowed a gem-like blue. Ducks floated across the water. The western walls of Triple Peaks, three unclimbed spires, came into view. Sheer rock faces, coated in frost and shadow, soared for thousands of feet into the sky. To Dave Johnston, the cliffs appeared like mirrored images of Yosemite's El Capitan, multiplied and enlarged into gigantic proportions before they vanished into the clouds. The mountains seemed infinitely high. It was hard to imagine anyone climbing to their summits. That night, eerie noises resounded as shards of ice tumbled through the air.

When the group headed south, images flickered by like scenes from a dream. The early winter of the glacial world was vanishing behind them. Green grass and moss, tinged with autumn gold, emerged from the snows. Birds called. Water flowed. Light rain returned while they wove around large boulders toward the Kichatna River. They thrashed through wet, clinging alder branches and forded icy currents until their clothes became drenched. On one occasion, a giant bull moose stood on a rise and looked at David, who seemed frail and vulnerable in comparison, his ice axe as small as a toy. He thought of how ice age human wanderers could have traveled by these frozen crags. Somewhere nearby, he realized, Herron's 1899 expedition might have camped.

Snowflakes began to fall again in damp, thick clumps. They shivered whenever they stopped moving. A square on their map indicated the possible presence of a hunting cabin. Inside the empty building, they lit a fire in its stove as a respite from the deepening chill. The next day, they hiked along moose tracks through snow-bent willows. Dave noticed that their footprints had turned purple—there were still blueberries and cloudberries underneath the early drifts. Hungry and weary, he crawled, picking at the fruit. One last obstacle lay ahead: the Happy River. Near a place where members of Spurr's expedition almost drowned in 1898, the 1966 team shook as the frigid waters rose to their hips.

At Rainy Pass Lodge, hunting guides offered them dry clothes, a blazing fire, and glasses of scotch. Already, David regretted the end of their journey.

In the *American Alpine Journal*, he concluded: "Our hike across those frozen stretches of land seemed to me alive with echoes of the wanderings of ancient tribes, of migrations in the wake of vast herds of reindeer, of the first superstitious voyages into the unknown north, and, finally, of the endless mythic journeys of our hearts.... What if we had climbed a certain mountain? It is still there, surrounded on every side by summits no man has ever visited, offering, as only the wilderness can, this world's last illusion of paradise."

---

IN 1968, DAVID PUBLISHED A GUIDE TO THE KICHATNAS IN SUMMIT "to shortcut, for future visitors, the problems of a Spires expedition by chronicling what is known about the place, and to entice serious mountaineers with a prospect of some of the most exciting mountains on earth." A few names on the hand-drawn map recalled choices from the 1965 and 1966 expeditions, though the Vulgarians' "Cool Sac Glacier" had already morphed into the statelier "Cul-de-Sac." Others were remnants of early exploration history: Augustin Peak, Gurney Peak, and Lewis Peak (of which David complained, "Today their untouched summits still officially bear the surnames of those three men whom obscurity would otherwise rightly have claimed."). Several glaciers were still only designated with numbers. Within a year, a trio of Californian climbers—Royal Robbins, Joe Fitschen, and Charlie Raymond—flew in to the Kichatnas to establish major routes to three unclimbed summits above 8,000 feet and to fulfill Yvon Chouinard's prediction that the techniques of Yosemite big-wall climbers would prevail on the "great granite ranges of the world." In the *American Alpine Journal*, Robbins raved about a future of difficult rock ascents in the spires, "a tale which promises to be long and exciting."

---

FOR A SHORT WHILE, SOME OF THE EARLY CLIMBERS KEPT GOING BACK to the Kichatnas, as if they couldn't let go of the original dream. In 1970, David made a second trip with Hank Abrons, another Harvard Mountaineering Club alum, "on a whim," David wrote in his expedition report. "We knew June was the wrong month, but greed at the prospect of Middle Triple Peak, second highest of the Spires ... interfered with our judgment." A snowstorm trapped them on the col between Gurney Peak and Kichatna Spire for four days. Although they managed to establish a base camp, David recalled, "the rest of the trip was a porridge of white-out, drizzling snow, and insincere patches of blue sky. We called our home 'Sunshine Glacier,' counting on future climbers to share in the irony." They named the pass they'd struggled to cross "Credibility Gap." When they trekked out to Rainy Pass Lodge, the waters were even higher than they'd been in October 1966. The two men faced a "truly hairy crossing" to escape with their lives. It was the last time David ever visited the range.

---

TWO YEARS LATER, AL DEMARIA RETURNED TO TRY TO CLIMB MIDDLE Triple Peak with Roy Kligfield and David Loeks. "Unfortunately," Al commented, "we did not attempt the peak by the route suggested by David Roberts in his *Summit* article." They landed, instead, on the west side of the mountain. "Our aim was to do an alpine-style ascent," Al noted with perhaps some understated humor. "Basically this was the main factor in our retreat." They spent an entire day toiling up sheer ice and snow to the col. From there, they faced a daunting surprise: what had looked like a ridge from below turned out to be a 1,500-foot-high wall. Higher up, a jagged edge of stone and snow sliced up and down for about a half mile. A rare blue sky reflected off the summits around them, but the flawless weather only deepened their gloom: they hadn't brought enough supplies for such a lengthy climb. Once more, Al left without attaining his fantasized peak.

Soon, promises of a hidden wonderland lured other climbers. Although the spires remained remote, steep walled, and storm battered, their summits were no longer "the epitome of inaccessibility" that Al DeMaria and Pete Geiser had called them. By the mid-1970s, the spread of water-resistant clothing and synthetic-fiber sleeping bags had diminished at least some of the misery of the Kichatnas' damp winds, cold rain, and wet sleet. And as alpinists became more adept at moving light and fast on steep walls, they could take better advantage of scant clear days. In the 1980 *Ascent*, Mike Graber described the Kichatnas as a "crowded *Klettergarten*." Four years prior, he and his partners had established *Illusory Ridge* on Middle Triple Peak, "route '3'" of the original lines inked on the Riesenstein photo. It was as if the fictitious mountains were emerging, at last, out of the imaginary and the sublime and into the attainable, the measurable, and the true.

Fragments of the backstory of the hoax also rose from the underground. While Graber was working on his article for *Ascent*, he'd become curious about the origins of the Riesenstein. Someone (Graber no longer remembers who) suggested he get in touch with Dee Molenaar, one of the most knowledgeable climbers in the Pacific Northwest. Molenaar told him to contact a certain notorious guidebook writer. "[Harvey] Manning was very reluctant [to talk] at first," Graber told me when I reached out to him in 2020. "He 'fessed up to being a participant in the hoax, but I recall him saying the other two participants were people who had respected scientific positions and he didn't want to compromise their credibility by tying them to a hoax." After a couple of persistent phone calls from Graber, and perhaps some time to talk the matter over with Austin Post and Ed LaChapelle, Harvey shared the names of his fellow conspirators. Finally, the basic details of the plot appeared in print.

As so often happens in mountaineering history, subsequent climbers questioned some of the topographic accuracy of the Vulgarians' story. In the 1981 *American Alpine Journal*, George Schunk wrote that he believed his own team of Andy Embick, Alan Long, and Randy Cerf had made the actual first ascent of the 7,785-foot mountain called "Vulgarian Peak" and that Pete Geiser and John Hudson had scaled a different 7,700-foot peak, now named "Whiteout Spire." When I sent Schunk's report and the most current map to Pete Geiser, he replied, "I can't dispute the *AAJ* record one way or another. We did climb a number of the 7,000-foot peaks, but which ones on your map are lost in the mists of time . . . also in the actual mists since a bunch were climbed in cloud, so we probably didn't know where we were anyway."

---

TO THE ORIGINAL RIESENSTEIN CLIMBERS, THE OUTSIDE WORLD HAD begun pressing in closer around the Kichatnas almost as soon as the first few expeditions ended. In 1968, Al DeMaria had picked up a local newspaper in Fairbanks to see headlines announcing the discovery of oil in Prudhoe Bay—a sign of battles ahead between environmental groups and oil companies over the construction of the Trans-Alaska Pipeline. For Al, this was the moment when he realized, starkly, "the difference between what was wild and what was not."

Conflict erupted over what, exactly, the fabled "Last Frontier" of Alaska meant. Some Americans saw it as a place where undeveloped areas might be rapidly settled and exploited with the help of modern technology, or they believed its landscape was so rugged it could protect itself. Others felt that wild places needed to be actively preserved for the sake of natural beauty, unrestricted adventure, or cultural history. In a 1974 book for Friends of the Earth, *Cry Crisis!*, Harvey Manning warned that the pipeline might be a rehearsal for a future doomsday, as the rise of energy demands and the burning of fossil fuels contributed to the melting of ice caps and the drowning of coastal cities. ("A fitting climax," he added, with bitter humor, to the "full-speed-ahead-and-damn-the-torpedoes down the road of America's hellbent highball ride.")

But many Alaska Native people, who had never given up their territories in treaties, would continue to struggle to protect their lands. As oil companies rushed to exploit the resources, executives found themselves legally bound to take into account the original residents' claims. During the 1960s and 1970s, Indigenous organizations interviewed elders to demonstrate that they had continued to dwell in these coastal and mountain regions since time immemorial. Paul Ongtooguk—a now-retired director of the Alaska Native Studies program at the University of Alaska, Anchorage—recalled that the elders' lists of "significant rocks, creek bends, outcrops . . . names and locations for collecting kinds of rocks, fish, plants, driftwood, shelter areas, slide-danger places, overflow locations, traditional trade routes and meeting places" proved much too vast and detailed for any previously published maps.

By the 1970s, conservationists such as Harvey found new allies—and new concerns—in the booming outdoor industry. As the American historian Roderick Frazier Nash wrote in *Wilderness and the American Mind*, many trends converged to bring people into the wild, including the countercultural ideals of getting back to the land, the advancements in backcountry gear, and the proliferation of guidebooks and outdoor media. In 1973, John Denver's song "Rocky Mountain High," about a man who climbs "cathedral mountains," was one of the top songs in the US. "Ironically," Nash observed, "the very increase in appreciation of wilderness threatened to prove its undoing."

As the number of climbers grew, the mythic allure of American road trips mixed with unease about overcrowding and overdevelopment. In 1974, Lito Tejada-Flores, editor of *Ascent* journal, described a popular route as "an ugly thoroughfare." He proposed that climbers should try to keep certain areas out of guidebooks, leaving "not only the cracks, but the sense of discovery intact." Proponents of the clean-climbing revolution urged others to abandon the use of pitons, which scarred the stone, in favor of removable gear. But the impacts were multiplying. Crowds of climbers trampled the ground at the base of crags. First ascensionists ripped rare plants from cracks to "clean" new routes—an act they called "gardening." In his memoir, David Brower described the damage from some of his own first ascents with deepening regret: "As long as you think there is an unlimited supply of something, then you think it will replace itself, if you think at all. . . . Today there aren't so many alpine gardens left."

The Vulgarians' friend Jim McCarthy had compared his generation of climbers to the free-ranging "mountain men" of nineteenth-century folklore. Now, in the November–December 1971 issue of *Summit*, he urged an increased sense of environmental responsibility: "Bluntly put, we can no longer do just as we damn well please."

Soon, *Summit* had multiple competitors. Newer magazines became more specialized, promoting the hardcore and the cutting edge. By the eighties, sport climbers were drilling expansion bolts like glittering trails up once unimaginably smooth, steep walls. To some readers, *Summit* seemed old-fashioned, its homespun appearance and gregarious accessibility a holdover from the mass outings of the Sierra Club. Its editorial vision had more to do with pure fun than with extreme sport, and its philosophy stemmed from the idea that "mountainlore" (as a letter writer put it) included not just one form of mountaineering, but all the multifaceted ways that people approach the hills.

In 1989, Jean Crenshaw and Helen Kilness sold *Summit* and retired to enjoy more time in the mountains with each other. A new owner relaunched the magazine as a high-end quarterly in 1990, but *Summit* closed for good six years later. In its place, many readers turned to glossy publications with images of lithe young people in brilliant Lycra hues and, eventually, to the unlimited, rapidly streaming social media images that flashed on computer screens and mobile phones.

CHAPTER 19

# The Exploration of No Place

BACK IN 1964, A CERTAIN "H. Hawthorne Manning" had published a satirical article in *The Mountaineer* that expressed sly pity for editors who become the targets of hoaxes. Among the origins of the problem, Harvey argued, was the exponential growth of climbing. Previously, news of first ascents traveled mainly by word of mouth, and since the protagonists were relatively few, they often knew about each other's accomplishments firsthand. "With so many new top climbers in operation," he noted, "this is no longer possible, and the journals play a necessarily enlarged role." Furthermore, as readers' expectations for ever-greater technical difficulties rose, some writers embellished the angle of a route, adding "overhangs" to every trip report or claiming "summits" that didn't exist:

> *One climber might attempt a mountain, get lost in the fog on the summit ridge, find himself baffled atop a nondescript block of rock, and scratch off the trip as a fiasco. Another climber, lost in an identical fog on the same summit ridge, might find himself atop the same block of rock, name it, and write it up for the journals as a first ascent. . . .*
>
> *. . . Consider [the editors'] situation—flooded annually with reams of copy from climbers they never heard of before. Since most of the copy sounds very much the same, how can editors decide which story deserves feature status, and which brief notice in fine print? Furthermore—incredible as it may seem—some climbers deliberately tell mistruths.*

In a tone of mock outrage, Harvey added his own hoaxes to a list of notorious deceptions (without, of course, confessing his role): "The Cook 'first ascent' of McKinley is the most infamous example. More recently, mountaineers have been scandalized by the 'No Name Peak' fraud, the 'Reisensteins' [*sic*] disgrace, and the 'sleeping system' outrage. There is no way by which editors or readers can distinguish between important ascents and pure hoaxes. Fact and fiction read the same in print."

Harvey wryly proposed a numerical system to determine the standing of each climber and the value of each peak. The CQNS ("cumulative-quantitative numbering system"), he insisted, would be much more exact than any other means of grading routes that climbers were debating at the time, particularly the YDS (Yosemite Decimal System) and the NCCS (National Climbing Classification System), which generated bursts of fiery rhetoric in the letters pages of *Summit*. According to the CQNS, Peak X—with 3,000 feet of trail hiking, 1,000 feet of bushwhacking, 100 feet of waterfall scrambling, 500 feet of snow slogging, and 25 feet of actual rock climbing—could be reduced to the equation of *[(3,000 x 1) + (1,000 x 4) + (100 x 7) + (500 x 3) + (25 x 1) = 9,225)]*. The variables presumably corresponded to the difficulty of each section and changed according to weather and route conditions. To ensure some sort of objectivity, he added, climbing also needed commissioners, referees, and leagues like those in mainstream sports. Participants could wear patches on their jackets that indicated their accumulated scores. "After a few years of adequate reporting on the sports pages, climbing can then seek to join skiing in the Olympic Games," he concluded.

If Harvey were still alive, he might have been amused and alarmed at the partial fulfillment of his prophecy. Sport climbing was scheduled to be an event at the 2020 Summer Olympics for the first time, before the outbreak of COVID-19 postponed the games. (In 1924, 1932, 1936, and 1988, officials gave medals to mountaineers for significant ascents, though climbing had never been a spectacle.)

The Peak X in this article represented another kind of imaginary mountain, one that could be reduced to numbers and equations, at least in the minds of Harvey's hypothetical climbers. It was as if the centuries-old tension between the quantifiable and the sublime had finally resolved. For its climbers, Peak X existed solely in terms of the status that could be extracted from it—a dystopian vision for the future of the pursuit.

Harvey had created his hoaxes and fictions partly to perpetuate a sense of mystery, a quality that seemed as endangered to him as the natural world itself.

Decades after the Riesenstein, in another one of his unpublished memoirs, "Gods, Devils, and Wilderness Pedestrians," he reexamined the changes that took place in British Columbia since the bygone era when Canadian climbers Don and Phyllis Munday had first imagined their own "Mystery Mountain" there. During the 1920s, after seeing a flash of spring light along a distant snowy range, the Mundays had spent weeks searching for an enigmatic peak, sailing up a fjord, stumbling through underbrush, dodging grizzly bears, and trudging up a glacier. In 1942, Fred and Helmy Beckey followed a similarly arduous itinerary on their way to the top of "Mystery," which the Canadian Geographic Names board had redesignated as "Mount Waddington." By the end of the 1970s, the use of helicopters transformed such lengthy expeditions into potential weekend outings. To re-create the scale and depth of past adventures, Harvey now believed, climbers would have to forgo the use of modern transportation and approach the peaks, once more, as the old mountaineers did: "They'd not be featured in journals but would achieve a deep satisfaction, feeling themselves the true kin of history-makers. Mountaineers of today could still devote an entire spring to climbing Denali—all of it. They would set out in the late blizzards, dog-sledding over the frozen muskeg, dodging the moose and the grizzlies. They would return in the season of snowmelt over bottomless bogs and raging rivers."

From his perch on Cougar Mountain, Harvey continued to stay up late, hammering at his typewriter to create stories to protect the wild. Sales of *Mountaineering: The Freedom of the Hills* enabled The Mountaineers to publish more books, many of them written or edited by Harvey, with a strong environmental emphasis. In 1964, The Mountaineers published *The North Cascades*, with photos by Tom Miller, words by Harvey Manning, and maps and drawings by Dee Molenaar, to promote the establishment of a national park. The contributors provided glimpses of the beauty of the land as it appeared to them: dark-walled towers wreathed with cloud-like glaciers, deep valleys draped with the shadows of trees, and hidden alpine-meadow basins like a multitude of Shangri-Las.

In 1965, Harvey contributed to another Cascades advocacy book, *The Wild Cascades: Forgotten Parkland*, published by the Sierra Club. Within its pages, Harvey praised climbers who'd learned how to love all of a mountain, not just its apex: "As they once bagged summits, now they bag cirques and cols, rivers and forests. . . . It's the same mountain, seen from the top, seen from the bottom, seen from across the valley, seen in spring, autumn, sunshine, and storm, yet every view is a new experience, a new dimension."

The ideal ascent of a mountain begins in as low a valley as possible, he explained, in the cool half-light under a thick canopy of trees. From there, the only distant view would be the one that revealed itself when travelers gazed directly upward—through the narrow spaces between the branches—deep into the sky. As they continued their journey, a window would open onto the first flashes of sun on alpine meadows and faraway snows, "a bright upper world impossibly remote from the low world of rivers, trees, and shadows." A cold, blue dusk would envelop them at a riverside camp. Stars would burst overhead. The next day, the trees would get smaller and their shadows thinner. (Here, they might pause and look for huckleberries, Harvey suggested). At last, the wanderers would step into the undimmed radiance of wildflowers set against the rock, snow, and sky. "Having paid one's way with many thousand steps and many pints of sweat, having learned to know the forest and river well, the third day is the *summit* day, duly earned," he noted.

Harvey extolled the practice of what he called "rain sleep," an immersion in the scents and sounds of woods and water and in the mountains of dreams and memories. On foggy days, he recommended that people concentrate on minute vistas beneath their feet: "Examine rocks crystal by crystal rather than cliff by cliff, and trace the path of a spider climbing up and down the suncups in a snowfield . . . experience flowers one by one, petal by petal, rather than in a thousand-flowered medley of meadow color, and thus, in the words of William Blake, 'see the world in a grain of sand, all heaven in a wild flower.'"

It was an approach that contrasted starkly with mainstream outdoor media's obsession with the fast, the first, and the cutting edge. "A mistaken notion," Harvey wrote, "is that there is a single sort of wilderness experience—strenuous and perilous—and a single sort of wilderness traveler—heavily muscled, highly skilled and fearless to the point of foolhardiness. . . . There are many varieties of wilderness experience."

While his writings, alongside the activism of many of his friends and contemporaries, contributed to the establishment of North Cascades National Park in 1968, Harvey wasn't entirely pleased with the boundaries drawn on maps. He'd been worried that only the realms of rock, ice, and snow would be protected, leaving valleys and forests exposed to logging. Although he was relieved to know that he'd never hear the buzz of chain saws in many ancient groves, some of his favorite sanctuaries still lay outside the new park. He kept writing frantically, working with members of the original Elderly Birdwatchers Hiking and Griping Society, the North Cascades Conservation Council, and other conservationist groups to continue the fight. After Harvey edited *The Alpine Lakes*, written by Brock Evans and published in 1971 by The Mountaineers, Washington State governor Dan Evans brought the book to the Oval Office. Its words and images inspired President Ford to endorse a bill to designate the 394,000-acre Alpine Lakes Wilderness, protecting more than seven hundred bodies of water, as well as the climbing areas of the Cashmere Crags and The Enchantments. Another Harvey Manning volume, *Washington Wilderness: The Unfinished Work*, helped persuade Congress to pass the 1984 Washington State Wilderness Act.

In his hiking guides—often coauthored with photographer Ira Spring—Harvey aimed to lead people on a journey that was as much imaginative and spiritual as geographic and physical, like the pilgrimage narratives of old. He designed his route descriptions to evoke a deeper sense of reverence, caring, and responsibility, advocating for low-impact travel in wildlands and composing specific notes about places that still needed to be saved. In a description of Golden Horn, an 8,366-foot peak beyond the borders of North Cascades National Park, Harvey decried "Washington City experts" who declared the region "not of national park caliber." He recounted how he "swooned" at the rose-gold color of the stone and the wind-brushed surface of the lakes until he finally shouted at the heavens: "Somebody in the National Park Service is not of national park caliber!"

During the late 1970s, as urban sprawl continued to swallow up forests and hills, Harvey turned, once more, to altering maps to protect "sky islands" of wild near the city. Beside Cougar Mountain, other gentle dark-green domes rise above Issaquah, including: Tiger, Squak, Rattlesnake, and Taylor. Harvey renamed the cluster of low summits "the Issaquah Alps," a ploy to associate them with images of higher, more Romantic peaks and to inspire more people to believe they were worth saving. He called this idea "name magic." And with members of the Issaquah Alps Trails Club (which he cofounded in 1979) and other activists, he worked to safeguard thousands of acres of these wooded uplands from the developers' bulldozers.

A vocabulary of conservation had emerged in Harvey's writings that included small spaces as well as vast ones, second- and third-growth forests as well as old-growth ones. There was the "wildness without" (high, remote mountain regions, which he wanted to protect as much as possible) and the "wildness within" (areas near cities and large towns, which he hoped would attract some of the crowds away from fragile alpine zones and still ensure that everyone got a chance to experience nature). He also referred to these concepts as the "Deeps" and the "Edges." Harvey and his friends came up with the slogan "Wilderness on the Metro," and they organized hikes to promote the use of public transportation as a more ecological and affordable way to reach trailheads—and to encourage the conservation of more accessible places. In 1990, the Issaquah Trails Club would lead an eighty-eight-mile march from Snoqualmie Pass to the Seattle waterfront. The trek became a catalyst in the movement to create the "Mountains to Sound Greenway." Today, its connected parks and open spaces form a 1.5 million-acre corridor of trails and recreation areas between Seattle and Ellensburg: a patchwork country of the wild.

Harvey's influence remains visible in meadows and forests throughout Washington that he helped preserve, a legacy quiet as the dusk that falls like rain from leaf to leaf in the valleys of the Olympics and the Cascades. But he was increasingly aware that guidebook writing itself could intensify environmental impacts by drawing large numbers of visitors to the most ecologically vulnerable places, where they might disturb skittish wildlife and crush rare plants. In one of his many imaginary math equations, he described his fears for the future: "If the number of bodies is q, and each body has a volume of x, during z time they occupy a space-time of qxz. If during z time they move over y distance, they occupy a space-time of qxyz, and as the values of q and y rise, it becomes impossible in an alpine meadow to find a clump of bushes or a boulder to squat behind."

The problem, as Harvey saw it, was partly the result of how modern life had continued to accelerate since the 1950s: crowds of people were moving so quickly through the world that they'd lost their connection to place, their ability to become immersed and to tread carefully in nature. The slower hikers went, he argued, the more they could regain a sense of "Thereness." Even better, they could merely sit still in one spot—in a meadow or on a mountaintop—for as long as possible. In some of his more outrageous satires, Harvey fantasized about shooting airplanes and helicopters out of the sky so their buzz could no longer startle him from his absorption in deep forests and mountain dreams. He penned an impassioned letter to REI, addressing the imaginary chief of an "Ethics & Soul Department," to protest the term "mountain bike," which he believed encouraged fad-following recreationists to bomb along trails in alpine wildlands, scattering hikers in their wake.

Harvey titled his December 1988 column in the *Mountaineer* magazine "It is Solved by Walking." Citing passages from Bruce Chatwin's *The Songlines*, he described the "dreaming tracks" of Aboriginal Australians who have recorded their knowledge of the land—and of geographic rituals, stories, and philosophies—through the paths they have traced across their continent for thousands of years. The importance of pilgrimages resonated across cultures, Harvey realized. "In Islam, and especially among the Sufi Orders," Chatwin had noted, "*siyahat* or 'errance'—the action or rhythm of walking—was used as a technique for dissolving the attachments of the world and allowing men to lose themselves in God." Harvey was drawn to the idea of meandering on foot as a means of expanding his perception of existence. "Walking lads, walking's the trick, / For fellows whom it scares to tick," he added. To his editor, Don Graydon, he explained that he was referring to the way that older people, such as himself, became increasingly aware of the sound of clocks and the passage of time. "I make my world large, / By going slow," Harvey wrote.

During one of my conversations with Paul Manning, he recommended his father's 1986 book, *Walking the Beach to Bellingham*, about the two years that Harvey spent ambling for nearly three thousand miles across the coastlines, hills, and lowlands along Puget Sound. In the introduction, Harvey explained that the pursuit of "low adventure" was the antithesis of trendy, jet-fueled travels to tour famous ranges and bag high peaks. His description of his shoreline journeys deliberately tangles up space and time, creating elaborately interwoven itineraries that would be impossible to repeat:

> *A further frustration to those trying to use this book as a guide is that while the story is told largely from south to north, sometimes it travels north to south, occasionally west or east, and some of the narratives combine walks taken over a number of years. If this isn't a guidebook, what is it? A book of sermons, perhaps. I preach that air travel be scaled back, as a start, to the level of twenty years ago, further reductions to be considered after all the Boeing engineers have been retrained as turkey ranchers. . . . I would discourage, if not ban, trekking to Everest base camp and flying over the Greenland Icecap. Generally, people should stay home. Forget gaining a little knowledge about a lot and strive to learn a lot about a little.*

In 1983, Harvey had gone on a four-day walking expedition to link the beaches along the coast from Tacoma to Seattle, similar to a mountaineering "enchainment," a term that describes the ascension of multiple peaks during a continuous journey. At night, he hid between piles of driftwood to sleep. On the last evening, he raced the incoming tide to Alki Beach Park. As the saltwater rose higher, an "impenetrable wall" of "trophy homes . . . thorny shrubberies, and stout fences" blocked his escape. Remembering that he knew one of the landowners, he clambered onto a nearby lawn.

A man glanced up from a hot tub and stared at the bearded, gray-haired individual loaded down with an archaic Kelty backpack, wearing ragged clothes and dripping with water, like an ancient mountaineer emerging from an old, strange tale. "*What* are *you* doing *here*?" the man asked.

"What were *you* doing on Everest?" Harvey responded.

The landowner, Jim Whittaker, the first American to climb the world's highest peak, invited him to stay for coffee. "Everyone's got to be someplace," Harvey observed.

It was the experience, not the specific destination that mattered. Whether or not Frederick Cook was telling the truth no longer seemed important to Harvey, if it ever had been. "The Pole was the excuse, not the reason," Harvey wrote. "The trip was the thing." He continued:

> *Nobody ever knows when or if they reach the Pole. You zig and zag back and forth across the white plain shooting the sun, and when you run low on pemmican, turn for home, shrugging, "It must have been around there someplace."*
>
> *. . . Dr. Cook's friends (he had more than Peary, being much the nicer man) think Peary lied too, more expertly and with the massive connivance of the Establishment. Personally, I don't care. Wherever Peary and Cook actually went, they had good trips, both of them. . . .*

And with a hint of his own sly humor, Harvey added, "So did I."

Sometime during the 1980s, in one of his many spiral-bound pocket notebooks, Harvey jotted down fragments of ideas that coalesced into a vision of the wild as a "suspension of disbelief." Because of the effects of air transport and mass tourism, he asserted, "increasingly we move into the era of make-believe wilderness." While early explorers confronted the challenges of unmapped or erroneously mapped terrain, modern wanderers would have to push their imaginations harder to create a sense of the unknown: "Everest now is make-believe compared to when Mallory was there. That's the bad. The good is, the same make-believe can be used everywhere." Harvey believed that adults needed to become more like children, who know how to transform a vacant lot into a trackless rainforest or how to turn a stroll down the street into a quest for the source of the Nile. To Harvey, these "next-door" wild places were necessary for those "who never will trek in Nepal or snowmobile to the Poles, perhaps never even hike in the Pickets—but [who] have in them that wild thing crying to get out—to go home." In page after page, he scrawled attributes that could transmute any natural place into a wilderness:

*to be at home*
*to be afraid*
*to be alone*
*to be friends*
*to look out*
*to look within*
*a reaching out*
*a soaking in*

Since "the experience requires vulnerability," he explained, it would be better to bring "a tarp than a tent" and to consider "going without guidebook or even map on purpose." In another attempt at a definition, he wrote, "A wilderness is a place where it is possible to get lost," which could happen even in the wooded outskirts of Seattle—as he had learned, decades ago, in the now-vanished forest of Hidden Lake. "Thus, wilderness experience in Seward Park can be the equal of that in the Brooks Range. Neither is real in the 1930s sense. But both are real, equally so, in the 1980s," he explained. "More of the wilderness seeking will be done near home," he hoped. "More must be done," he added, because of "the energy cost" of travel to distant places.

During the last decade of Harvey's life, he imagined staring into a crystal ball and seeing a future in which every scrap of remaining undeveloped space was preserved in the North Cascades, only to be ravaged by climate change. The heavy, luminous winter snows of the Cascades would turn to dreary rain. Summers would become longer and drier. Wildfires would burn through forests that had endured for centuries. Glaciers would vanish into thin air, leaving only outlines of their former glory on old topographic maps. Faced with the loss of beloved landscapes and the deaths of aging friends, Harvey became more vehement. Many late-twentieth–century hikers seemed impatient with his exhortations. They wanted to consume the wild as efficiently as possible, without "politics" getting in the way. In the introduction to *Best Winter Walks & Hikes: Puget Sound*, Harvey responded: "To readers' complaints that they want directions on where to go, not lessons in how to behave, we answer, 'If you don't want sermons, don't go to church.'"

It was the last guidebook that he and Ira Spring would work on together, and the last time that Harvey agreed to work with Mountaineers Books. Harvey's friendship with Ira had ruptured in part because of the growing differences in their approach to the wild. During the late 1950s, when they'd started collaborating on their guidebooks, the logging industry razed acres of trees in regions that relatively few hikers knew. "Do the North Cascades Really Exist?" conservationist John Warth had asked in the title of a 1961 article for *The Wild Cascades*. Warth had noticed so many errors and blanks in tourist maps and brochures of the time that the range appeared like a lost continent in the midst of the United States. By the beginning of the twenty-first century, Harvey and Ira had described hundreds of Washington peaks and valleys in words and images. Partly as a result, numerous regions of the Cascades had become protected from clear-cutting, but crammed with guidebook-toting excursionists. Ira had often spoken of what he called "Green Bonding," promoting trails to bring people closer to nature and to turn them into defenders of the woods. It was a goal that Harvey had shared with him, up to a point. Now, Harvey thought trail builders had gone too far. Too many paths strayed from the fringes of deep forests, where he felt they belonged, into the rare, trackless portions of the maps—into places that he thought should be kept quiet for wild creatures and perhaps for occasional solitary wanderers, thrashing through slide alder and devils club as they searched for their own version of the divine. "Over-building, over-civilizing is a threat just like wreckreating," Harvey wrote to Ira in 2001, combining the words "wreck" and "recreating" into one.

All Harvey's efforts couldn't prevent the advance of development up the unprotected parts of Cougar Mountain. Urban lights now turned the sky a sickly pinkish-orange at night. Rush-hour traffic roared like the rapids of a giant river. In a 2002 letter to conservationist Gene Duvernoy, Harvey explained that he felt besieged: "The very thought of venturing off this little island of green we (still) preserved . . . into the maw of the Beast inevitably reminds me that we are here as on a darkling plain swept with sounds of struggle and flight where ignorant armies clash by night." The description of the "darkling plain" was an allusion to Matthew Arnold's poem "Dover Beach," about "the Sea of Faith" that recedes, leaving only a world of "naked shingles" and "edges drear."

As Harvey struggled with his aging body, even walking short distances became difficult. He grew increasingly reclusive. Manuscripts piled higher in the loft office. Moss and ferns thickened on the roof. Dale Cole thought his friend was trying to freeze time. "I think he just did not want to see things move ahead, and yet invariably, inevitably, they were going to do exactly that." McMansions sprouted across Cougar Mountain, encircling ever-smaller patches of forest around the Mannings' and the Coles' homes. Dale felt as if he were watching his memories disappear, one by one. Unable to bear the loss, he and Lyn moved away.

Yet while his beloved geographies shrank, Harvey's imagination kept expanding. As a young man, he'd abandoned his boyhood dreams of climbing in the Himalaya and the Mountains of the Moon, but he'd found his "Shangri-La," first in the alpine basins of the North Cascades and the Olympics, and then in the backyard forests of the Issaquah Alps. As Harvey got older, he realized that a paradise of wonder existed in the jewel-bright multitude of birds' wings outside his windowsill.

On a typewritten scrap of paper attached to one of his notebooks, he'd written the words: "I had learned, by then, that a peak doesn't have to be remote to be wild—very wild. There is wildness next to our railroads, our highways, our lowland homes. I had relearned, as I'd known for some time, that at the far boundary of wilderness is . . . death."

Perhaps Harvey sensed that the common European idea of wilderness at its extreme becomes a void—an imaginary place emptied of human history and inimical to life. But he also loved to plant literary allusions in his writing. And "Death," as Hamlet pronounced in Shakespeare's play, is "The undiscovered country from whose bourn / No traveler returns."

Ever since college, Harvey feared that he'd die young from heart failure. But when the "tick" of his heartbeat did finally falter, he survived, recovering from triple-bypass surgery. He lived to age eighty-one before passing away on November 12, 2006, from colon cancer. Betty died nine years later. A new subdivision has consumed the Mannings' wooded lot—and with it, the spaces where their children explored and where their friends drank homebrew and philosophized under the stars. Dale has also lost his wife, and while he still goes hiking, the mountains seem haunted by the absences of friends. For him, the story of the Manning hoaxes now represents, most of all, his love of their instigators. "Where I kind of get choked up now and then about it is when it reminds me of not just Harvey but every one of those people I mentioned, and a lot of others," Dale told me. "In your mind, you'd like to keep them just like they were, wouldn't you? I can't help but, when I talk to someone like you, look back on my life and think how fortunate I was, . . . Harvey gave me a deep passion for the mountains and the outdoors that is carried with me right up to today. You could say, 'Now, how could you do better than this?' I don't really think you can."

In *The Wild Cascades*, a few months before he died, Harvey urged his readers to "take a look at the 2006 map of public land ownership in the state. . . . Do a bit of dreaming." For numerous people, one of Harvey's most lasting gifts was the power of imagination to see the world differently. Like many Cascades conservationists who try to carry on his work, Dick Fiddler recalled learning from Harvey the value of humor and creativity as forms of resistance, "how to make something that's ugly," such as human hubris in nature, "also look ridiculous." For Paul Manning, what captured "the Manning family appreciation of mountains is that we were always reading some book like *Lord of the Rings*. . . . The natural world and [Harvey's] literary imagination were always tied together." Because his father had written the guidebooks to "politicize" his readers as "spokespeople" for the wild, Paul explained, "some areas he was quite happy to tell everyone about. Other areas, he never really spoke much about in his writings, that is to say he didn't give very good directions to them." To reach one of the places that Harvey kept secret, you have to hike for miles into the mountains and find a junction where a clearly marked trail points to a well-known fishing destination, but a faint, eroded path—resembling a mere creek bed—leads to a concealed alpine paradise.

Claudia Manning remembers another hike she took with her father near Snoqualmie Pass when she was young. The sun beat down on them as they walked along a logging road, past stumps of trees, and up a steep mountainside. "I just turned to Daddy at one point and I said, 'You know, Daddy, you get no place exploring.' He thought that was so funny. When we got to the top of the peak and then there was this lake below that wasn't on any map. . . . He said, 'See, Claudia, you do get places going exploring.'"

I'm intrigued by the idea of experiencing "no place" as a place. Perhaps by slipping the bounds of ordinary cartography, we can start to glimpse something *elsewhere*—that "deep wilderness" that Paul says his father sought, a realm found only when you get truly lost. Long after he'd given up climbing to summits, Harvey kept exploring the flanks of mountains, searching for seemingly unnoticed cols and hidden valleys, finding wonders that he kept to himself or deliberately obscured in his published books. "To the day he died, when he was hiking, he had these little notebooks," Paul told me. The entries included "notes about flowers and things on the trail. There's little Xs on them. The little Xs were the places where his heart had a murmur. He marked it down each day, every day of his life." A map of the human heart.

CHAPTER 20

# What Lay Over the Horizon

AS I EXPLORED HARVEY'S IMAGINARY mountain worlds, I began to picture him as a kind of Prospero, the magician in Shakespeare's *The Tempest* who uses his enchanted books to cast spells across a fictitious island. There, visions of "cloud-capp'd towers" and melodies of strange music drift through the air. Prospero's "art" brings characters together into a wild plot that alters their existence long after the magician retires from the scene. I think Harvey would have been pleased to know that he, too, had a lasting impact on the people he duped and inspired.

While Frederick Cook's claims to have summited Denali still spark controversy and ire, most climbers who fell for the Riesenstein came to appreciate its whimsy. Or at least they accepted the purpose behind the hoax. The late George Whitmore, one of the first ascensionists of the Nose on El Capitan, was initially angry when he realized the Riesenstein story was false. "I did not take kindly to people who found it humorous to mess with the facts and create confusion," he explained to me in 2019. Yet his opinion had changed since the 1960s. "I used to be obsessed about first ascents, too," he admitted. "But there certainly wasn't much glory involved—most climbers had no idea what I was doing, and didn't care." The challenges George faced were with the unknown, and with himself. "What is in this area where there is a blank on the map? What is beyond that ridge? Can I ford this river? That mountain looks pretty formidable—I wonder whether I can get up it?" George, too, thought that self-promoting peakbaggers were climbing for the wrong reasons. Like Harvey, he ended up devoting much of his life to conservation. "So Harvey and I might have had something in common," he concluded.

After I shared what I'd been able to glean of Harvey's motivations, Art Davidson told me that the hike out from the Kichatnas—when he and his climbing partners had immersed themselves within neglected contours of the maps—conveyed its own lingering wonder. "It's just the magic of not knowing what is going to lie around the corner. . . . A hoax like the Riesenstein, it wouldn't happen again, now, because so many things are known, right?"

By the late 1960s, Art had found a new symbolic "mountain" to climb through his work with environmentalist groups and Alaska Native activists to protect some of the regions he'd come to love and to preserve the rights of their Indigenous stewards. Still, Art wishes he could persuade his aging teammates to go back to the Kichatnas, even just to camp there one more time. "I think we all had this feeling that we just shared something very, very special. Even in that era when there were so many unclimbed mountains."

Some Kichatnas climbers sought out similar experiences again and again. Several months after their expedition, Art and Dave Johnston participated in the first winter ascent of Denali. For Art, the climb was part of his ongoing search for a way to enter "an unexplored land." In the long Northern twilights, the upper regions of Denali seemed like another unseen world, lit by drifting shapes of moon-silvered clouds, changing hues of aurora borealis, and translucent crystals of falling ice, like "a dream half remembered, like a memory from earliest childhood," he wrote in *Minus 148°*. That summer, Art and David Roberts joined Matt Hale, Rick Millikan, Rick's brother George, and Ned Fetcher on a six-man expedition to a cluster of distant towers that they'd noticed from high on Kichatna Spire. The Revelation Mountains, as they'd named the peaks, contained unclimbed formations as fantastical as those of the Riesenstein. One of them, the Vanishing Pinnacle, seemed to fade into a wall behind itself when viewed from certain angles. The team made the first ascents of nine peaks. But the very top of the most desired mountain eluded their six attempts. Only 750 feet below the summit, under a crystalline sky, Matt and David turned back. The final ridge glistened, white and frozen, in the dwindling late-summer light, and they'd brought only one axe and no crampons or headlamps on that foray. They called the peak "The Angel" because its ridges lifted above the icy land like outstretched wings.

Looking back on his Riesenstein days, Rick Millikan told me, "I feel so fortunate to have been able to climb when it was possible to be that remote, to have no contact with anybody." A few years after the Revelations, he began to drift away from mountaineering. As a youth, he'd felt a sense of pride in the attempts of his illustrious grandfather George Mallory to climb Mount Everest. But after his own children were born in 1970 and 1972, Rick's perspective changed. "I do fault someone that takes those kind of risks when they have a family," he said. "[Mallory] left three children, including my mother. [His disappearance] had lasting scars. So I don't glamorize him too much."

Dave Johnston kept climbing in Alaska for much of his life, working as a state park ranger and building trails. There was so much to explore, he recalled when we talked in 2020, that "every now and then, when another mountain beckoned, you had to go AWOL and join friends on a climb." Even over the phone, in the midst of the global pandemic, I could hear the smile in his voice. In 2001, he and his wife, Cari, had accompanied their eleven-year-old son, Galen, as he became the youngest person to summit Denali. Although the effects of a 2015 stroke have likely ended Dave's own exploratory mountaineering days, he assured me there are still plenty of unclimbed routes in the Alaska Range. "Even if I never get out there, it's heartwarming to know that they are there." He added, with self-deprecating humor: "I guess I'm just a peakbagger at heart. But you can get the same thrill just on an ice gully that no one has been on before or a big boulder. And in the end, friendships forged in the mountains are still strong and as meaningful as when we were in the hills."

Though he never made it to the Kichatnas, Don Jensen looked for his own version of the Riesenstein myth in other places, pursuing an elusive ideal that transformed from granite spires into something radiant and undefined. In 1967, he made one last attempt on Mount Deborah with Pete Carman, Frank Sarnquist, and two Vulgarians, John Hudson and Art Gran. Among the books that Don brought with him was Hermann Hesse's *Journey to the East*, the 1930s novel that depicted seekers of paradise wandering freely across mythic space and time. A storm shook the walls of Don's tent as he read, and new ideas stirred in his mind. "Seldom specifics now, but just feelings," Don wrote in his diary, "and I would like to be able to put them (if they really are) in practice as love with Joan," his future wife.

Unwilling to return to his misery at Harvard, Don completed his BA at Fresno State and got a PhD in mathematical logic at the University of Southern California. He became the chief guide at the mountaineering school in the Palisades. He and Joan celebrated their wedding feast atop a giant, flat-summited rock, the "Banquet Boulder," along the North Fork of Big Pine Creek. Over the following years, they visited many alpine sanctuaries amid the spiny ridges, splintered arêtes, and stark light of the Sierra. In 1969, with his client Rex Post, Don and Joan made the first traverse of all twelve pinnacles of the Palisades Crest, naming each summit after characters in J. R. R. Tolkien's books. But Don never forgot the horrific ending to the Mount Huntington expedition. "I guess I will suffer Ed's death over and over again thousands of times," he wrote to Joan, "because, in my heart, I believe that exposing people to the mountains will make them more happy."

By 1970, Don realized that his true "career" was to build a "Happy and Productive Life" with Joan. They made plans to homestead in the North, staking a claim in the Yukon to have a base for future explorations. "I felt I could have become the greatest of mountaineers," he told her, "but chose to integrate the joy of the mountains into my life—instead of making it control my life." He never got a chance to complete their personal utopia. In 1973, he and Joan moved to Scotland for a year so he could accept a post-doctoral fellowship. That November, Don was bicycling to school on an icy road when a truck hit him. He died at age thirty, leaving behind his own geographic enigmas. Fellow guide Doug Robinson recalled a recipe box in a Palisades mountaineering school tent where Don kept notes of unpublished first ascents. The box is now missing. Still, Doug explained, subtle "clues" might be found in the rock itself. Don had a habit of polishing sharp edges where the strands of a climber's rope might break. The traces of his work create a faint trail, only distinguishable to those who know how to look: small dots of mirrored sunlight on burnished stone.

In 2016, faced with a diagnosis of terminal cancer, David Roberts looked back on his friendship with Don and felt a keen longing. "However ephemeral it proved," he wrote in *Ascent*, "the bond that linked us made its founding credo self-evident—that not only was climbing the most important thing in life, it was worth more than all else combined. That state of grace was like first love: a glimpse of a forbidden paradise." While he recovered from rounds of radiation and chemotherapy, David continued to ponder what desires drew mountaineers like themselves to search for "lost and unknown places." Unsettling thoughts filled his mind as he composed his next book, *Limits of the Known*. With the prospect of death before him, he rejected the delusory promises of *terra incognita* and the fantasies of transcendence that lured adventurers away from their loved ones: "For one who does not believe in God, prayer is a waste of time. In its place, I have only hope, or wish. What I wish for, then, in that last conscious moment before the darkness closes in forever, is not the shining memory of some summit underfoot that I was the first to reach, not the gleam of yet another undiscovered land on the horizon, but the touch of Sharon's fingers as she clasps my hand in hers, unwilling to let go."

The Vulgarians, too, faced inconsolable grief. In 1967, before he left to spend a year working on an oceanographic research ship, John Hudson gave his motorcycle helmet to Aaron Schneider. "You have a closet," John said to him, by way of explanation. In November 1968, his job over, John met up with another Vulgarian, Roman Laba. The two friends headed to the rime-feathered granite spire of Fitz Roy in Patagonia, where they remained for one hundred gale-plagued days, waiting for better weather and making repeated attempts. After they'd been stormed off twice from high on the mountain, Roman mentioned a surreal route, still unclimbed, in the Cordillera Real of Bolivia: a crest of ice and stone that separated the high desert of the Altiplano from the green shadows of the rainforest. The northeast ridge of Huayna Potosí would be the most difficult climb anyone had accomplished on the mountain so far, Roman promised. Several other teams of American, Bolivian, French, and British climbers had attempted it, and Roman suggested asking one of the English aspirants, Roger Whewell, if they could join forces for another try.

John whiled away the time before their expedition by studying Spanish in La Paz, Bolivia. In late June 1969, he started up Huayna Potosí with Roman and Roger, staggering through heavy winds beneath a hanging glacier that seemed about to calve. After John's crampons snapped and Roger's fell off, they retreated. About a week later, the three men were back with British climber Keith Miller. All night, gusts blew snow on them and cold air seeped into their bivouac sacks. "The Englishmen looked dour and hard," Roman recounted. "We Vulgarians giggled." The next morning, the Vulgarians climbed on, leaving their grim-faced partners behind. Ahead, the slope hardened into metallic blue ice, veined with bands of rocks. Below them, mountainsides plunged into deep-green woods. At the instant before nightfall, the summit flashed like a candle flame in the tropical dusk. The next day, from the apex, John and Roman released balloons and watched them float above the rainforests. "What more could we do," Roman thought, "but dream of future climbs under the clear morning sun?"

Weeks later, while the two men were attempting a new route on Huascarán in Peru, their crampons sliced through what looked like a firm layer of snow. Then the slope cracked. John slipped, struck a ten-foot rockband, and continued tumbling to his death. When Pete Geiser heard the news, he remembered their first attempt on the mountain they called "Vulgarian Peak." There, too, the surface of the snow kept breaking like a series of trapdoors until they were up to their waist in sliding debris. Looking back at Austin Post's photos of the

Kichatnas, Pete realized just how close he and John had been to the summit of the Spyder when they retreated. Now all that mattered was the time they'd spent together. For Pete, as well, perhaps the real lost paradise was a bond with a departed friend. "We were soulmates," he realized.

In a June 1968 letter to fellow Vulgarian Joe Kelsey, John Hudson had mused: "Perhaps we should start our own journal. We could hopelessly confuse real and imaginary events—indiscriminately mix reality and fantasy—until even we would forget whether [J. R. R. Tolkien's] orcs had appeared on the summit of Geikie or had merely been seen at a distance as they scurried from our tent when we returned to the meadow." When the first edition of the *Vulgarian Digest* came out in the spring of 1970, the editors included a commemorative photo of John, his middle finger in the air. For three issues, the magazine blended ribald tales, fictional stories, real trip reports, made-up routes, and invented peaks with sharp and whimsical satire that would have made Harvey Manning proud. One anonymous contributor critiqued *And Not to Yield*, a book about an imaginary Himalayan peak where "there was only the purity of snow and stars." The author, James Ramsey Ullman, was known for his gripping adventure tales. (In one of his memoirs, Harvey referred to "the allegorical solemnity" of Ullman's novel *The White Tower* as a "favorite joke.") In a passage quoted from *And Not to Yield*, Ullman's protagonist declares, "As a boy his mountain dream had been Everest. But no longer. Let the British have their Everest; they had tried it seven times and they deserved it. For him, Eric Venn, it would be Dera Zor. . . . He would climb it, top it. It would be his." The Vulgarian reviewer commented sardonically that "Venn has, in 444 pages, an affair with every known stereotype of woman. . . . One lovely tells Venn he will freeze his balls off. Sure enough, ten pages later . . . 'his private parts, he realized, had gone numb with cold. Somewhere, a long way off, someone seemed to be grinning.'"

Some Vulgarians continued to wander in search of ideal places. As the Vietnam War continued, Aaron Schneider became more active in protest movements and he grew discouraged with American politics. After Ruth finished her PhD in English, the couple bought land in the St. Ann's Bay area of Cape Breton, Nova Scotia—an old farm down a remote gravel road. Eventually, they settled there year round. Aaron patched together a living as a substitute teacher, kayak guide, freelance writer, and fish farmer. Ruth found work at Cape Breton University and penned short stories. In an anthology called *Local Hero*, she described the 1964 crevasse fall on Mount Marcus Baker: "I emerged like a new born snowbaby." Looking back, she realized that her concept of a meaningful life for herself and Aaron had coalesced in that moment when she first understood she could die. "We had children, created a home, and built careers," she wrote "Now . . . sitting in the warmth of my study with the map of Alaska in front of me, I know that I had to go to the edge before I could find the core." The couple chose to focus their love of exploration on the forests and coasts near their new home. "It's these little places that you discover that are interesting," Aaron told me. "People know about them, but not a lot of people. . . . Little gem places and holes in the woods." They got involved in local environmental activism, and Aaron wrote poetry. His 1998 collection, *Wild Honey*, includes an elegy for John Hudson: "You outclimbed us all / in your ass-torn pants, / bootsoles held on by the laces.'" He pictured John's fall down the mountainside, his body turning into a speck and vanishing beneath the snows: "Through vertical acres / nothing could be found, / but one door opens like a memory. / It is what the dead tell us / about our lives: / 'Fear only suffering,' / your helmet, / still hanging in my closet."

In 1975, bush pilot Don Sheldon died of cancer. By then, the silver speck of his plane had flashed across the Alaskan sky in countless mountaineering tales. Aaron Schneider memorialized his hero in a poem about the 1965 Kichatnas expedition. Its verses are full of nostalgia for a place where "the glaciers lay in the spaces between / the spread fingers of a granite hand" and "the wind sang." With Don's help, Aaron recalled, he and his friends had "searched for a way to the sheer icy tower" that remained "inviolable." The light of the North's long summer days had appeared eternal, and for a moment, an escape from world and time seemed possible. "I wondered how we flew so free from fear / as (it is believed) the soul flies out at death," Aaron concluded, "freed from the gravity of living."

Claude Suhl had never stopped looking for enchantment. Among other jobs, he and Al DeMaria had both worked as teachers, and they'd taken many summer climbing trips together. One year, they went on an expedition to the Logan Mountains in Canada's Northwest Territories, near the Nahanni River. It was not far from there that early twentieth-century explorer Raymond Patterson once encountered, as Claude described it, "a magic valley surrounded / rimmed by cliffs and accessible through a narrow slot—laden with crystals and other wonders." Although Claude didn't rediscover the valley on that trip or on any of his subsequent ones, he has stumbled upon plenty of other "magical spots" since then, he assured me—even just bushwhacking and hunting around the low summits of the Catskills and Adirondacks in New York.

Meanwhile, Claude had also settled into family life. He married Alice Bridges in 1978, and her adventurous six-year-old daughter, Susan, soon joined her new stepfather on climbs at nearby crags. Around the start of the new millennium, Claude returned to Alaska to revisit his Riesenstein memories with his and Alice's son, Jean-Claude. In Talkeetna, Claude recalled, "The Ranger station seemed unimpressed by my eager display of 'pictures from the first human visitors ever to the now National Parked Kichatna Spires,' but assured us that some Ranger was keeping historical stuff." As he looked back at the Riesenstein Hoax, Claude thought, "The story, is / was just a story—a corollary fragment—amazing but true—as are lots of other phenomena, when we were there, climbing, eating, getting trench foot. . . . Everything about climbing and Alaska is / was mythic—that is why I do it and why I travel and why sometimes I stay at home!"

Over time, the Vulgarians themselves became legends. Year after year, as so often happens with folklore, the most frequently told stories amplified the eccentric, dramatic, and humorous details of their antics and pranks. "It's all myth," Claude reflected in a recent email, "or as [Joe] Kelsey quotes Ken Kesey in at least one of the now mythical *Vulgarian Digests*, 'It's the TRUTH, even if it didn't happen.' Often it does and did happen . . . holy shit???" Roman Laba recalled that as late as the 1990s, he'd hear rumors among Wyoming climbers that the Vulgarians were returning to wreak more havoc in the Tetons. "I didn't tell them that the Vulgarians are [now] old," he said to me. "They don't have the energy to come out West anymore."

Today, Claude and Al still live near each other, close to the Gunks. When I visited them in 2014, the bands of cliffs shone golden-gray in the late autumn light. Nearly fifty years had passed since they'd headed to the Kichatnas on their "treasure hunt," but when Al got out the map they'd made of the spires and spread it on a table in his house, the paper was still crisp, their invented place names inked clearly in blue. In Claude's wide eyes, I could still see the startled wonder and madcap creativity of his Riesenstein tales.

Their friend Pete Geiser had since moved to the hills north of Lyons, Colorado, near the occasional home base of his grown daughter, Alisa May, an adventure filmmaker who inherited his wanderlust. On a visit three autumns later, I found myself surrounded by small, mist-wreathed summits and pinnacled crags. It was like a landscape from an old painting or a dream. "I look at mountains," he told me. "I kind of toddle among them." Throughout his long career as a geologist, the Riesenstein stayed in his memory, an image of misty summits that drew him onward. As Pete and his colleagues studied how the earth's crust resonates, they learned how to hear the sounds the planet makes while mountains form, like string music "plucked by the stress waves of earthquakes and tides," he said. "Nearing the end of my journey," he later wrote to me, "[I realize] the Earth sings to me and to all of us. It is an incredibly moving gift." He still struggles to understand what it was that he experienced in the Kichatnas. "Not necessarily a warm and nurturing place, but a place that you can learn from. But again, I come back to why do we have that connection? Why do [mountains] have that power? Why is that part of our collective psyche? I don't believe that it's something just restricted to people who climb. Possibly it goes back to when humans first left Africa and started to spread across the world. There's always that mystery of what lay over the horizon."

---

AND WHAT OF HARVEY'S CO-CONSPIRATORS, WHO HAD HELPED HIM set the adventure in motion? In the decades after the Riesenstein Hoax, they, too, searched for other mysteries in the mountains. Ed LaChapelle sometimes affixed a tape recorder to his skis so he could listen to notes created by ripples of snow. The differing shapes of the crystals altered the natural music he heard, and he became aware of changes otherwise too faint to perceive. "This raises the question of how much of the 'feel' of snow is a subconscious perception of similar vibrations," he wrote in his last book, *Secrets of the Snow*. Ed's scientific writing was often poetic. He'd compare crystals of surface hoar to "small, flat leaves" that sparkled under the sun and rustled under swift-moving skis. He'd describe the way the light blazed over firn or softened over rime; how separate crystals bumped into each other and linked together as they drifted down through the air, their "intricately branching arms" intertwined.

Beyond what could be quantified, Ed maintained, lay realms of persistent mystery: "All the rest of the information, less easy to define or describe, also keeps flowing through our senses and influences our decisions.... These kinds of data are just as important as measurable information like air temperature or wind velocity or slope angle, or visual information like the curve of a cornice... but are relegated to the realm of seat-of-the-pants feel or intuition because they are difficult to communicate."

Ed never stopped recording the weather, ice, and snow. After his marriage to Dolores dissolved, he spent his final twenty-five years with Meg Hunt in a remote, off-the-grid home in McCarthy, Alaska. The two of them went on frequent hikes to observe the Kennicott Glacier. "It was always changing form," Meg told me, "and the glacier was always, of course, backing away." In 2007, at age eighty, Ed died of a heart attack after a morning of flawless powder skiing at Monarch Pass in Colorado. He'd recently driven to nearby Silverton to attend a memorial service for Dolores, who had passed away just eleven days before.

Today, Ed's and Dolores's legacies remain intertwined. In now-classic books such as *Deep Powder Snow*, Dolores had pieced together a philosophy of ecology and outdoor mysticism influenced by some of their shared adventures. While gliding through powder, she wrote, she'd attained a sense of flow in which there seemed to be no borders between herself and the myriad crystals of ice and snow that drifted beneath her skis. The world, as she saw it, was formed of interrelationships in which all individuals are inextricably linked to a greater, natural, luminous whole. In the best moments, she felt herself making turns with other skiers, each following a natural, individual path down the mountain and "still flow[ing] with one another and with the earth. . . . Just as in a flight of birds turning through the air."

Blending ideas from both his parents, their son, David, imagined that he could uncover metaphors in the peaks and glaciers his family loved, signs to help him find his way in an increasingly precarious world threatened by environmental degradation and climate change. In one fiction story published in 2001, eight years before his own death, David described a scientist's search to find "the map of hidden realms of matter" concealed within crystals of frost. David also thought back to his own alpine childhood, to a day after a storm when he tossed handfuls of snow into the air and watched them fall, just as his father had done many times before. "Something about the light-illuminated snow crystals shimmering against the deep blue sky broke me open," he wrote in *Navigating the Tides of Change*. He felt as if the star-like rays drifted both outside and inside of him. "At that moment I was in a state of coherence with myself, with the world, and with the subtle source of the bliss. . . . The word 'coherence' comes from a Latin root meaning, 'to stick together.' Its dictionary definition is worth noting: 'A cleaving together; an agreement of ideas; consistency; to adhere, to be attached physically, or by affection or some other tie.' Coherence, then, is the cleaving together of the parts into a whole. . . . Underneath the turbulence of our times is an invitation to join in the coherence of our cosmos."

For modern readers, perhaps it's a similar message of coherence that emerges most from Ed LaChapelle and Austin Post's book *Glacier Ice* and from its picture of the Riesenstein: the wonder of the bodies of ice that shaped the world's topography as we know it, the awareness of growing absences that haunt our fates as humans on this earth. By the early twenty-first century, Austin Post had taken more than one hundred thousand photos of glaciers. Researchers compared his older images with that of his younger protégé, Cascades pilot and photographer John Scurlock. Ice had shriveled in many regions, leaving swaths of bare rubble against the shadows of trees. Through his own studies of surging and calving glaciers, Austin had helped develop a methodology for understanding the curious behavior of worlds that were now in peril. In a conversation with his friend Kevin Ward, he imagined the lost, cherished ice realms returning long after humans vanish from the earth.

Around the world, rising temperatures were melting bodies of ice on summits. Ridges were disintegrating as the permafrost that bound their rocks together thawed. Some of the peaks above the McCall Glacier had begun to shrink. Mount Hubley, for now, rises to the same height as it did in the 1950s. Its name still offers a testament to the loss of one of Austin's best friends, a reminder of how people try to fix on a map, and in their memories, all that seems at risk of changing or disappearing with time. But it also recalls the echoes, beneath the surface of paper and layers of snow, of all that abides, immeasurable as grief or love.

During his final years, Austin continued to explore fading worlds of ice and snow by plane, by camera, and on foot. "He never lost his desire to look further into things," his photo assistant David Hirst told me. Austin's son Richard recalled that his father was fascinated by Google Earth, though some people saw it as a replacement for the work of aerial photographers like him. In 2003, Austin became absorbed by the idea of solving another geographic mystery—finding the location of the easternmost glacier in the North Cascades. Despite all that had been mapped by air and by satellite, no one, it seemed, knew the answer for sure. "When you get into the realm of these vestigial glaciers, or ones that are almost extinct, they're not obvious to the unpracticed eye," John Scurlock explained to me. "They might be covered by talus from cliffs above, or they might be in inaccessible pockets in the mountains that are hidden, that are off the beaten track." Since small bodies of ice can be snow-covered for much of the year, or found in deep shadow, sometimes it's not enough to look at images taken from above. "You have to go there and walk around on it," Scurlock said, "and find out if it has glacial characteristics like ice movement, crevasses, evidence of old moraines."

Austin referred to the hypothetical glacier as "Eacas," for eastern Cascades. When Scurlock took Austin on an aerial survey of the north side of Mount Bigelow, Austin thought he glimpsed hints of something hidden in the rocks. Two years later, at age eighty-three, Austin returned with Scurlock and others to search from the ground. The group hiked six miles through the dry autumn forests of the eastern North Cascades. Yellow larch needles shone like slivers of stained glass against a deep-blue sky. After a night at 6,300 feet, they meandered to the edge of a boulder field. A few rocks tumbled down the scree—signs that remnants of a glacier might be creeping beneath the surface.

Something glittered like a diamond in the precipices above. "Can one of you youngsters get up there?" Austin said. One of his companions, Jim Lane, scrambled higher and found a field of ice, split by a crevasse. He climbed partway down into the chasm. As the walls drew closer, he could see the glint of more ice far below. "We can call it 'Eacas Glacier' for sure," Austin announced. In a photo that John Roper took that day, Austin sits on a boulder next to his son Richard, surrounded by sun-dappled rocks. Austin looks up, a camera around his neck, the start of a wry smile on his face, his silver hair aglow. It's as if time has vanished. His figure exudes the energy of a twenty-year-old man.

When Scurlock asked Austin if there might be hidden North Cascades ice even farther to the east, Austin suggested somewhere near Remmel Mountain, in the Pasayten Wilderness. But that hike was too far for him to undertake. "I think if Austin were alive," Scurlock told me, "he would say that the Eacas Glacier is not necessarily the easternmost glacier in the North Cascades, but it's the easternmost glacier that we've found." Another hidden glacier—if it exists under a field of rubbly talus or in the shadows of a mountain crevice—might well melt away before it is ever mapped.

During the 1980s, Austin started building a house in the shape of a ferryboat on Washington's Vashon Island. There, he lived with his wife Roberta until 2007, when the aging couple moved into an assisted living home. After other marriages that didn't last, including one to Dolores LaChapelle's sister, Austin had found happiness with Roberta, a longtime singer in the Seattle Symphony Chorale. In a memoir written for his sons, Austin explained that he'd fallen in love with the sound of her voice during their first telephone call. The windows of the "Ferry Boat House" looked out on Rainier glaciers that seemed to float above the blue waters of Puget Sound. Each morning, she tenderly braided his long silver hair. According to one friend, he refused to get it cut again after a barber charged him twenty dollars. Despite all the recognition he'd earned for his work, Austin remained a deliberate outsider. During the early 2000s, Austin's colleagues nominated him for an honorary doctorate at the University of Alaska, Fairbanks. Bradford Washburn and Ed LaChapelle—by then a professor emeritus of geophysics and atmospheric sciences at the University of Washington—were among the many admirers who wrote enthusiastic letters of support. But Austin refused to go to the ceremony in May 2004. "My father dreaded being up on stage in front of people," Richard recalled. In the end, university officials agreed to travel to Vashon and award Austin the degree at his home, where they insisted that the newly minted Dr. Austin Post at least put on a graduation gown.

The notion of "doctoring," Austin joked afterward, in the sense of altering realities, seemed "uncomfortably close to home." Like Harvey Manning, he'd retained a playful approach to cartography, moving landforms and names around on the maps inside his office. Austin also kept writing fiction stories, including one about an expedition outfitter who gets lost with a scientist deep in the Alaskan wild. On the brink of death from hunger and exhaustion, after staggering over avalanche debris and through a dense forest, they stumble upon a recluse's cabin stocked with food. There, they rest until they're strong enough to find their way back to their original base camp, where their pilot picks them up. Later, when the outfitter tries to return to replenish the supplies they'd used, he can't find the place again: the surrounding alpine basin doesn't exist on the map, and the cabin has vanished amid the endless, shadowed trees. Past explorers, too, had similar experiences, he learns, and he concludes they must have all fallen through a portal in the earth into a "dream world."

Austin's USGS colleague Carolyn Driedger remembered that he also told the story of the Riesenstein Hoax repeatedly and that he laughed every time. "He was very proud of it," she said. "He had no time for anything having to do with pretentiousness. If there were alpine climbers who thought they were going to get credit for some big new climb, he was going to send them on a goose chase." In our 2011 correspondence, Austin explained with pride that he'd helped make "Kichatna Spires" (rather than "Cathedral Spires") the official designation for the entire group of mountains—a term that is closer to the original Dena'ina word K'its'atnu. "What I do regret," he added, "is the name

Riesenstein wasn't retained for that wonderful peak [the tallest point in the original hoax photo]!" Austin's pleasure faded, though, when he described the real transformations taking place in the Alaska Range: "It's criminal what has happened to the forests, even the icefields are taking a beating." By the time a second edition of *Glacier Ice* appeared in 2000, its observations about the connection between climate and glacier size had become more urgent than ever. In the conclusion, Austin and Ed warned, "This world is a habitable spot in a hostile universe. . . . Much of modern civilization exists by virtue of a delicate balance. . . . Were the polar ice caps to melt, much of the world's urban area would be flooded by the rising sea." They urged scientists to continue looking for clues to predict the earth's possible futures: "The answers to this question are hidden somewhere in the glacier ice."

---

AUSTIN, TOO, IS GONE NOW: HIS ASHES WERE SCATTERED FROM A PLANE above his beloved Pyramid Mountain, where as a young boy, he'd first glimpsed the possibility of an ideal life among glaciers. It's impossible to read his and Ed's words now without thinking of how little time is left for any of us to find the answers they sought. The landscapes of all these histories and myths are changing beyond recognition. Layer by layer, records of past eons melt. Rockfall turns alpine walls into ghostly clouds of dust. Islands, in an echo of mythic Atlantis, may vanish beneath the waves. Once-imaginary places, such as an ice-free Northwest Passage, are becoming real. Once-real places exist only in imagination. Each year, in late spring, as I head higher up the mountains to look for ice flows still solid enough to climb, snowfields still large enough to ski (or at least to cool the stifling air), I realize how much smaller these countries of winter are growing in space and time. One day, many of the white-and-blue spaces on topographic maps may be gone, and their delicate crystals of frost and wild scrolls of cornices will become as wondrous, but as wholly mythical as the strange beasts on the edges of ancient cartographies.

PART III

# THE INNERMOST RANGES

Why do we want to have alternate worlds? It's a way of making progress. You have to imagine something before you do it.

—Joan Aiken, *Locus Magazine*

CHAPTER 21

# The Afterlife of Hoaxes

BY THE START OF THE twenty-first century, the Riesenstein Hoax had retreated into obscure corners of climbing lore. But the No Name Peak Hoax had an unexpected afterlife. A strange sense of reality clung to the tale: the walls of both the mythical and actual mountains appeared equally mist-wreathed, hazardous, perhaps forever unclimbable. In 1968, Fred Beckey had attempted the east face of Southeast Mox, the No Name Peak route extolled by the imaginary characters. Afterward, he wrote to Harvey with little optimism: "No good—bad rock and limit where cracks go."

Thirty-seven more years passed before someone managed to complete a first ascent of the real east face. Washington climber Michael Layton became intrigued by the route during a reconnaissance flight with John Scurlock. In the late summer of 2005, he and Erik Wolfe took seven hours to bushwhack the first one and three-quarters miles of the approach. Devil's club tore at their skin, and slide alder soaked their clothing. Like Thiusoloc and Henry Custer on their 1859 North Cascades expedition, Layton and Wolfe clung to tree roots and balanced on branches to pull themselves uphill. At the base of Southeast Mox, they confronted some 2,500 feet of steepening gneiss. After a bivouac partway up the wall, they teetered across meandering ledges and overhanging stone. Loose rocks whistled through the air. Layton felt like bursting into tears. He knew the holds might vanish ahead, and their gear could rip out if he fell. By the time they reached the top of the East Face, they were out of food and nearly out of water. There was no question of continuing to the apex of the mountain. They left a joker playing card as a sign of their presence, and they began a long series of rappels toward the darkness of the tangled woods.

In the *Northwest Mountaineering Journal*, Layton reported encountering a button-head bolt on the east face. He assumed it had been left by Paul Williams's expedition to No Name Peak, as if Harvey's invented attempt had, in fact, taken place. When I contacted Layton in the summer of 2017, he said he had no idea the original *Summit* story was a hoax. He wasn't the only one confused. Other climbers and Cascade chroniclers had made references to the 1959 Williams attempt as if it were simply part of the actual history of the mountain.

As I continued my research, I found more and more coincidental details that seemed to corroborate the No Name Peak account attributed to "Paul Williams." I started to feel disoriented. When I sent a copy of the May 1960 *Summit* article to Layton, he responded, "The topo on the hoax looks remarkably similar to the initial portion of our climb (more or less) and their high point is pretty much where we saw the old bolt." On a 2005 Cascade Climbers.com thread about Southeast Mox, someone else posted, "The Paul Williams mentioned in the article is my father-in-law." This real Paul Williams, I learned, had been an active Cascades climber around 1959, a founding member of Seattle Mountain Rescue, and an ardent conservationist. He'd once led an Arctic expedition to look for signs of the missing crew of John Franklin's Northwest Passage expedition. He'd also guided a group of clients who hoped to find traces of Noah's Ark on Mount Ararat in modern Turkey, near the borders of Iran, Azerbaijan, and Armenia (likely the same peak mentioned in Marco Polo's tale). Like a character in a Harvey Manning tale, he was a seeker of geographic mysteries and legendary lands.

A thought kept creeping back, as implausible as I knew it was: Could the No Name Peak story have been true after all? Was the actual hoax the notion that it was a hoax? I had plenty of evidence for the plotting of a fake peak. There was Harvey Manning's letter to Ted Beck outlining his idea for a fictitious climbing area (initially to be called "Crazy Creek Crags"). There was Harvey's note to his father-in-law admitting that he'd borrowed the name "Paul Williams" for the author of the No Name Peak tale and explaining the ruse ("The mountain is <u>not</u> missing. It's just misplaced."). And there was Dale Cole's earnest recollection of the practical joke, recorded in his interviews with me and in the obituary he wrote about Harvey for *The Wild Cascades*. Still, that post on CascadeClimbers.com and that bolt on the spire stuck in my mind, like hairline cracks in a giant edifice that threatened to bring the whole structure down.

But when I finally got in touch with Brian, the son of the real climber Paul Williams, he assured me that his father couldn't have been involved in the No Name Peak story. This Paul Williams wasn't from Portland, and he had no mountaineering partners with the names of the characters in the *Summit* article. So, whose traces were found on Southeast Mox, if they weren't those of any actual person named Paul Williams? Were they from Beckey in 1968? Or from someone else? After I'd emailed many Cascades climbers, Alan Kearney suggested I ask Alex Bertulis, who told me that he and Scott Davis might have left that bolt when they retreated during "inclement weather" in the 1980s. I could almost hear Harvey Manning's quiet laughter: after all these decades, his hoax had nearly become real.

"So, did I ever feel any remorse about any of this?" Dale said to me as we continued to talk about No Name Peak. "Of course not. In fact, as I look back at that time, it really provides some wonderful memories." Compared to the pernicious false stories of our current time, Harvey's 1960s hoaxes have an aura of innocence. The climbers lured to Harvey's "Great Wall of No Name Peak" had an unforgettable experience of a wild and beautiful mountain. "I don't think many people get the chance to feel that way about anything," Layton recalled. He felt fortunate to have been a part of the history of Southeast Mox, to have been immersed in that "excitement of adventure, the beauty of such a remote area and the camaraderie of friendship."

A year after the 2016 US presidential election, Kevin Young wrote in *Bunk: The Rise of Hoaxes, Humbug, Plagiarists, Phonies, Post-Facts, and Fake News*, "Today the hoax mostly traffics in pain." During the Trump era, Americans confronted avalanches of fabricated information designed to undermine the credibility of journalism and the survival of democracy itself. False claims by then-president Donald Trump and others about widespread election fraud became a catalyst for the January 6, 2021, attack on the US Capitol building in Washington, DC. Yet while Trump derided any realities he didn't like as "fake news" and while right-wing conspiracy theories still surge across the internet, pro-democracy activists have also figured out ways to turn some hoaxes against their perpetrators. In 2017, Trump's senior counselor Kellyanne Conway cited a nonexistent "massacre" by Iraqi terrorists in Bowling Green, Kentucky, to try to justify a travel ban against immigrants from seven predominantly Muslim countries. People responded with an outpouring of memes, T-shirts, songs, and mock memorials parodying the false story and demonstrating, as folklorist Timothy H. Evans observes, that at times the "lies of those in power could be mocked in a carnivalesque way." Harvey, whose own satires were partly aimed at the destructive fallacies of dominant groups, would certainly have approved of such ingenious forms of resistance.

In 2017, I'd been surprised that some modern climbers and history writers still thought the No Name Peak story was a genuine, though error-ridden, account of an actual expedition. Now it seems plausible that there are many more Harvey Manning hoaxes tucked within the pages of obscure mountain journals. Given the success of the pranks we know about, why wouldn't Harvey have been tempted to keep going, changing the hidden messages to suit the issues of each decade and making the riddles more elaborate and harder to solve? Maybe other authors, knowingly or unknowingly, picked up a few of his fabricated details and transformed them into accepted lore in climbing histories and guidebooks—now awaiting some diligent mountaineering detective of the future to uncover the secret fiction.

Among the many boxes of Harvey's letters, notes, and unpublished manuscripts, I found numerous accounts of hidden ranges that blended reality, fantasy, and dreams. In one fragmentary paragraph, he wrote of a character who "was given a map by a dying prospector and followed it to a cave whose walls and floor and ceiling were glittering crystal quartz veined with eighteen-carat gold." In the 1960 *Mountaineer*, Harvey had claimed that he himself had made a similar expedition to a "Peak X," but failed to find the treasure. Was this other story a plan for an unrealized hoax? Or was it Harvey's way of imagining a different ending, in which a mountain of incalculable desire becomes attainable? In a 1996 *Backpacker* interview with climbing journalist Mark Jenkins, Harvey described his "favorite dream" as "revisiting a mountain range I first dreamt of 50 years ago and have returned to regularly." Did the inspiration for this mysterious range, seemingly older than No Name Peak or the Riesenstein, exist as a real place on Earth? Or did it merely arise from a blend of mythologies, adventure stories, and his unconscious mind?

Harvey was no longer around to answer any of these questions. If I wanted to understand more about the meanings behind such peaks, including my own, I'd have to look elsewhere—in the stories of imaginary ranges that continued to spread after his death and in the phantom geographies that still arise today.

---

THE QUEST FOR FABULOUS MOUNTAINS DIDN'T STOP WITH THE UNdiscovery of the Riesenstein. As they had so many times in history, seekers moved on to other places. During the late twentieth century, American mountaineer Galen Rowell became fascinated by the legends that surrounded the elevation of Amye Machen in the eastern Kunlun of Tibet. Decades after Terris Moore's expedition decided to investigate Minya Konka instead, rumors persisted that Amye Machen might be the mountain taller than Everest.

"No survey [of Amye Machen] had been precise enough to convince geographers," Rowell noted in the *American Alpine Journal*, "until a sensational news story appeared to confirm the mountain's height during World War II. A U.S. pilot ... reported coming out of the clouds at 30,000 feet ... only to see a mountain rising above him." In 1948, Bradford Washburn set out to try to ascertain the truth, accompanied by a former Minya Konka expedition member, Jack Young, and the ballpoint pen magnate Milton Reynolds (who paid for the trip). Their quest ended in infamous absurdity: leaving Washburn and other teammates behind in Beijing, Reynolds attempted an unauthorized flight over Amye Machen, quarreled with Chinese authorities, and then made a dramatic escape from the Shanghai airport in the expedition plane. Later, Reynolds claimed that he'd hurled fistfuls of his sample pens at Chinese guards who tried to stop him. In some versions of the story, the pens were made of gold.

A year later, an American explorer and World War II intelligence agent, Leonard Clark, reported making his own reconnaissance of Amye Machen on behalf of a Chinese nationalist warlord. Clark returned with the intriguingly specific number of 29,661 feet. In his memoir, he suggested the mountain was cursed: "Death and misfortune, notoriety, misery and failure, have followed all the travelers (adventurers, flyers, explorers) who have ... sought the mystery mountain."

It was somewhere around there that British novelist James Hilton had located his mysterious peak of perfect beauty. According to one of Hilton's characters, rumors existed of "mountains actually higher than Everest" in the Kunlun, where summits "had never been properly surveyed," a statement that seemed possible to some explorers as late as the mid-twentieth century. In contrast to the peaceful tranquility of Shangri-La, the real landscape of Amye Machen had been fraught with strife—one reason that so few outsiders were able to visit the peak. In 1956, air raids forced Golok fighters to surrender to China after they had twice defeated communist soldiers' efforts to subdue the region. Amye Machen remained an important symbol to the surviving Golok people, the abode of Buddhist deities and one of the most sacred mountains within their traditional territory.

In 1981, curious to see Amye Machen, Rowell helped organize an expedition of Americans trekkers to take part in the Buddhist pilgrimage around the mountain. While Rowell was negotiating for permits, Chinese Mountaineering Association officials told him that an eight-person Chinese team had made an ascent of Amye Machen in 1960 and had found its elevation to be 23,490 feet. They said its mountainsides were a refuge for "a wealth of rare birds and animals," a "Shangri-La" of wildlife. Later, the officials offered a correction: it turned out that the 1960 expedition had actually reached one of the mountain's lower summits. The highest point of Amye Machen was still unclimbed, but its measurement had been revised to only 20,610 feet.

Rowell learned that several other foreign teams planned to attempt a first ascent of the mountain's apex, including an American group led by his friend Kim Schmitz. Rowell joined forces with Schmitz's team, intending to climb Amye Machen before he met with his trekkers. But while the American mountaineers were hiking toward the peak, through a deluge of rain and blizzard, they met Chinese glaciologists who informed them that a Japanese expedition had just attained the tallest summit.

After the skies cleared, Rowell, Schmitz, and Harold Knutson set out from an advanced base camp at 15,000 feet and slogged through new-fallen drifts toward a narrow, blade-like ridge, encrusted with seracs. The next morning, much to their relief, they realized the storms had coated most of the ice with a solid layer of snow and they could easily plod around the seracs. When they arrived on the summit plateau, however, they discovered that the real apex was still another mile distant, across soft powder that rose to their thighs. After hours of wallowing, they staggered onto the highest visible point, where their altimeter recorded an elevation of 20,700 feet. (The current measurement is 20,564 feet.) They observed no traces of a previous team, though perhaps the signs were buried under all the layers of snow. "We were uncertain," Rowell noted, "whether we had made the first, the second, or the third ascent." (According to John Town's subsequent analysis for the British *Alpine Journal*, the Japanese team expedition did, indeed, beat Rowell's group to the summit.)

Rowell descended to join the trekkers, and they followed Golok guides along the pilgrimage route. As they hiked across foothills between 13,000 and 16,000 feet high, Rowell started to comprehend how early explorers might have misjudged the height of Amye Machen. For days, he gazed at its now-distant summit until the pearl-like sheen of ice blurred into the glow of high clouds, as if the mountain had spread into the sky. One day, he set off for a run alone toward a hilltop shrine. A Golok guide, Chong Hun, followed him on horseback. "A low sound that seems born of the earth itself grows louder," Rowell recalled. "At first I do not realize that it is not coming from the hill but from behind me. The Golok [man] is chanting a Buddhist incantation in perfect rhythm with my footsteps."

After Rowell's Chinese translator, Gung Jian Chun, caught up with them, Chong Hun shared stories of the place. "When I was eight years old," he said, "I came here with my family on a pilgrimage around the mountain as you are doing now. . . . We saw wolves, bears, musk deer, great herds of gazelles, blue sheep, and nyan [an endangered mountain sheep]. . . . I saw my last nyan when I was 18; now I am 43. . . . There are more people, more yaks, more goats, more guns, more bullets, and no more nyan."

When Rowell got back to California, his mother gave him a letter from Dick Leonard, a friend of the family and one of the groundbreaking Yosemite climbers of the 1930s. Leonard had an unusual story about Amye Machen to relate. In October 1944, he'd been flying over the Himalaya with an air force captain. "Major, you seem to know a lot about the Himalaya," the captain said to him. "Have you heard of the peak higher than Everest?"

"Oh yes, Amye Machen is one of the greatest geographical discoveries of the century," Leonard responded.

"Well, it's all a fake," the captain said. "We made it up. Those British correspondents kept pestering us for exciting stories to cable home, so we told them of a DC-3 that got blown off course in a terrific storm and discovered a mountain over 30,000 feet. . . . Of course a fully loaded DC-3 can't fly anywhere near as high as we said, and it couldn't carry enough fuel to get back from that far off course. . . . It was a great practical joke, and serious reports of it were published all over the world."

Other hoaxes may still lurk within the route descriptions of climbing guidebooks. At least one late-twentieth–century writer followed in Harvey Manning's tradition of inventing imaginary peaks to convey a message. In Bruce Fairley's 1986 edition of *A Guide to Climbing & Hiking in Southwestern British Columbia*, there is another curious reference to a mountain "reportedly quite high." The text, at first glance, seems to be written in a traditional guidebook style. On a closer look, quirky or incongruous details appear. For example, the author credits K. Ricker and W. Tupper with the first ascent of the west glacier route and includes an odd request: "The next party is asked to retrieve a theodolite inadvertently left on a glacial boulder pedestal. A round of readings would be appreciated." The description of the south-southwest ridge states, "*FA (although they deny it): M. Feller, R. Wyborn.* The approach is incredibly bushy and dismal. Only those of very tough mettle should even consider it." The peak's name, "Bogus Mountain," provides an obvious clue, as does its location "roughly N of the Reality River," that this entry is a parody.

Over email, Fairley told me that he'd dreamed up Bogus Mountain as a humorous means to honor people who played significant roles in the region's climbing history. The fake route descriptions include private jokes about real climbers' habits. Riesenstein debunker Glenn Woodsworth was among the chosen protagonists, and he acknowledged a certain appropriateness in the references to "indescribably rotten rock" and necessary "prospecting experience" on the fictitious climb attributed to him and Dick Culbert. Glenn added that Tupper of the purportedly forgotten theodolite was, in fact, a surveyor and that Feller thought guidebooks detracted from the "mystery of an area," hence the allusion to their refusal to report a first ascent.

One of the researchers for the guidebook, Anders Ourom, confirmed that "C. S. Bungi," an alleged first ascensionist of the northwest rib (described as "an obvious" route, "quite suitable for dogs and small children"), was an imaginary climber. Members of the University of British Columbia's Varsity Outdoor Club had created Bungi around the 1960s. "He would be referred to when discussing the finer points of dancing the notorious 'Salty Dog Rag,'" Ourom said, "Also, of course, he was a convenient 'person' to blame naughtiness on. A sort of Cheshire Cat."

If it takes a moment for some of Fairley's readers to recognize that Bogus Mountain is a joke, perhaps that pause is a testament to how quickly we still grant authority to writers' or mapmakers' depictions of the world. "The tale reminds us," Ourom reflected, "that the history of all mountains, their exploration and climbing, is a human construct." Although this fictitious mountain is, in the words of its own inventors, "bogus," like all parodies, it gets us to think a little more critically about the ones we believe are real. Geographic names often conceal disparate realities, such as the unacknowledged existence of Indigenous histories or the complex layers of anecdotes and myths behind the choice to christen a mountain after a particular human figure. Or the notion that the entirety of a mountain—the intricate and shifting permutations of soil and stone, flowing water and still ice, the fleeting tracks of rabbits between winter crags and frozen pines, the flash of birds' wings against a snow-white sky—might be condensed into a brief set of alphabet letters.

Like Harvey Manning's hoaxes, the Bogus Mountain entry takes the usual dryness of guidebook writing and turns it into something unexpected, hinting not only at the absurdity of exploration itself, but also at the possibilities of reimagining it in new forms. In a fake interview published in the 1990 *Varsity Outdoor Club Journal*, Bungi was asked, "Is there anything you'd like to say to your admirers?" He replied, "Well folks, if you want adventure, put your boots on and go."

Climbers and hikers still have an insatiable appetite for the treasure hunts of folklore and myth, and other modern-day eccentrics have manufactured quests for them. In 2010, New Mexico art dealer Forrest Fenn composed a cryptic poem with clues to a box of gold and gems that he'd claimed he'd hidden somewhere in the Rockies. Thousands of people headed into the mountains to look for it, as if gripped by the fervor that ignited the nineteenth-century search for the Diamond Mountain. In 2018, Fenn explained that he, too, had wanted to send a message: he'd hoped to perpetuate "the thrill of the chase," to resurrect a time before the "internet and technology" made it hard to imagine marvels and mysteries in the wild.

Unlike the search for the Riesenstein, however, the Forrest Fenn adventure lasted a decade, and several seekers died after they wandered off course (despite Fenn's insistence that technical skills weren't required to reach the treasure chest). In early June 2020, Fenn announced that someone had finally unearthed the prize, "under a canopy of stars in the lush, forested vegetation of the Rocky Mountains," but when Fenn refused to reveal the finder's name, some of his readers became suspicious. A few months later, Fenn passed away. A sense of mystery hovered over the question of whether the discovery of the treasure was a hoax At last, in December, prompted by a pending lawsuit, a medical student named Jack Stuef admitted that he was the one who located the box. "I thought that whoever found the chest would be absolutely hated because it ends everyone's dream," he confessed to author Daniel Barbarisi in *Outside* magazine. "I realize I put an end to something that meant so much to so many people."

CHAPTER 22

# Not to Escape the World, but to Enter It More Deeply

SINCE THE EARLY DAYS, AS American and European mountaineers have sought to claim superlative heights, untrodden summits, or fabulous riches, their quests have often remained entangled with legacies of colonialism and imperialism. But explorers from other cultures have also continued to look for mythic peaks. And their accounts suggest alternative cartographies of dreams—ways of approaching the world's mysteries without trying to conquer them.

In 1917, decades before Galen Rowell's ascent of Amye Machen, a Tibetan visionary named Sera Khandro went to look for a treasure that existed not on the apex of the peak, but deep within its interior. In her memoirs, she recalled that as she approached the mountain with her daughter and other companions, swirls of rainbows lit the sky. Images of female deities appeared above the clouds, their hands outstretched as if to offer gifts.

While the others circumambulated Amye Machen, Sera Khandro's daughter remained nearby as she opened a portal into the peak. Sera Khandro took out sacred writings, medicines, and chests made of turquoise and semiprecious stones. As fragrance suffused the air, a miraculous spring gushed forth. Later in the pilgrimage, Queen Drakgyelma, a goddess of the mountain, appeared, adorned in blue silk and flashing jewels, and she gave Sera Khandro a crystal vase. "If you hide this in the realm of the four elements . . . it is certain that many sentient beings' rounds through the lower realms of samsāra will stop," Queen Drakgyelma told her.

Although Sera Khandro was following a tradition of quests for alpine paradises—in her case, Buddhist beliefs about the existence of *beyul*, or "hidden lands"—her goal wasn't to satisfy any personal longing for dominion, fulfillment, or gain, as Sarah H. Jacoby, a professor of religious studies, observes. Instead, Sera Khandro sought a treasure of sacred knowledge that could help all people, and she compensated the land for anything she removed from it by leaving offerings of great value in return.

Similar tales exist throughout the Himalaya. According to tradition, Indian teacher Padmasambhava traveled across the mountains of Tibet during the eighth century, converting local deities to Buddhism. As he went, Padmasambhava and his companion Yeshé Tsogyal concealed some religious teachings in the form of *terma* or "treasures" inside beyul, often within the walls of Himalayan peaks. Many of these hidden lands could be found only in times when people desperately needed a sanctuary from war or other horrors. Only the right *tertön* (a lama or visionary who has the ability to find terma in the landscape) could open the door to these places, usually with the help of a *khandro* or *dākinī*, a female spiritual being who may have taken human form.

In 1962, the same year that the Riesenstein Hoax appeared in *Summit*, a tertön from the Golok region named Tulshuk Lingpa and three hundred of his disciples journeyed toward the immense snowy massif of Mount Kangchenjunga, a 28,169-foot peak on the border of Sikkim and Nepal. There, Tulshuk Lingpa hoped to open the Beyul Demoshong, a hidden land of extraordinary natural beauty, with green meadows and bright cascades, as well as treasures that offer spiritual teachings, healing plants, and longevity. In a guidebook for the journey, he recounted a vision of Yeshé Tsogyal, who told him, "Tibet is being overrun [since the Chinese invasion] and those who aren't slaughtered have nowhere to go. The time is coming for the opening of the beyul in Sikkim."

Another religious leader, Rigdzin Godemchen, had described locating the way into the beyul during the fourteenth century, in the midst of a chaotic era of Mongolian rule and civil war. Legends also told of a seventeenth-century lama, Lhatsun Chenpo, who had discovered a doorway in a stone cliff somewhere below the massif. Since then, other Buddhist lamas and pilgrims had searched for the entrance without finding it again. During Tulshuk Lingpa's quest, when a suspicious police commissioner insisted that Tulshuk Lingpa point to the location of the beyul on a map, he replied, "If Beyul map, it wouldn't be Beyul."

One disciple, Wangyal Bodh, later told American author Thomas (who wrote a book about their quest) that he and Tulshuk Lingpa eventually glimpsed the margins of the hidden land. On the Kangchenjunga massif, Tulshuk Lingpa left the other disciples behind at a high camp while he and Wangyal Bodh continued up a steep glacier, carrying only one ice axe. When an avalanche roared toward them, Tulshuk Lingpa warded it off with his *phurba*, a ritual dagger. Above the glacier, the snow and ice vanished. The edge of a green meadow appeared, shimmering with rainbows like translucent flowers. The scent of saffron filled the warming air.

When they were only about ten steps away, Tulshuk Lingpa said they should go back for more members of their group. The next day, as Tulshuk Lingpa and three companions climbed ahead of the rest of the party, the slope cracked and an avalanche engulfed them. Tulshuk Lingpa was found dead. Some people thought that the moment to open the beyul hadn't arrived yet. Others believed that Tulshuk Lingpa must have attracted too large a group of followers, not all of whom had sufficient faith. Or they asserted that a beyul is more a state of mind than a geographic place, attainable to an enlightened person anywhere.

Tibetan Buddhists aren't the only ones who tell stories of a paradise concealed inside Kangchenjunga. Lepcha people of Sikkim believe the deity Itbu Debu Rum created them from the mountain's snows, and they recount legends of a secret place, Mayel Kyong, that exists somewhere within the vast labyrinths of rainforest, ravines, and glaciers below the summit. Its doorway is blocked by a giant rock that can only be opened by a Lepcha with a pure mind. Inside, there is no illness, hunger, or death. As Charisma K. Lepcha, a Sikkim University professor, relates the tale, "There are seven couples who live in Mayel Kyong who are children in the morning, young people during the day and old people by night, hence they are immortal." In some accounts, Lepcha people have occasionally found their way into Mayel Kyong, and received food and other forms of assistance. Once they left, they were unable to find it a second time. Legend has it that after an apocalyptic disaster in the future, the inhabitants of Mayel Kyong will provide Lepchas with seeds to replant the earth and restore civilization. In 2007, one villager told visiting scholar Claire S. Scheid that the hidden paradise had become an internal place, reached through living in peace.

From 1993 to 1998, American anthropologist Ian Baker undertook eight expeditions in search of the geographic coordinates of another beyul, called Pemako. It was said to lie at the eastern end of the Himalaya, in an unmapped region of the Tsangpo Gorge, near the disputed border of India and China. Nineteenth-century British explorers once hoped to find the earth's largest waterfall there. The description of the superlative cascade first appeared in a Survey of India report dictated by the Indian pundit Kinthup. The waterfall's purported size later turned out to be a transcription error: Kinthup's actual account had told of a smaller cascade on a tributary of the Tsangpo. But the discovery of the mistake didn't stop adventurers from dreaming.

At the advice of the Buddhist lama Bhakha Tulku, Baker journeyed to Kundu Dorsempotrang, a mountain that had long been a pilgrimage destination, though he could find no map that showed its location. Still, he learned that, during the 1950s, a lama named Kanjur Rinpoche and his companion had passed through a nearby waterfall into the hidden land. Inside, they'd found a valley of abundant fruit and healing plants, walled by snowy mountains in the shape of a heart. When Kanjur Rinpoche tried to lead others there, he could no longer uncover the way.

While Baker and his fellow pilgrims circumambulated the peak, they paused by a slab of steep rock on the western side. About one hundred feet up the cliff, under rivulets of rainwater, lichen created a pattern like ancient script. One of his companions, the lama Kawa Tulku, explained to Baker that the "key" to the hidden land might be discovered here. Then the lama climbed up and down the cliff, unroped. No portal opened that Baker could see, but he remembered what other lamas had told him about the beyul: that it might only reveal itself at certain times to those who had already opened a doorway within their minds, that it might not exist in a single geographic place at all, or that it might represent a concealed reality reachable anywhere through dedicated Buddhist practice.

In 1998, Baker's expedition headed farther down the Tsangpo Gorge than any previous foreign team had gone. Using modern climbing gear, they navigated a maze of steep cliffs not unlike the landscape of the Rishi Gorge that leads into the Inner Sanctuary of Nanda Devi. By the end of the trip, Baker realized the nineteenth-century British adventurers were wrong: the giant waterfall they'd dismissed as an error or a myth did, in fact, exist in the depths of the gorge. It wasn't the one that Kinthup had written about, and it wasn't the biggest in the world. But it was, nonetheless, more than one hundred feet tall. And it already had a local name, according to Buluk and Jayang, Ian's Monpa guides: the "*chinlap*" of the deity Dorje Phagmo, "her blessings or, in literal translation, her transformative flood of power."

Beside the waterfall, Buluk showed Baker patterns of lichen on a rock wall and suggested the door to the beyul might exist in that spot. A nearby tunnel appeared to lead deep into a mountainside, though its entrance was unreachable, blocked by hundreds of feet of surging rapids. Even if they got there and the beyul existed, Baker thought, the paradise would probably remain invisible to him. Watching the dazzling interplay of light, water, and stone, he contemplated how meaningless it was to think that measuring a waterfall mattered: the height of cascades altered constantly over time as the water eroded the rock below. It was even more absurd to talk about discovering a place that local Monpa hunters had known about for so long. The belief in a secret, unseen cascade had merely been another form of *terra miscognita.* The quests for the waterfall and the beyul might have resonated so much for generations of Western adventurers because of the resemblances to centuries-old dreams. "Pemako enjoys many of the attributes of the lost Eden," Baker mused, "a promised land east of India sealed in by towering mountains and hazardous terrain, duplicitous serpents and magical flora somewhere at its heart." A giant cascade had also appeared in legends of a mountaintop Earthly Paradise. While those myths had sometimes inspired Europeans to conquer foreign lands, perhaps stories of beyul could have a different effect on modern-day adventurers. "The perspective offered by Padmasambhava's scrolls," Baker reflected, "invite us to grow beyond nineteenth-century models of exploration and to open to the blank spaces within our own understanding—to explore not only the physical terrain but, to the best of our ability, to comprehend what the earth's wildest places mean for those who have always lived there or dreamed them into existence."

In the introduction to Baker's book *The Heart of the World*, the Dalai Lama wrote that beyul are "not places to escape the world, but to enter it more deeply," sanctuaries that "deepen awareness of hidden regions of the mind and spirit," where geographic location, ultimately, matters less than "the journey itself."

CHAPTER 23

# Selective Availability

WHEN DAVID ROBERTS STARTED RESEARCHING *Great Exploration Hoaxes* in 1979, he thought many readers might simply shrug at his efforts to uncover the truth or falsity of specific claims. "Does it really matter who climbed a certain mountain first?" he imagined them asking. To his surprise, most people cared, even those who weren't normally interested in exploration stories. As I worked on this book, I encountered a different reaction. Particularly after the 2016 US presidential election, almost all the people I spoke with—climbers and non-climbers—were aware of the serious dangers of fabricated news stories about political or scientific issues. At the same time, many of them lamented the idea that geographic jokes, such as the ones that Harvey Manning perpetrated, might no longer be possible. "The world has become so well known," they said. "The world has become so small."

In 2011, Fred Beckey, longtime ferreter-out of secret places, had emailed me one of the characteristic all-cap shouts of his later years: "NOW YOU CAN STUDY GOOGLE MAPS AND FIGURE OUT THE BEST ROUTE AND ACCESS WITHOUT GETTING OFF YOUR DUFF. COMPARE THIS WITH WHAT THE MUNDAYS HAD TO DO IN FIGURING OUT MT WADDINGTON. I THINK . . . GEOGRAPHIC INFORMATION HAS GONE TOO FAR."

In some respects, Beckey was right. The availability of detailed information has removed many of the uncertainties from expeditions. But there are places that remain beyond the reach of satellite maps. Like the Eacas Glacier of Austin's final quest, they can only be verified on foot, or like the beyul of the Himalaya, they might exist in an interior world, opening merely at certain times to certain people.

Moreover, digital mapmaking technologies don't eliminate all possibilities of illusions and myths. While the spread of GPS has demystified much of the world, its history is also full of errors, both inadvertent and intended. In 1978, the US Department of Defense launched the first satellite in the Navigation System with Timing and Ranging (NAVSTAR) Global Positioning System, the beginnings of today's GPS. Five years later, President Reagan made GPS available to civilians, after 269 people died aboard a Korean Airlines plane that had accidently strayed into forbidden Soviet airspace and been shot down by Russian pilots. Until 2000, however, the US government programmed a deliberate level of inexactness, called "Selective Availability," into civilian GPS models to prevent potential enemies from having access to precise geographic knowledge for military operations.

Even with the most accurate measurements now accessible, current navigation devices that use GPS (or apps simulating them) aren't all-knowing. The satellite technology merely indicates a coordinate location on the earth's surface. The depiction of what is actually present at that spot still comes from map databases that have been linked to the device—information that may occasionally contain incorrect or outdated details. In remote parts of Death Valley, phantom roads still haunt the digital screens of visitors, leading them astray, just as phantom islands of older cartographies lured and imperiled sailors. The very elevations of peaks are still referred to as height above sea level, "a term that can lead to much confusion, especially in this time of rising sea level in response to climate change," explains Jim L. Davis, a geophysicist at the Lamont-Doherty Earth Observatory of Columbia University. Cartographers and earth scientists are continuing to correct old numbers on maps as they revise the systems they use to define height (relative to a mathematical model of the earth's true surface), calculating how gravity's varying pull affects GPS measurements at different locations and taking into account the complex and changing shape of the planet itself. In December 2020, surveyors from Nepal and China announced a new measurement of Chomolungma as 29,031.69 feet, more than three feet lower than the elevation delivered by Bradford Washburn's National Geographic expedition in 1999. To supplement their use of satellite navigation systems and laser theodolites (a high-tech version of the centuries-old triangulation tools), the Nepali summit team had relied on ground-penetrating radar to determine how many feet of impermanent snow concealed the true rock apex.

Imperfect as they are, GPS units have transformed the practice of exploration in geographic regions much less known than Everest, helping mountaineers attain remote and still-unvisited summits, and facilitating high-altitude search and rescue by indicating their locations if they falter. But the successful aspects of the technology can forge "an electronic tether to the world we were trying to leave," as Australian mountaineer and mapmaker Damien Gildea has observed. That same tether can foster an overreliance that becomes dangerous when the device fails. In *The Shallows*, American technology writer Nicholas Carr noted that the invention of each new cartographic tool, beginning with mass-produced paper maps, may have reshaped not only our relationship to our environments, but also the internal landscapes of our minds, shrinking the parts of the hippocampus used for spatial representation.

I learned the wooded hills of my childhood by roaming through them, imprinting each bend and curve in my memory. Before long, I could sense the direction of landmarks even when they were hidden by thick summer leaves: the sky-blue flicker of a pond west of our house, the faint hum of a road to the east, the warm air that rose from a marsh between them. One by one, each feature seemed to become part of me, until the whole forest—the shiny acorns and oak leaves, the cool moss and damp stone, the crisp twigs of sweet birch and soft branches of white pine, even the undulations of low hills—mirrored itself inside my mind. How much would I have noticed if I'd been following a GPS track on a screen? Would I have been too focused on a preprogrammed destination to meander off course, my curiosity stirred by the heft of an old tree or the glint of a vernal pool? As an adult climber, while I've frequently stopped to check that the features of a cliff matched up with those of a photocopied topo map, I've rarely remembered to look at anything outside the lines. Maybe what some of us need are more maps like the ones Harvey made—to get off track and expand our imaginations again.

Back in 1972, a historian of imaginary places, Raymond H. Ramsey, had wondered, "Are the factors that in the past placed nonexistent regions on the map still operating?" While Ramsey thought that new fictitious lands were unlikely to be believed, he acknowledged that questionable older islands still appeared in the vast blue spaces of oceans on modern maps, waiting for their existence to be proven or disproven. Nearly forty years later, in 2009, a group of researchers from the National Autonomous University of Mexico set sail to search for the island of Bermeja, which had appeared on maps of the Gulf of Mexico since the sixteenth century. When they arrived at the island's coordinates, only empty water glimmered before them. But the existence of Bermeja had international importance—the presence of a landform would have extended Mexican claims to oil within that part of the Gulf—and so people kept searching. Theories abounded: Had Bermeja disappeared because of an earthquake or rising seas? Did a long-ago mapmaker invent the island to see if other cartographers were plagiarizing his work? Was its presence on the map a simple mistake, a result of the classic blend of second-hand information, inaccurate longitude readings, and vivid mirages?

Today, many mapmakers do much of their work in offices, compiling data from faraway places that they may have never seen, not unlike the early cartographers who pieced together explorers' reports into world atlases. A more intricate and nuanced understanding of a place still requires visiting it in person. In the end, we still experience forms of selective availability: gaps in digital sources, glitches in systems, outdated information, undiscovered mistakes, margins of error that allow adventurers not only to get off route, but also to pursue creative dreams. When the nonexistent Sandy Island finally vanished from Google Maps in 2012, users uploaded fantasy photos of extinct dinosaurs and otherworldly temples in its place. "Although we live with the expectation that the world is fully visible and exhaustively known," geographer Alastair Bonnett explained in *Unruly Places* "we also want and need places that allow our thoughts to roam unimpeded.... Sandy Island's disappearance established it as a rebel base for the imagination."

---

BACK WHEN FREDERICK COOK AND HARVEY MANNING WERE ASSEMbling the pieces of documentation for their tales of imagined summits, they relied primarily on paper maps, drawings, photographs, and vibrant storytelling. What neither of them might have imagined were the ways that new media could make future hoaxes easier to create and harder to eradicate. In 2016, two mountaineers received official Nepali government certificates for climbing Everest. They claimed to be the first Indian couple to summit together. A month afterward, another Indian climber, Satyarup Siddhanta, announced that the couple appeared to have Photoshopped themselves into pictures that he recognized as his own. Other, more sophisticated forms of hoaxes may be more difficult to identify. With the rise of "deep fakes," fictional photos and videos can look nearly indistinguishable from genuine ones. Advances in artificial intelligence make it feasible to swap faces in digital images and to mimic voices in audio messages. Entire identities can be invented, convincingly, online.

Technology, which seemed to promise the potential—welcome to some, dystopian to others—of surveilling climbers' movements on high peaks, often remains inadequate as a means of definitive evidence. While digital media can give the impression of close-up views of distant ranges, these glimpses, like the mirages of old, are vulnerable to distortions. For decades, Nepali journalist Kunda Dixit worked with the late American chronicler Elizabeth Hawley, who became one of the founders of the Himalayan Database, a comprehensive source of information on climbing in Nepal. When they began reporting on ascents together, Dixit told me, they filed stories "by feeding a punched paper tape through a rattly telex machine" in Hawley's Kathmandu living room, far from the mountains. Now, with modern communication devices, Dixit said, there's "instant transmission of climbs and even phone calls from the summit." As a result, participants whose voices were once rarely heard in international newspapers and books—such as expedition staff—can now share their experiences directly through social media, increasing both the accuracy and inclusiveness of some climbing stories. Yet more powerful groups can easily spread misleading news online, bypassing the gatekeepers of traditional journals. French chronicler Rodolphe Popier, a current Himalayan Database team member, points out that there is still no "standardized international system" for fact-checking climbs. Generally, an ascent is considered valid if an alpinist has a reasonably sufficient collection of proof—or if members of the climbing community decide to take their word for it, "in the absence of a set of negative clues." If enough hints of falsehood arise, a climb might become disputed, and if enough actual evidence emerges, it could be invalidated. But there's no clear, widely accepted threshold for how much doubt must exist before fact checkers should openly challenge a claim. In this sense, little has changed since the days of Fake Peak and the Riesenstein.

The lack of a universal system of validation means that influential individuals, brands, and organizations can become default authorities, whether or not they are the most objective or knowledgeable sources. Even with stringent efforts to ascertain what happened on a mountain, when there are no eyewitnesses, uncertainties are inevitable. As Popier notes, altitude, weather, and stress can all muddy how alpinists perceive terrain. Wind and snowfall can erase the traces of their passage. Details can refract or fade in memory. Critics can argue that a team's reported speeds are implausible, Popier adds, but climbing communities might only consider the most "drastic variations" from the norm to be signs of deceit. Journalists and editors can compare the difficulty of a climb with that of a mountaineer's previously demonstrated abilities, though they might have trouble pinning down just how much improvement is unbelievable. They can try to analyze individual climbers' psychologies—for example, does someone's facial expressions and speech patterns during an interview suggest that he's telling the truth?—though such an approach is inherently subjective and open to bias.

Summit photos remain a preferred method of proof, despite the history of mountaineers such as Frederick Cook attempting to fabricate them. But growing skepticism of visual media now means that even truthful climbers may find their unaltered images disputed. In one of his emails to me, Popier recalled the story of Hungarian mountaineer Suhajda Szilárd, who had made a well-documented report in July 2019 of his ascent of K2's Abruzzi Spur, only to be beset by rumors that he'd somehow faked his extensive photos and film footage. Several of the world's top mountaineering chroniclers examined the landscapes and metadata of Szilárd's images and considered the speed with which he'd been able to provide such detailed evidence. In this instance, they determined, the climb must be real and the accusations must be false.

What might all these enduring debates and ambiguities mean for the future of climbing media? For decades, historians confronted the late Italian alpinist Cesare Maestri with an ever-growing mountain of evidence against his claim to have summited the 10,262-foot granite spire of Cerro Torre in Patagonia. In a 2014 book on the controversy, *The Tower*, longtime climber and mountaineering editor Kelly Cordes recalled that Maestri kept reiterating the same defense: "If you doubt me, you doubt the history of mountaineering." Much of climbing history depends on the assumption that ascensionists are telling the truth. Take away that foundation, Maestri seemed to suggest, and the entire edifice will fall.

But, as Harvey Manning might retort, some additional skepticism could result in a more nuanced and meaningful, if less orderly, approach to history. Many readers are all too apt to see protagonists of climbing stories as flawless, strong heroes and to accept aggrandized versions of ascents without looking closely at what authors frequently leave out of their tales: the contributions of the expedition staff; the uneven opportunities for who can become (or who can be recognized as) a "significant" climber; the possibility that a lesser known mountaineer, perhaps a local resident, might have long ago climbed the same peak that a visiting alpinist has just claimed as a first ascent. Let that architecture of preconceptions and myths fall apart, accept that history is not something fixed for eternity, that it's always open to revision, and, out of the chaos, a far more diverse and accurate vision of the truth might arise.

At the same time, the sheer volume of climbing reports, the ceaseless flow of twenty-four-hour newsfeeds, and the decrease in funding for modern journalism can make it impossible to dig deeply into every story. "While editing the *American Alpine Journal*," Cordes admitted, "I didn't scrutinize the veracity of every new route claim . . . but we probably get duped more often than we realize. Usually, you scrutinize only when red flags arise." Catching less obvious errors is a kind of virtuoso art that requires multiple talents. Fact-checkers and editors must be able to notice discrepancies, sometimes deeply hidden, in climbers' reports. They must be able to filter claims through an intimate, on-the-ground knowledge (either their own or that of trusted sources) about the complexities of a particular region. Finally, they must be able to use their knowledge of a local history, studied for decades, across numerous published and unpublished sources in multiple languages, to help writers recall an under-reported ascent, an oral tradition, or a disproven fact that they might have missed.

Fact-checking in the mountaineering world still often relies on extensive libraries of information archived in individual memories that remain subject, eventually, to aging and loss. When Elizabeth Hawley passed away in 2018, it was as if an oracle had vanished. In a 2011 *Outside* article entitled "The High Priestess of Posterity," Eric Hansen echoed the feelings of numerous climbers: "It doesn't matter if you're Reinhold Messner or Ed Viesturs; your summit never happened unless Elizabeth Hawley says it did." During her lifetime, friends and colleagues say, Hawley didn't consider herself an absolute authority. Her critics were quick to note that she had no climbing experience herself. Yet if her iconic status reverberated with a sense of power and ritual for so many fans, perhaps it was partly because of her phenomenal fact-checking abilities, and partly because of a deep, communal longing that someone, somewhere, might be an ultimate arbiter of elusive truths.

Hawley once told her biographer, Bernadette McDonald, that paying attention to the "body language" of climbers was an important method for verifying the truth. When we refer to a body of work, a body of knowledge, it's easy to forget the human bodies that create them. Hawley's colleague Eberhard Jurgalski, in his late sixties, still spends long hours at his computer in Lörrach, Germany, maintaining lists of mountain data he has gathered for more than forty years. On his website, 8000ers.com, he houses up-to-date measurements of high peaks, a history of alpine record keepers, and a lengthy examination of the definitions of mountains around the world. He describes himself to me as a "map lover," saying, "You cannot explain it better than it's a passion." Like so much of journalism, however, he notices that fact-checking has become increasingly undervalued, often expected as a service for free. He has struggled to get enough donations even to maintain his website. Without financial support, the work of expert chroniclers like him may one day come to an end.

In the summer of 2019, questions about the accuracy of topographic knowledge arose again, this time on some of the most famous mountains in the world: Manaslu (26,781 feet/8,163 meters), Annapurna I (26,545 feet/8,091 meters), and Dhaulagiri I (26,795 feet/8,167 meters). After years of closely examining climbers' photos and social media posts, as well as new satellite imagery, an international team of researchers—including Jurgalski, Rodolphe Popier, Bob A. Schelfhout Aubertijn, Thaneswar Guragai, Damien Gildea, and Tobias Pantel—ascertained that many mountaineers didn't actually reach the real apex of the mountains they claimed to have climbed. Often, simply by error, they'd stopped at lower points that looked like summits instead. On 8000ers.com, Pantel noted a "hazy summit topography" on Manaslu where a ridge rises and falls over a series of fore-summits and a 90-degree bend hides the highest point from view. In another report by Popier, a satellite photo of the immense summit ridge on Annapurna I shows numerous bumps, the lowest of which is 26.8 meters below the tallest. And on Dhaulagiri I, a similarly confusing summit landscape includes a metal pole stuck in the wrong place. Jurgalski has suggested that historians could agree upon a "tolerance zone" for past ascents that ended, unbeknownst to the climbers, within a certain distance of the apexes. An "elite list" could be reserved for those who truly reached the top. Nonetheless, he concluded, given the potentially large number of inaccurate claims, "the whole 8000ers history should be rewritten."

By December 2019, Jurgalski told me there had been relatively little reaction to his fact-checking team's reports of missed or mistaken summits on Manaslu, Annapurna I, and Dhaulagiri I. For climbers who have based their careers on publicizing ascents, perhaps there's so much at stake that they might want to ignore or reject any news that puts their past assertions, explicitly or implicitly, into question. Social media is awash with embellished tales, and maybe many people have simply become accustomed to them.

In his 2020 *American Alpine Journal* report, Damien Gildea noted that for some alpinists, reaching the actual top doesn't seem as important as exploring difficult new terrain to a summit ridge or to an intersection with a previously established route. But in the case of peakbaggers, he affirmed, the matter is different: "These are trophy peaks, and you don't get a trophy for stopping at 90 meters in the 100-meter sprint." In the midst of a global pandemic, the correction of mountaineering records may appear increasingly futile and trivial. But we can imagine a future in which historians could add asterisks or footnotes to lists of past climbs. Mountaineers might one day return to complete ascents they now feel they'd left unfinished. New aspirants might race to become the first-of-whatever-category-to-reach-the-actual-apex of every 8000er. "This is history," Jurgalski said to me. "Why not tell the truth to people?"

There's another potential outcome to such discoveries, which overturn prior assumptions: a growing awareness of the limits of common ways of envisioning climbing. In the 1977 memoir *The Living Mountain*, Nan Shepherd wrote that alpine mirages and topographic illusions "drive home the truth that our habitual vision of things is not necessarily right: it is only one of an infinite number." Like Harvey in the North Cascades, she strove to encounter the "total mountain"—each crystal of ice and quartz, each arc of ridge and cadence of line, each light-struck hill and shadowed chasm, each curve of leaf and petal. This form of ascent can never be completed: the top of one peak is only part of an endless journey, far more demanding than any record book could ever contain. "If I had other senses, there are other things I should know," she wrote, and she added, "the thing to be known grows with the knowing."

---

SOMETIMES, AS HARVEY HAD KNOWN FROM HIS DAYS AT HIDDEN LAKE, the best way to escape from delusions of a thoroughly measured, finite world is to get absurdly lost. In 1939, after straying off route in the Italian Alps and erring up a summit that he couldn't find on his map, British poet Michael Roberts imagined compiling a compendium of disoriented climbers' accidental ascents, *The Climber's Guide to the Wrong Mountains*. "These exhibitions of our own foolishness are an intrinsic part of climbing," he argued in an Alpine Club lecture. Such reminders to maintain a sense of self-deprecating humor about our pursuits, he added, could help undercut tendencies to grandiosity and excessive Romanticism and provide a valuable "companion volume" to another proposed book, *The Climber's Guide to Imaginary Mountains*, which would list "those nameless symbolic mountains that haunt our imagination." By wandering off course on a mountain, we occasionally recover something more valuable than our original goals: a recollection of how to navigate beyond predetermined locations, a restored feeling of humility and awe.

One summer in the Tetons, a friend told me a story about a climber who became so disoriented by gaps between a terse guidebook description and the actual topography near a mountaintop that he thought, for a moment, he was making a first ascent. He was not actually lost, he only believed he was, but in that instant he experienced the illusion of climbing a new route on an unidentifiable peak. Soon afterward, I followed that same established route, and despite the warning I'd been given, I became nearly as baffled. In fragments of memory, I recall staggering through what seemed like a dream: across a deep-green sweep of meadow, over a dark spine of crumbling rock, into a realm that existed in the silences between words on the page. Had the effects of sleep deprivation, altitude, and exhaustion—and the influence of my friend's story—tinted my surroundings with an aura of enchantment? Or was it simply that I'd managed to become, for a moment, entirely adrift in wonder at the real, known world?

The abundance of crowd-sourced route descriptions and internet trip reports is often derided as removing the adventure and uncertainty from climbing. But while YouTube videos can display close-ups of each move on a difficult pitch, written information still depends on human memories, and its reliability is uneven. Vertical spaces remain notoriously difficult to convey in exact cartographic detail. Even small mountains have infinite fastnesses, formed of secluded alcoves and miniature crenellations like fragments of hidden interiors and fortress walls. In the summer of 2016, clutching a printout of an online topo, I scrambled just a few hundred feet from a crowded trail and into a bewilderment of arêtes and ravines. All sight and sound of other people vanished. Already, I was invisible, lost within a mountain's folds, the tangles of krummholz trees, and the mazes of jagged boulders. None of the geographic features around me matched the route lines or directions in the topo. Had the author of the trip report taken incorrect notes? I wondered. Was the topography simply too convoluted to capture in words?

As I traversed diagonally across a buttress that didn't exist on my piece of paper, I glanced down. Forests sank into the blue of distant valleys. A faraway lake shrank to an eye. The terrain below me now looked dangerous to descend: jumbles of steep, loose rocks. Above me, the way was clean and sharp: lines of white quartz and dark cracks, ramparts of stone and air. I made imaginary maps in my mind—this rock horn for one hand, the side of this wall for a foot, this edge so sharp it tore my fingers and would not let me fall. I tried to avoid touching any of the miniature gardens of alpine flowers that had grown in the crevices, perhaps undisturbed, for many years. Beyond the top of the buttress, I regained the trail, and I felt as if all that secret terrain had folded back inside my mind: a fragile, possibly forbidden, realm encountered by accident, never to be visited again.

Since that climb, I've come to think of the Riesenstein as a kind of alpine psychogeography: a map that misleads its readers in order to guide them toward a deeper perception of the wild. Some of the ideas behind the hoax might be even more popular now than they were in the 1960s. Many twenty-first–century authors have written nostalgically about "the lost art of getting lost." A plethora of books explore places that have disappeared from ordinary maps or that never existed in the physical world at all: *The Phantom Atlas* (2016), *Atlas of Vanishing Places* (2019), *Atlas of Lost Cities* (2016), *The Un-Discovered Islands* (2017), and so on. An entire online magazine founded in 2009, *Atlas Obscura*, is devoted to hidden, bizarre, or unconventional destinations.

In *A Place in Which to Search*, Vulgarian Joe Kelsey wrote of his own decades-long quest to experience a single region fully, including the corners that had been forgotten or misplaced on maps. After years of editing alpine journal trip reports, he recalled, "I became increasingly detached, disinterested in deeds of derring-do...while at the same time becoming more interested in simply being in the mountains." As he investigated cartographic gaps and errors in the Wind River Range for a local guidebook, Joe kept track of small things, such as an arrowhead on a summit ridge or a flower in a stone niche. "Simply seeing—seeing clearly, seeing detail—could be the ultimate gesture of reverence," he concluded. At night, he, too, began to have recurring dreams of an invisible, unattainable peak concealed behind a dense labyrinth of contour lines. To find it, he realized, he might have to learn how to go astray. "I, who consider intimacy with the landscape to be the goal of our wanderings, believe that the ultimate intimacy is being so lost that I have not the slightest idea where I am," he wrote. "I am not somewhere on a map; I am simply *there*."

There's a distinction, as the philosopher Walter Benjamin once wrote, between getting lost in a place and losing yourself there. The first is usually a result of inadequate information or human error. The second requires a deliberate, meditative, total immersion. In *A Field Guide to Getting Lost*, Rebecca Solnit explained that "to be lost [in the latter sense] is to be fully present, and to be fully present is to be capable of being in uncertainty and mystery. And one does not get lost but loses oneself, with the implication that it is a conscious choice, a chosen surrender, a psychic state achievable through geography." Solnit imagined a different kind of phantom range: peaks that turn translucent blue along the horizon. "The blue at the far edge of what can be seen . . ." she called it, "the color of longing for the distances you never arrive in." These blue mountains can never be truly climbed, since their enchanting color vanishes when we draw near. Instead of trying to satisfy this desire, she wrote, we could let go of the fixation with arrival or possession and realize the beauty of what cannot be reached or claimed.

In early 2020, having wrangled a six-month sabbatical from my job, I left Vermont for what I thought would be a short stay in the Bangtail Mountains of Montana. My plan was to spend a couple of months writing at the house of a family friend before traveling to some of the real ranges that inspired the fictitious ones. Instead, when the global pandemic arrived, I found myself sheltering in place for more than half a year. Day after day, I read books about imaginary mountains and gazed out the window. Foothills, spread in waves below me, turned white with winter snow, then green with the rain-rich hues of spring, and finally orange, gold, and brown with the searing heat of wildfire season. The faraway city of Bozeman vanished in the haze of midday, only to glitter at sunset like a field of crimson stars as the light struck thousands of west-facing windows.

Farther still, the Madison Range formed a pale, luminous skyline, its colors shifting from cerulean to lavender. One peak rose above the rest, at the vanishing point where all the lines of the landscape converged. Each evening, when the pyramidal summit caught the last fires of alpenglow, its beauty startled me into wonder. At times I dreamed of climbing it, but as the quarantine eased and I ventured farther from the house, I no longer wanted to reach its summit or even to know its name. The peak that held me spellbound wasn't one that I could ever trample with my feet. As Solnit might say, it existed only in the blue-tinted distance.

Lyrical descriptions of natural thresholds—such as alpine cols—appear throughout Harvey's guidebooks. His favorite kind of trail was one that took hikers right up to the edge of an unmarked space on a map, without actually venturing inside. Maybe there was another reason for this preference beyond his desire to protect the most fragile areas: an appreciation for the enchantment of gazing at unattainable places. The dusky mountains he saw from Marmot Pass as a boy could represent the *wild* to him because he couldn't yet climb them. There's something ineradicable about the way that human longings attach themselves to distant, gleaming summits—along with an inextinguishable hope, perhaps, that the improbable, the fantastical, and the transcendent might exist in some hidden part of the earth.

Joe Kelsey recently told me that as he has aged and become "content to merely *be* in the mountains," his own recurring dreams of imaginary peaks have changed. Now, instead of attempting to approach the unreal summits, he finds himself back at his desk, "trying to match a bewildering array of peaks with names on a map." And my repeated questions about the Riesenstein have had an effect, he said: "I remember waking from an imaginary-geography dream and being so impressed with its profundity—and with your project in mind—that I actually bothered to get up and sketch the map. I also remember thinking that the dream conveyed such an unforgettable message that I needn't write it down. If the unforgettable message ever comes back to me, you'll be the first to know."

---

WHEN I WAKE FROM MY MOUNTAIN DREAMS, AFTERIMAGES LINGER: A sheen of frozen waterfalls rising in tiers of incandescent blue, a broad slope of pine-shadowed snow. Faint contours of peaks evaporate into thin air leaving only vague impressions, like forgotten words at the rim of my memory, or a map burned to ash before I can finish tracing its lines.

Some of the messages of the Riesenstein and of other imagined peaks still await beyond the boundaries of ordinary cartography. There are infinite worlds of ice-lit citadels, alpine basins, and dark forests in the invisible places of the human heart. Faced with the sheer amount of modern data and satellite imagery, some modern mapmakers no longer feel the need to focus on pinpointing the exact locations of roads, hills, and rivers. Instead, they explore terrain in a multitude of imaginative and intuitive ways. The resulting work is "faithful to more than the measurable," as English artist and cartographer Tim Robinson wrote in *Setting Foot on the Shores of Connemara*, "that mysterious and neglected fourth dimension of cartography, one which extends deep into the self of the cartographer." A practitioner of what is now called "deep mapping," Robinson sought different vantage points to hint at the many subjective experiences of the Aran Islands of Ireland, sketching a "seagull's eye perspective" of their undulating coastal cliffs or laying a giant map of their hills on a gallery floor so visitors could wander across them and write their own stories of the land.

In certain ways, recent artistic cartographies resemble the *mappa mundi* of the Middle Ages: their summits are landmarks along inner journeys; their topographies suggest directions for how to reach particular states of mind. "Continually being mapped and unmapped," British geographer Richard Phillips observes, "the geography of adventure, like the space of the map, is more fluid and adaptable than is sometimes apparent." While charts and stories of exploration can replicate old forms of colonialism and imperialism, they can also shatter them, Phillips suggests, offering "sites of resistance," settings for the transgression of "boundaries and conventions." If an imaginary peak is a creation of desire, its very elusiveness can hint at something unconquerable. As Harvey knew, the invention of mythic landscapes can be one way to try to change the real world—an act of revolt. "Why do we want to have alternate worlds?" asked the fantasy writer Joan Aiken in *Locus Magazine*. "You have to imagine something before you do it."

Harvey had a penchant for making up peak names—whether the Issaquah Alps or No Name Peak or the Riesenstein. But he also advocated for some real Native names. He knew that the "Big Steal," as he called white settlers' appropriation of Indigenous lands, was still going on in his time. In a May 1988 article for the *Mountaineer*, Harvey urged his readers to write to the Washington State Board on Geographic Names and to demand a restoration of the Lushootseed term *Whulj* to at least part of the area around

Puget Sound. Observing in *Cool Clear Water* that local Quinault people were doing a much better job of ecological conservation than white land managers were, he also suggested that the beaches should be placed under Indigenous administration again.

A corollary to the imagining of ideal, unmappable places is the realization that what is truly important has never been on colonialist maps at all. Far too frequently, non-Indigenous mountaineers have assumed that their pursuit of spiritual experiences was more important than the religious practices of people who have been stewards of the land for thousands of years. Even in recent years, some climbers have refused to respect the voluntary June closure of Bear Lodge (Devils Tower), a policy enacted to make space for the ceremonies of Lakota, Tsitsistas and Arapaho people, as well as those of other Native American tribes. But current writers, artists, activists, and cartographers also use mapmaking tools to retrace the heritages of marginalized groups or to reclaim ancestral lands. "Mapping has been the tool of empires and governments for 500 years," Hofstra University geography professor Craig Dalton reflected in an interview with MapLab. "What happens when maps get into the hands of people who've been victims of cartographic sleights of hand?" In a 1995 article for *Antipode*, Nancy Lee Peluso described how residents of Kalimantan on the island of Borneo drew their own maps to reassert their traditional rights to forests: "Local groups can claim power through mapping by using not only what is on a map but what is *not* on it. . . . Alternative maps, or 'counter-maps' . . . greatly increase the power of people living in a mapped area to control representations of themselves and their claims to resources."

In a multimedia installation filmed by the Art Gallery of Ontario in 2014, artist Bonnie Devine applies bright brushstrokes across a nineteenth-century map of Canada and beyond its margins onto the surrounding gallery walls. A member of the Serpent River First Nation (Anishinaabe and Ojibwe territory), Devine paints images that narrate how European settlers transformed the landscape: the incursions of white soldiers, the loss of woodlands, and the fleeing of wildlife. With those changes, she explains, came "the gradual erosion of the understanding that this was our land and that we had free passage here." In contrast to colonialist notions of North American "wilderness" as a place devoid of previous history or of Native residents as "vanished races," she creates basket-woven sculptures of human figures that remind audiences of the abiding presence of modern Indigenous people. This form of artistic cartography can be more accurate than official maps: it demonstrates ways of envisioning the world that are closer to what was and to what still is there.

The rise of diversity among North American climbers is also helping to change representations of vertical landscapes. Activists from a wide range of backgrounds are demanding the removal of sexist, racist, and anti-LGBTQA+ climbing route names from print and online guides. Navajo/Diné mountaineer Len Necefer now geotags ascents with Indigenous names of each peak as a way to remind his Instagram followers of the original stories and residents of mountain ranges. Similarly, an interactive digital atlas, hosted on the Pan Inuit Trails website, depicts traditional Inuit routes and place names in regions that were known to Indigenous people long before European explorers searched for the Northwest Passage or John Ross sighted his imaginary "Croker's Mountains." In 2015, after generations of advocates had pushed for a return to the Koyukon Dene name, "Denali" finally replaced "McKinley" as the designation for North America's highest peak.

There are other invisible cartographies that can be restored behind the maps of the Kichatnas and the Riesenstein. Shem Pete (K'etech'ayutiłen), a Dena'ina storyteller, was born around the time of Spurr's and Herron's expeditions. By the end of Shem Pete's life, he'd traveled by boat and on foot across almost 13,500 square miles of Alaskan backcountry, becoming familiar with Indigenous names, tales, and songs "all over the hills and mountains," as he recounted. During the 1970s and '80s, he and other Indigenous people worked with linguist James Kari and anthropologist James A. Fall to compile an atlas of Native geography. First published in 1987, *Shem Pete's Alaska* places the actual Dena'ina terms back on top of the sepia-hued map that Herron had created of the range so many years ago.

CHAPTER 24

# The Return to Marmot Pass

FOR DECADES, HARVEY MANNING DIDN'T go back to Marmot Pass. He was afraid that the forests and meadows, where he'd first experienced that sense of revelation, would be thrumming with motorcycles and pockmarked with stumps. In 1984, after the passage of the Washington State Wilderness Act, he felt ready to return: "The new Buckhorn Wilderness meant I could . . . go home again. Not the whole of it, of course. The Forest Service had pushed the road beyond Bark Shanty. . . . At the shelter cabin by the creek where in 1938 we'd stopped for a lunch of Sailor Boy pilot bread, cheese, raisins, and chocolate, the cars now were parked—and exactly there was the brandnew sign announcing (be still my heart) 'wilderness boundary.'"

Many more visitors had stayed at Camp Mystery since Harvey and the other Boy Scouts had curled up in sleeping bags beneath the branches and the stars. Yet on the day that Harvey arrived with his pet Shelties, curtains of soft, cold rain brought "an old-time solitude," he wrote. "I felt like somebody not me . . . a time traveler, an explorer of alternate, parallel worlds." As Harvey plodded up the old trail, he felt like a young boy again. He imagined George Mallory and Sandy Irvine vanishing into the mists on Everest. He pictured Scouts tromping up the broken, ruddy stone of Iron Mountain—a peak that first aroused, and then extinguished, the dreams of prospectors. He shuddered in the damp air and he could see his childhood self, once more, hiking toward Marmot Pass to stay warm. "I was alone in the fog at Marmot Pass," he recounted. "Everything was as it had been. . . . Except for the sunset, of course, though through the rain I could reconstruct the one of 1938."

One by one, Harvey conjured old memories: of the meadows that arched ever higher until they blurred into a rose-colored sky, of the darkness that drifted up the valley on the other side, of the distant sound of cascading water from the river that ran, invisible, through the twilit shadows far below.

The next morning, the mists parted, he recalled, "and as in a dream I drifted through flowers again to Marmot Pass and contoured the meadow slopes to . . . The Encounter." Here, as a boy, he'd once thought he'd had a vision of "the World-as-it-Should-Be." Now, he saw a coyote a few dozen feet below him, and he remembered some of the tales told by Indigenous people—who explored and lived in the Pacific Northwest long before his own wanderings, hoaxes, and dreams, and who still maintained their deep connection to the range. "He loved to play practical jokes," Harvey wrote of the trickster hero Coyote, "but he was a nice guy, knew his way around the country, knew things the People needed to know." As Harvey watched, the coyote lifted his head to the sky and began to ululate. "He may have been talking to the Shelties," Harvey recalled. "No interest in me at all. . . . Half an hour he sat there, interjecting into the song occasional sharp barks and long howls. Then, abruptly, he turned and disappeared down the mountain, having told me (and/or the Shelties) all he had on his mind. I now know everything I needed to know."

---

IN AUGUST 2019, I MADE MY OWN PILGRIMAGE TO MARMOT PASS. AT the trailhead, green shadows of the trees closed in around me as if I'd stepped into a vernal pool. Camp Mystery was empty: silent spaces and evergreen groves. Higher up the trail, meadows dazzled with flowers, just as Harvey had described, though the grass was turning golden with autumn. A bright sea fog blew across the pass, hiding and revealing craggy summits. When the mists parted, I, too, stared into a tree-darkened wild so deep it seemed to resonate with its own low chords. Above the pass, I continued to Buckhorn Mountain. Somewhere near the summit, Harvey had watched Monie climb a short, glassy cliff that seemed to lack even the vaguest ripples of holds. I imagined myself following her ghost as I scrambled up one of the reddish summit boulders. Its polished surface reflected back only the sun and sky. I perched on the top for a while, bewildered by wind and light.

On another evening, I stopped in Issaquah to see the bronze statue of Harvey that sits on a rock in a small park. He looks up, with an expression that seems almost plaintive, at the forest-green summits high above the streets. In his shirt pocket, there's a spiral-bound notebook and a hole where a pen might go, or where visitors might place the stem of a flower. A nearby board displays tributes. In one, Ken Konigsmark of the Issaquah Alps Trails Club wrote: "Two words immediately come to mind when I learned that Harvey Manning had died: 'legend,' and 'cantankerous.' He was both. Why a legend? We simply wouldn't have the open spaces we enjoy today were it not for Harvey's efforts. . . . Why cantankerous? Anyone who knew Harvey knew that he could mercilessly skewer his target by pen or spoken word, and it usually didn't matter if you were friend or foe."

"Curmudgeon" was another word that Harvey's friends often used to describe him. And as a satirist, he could be hard to pin down. Particularly in his unpublished writings, his prose appears to shape-shift continually, not only between fact and fiction, but also between serious meaning and parody, between mockery of others and of himself. He couldn't always be idealized, nor, it seemed, did he want to be. John Edwards, an editorial board member, acknowledged in *The Wild Cascades* that Harvey would "almost certainly . . . not have approved" of being sculpted in bronze and placed on a pedestal. I remembered something that Harvey's son, Paul, had said: "Statues don't talk back. A person, when they die, becomes communal property. . . . Heroes, of course, live in a totally different kind of universe and are a totally different kind of being than a living, breathing person." With his death, Harvey himself had become a quasi-imaginary figure—a projection of other people's memories, rumors, and ideas. I'd spent more than five years sifting through his notes and manuscripts, and talking with his family, colleagues, and friends. As I'd explored Harvey's imaginary worlds, how could I be sure that I wasn't just re-creating more regions of my own dream mountain, filtering each discovery through my expectations of what I might find?

Near nightfall, I drove to the Harvey Manning Trailhead (named in 2016, a decade after his death) at the edge of Cougar Mountain Regional Wildland Park. As the first branches arched above the asphalt road, I gasped: the subdivisions of Issaquah blinked out in an instant. The forest ahead was hardly a wilderness in the usual sense of the term, and yet it appeared haunting, almost primeval. Soon, even the recollection of houses, pavement, and yards seemed lost within the verdant darkness of tall trees, thick moss, and giant ferns. Dusk drifted through the bluish air as I walked past the junction with the Shangri La Trail. There was no one else in sight. In the growing dark, the woods seemed to multiply. The last light flared and then turned ashen as it faded between endless leaves.

I continued driving deep into the Cascades the next day, hoping to find a place that Harvey had considered his "home," where his family had scattered his ashes. Near a parking lot, a picture of official paths showed wriggling burgundy lines. My destination lay somewhere in the blank orange space beyond them marked "Wilderness Boundary." I was looking for a particular location within an alpine basin concealed behind steep ridges: a realm of wildflower meadows below a waterfall and a snowy peak. It sounded like something from an old legend or from one of Harvey's fantasies. The unmarked trail that was supposed to lead me there didn't appear on any of the paper maps I'd found. But I was certain this spot was real. Paul had emailed me a digitized map with a line he'd added to show the path. Harvey's daughter Claudia had sent me photos of the family's most recent visit. As with many seemingly hidden places in the internet age, patchy information appeared in obscure parts of the Web. (Later, I noticed sparse references in a few of Harvey's older guidebooks.) It still didn't seem easy to find. Long before you reach the unmarked path, one blogger warned, the named trails branch in confusing ways, not always corresponding to lines on any maps.

When I left the parking lot, late summer sun filled the woods and fields with a dusty shimmer of gold. I've never gotten in the habit of using GPS. Instead, I paused at each bewildering junction to stare at a crumpled stack of contradictory printouts and topographic maps. Often, I simply guessed which was the correct way. As I contoured a mountainside of dark evergreens, I kept looking for the unmarked trail, wondering at each dim imprint of footfalls amid the grass and rocks. A backpacker appeared around a corner, and he told me that he was just returning from the place I sought. He and his friends had built a cairn to mark the path. He said the alpine basin exceeded any of his expectations. It was, he believed, the most beautiful place in the world. I walked on, following his directions, to a narrow track that led up a steep hillside, around a rampart of cliffs, to the top of a sudden pass, and through the space between two giant evergreens that rose like an opened doorway to another realm.

It was as if so many wanderers' dreams had coalesced into one place: the green-gold grassy slopes that sparkled with flowers, the snowy dome that glowed beyond dark fins of rock, the jagged peaks that surrounded this inner world and concealed it from outside view. I remembered the Buddhist stories of beyul and the Xanadu of Coleridge's poem: "With walls and towers . . . girdled round . . . forests ancient as the hills, / Enfolding sunny spots of greenery." I recalled Shipton's description of Nanda Devi: "My most blissful dream as a child was to be in some such valley, free to wander where I liked. . . . Now the reality was no less wonderful than that half-forgotten dream; and of how many childish fancies can that be said, in this age of disillusionment?" Perhaps, Harvey also felt, for a moment, that he'd found the ideal imaginary peak of his childhood in the real world. This wasn't the Riesenstein, of course, but it might have come closer to the wild regions of Harvey's heart than any sleet-battered spire in Alaska. Here, there wasn't even the illusion this was untouched land. Dirt paths were worn into lush meadows. Old campfires were marked by charred logs. Sunlight reflected off the faint indents of feet in the tall grass. The wonder was undiminished.

I tried to memorize how the sun blazed through clusters of yellow petals, how a cascade glittered across polished, almost iridescent rocks, how groves of evergreens encircled meadows within meadows, worlds within worlds. At last, I realized I should hike back out, through the maze of branching paths, before dark. With each step, I felt the steady loss, in my own life, of this place. Even if I returned, I would never again see it this way: in this fleeting burst of late-summer light, in the startled awe of encountering it for my first time.

By the time I neared the parking lot, after hours of continual walking, my body felt almost weightless, as ephemeral and transparent as the dust that hung, suspended, in the twilit air. The final rays of sun lingered on the hillsides above me, illuminating boughs of evergreens with a beauty that seemed almost unbearably gentle and fleeting. Close by, crisp shadows outlined countless blades of grass, petals, and leaves. I thought of Harvey's many trips here and of the hike that he might have guessed would be his last. I thought of what it means to move through a landscape that someone else has deeply loved, whether something of that person remains in it. I imagined how he might have known each tree and branch, each gentle curve and ragged line of peak and ridge; how he might have recognized the way the small, bright faces of flowers still turned toward the fading light as the soft gold of evening lit the pines. It was hard to believe that kind of love, for any place or anything, could ever be wholly lost.

A few days later, on September 2, I learned that Jean Crenshaw had died at age ninety-five, a year after her fellow *Summit* editor Helen Kilness had passed away. From the clifftop of Summit House, like Harvey on Cougar Mountain, they, too, had kept an eye on the ongoing issues of the mountaineering world. During my visit in 2014, Jean had shared her indignation about the recent deaths of sixteen Nepali expedition workers when an avalanche roared through the crevasses, pinnacles, and ladders of the Khumbu Icefall on Everest. "Sherpas need the money to support their families," she told me. "Climbers select the danger. It's their lifestyle, their choice." Of the commercialism that creeps into high-mountain tourism and the apparent disregard for human life, she added, "It's horrible even to think of."

In their quiet way, Jean and Helen had offered an alternative approach to climbing: through the articles they'd chosen to publish in *Summit*, through the humble layout of its pages, and through the collections of words and images that emphasized the camaraderie of their formative mountaineering days and their earnest delight in the beauty of the natural world. Although they rarely printed anything in their own voice, their spirit is everywhere in old issues of the magazine. Climbing history tends to focus on measurable peaks and quantifiable records. But there are other layers buried beneath accounts of the first, the hardest, the fastest, and the highest: the perspectives of lesser-known climbers, writers, and mountain wanderers, who have no interest in setting records or claiming conquests, but who simply seek, as Eric Shipton once put it, a means of "identifying . . . with this enchanting world." There's the drifting of winter light over a flow of blue ice, the slow growth of a bristlecone pine, the quickening of a mind to wonder—all those elements that mostly vanish through the lacunae of history and that *Summit*, in its own way, documented so well. Doug Robinson, an early reader, told me that as he leafs through old issues, "bits and pieces come surging back into memory," entire private worlds of glistening domes, alpine meadows, and distant laughter, hidden between the covers for decades, released at the touch of a hand.

I can still dream my way back to Summit House. I can glimpse the golden oak leaves that shone beneath my feet when Helen and I went for a walk along the mountainsides together. I can feel the rough crystals of granite beneath my hands as I climbed the boulders in their garden, while Jean pointed out routes with her cane. I can squint and see the sapphire glimmer of the distant lake between the trees. I can walk through their doorway in my mind, into the interior of the building, cool as a mountain cave, where Jean took out a series of black-and-white photos from a box she kept tucked away. I can summon up the image of her in a white military uniform, her smile full of authority and charisma. I can recall the photo of Helen where she leans back against their motorcycle, gazing, wide-eyed, curious and gentle, at the world. Jean told me that she was briefly engaged to an enlisted man. "But he went down with his ship. Afterward, I said I would never get married. And I never did. The magazine became my life."

Between the lines of the stories that appeared in *Summit*, there's another, invisible, history of life lived at the rhythm of pitches, the running of a press, the shuffling of feet on forest trails, and the moment of sitting down before a blank piece of paper, that, no matter how often repeated, feels endlessly new. There's the bond between two women that lasted for three quarters of a century. And there's the house they shared, grown increasingly precarious with age, and yet still wondrous, still perched improbably on top of its crag.

"It's been real nice living here," Helen told me. "I enjoyed every moment, just living surrounded by birds, deer, trees, being out in the mountains." On the evening of my last day with them, the light deepened to rose and gold. One of their two small terriers gently washed the face of the other, now ailing. "Climbing gives you a good attitude toward danger," Jean said, when I asked her what she loved about our pursuit. "Climbing makes you accept life as it is. It's a good, clean life, to climb mountains. A good feeling when you get to the top." She knew the risks her writers faced. In quiet moments, she faced them, too. "I would always leave my desk in order because I might not come back," she said. She accepted the idea of her own death. "It just means that you might not come back."

Night fell on us so quickly it happened without warning. One minute the sky was still lit, and then it was dark. Soon the first snows would pile drifts as high as six feet; soon they'd have to move down to their second house in the valley. Someday, they would no longer be able to maintain this mountain home at all. Jean said she thought she was still strong enough to run the tractor to plow the road. She insisted they could spend one more winter here. "I'm dragging my feet," she told me. "I don't want to go."

I didn't want to go either. Summit House remains a haven in my memory, an emblem of how my life might be if I could build my own realm to devote to work, to mountains, to a community, and to another person. Among all the tales of imaginary ranges, I find myself returning to a 1979 German novel by Michael Ende, *The Neverending Story* (the 1984 movie adaptation includes only a fragment of the original plot). In the book's imaginary world of Fantastica, the Mountain of Destiny rises all the way into the heavens. Snowstorms and avalanches swirl into every nook and cranny of its icy pinnacles and twisted gullies. Nobody can reach its summit until all previous ascents have slipped from memory. When the protagonist, Bastian, enters Fantastica, he re-creates its landscapes and history with each conscious and unconscious longing that he feels. He soon learns that his desires can have unexpected consequences, resulting in violence, oppression, and war. The only way he can redeem himself and stop destroying Fantastica is to uncover his true innermost wish, beyond all illusions. So he continues wandering and erring, uncertain whether he's getting any closer to his destination. He never climbs the mountain. Instead, he finds that the answer to his search is a kind of all-encompassing, self-relinquishing love.

As a conclusion for a story, love seems simple and commonplace. Yet at the same time, it remains mysterious and irreducible, requiring fathomless caring and responsibility. A number of the climbers who were drawn into Harvey's plot ended up discovering something far more significant than the possibility of first ascents: a deep love for each other and for the earth. During the most focused moments of any climb, all prior knowledge seems to fade. We re-create a world for ourselves, at once ephemeral and eternal. Its cartography might fluctuate like patterns of light through stained glass, radiant and shifting, both real and intangible. To Swiss psychologist Carl Jung, whose ideas on myth rose to prominence in the early twentieth century, dream mountains were metaphors for the unconscious self, a realm that offers unlimited space for exploration. René Daumal unfortunately died before he could finish his novel *Mount Analogue*, but in the last chapter he planned to ask his readers: "And you, what do you seek?" Daumal's notes make it clear that he believed some answers had dangerous consequences. He wrote of a second group that went to look for Mount Analogue. This team wasn't motivated by the spiritual aspirations of the first expedition, but by a belief that they would find "oil, gold, and other earthly riches" hidden within the superlative peak. They set out in a warship, intent on conquering the mountainous island for themselves. Yet as they prepared to open fire on the local residents, they found themselves trapped in a whirlpool. "Condemned to turn around and around," Daumal wrote, "they were still able to bombard the coast, but all their projectiles came back to them like boomerangs."

Symbols of aspiration and transcendence, the shapes of imaginary peaks have mirrored back a multitude of conflicting answers about what it is that dreamers most desire: a union with the divine, a pursuit of conquest, an act of resistance, a search for glory or wealth, an escape from the real world, an elixir of immortality or at least longevity, a shedding of egoism for transcendent love, or a means to reconnect with nature, cultural traditions, communities and friends. "In the middle of the night," climbing novelist Jeff Long once said to my fellow *Alpinist* editor Paula LaRochelle, "stands a mountain all your own, an invisible mountain. . . . Like René Daumal's Mount Analogue, it is a mountain you will never summit. Or maybe, like Mallory on Everest, one that you may finish but out of sight in clouds of mystery or smoke." I'm still not sure what my own dream mountain represents. All I know is that my longing for something nebulous and unnamed persists. If I had to pick a word, the closest one I can think of, now, is *hope*.

---

LIKE HELEN AND JEAN, I'VE ALSO WONDERED ABOUT THE HOAXES I might have missed as a climbing magazine editor. One of my writers, Ueli Steck, was accused of fabricating his report of a solo first ascent of a route on the South Face of Annapurna in 2013. I couldn't believe he was guilty. While working with him on a story about the climb, I'd felt as though I could see, hear, and feel the mountain at night: the light of a headlamp glancing off silver runnels of ice and snow, the explosion of stars above the summit ridge, the sounds of frozen shards falling beneath an axe like broken crystal, and the numbing creep of high-altitude cold.

All the clues for or against him—the lack of summit photos because of a dropped camera, the absence of evidence from his GPS tracker (which he hadn't turned on), the two members who spoke of a headlamp seen high on the South Face and the one who noticed only empty darkness when he glanced up, the sheer number of investigations across media platforms, and the accumulated words of climbers, friends, and critics who weren't present at the time but who nonetheless supported Ueli or doubted him—none of it added up to definitive proof beyond the shadow of any doubt that he had or hadn't reached the summit. In the end, these decisions are still influenced by what we think we know about a person's character, so often based on intuition or wishful thinking. In 2017, Ueli was climbing alone, again, on the icy north face of Nuptse, a high peak in Nepal, when he somehow slipped and fell thousands of feet down the mountain. His loss left a void as stark and cold as a crevasse. I cared about Ueli, and I grieve his death.

More than a decade prior, during the 2005 Banff Centre Mountain Film and Book Festival, I sat in the now-vanished Kiln Café, listening to a well-known alpinist complain about modern climbers who seemed to overhype and embellish their trip reports. "It would not be that hard," he said, as he turned to me, with a sudden focus in his gaze, "to pass off a fake climb in today's media." I stared back at him. Back then, I was new to working at *Alpinist*, and I wasn't sure what would be best to say. Part of me was afraid to confess how vulnerable I felt. Of course, I knew that inadvertent errors big and small crept into any publication, including ours. It was certainly possible that we'd been duped before and that we would be again. But what about an entirely false ascent, from beginning to end, by someone who hadn't even arrived at the base camp of a mountain? A hoax designed by someone like this grinning man before me, who had no desire to inflate his resume or to make any lasting false claims, but who might just want to prove a point about the unreliability of all narratives?

I considered the reams of questions our fact-checkers asked and the hours we spent poring over maps and archives, but I also remembered the times when we'd had no choice except to decide whether or not we trusted someone. Then I thought about how the digital age had pressured us to publish faster and faster, about the readers who expected news reports almost as soon as events happened, and about the late nights that reporters worked to give them what they wanted. It's all too easy to cut corners or to miss something when you're rushed and tired. It's hard not to assume that a well-respected climber is telling the truth. "Yes," I conceded, though I no longer remember whether I dared to speak these words out loud. "It could be done." I do, however, recall saying in an embarrassingly pleading tone: "Please, if you're going to try that kind of hoax, don't do it to me." The alpinist laughed and left the café.

Outside, the lambent gloom of early November filled the air with a perpetual slate-gray twilight. Beyond the town of Banff, Alberta, the woods seemed to stretch forever into dark-green stillness. Sharp, rocky peaks rose, in hues of silver and ash like shards of dreams. Humans have lived here, too, for thousands of years. When early colonial mountaineers arrived to make their "discoveries," they were often led by Īyāȟé Nakoda guides who knew the ranges well and who had their own names for the summits. A few unclimbed alpine routes remained scattered here and there above the valleys—nooks and crannies of untouched stone, fleeting wonderlands of ice that formed and melted again. But it wasn't the remnants of *terra incognita* or *terra miscognita* that I longed to encounter. Each vista of limestone and evergreen, each shift of light and shadow over the ridgelines, each curve and contour of the land, each crystal of snow and eddy of wind, possessed far more presence and mystery than I could ever understand. As Arctic explorer Robert E. Peary had predicted in 1904, communications technology has continued to advance since the early days of wireless telegraphs and "the atmosphere of the globe" now "throb[s] incessantly with countless messages." Amid the unrelenting streams of information, however, persist innumerable fragments of inaccuracies, hypotheses, and dreams. So much irreducible mystery remains—even in what many of us think of as the *known*.

In the 1946 fiction story "On Exactitude in Science," Argentine writer Jorge Luis Borges envisioned a map that would be the same scale as the territory of an imaginary empire, each mark on paper corresponding exactly to each feature in the landscape. I've tried to picture what such a map might look like. Perhaps it would paper over the entire earth, replicating mountains in three-dimensional forms instead of distorting them into symbols on a two-dimensional page. Or maybe it would update instantly to portray the calving of a glacier, the fall of a tree, or the washing away of a grain of coastline sand. Could it capture each facet of quartz along a ridge of stone, each minute bend in a glacial river, with infinitely spiraling, fractal-like forms? Would this map show the world as a deity might see it, displaying some transcendent vision of truth beyond the limits of representation? Would it include all the particular, shifting perspectives of cartographers and map readers and their relationships with the land? Or would it simply be redundant, a 1:1 copy of terrain that we might experience better by physically walking outside rather than by perusing any virtual simulacrum?

The inhabitants in Borges's story decided that their map had no use, and they threw it out. Over time, the sun bleached away its lines and colors, while the rain, snow, and wind tore apart its surface. In the end, only ragged pieces remained, fluttering in the deserts of the West. Perhaps it became just another replication of multiple experiences of reality, refracted through the subjective visions and beliefs of countless individuals, a vision as ultimately baffling as the world that stretches out before us. All maps, in the end, will always be imaginary.

---

THERE'S A MOMENT NEAR THE BEGINNING OF *MOUNT ANALOGUE* WHEN the narrator has just published a story about a far-fetched, superlative peak, an account that he believes is merely a literary exercise. He is then astounded when a reader shows up at his office, tells him that the mountain actually exists, and invites him on an expedition to search for it. Nearly a decade has passed since I first read about the Riesenstein. While I know the imaginary version of those mountains exists only as fantasy, satire, and allegory, I, too, can't help wishing I could keep looking for them. Perhaps, like Glenn Woodsworth, I'll venture one day to that tangled region of woods, peaks, and stories near the Skeena River. I'll carry the hoaxers' map to the place where the Klawatti River doesn't flow, and I'll see what I might yet encounter in that confluence of the real and the unreal.

Even so, I realize that I'm more likely to stumble upon the Riesenstein in my dreams than in the waking world. "There are some things of which I cannot at once tell whether I have dreamed them or they are real: as if they were just, perchance, establishing, or else losing, a real basis in my world," Henry David Thoreau wrote in his journal on October 29, 1857. "This is especially the case in the early morning hours, when there is a gradual transition from dreams to waking thoughts, from illusions to actualities, as from darkness, or perchance moon and starlight, to sunlight." Throughout his writings, Thoreau used language from the history of imaginary voyages to urge his readers to explore wild spaces near their homes and within their minds instead. In his own memoirs, Harvey Manning recounted with admiration that "Thoreau, having listened patiently to hours of gushing by a gadabout just returned from a Grand Tour of Europe, was asked, 'So Henry, what have you been up to?' His answer: 'I have traveled a good deal in Concord.'" Unlike John Muir, Thoreau didn't desire the illusion of an Edenic "wilderness" without human residents. And in his most well-known book, *Walden*, Thoreau rebuked some of the protagonists of the quests for the Mountains of Kong and the Northwest Passage: "Be rather the Mungo Park, the Lewis and Clark and Frobisher, of your own streams and oceans; explore your own higher latitudes."

Often, when Thoreau woke in his home in Concord, Massachusetts, the same vision receded from his mind: asleep, he'd crossed the boundaries into an otherworld to the east of town, where a dim wood fringed the base of a great mountain. Alone, he'd trembled as he scrambled up its stony crest, past the bent shapes of krummholz trees and the shadows of feral creatures. "I lost myself quite in the upper air and clouds," he recalled, "seeming to pass an imaginary line which separates a hill, mere earth heaped up, from a mountain, into a superterranean grandeur and sublimity. . . . It can never become familiar; you are lost the moment you set foot there. You know no path, but wander, thrilled, over the bare and pathless rock, as if it were solidified air and cloud."

The summit remained half-hidden, a blocky silhouette in a shimmer of clouds. For a moment, he felt as though he'd been transported into an ethereal realm. Then the contours of the peak dissolved in the morning sky, like the facets of a giant ice crystal melting before the New England farms and the low hills. "It is a promised land, which I have not yet earned," he concluded.

I grew up only a short walk from Thoreau's cabin. From my mother's house, I often descended through the dark hemlock groves, contoured the green-leafed shores of Flint's Pond, and hiked over the faint swell of Pine Hill. Ahead, summer crowds of tourists and pilgrims tramped beside Walden Pond, seeking communion with Thoreau's memory, while the sound of a commuter train echoed loon-like from the far side. In those days, I thought of Walden as simply a place to swim. It wasn't until recently that I read Thoreau's writing in depth. When I came across his October 29 journal entry, the familiar landmarks of my childhood, described in nineteenth-century prose, stirred memories of August haze thick as maple syrup, of vistas hemmed by branches, of slopes too gentle and rocks too small for climbing. I remembered my own explorations of an imaginary summit near the same place. "Dreams are real," Thoreau asserted, "as is the light of the stars and moon." And when I finally read those words, I felt a sudden recognition: Near Concord, of course. That mountain exists. Night after night, I've attempted it, too.

I still think it's possible to find places beyond the gridlines of longitude and latitude or the furrows of contour intervals and marked boundaries. Even the most sophisticated modern cartographers can't capture all the infinite complexities of ice and stone. They can't fully express the changes with time or the vagaries of our emotions and perceptions. Far too often, stories and maps of climbers have erased the prior knowledge and worldviews of local and Indigenous peoples, replacing them with new, imported symbols and fantasies. In some ways, the tales of the Riesenstein reflect these problems. Yet by comparing physical and imagined geographies, we can remember that there are other reasons for approaching mountains besides those of conquest, appropriation, and possession. And we can ask ourselves what it might mean to unmake the maps. To search for everything that escaped from them—and everything that only seemed to be lost.

Dale Cole once told me that "Harvey Manning and I spent much time thinking on how we could make the world a better place. A hoax now and then seemed a likely way." To explain what he meant, Dale added that Harvey loved to quote a few lines from *A Shropshire Lad*, a collection of poems written by A. E. Housman in 1896:

> Ale, man, ale's the stuff to drink
> For fellows whom it hurts to think:
> Look into the pewter pot
> To see the world as the world's not.
> And faith, 'tis pleasant till 'tis past:
> The mischief is that 'twill not last.

---

IMAGINARY PEAKS INVITE US "TO SEE THE WORLD AS THE WORLD'S not." But they might also show us how the world could be. How can we explore such landscapes of possibility? Rebecca Solnit provides one of the best answers in *A Field Guide to Getting Lost*: "Mystery. That much is certain. It can be a kind of compass."

I'm still trying to follow that compass in my dreams. Since childhood, I've wandered up and down knobby ridgelines that vanish into mist, or traversed along narrow ledges and broken staircases that spiral up ancient tower walls. I've never arrived at a final high point, though I've met many other seekers and learned of endless, untold quests. Once you begin to look for imaginary peaks, you start to see them everywhere: each furrow of crag and hill has its own local myths; each square of map conceals forgotten phantom heights. Each human mind contains innumerable ranges, sparkling like starlight and like snow.

The real Kichatnas of Alaska have been climbed. But no one, it seems, has ever reached the last invisible summit of the Riesenstein. As the editors of *Summit* once asked: "Who will be the first to climb it?"

# ACKNOWLEDGMENTS

A MULTITUDE OF PEOPLE MADE this book possible. Many answered research questions or contributed interviews, advice or information, including: Margaret Anderson, Anka and Burt Angrist, Paul Longley Arthur, Meera Baindur, Ian Baker, Lawrence Bamblett, Daniel Barbarisi, Thomas Bassett, Irene Beardsley, Judith Hudson Beattie, Randi Beck, Fred Beckey, Donald Beecher, Jeff Benowitz, Brownell Bergen, George Bloom, Whitney Boland, Cynthia Brewer, Amy Brockhaus, Heidi Brooks, Jerry Brotton, Robert Bryce, Katia Buffetrille, Colin Calloway, David Cameron, Ernesto Capello, Keith Thor Carlson, Siobhan Carroll, Bill Chapman, Albrecht Classen, Dale Cole, Kelly Cordes, Jean Crenshaw, Craig Dalton, Lauren Danner, Art Davidson, Jim Davis, Bernard Debarbieux, Veronica della Dora, Al DeMaria, Amrita Dhar, Kunda Dixit, Ed Douglas, Carolyn Driedger, Jaś Elsner, Timothy Evans, Bruce Fairley, Unn Falkeid, James Fall, Phil Fenner, Doug Fesler, Dick Fiddler, Joe Fitschen, Richard and Shirley Flint, Dave Fluharty, Ananda Foley, Andrew Fountain, Christian Fracchia, Claude Gardien, Frances Garrett, Pete Geiser, Damien Gildea, Stephen Goodwin, Mike Graber, Maggie Greene, Virginie Greene, Rachel Gross, Andrew Gulliford, Peter Hansen, Tyler Harvey, John Hessler, David Hirst, Tami Hohn, Martin Hood, Meg Hunt, Maurice Isserman, Jack Ives, Sarah Jacoby, Joan Jensen, Lin Jensen, Steven Jervis, Erik Johnson, Dave Johnston and Cari Sayre, Eberhard Jurgalski, Harish Kapadia, David Kappler, Sarah Kareem, James Kari, Joe Kelsey, Michael Kennedy, Helen Kilness, Kerwin Klein, Tami Knight, Peter Kuznick, Roman Laba, Lisa Labovitch, Michael Layton, Charisma Lepcha, Louise Lindgren, Jeff Long, John Long, Siwei Lyu, Ian Mabbett, Claudia Manning, Paul Manning, David Mark, Rich Marriott, Elaine Matthews, Ridwan Maulana, John McCannon, Jim McCarthy, Doug McClelland, Rick McGuire, Jerry McLain, Jennifer Mercer, Murat Cem Mengüç, Cole Messa, Rick Millikan, Christopher Minster, Dee Molenaar, Theresa Mudrock, Len Necefer, Matt Nolan, Norbu Tenzing Norgay,

Paul Ongtooguk, Randall Osczevski, Anders Ourom, Ron Perla, Richard Phillips, Rodolphe Popier, Austin Post, Richard Hubley Post, Jeffrey Punske, Daniel Prior, Brandon Pullan, Josh Reid, David Roberts, Doug Robinson, Zac Robinson, John Roper, Morris Rossabi, David Roxburgh, Joan Pau Rubiés, Jan Sacherer, Neil Safier, Alessandro Scafi, David Schaepe, Caroline Schaumann, Aaron and Ruth Schneider, Chic Scott, John Scurlock, Andy Selters, Don Serl, Maria Seton, Thomas Shor, Lowell Skoog, Stephen Slemon, David Smart, Barry Smith, Gerad Smith, Bill Snow, Mark David Spence, Stephen Spurr, Matt Stirn, Richard Strassberg, John Studley, Claude Suhl, Steve Swenson, Geoffrey Symcox, Pete Takeda, Joseph Taylor, Hugh Thomson, Coll Thrush, Yi-Fu Tuan, Jack Turner, Chet Van Duzer, Laura Dassow Walls, Kevin Ward, Jacey Warne, Jon Waterman, Stewart Weaver, Eric Wehrly, David Welky, Mark Westman, George Whitmore, Jim Whittaker, Brian Williams, Dick Williams, Knox Williams, Jim Woodmencey, Glenn Woodsworth, Milo Yellow Hair, and Lobsang Yongdan.

Brad Rassler provided early research assistance. Roberta Post helped with my interview of Austin Post. Paula Crenshaw arranged my visit with Jean Crenshaw and Helen Kilness. Joan Jensen mailed copies of Don Jensen's letters. Richard Hubley Post emailed reams of Austin Post's manuscripts. Megan Bond assisted with my research of Fred Beckey. Katie Sauter and Dan Cohen at the Henry S. Hall, Jr. American Alpine Club Library scanned extensive archival material. Alle Monheim and other staff of the University of Washington Libraries Special Collections, as well as Lowell Skoog of The Mountaineers Archive, helped locate Harvey Manning's papers. Laura Kissel of Ohio State University's Byrd Polar and Climate Research Center Archival Program scanned pages of Frederick Cook's papers.

Bob A. Schelfhout Aubertijn, Anders Ax, Anna Callaghan, Carolyn Davis, Russ Gershman, Katherine Indermaur, Bill Ives, Kathy Ives, Kaelyn Lynch, Samantha Yadron, and Larissa Zhou helped with fact-checking. Jerry Auld, David Burgess, Kathy Ives, Amanda Lewis, Brad Rassler, Stephen Slemon, and Alice Waugh gave feedback. Many people at Mountaineers Books worked on editing and layout: Kate Rogers, Mary Metz, Ellen Wheat, Laura Lancaster, and Jen Grable. Lynda McGilvary at the Geophysical Institute, UAF, provided the Kichatnas photo. Paul and Claudia Manning, Charlie Lieu, and Emily White helped locate Harvey Manning's favorite place. Irene and John Briedis let me spend months writing at their house. Coworkers at Height of Land Publications—especially Paula LaRochelle, Derek Franz, Tyler Cohen, Adam Howard, Mailee Hung and Anna Callaghan—worked especially hard during my leaves of absences while I was finishing the book.

# NOTES

## AUTHOR'S NOTE

9 *"To a large extent," American geographer*: See Roderick Peattie's *Mountain Geography: A Critique and Field Study.*

## A QUEST FOR THE RIESENSTEIN

13 *In June 1962, readers of* Summit: "Know Your Mountains," *Summit*, June 1962. The following retelling of the hoax is a work of creative nonfiction. While the listed "facts" reproduce what was in the published article, I have also—as indicated in my text—included some readers' imaginings about what the alleged Austrian climbers might have experienced, based on studies of the printed photo and reactions to the authors' words.

15 *Beckey himself was becoming half-myth*: Brad Rassler discussed Fred Beckey as a folkloric figure in "The Beckey Effect," *Alpinist* 61, Spring 2018. According to Megan Bond, Beckey's biographer, "By design, Fred kept his biggest secrets in his head," and he wouldn't have written down names of coveted unclimbed peaks in a notebook that could be lost, read without permission, or even stolen. Beckey told me about his reaction to the Riesenstein Hoax in a 2011 interview.

20 Terra miscognita: I first encountered the term *terra miscognita* in Coll Thrush's book *Native Seattle* and have evolved my understanding of it through correspondence with him.

21N1 *One of the Riesenstein hoaxers*: As narrated in *Walking the Beach to Bellingham.*

21N2 *"Suddenly it came to me . . ."*: This quotation from "Mount Everest and Me" comes from manuscripts generously scanned by Paul Manning and made available in the North Cascades Conservation Council online archives.

## CHAPTER 1

24N1 *In 2012, scientists aboard the Australian ship*: This account of the un-discovery of Sandy Island, reported by AFP and other news sources, also draws from correspondence with Dr. Maria Seton. In addition, see the report of the *Velocity* in the 1879 *Australia Directory,* as well as Captain James Cook's *Chart of Discoveries made in the South Pacific,* published in 1776, and Alastair Bonnett's *Unruly Places.*

24N2 *Nautical charts stopped including Sandy Island*: More about the history of Sandy Island from the perspective of French surveyors—who proved its nonexistence long before it vanished from Google Maps—can be found in the following press release: "Sandy Island: Le Mystère de l'Île Fantôme Dévoilé depuis Déjà 33 Ans," Service Hydrographique et Océanographique de la Marine (SHOM), December 12, 2012.

25 *where "the Sun is hidden"*: As cited in Thomas Reinertsen Berg's *Theater of the World*.

26 *As historian Murat Cem Mengüç notes*: See Mengüç's article in *Hyperallergic*, December 23, 2016.

27N1 *In 1154, Moroccan geographer al-Idrīsī*: Valerie Hansen described the silver map in *The Year 1000*, and Ernesto Cappello analyzed al-Idrīsī's other maps *in Mapping Mountains*.

27N2 *As the fifth-century bishop*: See Saint Eucherius of Lyon's *Formulae*.

27N3 *Since sea voyages in the Middle Ages*: For the uncharted spaces and wildwoods of early European maps, see Alessandro Scafi's *Mapping Paradise* and Graham Robb's *The Discovery of France*.

28 *In the introduction to* Mountains of the World: Various scholars and organizations have attempted to come up with universal definitions. See Eberhard Jurgalski's website, 8000ers .com, and the 2000 map described in Martin F. Price's *Mountains: A Very Short Introduction*.

29 *Swiss geographers Bernard Debarbieux and Gilles Rudaz*: See Debarbieux and Rudaz's *Mountain: A Political History*.

30 *Mahameru or Meru, a sacred mountain*: Meera Baindur explored the mythic and geographic Merus in "Meru: The Axis of the World," *Alpinist* 54, Summer 2016.

31N1 *Historian Alessandro Scafi has described*: See Scafi's *Mapping Paradise*.

31N2 *Fourth-century monk Saint Ephrem*: See Saint Ephrem's *Hymns on Paradise*.

31N3 *a woman known as Egeria*: Little is known about Egeria's origins, and scholars debate whether she came from Gaul or Galicia. Jaś Elsner and Joan-Pau Rubiés's introduction to *Voyages and Visions* recounts the implications of her legacy, from the assessments by seventh-century monk Valerius to modern reflections of an "always unachievable paradigm."

33 *Among them, Banryū*: For a discussion of *Banryū*, see Scott Schnell's "Believing Is Seeing," in *Nature, Science, and Religion* (2012), edited by Catherine Tucker. For Bai Juyi (Po Chü-i), see Amrita Dhar's essay in the 2019 *Cambridge History of Travel Writing*.

34 *Fourteenth-century Moroccan writer and Muslim pilgrim*: See *The Travels of Ibn Battutah*.

35N1 *In 1498, as Christopher Columbus sailed*: Christopher Columbus's speculations about a pear-shaped planet come from a letter he wrote to Spanish monarchs Isabella I and Ferdinand II.

35N2 *Sixteenth-century Swiss naturalist Conrad Gessner*: Conrad Gessner's celebrations of the paradise-like "spectacles" of the Alps appear in W. A. B. Coolidge's *Josias Simler et les Origines de l'Alpinisme jusqu'en 1600*.

36N1 *To explain why compasses point north*: For various interpretations of the imaginary magnetic peak, see Ernesto Capello's book *Mapping Mountains* and Chet Van Duzer's 2006 article "The Mystic Geographer" in *Culturas Populares*, no. 2.

36N2 *In Islamic cartographies*: For some of the legends of Mount Qāf, see John Hessler's "Mount Qāf: The Home of the Clouds," *Alpinist* 54, Summer 2016; Daniel G. Prior's "Travels of Mount Qāf: From Legend to 42° 0'N 79° 51'E," *Oriente Moderno Nuova Serie*, Anno 89, no. 2, *Studies on Islamic Legends* (2009); and Ḥamd Allāh Mustawfī al-Qazwīnī's *The Geographical Part of Nuzhat al-Qulūb*. For Gottfried Merzbacher's account of his quest (quoted here) see his *An Expedition into the Central Tian-Shan Mountains*.

## CHAPTER 2

37 *Early alpine guides, known as marrons*: Coolidge preserved the history of the *marrons*, as well as anthologized stories of Mount Etna and Rochemelon (referred to here) in *Josiah Simler et les Origines de l'Alpinisme.*

39N1 *Philosophy professor Unn Falkeid*: Unn Falkeid discussed this idea in "Petrarch, Mont Ventoux and the Modern Self" in *Forum Italicum.* Vol. 43. No. 1 (2009).

39N2 *As alpine historian Peter Hansen muses*: Peter Hansen's quoted words here derive from our correspondence, but I am also indebted to his book *The Summits of Modern Man.*

39N3 *"Ever since the very beginnings of cartography,"*: Library of Congress cartographer John Hessler's years-long correspondence with me—as well as his essays, including "Verticality: A Short History of the Other Blank on a Map," *Alpinist* 41, Winter 2012–2013—has been a key source for my understanding of mapmaking history. (Any errors are my own.)

40N1 *Alongside attempts to calculate*: Readers can find more-extensive descriptions of Johann Jakob Scheuchzer's work, the development of barometer use in the Alps, and the relationship between science and the sublime in Caroline Schaumann's *Peak Pursuits* and in her article "Tool Users: Barometer" for *Alpinist* 71, Autumn 2020. See also Florian Cajori's "History of Determination of the Heights of Mountains" in *Isis.* Vol. 12, no. 3 (December 1929).

40N2 *such hatchwork made summits look like "hairy caterpillars"*: See John Noble Wilford's *The Mapmakers.*

42N1 *As humanities professor Paul Longley Arthur*: Paul Longley Arthur's *Virtual Voyages* and Siobhan Carroll's *An Empire of Air and Water* examine the link between imaginary voyages and colonialism.

42N2 *"One must have a long sojourn . . ."*: as quoted in Neil Safier's *Measuring the New World.*

43 *In 1749, the French cartographer*: See Jean Baptiste Bourguignon d'Anville's *A Geographical Illustration of the Map of India.* For Carroll's quotation, see *An Empire of Air and Water.*

## CHAPTER 3

45N1 *Far from diminishing a sense of wonder*: These scenes appear in Alexander von Humboldt's *Cosmos* and *Reise auf dem Río Magdalena, durch die Anden und Mexico*, translated and excerpted in Caroline Schaumann's *Peak Pursuits.*

45N2 *as University of London professor*: See Veronica della Dora's *Mountain: Nature and Culture.* London: Reaktion Books, 2016.

46N1 *Stephen was writing during an age*: For the connection between nineteenth-century agnosticism, alpinism, and secular mysticism, see Michael Reidy's "Cosmic Emotion," *Alpinist* 39, Summer 2012.

46N2 *"The steepest places," cartographer John Hessler observes*: See Hessler's "Verticality: A Short History of the Other Blank on a Map." *Alpinist* 41, Winter 2012–2013.

47N1 *By the 1860s, climbers had started to create*: Paula Wright (LaRochelle) offered an overview of the early evolution of topos in *Alpinist* 68, Winter 2019–2020.

47N2 *"Ideas lose their form when they decay . . ."*: Francis Spufford investigated this idea in *I May Be Some Time.*

47N3 *One element that contributed to myths*: For an in-depth history of the invention of the chronometer and the misadventures that preceded it, see Dava Sobel's *Longitude.*

48N1 *"outposts in the homelands of others"*: Darran Anderson's *Imaginary Cities* provides an exploration both poetic and critical of the complex legacy of imaginary places.

48N2 *Within legends of storied lands*: See the primary sources in Richard and Shirley Flint's *Documents of the Coronado Expedition, 1539–1542*. The reference to "gold fever" appeared in their correspondence with me.

48N3 *Flemish explorer Eustache de la Fosse*: See Eustache de la Fosse's *Voyage à la Côte Occidentale d'Afrique en Portugal et en Espagne* and Edward Brook-Hitching's *The Phantom Atlas*.

49 *An enslaved Black explorer known as Esteban*: In *No Settlement, No Conquest*, Richard Flint noted, "There is some evidence that Mendoza had manumitted Esteban after purchasing him," but no definitive formal document has been found.

50N1 *Inside aspiring settlers' imaginations*: In selecting anecdotes for the section on "the Garden of the World," the "Northwest Passage," and the "Shining Mountains," I was influenced by John Logan Allen's *Passage through the Garden*, Roderick Frazier Nash's *Wilderness and the American Mind*, and Zac Robinson and Stephen Slemon's "The Shining Mountains," *Alpinist* 50, Summer 2015.

50N2 *US diplomat Benjamin Franklin*: On March 10, 1779, Benjamin Franklin wrote a letter to American sea captains urging them to give Captain Cook and his crew safe passage "as common Friends to Mankind." Unbeknownst to Franklin, Cook had been killed less than a month prior in Hawaii while attempting to kidnap King Kalaniʻōpuʻu.

50N3 Father Louis Hennepin's quotation appears in *Passage through the Garden*; Gabriel Franchère's is from *Narrative of a Voyage to the Northwest Coast of America*.

51N1 *Peter Fidler, a British surveyor*: As described in Judith Hudson Beattie's "Indian Maps in the Hudson's Bay Company Archives: A Comparison of Five Area Maps Recorded by Peter Fidler, 1801–1802," *Archivaria* 21 (Winter 1985–1986).

51N2 *Some US geographers dreamed that these peaks*: For this and other examples of speculative cartography before Lewis and Clark's expedition, see Allen's *Passage through the Garden* where Thomas Jefferson's instructions to the explorers can also be found.

52N1 *Mandan villagers and other Indigenous residents*: See Lewis and Clark's journals and John Noble Wilford's *The Mapmakers*.

52N2 *A long and arduous journey*: During the journey home, as members of Lewis and Clark's expedition staggered near the edge of the Rocky Mountains, one of them, an enslaved Black man known as York, set off with another teammate on a mission to save the group from hunger. They returned with roots and bread they'd persuaded Nimiipuu people to give them in exchange for tin boxes, medicine vials, and buttons (cut from Lewis's and Clark's own coats). When the team got back East, Lewis and Clark were lauded as heroes. York, whose efforts had contributed to their survival, lived in poverty even after he finally gained his freedom. See Robert B. Betts, *In Search of York*.

52N3 *In 1818 John Ross*: For John Ross's account of the "discovery" of Croker's Mountains, see his 1819 memoir *A Voyage of Discovery*. See also Brooke-Hitching's *A Phantom Atlas* and Anthony Brandt's *The Man Who Ate His Boots* for the expedition and its aftermath.

53 *"The view from the summit,"*: See *Journal Kept by David Douglas during His Travels in North America, 1823–1827*. (This published journal differs from Douglas's original field notebook, where he listed the height from base to summit of Mount Brown as "about 5,500 feet," as cited in James Monroe Thorington's *The Glittering Mountains of Canada*.)

54N1 *A railway surveyor, Walter Moberly*: Quoted in *The Glittering Mountains of Canada*.

54N2 *Finding them proved unexpectedly hard*: University Alberta professor Zac Robinson responded in an email that the 1846 Oregon Treaty likely played a role in the longevity of the Mount Hooker and Mount Brown myth: "The HBC [Hudson Bay Company] lost access to the fur-wealth of the Columbia District, and with that loss, Athabasca Pass fell suddenly into absolute abandonment. . . . The relative inaccessibility of the pass meant that the area's inflated heights remained in the public record much longer than they would have otherwise."

55 *Lines from a Kipling poem came into Collie's mind*: As J. Norman Collie recounted in the 1924 *Canadian Alpine Journal.*

56 *In 1920, a Canadian Interprovincial Survey expedition*: Thorington discussed this expedition and his own quest in *The Glittering Mountains of Canada*, which includes a deeply researched analysis of the Mount Hooker and Mount Brown myth. Zac Robinson and Stephen Slemon presented a modern-day interpretation in "Deception in High Places: The Making and Unmaking of Mounts Brown and Hooker," a chapter in *Sustaining the West.*

## CHAPTER 4

58 *"Is there something particularly American . . ."*: In *Bunk*, Kevin Young explained: "Where the eighteenth century was the hoax's height in Britain, the nineteenth century starred the United States, so much so that someone at the time called it 'the age of imposture.'" Young's book offers a brilliant investigation of the negative impact of these trends from the nineteenth century to the Trump era.

59N1 *Out West "stretched the land of enchantment . . ."*: Asbury Harpending's exuberantly titled memoir, *The Great Diamond Hoax and Other Stirring Incidents in the Life of Asbury Harpending*, paints a colorful picture of a speculator's activities during post–Civil War America.

59N2 *climbing novelist Jeff Long*: See Jeff Long's "Glass Mountain: A Fable" in *Alpinist* 54, Summer 2016.

60 *"fairy tales of sapphire paved courts . . ."*: As quoted in Bruce A. Woodard's *Diamonds in the Salt*: *The First Authentic Account of the Sensational Diamond Hoax Chicanery.*

61N1 *"four distinct types of diamond . . ."*: As cited in *Diamonds in the Salt,* along with an in-depth account of Clarence King's debunking of the hoax. For King's tales of his ascents in California (including the quotation "like an Indian arrow-shaft"), see *Mountaineering in the Sierra Nevada.*

61N2 *Twenty-first–century climber Daniel Arnold*: From Daniel Arnold's *Early Days in the Range of Light.*

62 *John Muir, among the most influential mountaineering writers in US history*: In his now-classic account, *Dispossessing the Wilderness*, Mark David Spence discussed the link between the ideal of a pristine wilderness—as embodied in some of Muir's writings—and the removal of Indigenous people from both the land and the history.

63 *According to geographers Thomas J. Bassett and Philip W. Porter*: Thomas J. Bassett and Philip W. Porter's "'From the Best Authorities': The Mountains of Kong in the Cartography of West Africa," *The Journal of African History* 32, no. 3 (1991), examines the creation and deletion of the Mountains of Kong within the context of political and cartographic history. See also Anders Ax's "Mountains of Kong: The Vanishing Range," *Alpinist* 54, Summer 2016.

65 *At last, for many*: An extensive literature exists on the role of Shangri-La in cultural and political history, from scholarly books such as Peter Bishop's *The Myth of Shangri-La* to would-be practical guidebooks, such as Michael Buckley's *Shangri-La*: *A Travel Guide to the Himalayan Dream.*

66 *as the Tibetan scholar Lobsang Yongdan observes*: From Lobsang Yongdan's chapter in *Mapping the Modern in Tibet* and from correspondence with him. See also Ed Douglas's *Himalaya*: *A Human History.*

## CHAPTER 5

68N1 New Yorker *writer Ed Caesar later quipped*: From Ed Caesar's book *The Moth and the Mountain.*

68N2 *In March 1930, American mountaineers*: For Moore and his teammates' account of this story, see the book *Men Against the Clouds.*

69 *Cecil Pereira, the late brigadier general's brother*: From the 1924 *Geographical Journal.*

71N1 *During the 1940s, US explorers*: For the story of Vinson and Nimitz, see John Pirrit's *Across West Antarctica* and Damien Gildea's *Mountaineering in Antarctica.*

71N3 *While surveyors kept correcting elevation errors*: From 2001 to 2008, Australian mountaineer Damien Gildea participated in expeditions to remeasure Antarctic peaks with GPS, discovering many inaccuracies. In *Alpinist* 44, Autumn 2013, he wrote: "The Antarctic programs of the 1950s, ['60s, and '70s] had mapped the continent using ground surveys and aerial photography. But . . . readings taken from slowly moving ice have their limits."

72 *For Western visitors, the place recalled*: In *Mapping Mountains,* Ernesto Capello described "a second tendency," in the mythology of the Earthly Paradise, "namely the use of a ring of mountains to demonstrate the hiding place of the Garden of Eden." In their accounts, Pete Takeda and Hugh Thomson also noted similarities between the landscape of Nanda Devi and Western myths of Eden.

73N1 *A snow pigeon flew by*: Tilman's account of the summit day and its aftermath, including the response by an Indian newspaper, appears in *The Ascent of Nanda Devi.*

73N2 *Despite requests from the other Sherpa workers*: In *Tigers of the Snow,* Jonathan Neale narrated the series of events that led to Kitar's death from the perspective of Sherpa staff.

74N1 *"Lost civilisations beyond the ranges. . ."*: From Shipton's 1943 book, *Upon That Mountain.*

74N2 *"an environmental disaster"*: From Harish Kapadia's article in the 2002 *American Alpine Journal* and from our correspondence.

## CHAPTER 6

76 *As a young British soldier*: Unless otherwise specified, the J. R. R. Tolkien quotations come from his letters. For some writers of Tolkien's generation, the grim realities of the First and Second World Wars shattered any gauzy remnants of Romanticism, leading to such famous works as Wilfred Owen's poem "Dulce et Decorum Est." Others, however, turned to fantasy as a means to hint at inexpressible horrors. As Verlyn Flieger explained in *A Question of Time,* the "extremes" of "War and Faërie . . . can change those who return so that they become 'pinned in a kind of ghostly deathlessness,' not just unable to say where they have been but unable to communicate to those who have not been there what they have seen and experienced." Tolkien wasn't seeking "imaginary opiates" to distract himself, John Garth emphasized in *Tolkien and the Great War,* but rather a form of creative resistance.

77 *The onslaught of "rationalisation"*: In 1918, German sociologist Max Weber termed a similar concept "the disenchantment of the world."

78N1 *as Macfarlane put it, "in a cloud of unknowing"*: The phrase "cloud of unknowing" derives from the title of a fourteenth-century Christian mystic guide to prayer.

78N2 *Once a forbidden place*: The quotation from Tenzing Norgay comes from *Tiger of the Snows.* Tenzing Norgay's son Norbu Tenzing Norgay explained in an email: "Climbing the mountain was a pilgrimage, and for him it felt like he was in the lap of his mother."

79 *In 1936, W. H. Auden and Christopher Isherwood*: W. H. Auden's brother John was a mountaineer who accompanied Eric Shipton and Bill Tilman on a 1937 expedition to the Karakoram. Climbing writer David Roberts, who named his first book, *The Mountain of My Fear*, after a line from a W. H. Auden poem, described his encounter with the poet in *Alpinist* 59, Autumn 2017.

80 *"My friends and I have . . . "*: As cited in Hubert Odier and Sylvain Jouty's "Mount Analogue: On the Other Side of the Door," *Alpinist* 54, Summer 2016.

## CHAPTER 7

84N1 *I'd begun my search with Austin Post*: The following section on Austin relies on a number of sources: in addition to interviews with Austin, Austin's son Richard Hubley Post, his protégé John Scurlock, and other colleagues and friends, some details and quotations come from Austin's published memoir, *Pyramid Mountain*, or from his unpublished stories scanned and sent to me by Richard.

84N2 *"I can't recall a single close call"*: From Austin's essay "Annual Aerial Photography of Glaciers in Northwest North America: How It All Began and Its Golden Age" in *Physical Geography* Vol 16 (1995).

89 *Meanwhile Hubley flew out*: For information about Hubley's death, see Walter Sullivan's *Assault on the Unknown.* For the climbs that Hubley and Post and their partners did on the McCall Glacier, see Robert W. Mason's 1959 *American Alpine Journal* account.

90N1 *a term derived from a misspelling*: Austin Post attributed his choice of "Klawatti" to a misspelling of "Kahloke." The word appears in an online dictionary of Chinook and Chinook Jargon (archive.org/details/chinookjargonhow00shawuoft/page/34/mode/1up). Sam Sullivan, co-founder of the BC Chinook Wawa Project, points out that "the traditional language" near what Austin named the "Klawatti Glacier" would actually have been "a Salish language like Lushootseed or Columbian." His colleague Rein Stamm adds, "There is more of a chance that Klawattii is a misspelling of "klatawa," meaning 'to go,' 'flee,' 'travel,' 'move away,' 'migrate' . . . and more."

90N2 *But Washburn hadn't bothered to take pictures*: David Roberts explained to me: "[Washburn] was never interested in rock spires. . . . What turned him on were the big snow giants. . . . He once told me he'd never pounded a piton in his life—and he was bragging."

91 *Ed had also worked and climbed*: For my biographical sketches of Ed LaChapelle, I am indebted to interviews with his colleagues, friends, and loved ones, as well as his books and the memorial articles published in the *Avalanche Review*, April 2007. Ed's letter to Dolores was cited in David LaChapelle's tribute to his father in *The Avalanche Review*, where David's story of the dragon can also be found.

93 *The trio composed the story from the point of view*: The information about the alleged Canadian writer and Calgary mailing address comes from Mike Graber's account of the hoax in *Ascent*, 1980, and from my phone interview of Graber in 2020. Graber's article identifies the location of the plot as Harvey Manning's house, but I have decided to go with what Austin Post wrote to me in 2011—that it was Ed LaChapelle's house.

94 *as other readers have suggested*: The suggestion about the meaning of the "misspelled" version, "Riensenstein," comes from *Alpinist* reader David Burgess and from my mother, in separate correspondence.

## CHAPTER 8

95 *When Harvey Manning first stood on Marmot Pass*: The chapters on Harvey Manning draw mainly from his unpublished manuscripts, letters, and notebooks (preserved in the University of Washington Libraries Special Collections, in the North Cascades Conservation Council's online archives, and in The Mountaineers Archives), as well as from interviews with his family, friends, fellow conservationists, and climbing partners, unless otherwise noted.

98 *These powerful beings arrived to change*: Information about the Indigenous history and cartography of the North Cascades appears in "Stó:lō Mapping and Knowledge of the North Cascades," by Daniel L. Boxberger and David M. Schaepe, in *A Stó:lō Coast Salish Historical Atlas,* edited by Keith Thor Carlson. See also Forest McBrian's "Mountain Profile: The Picket Range" in *Alpinist* 47, Summer 2014. Henry Custer's words appear in the *Report of Henry Custer, Assistance of Reconnaissance Made in 1859.*

99N1 *In an 1870 journal entry*: As described in Lowell Skoog's essay in John Scurlock's *Snow and Spire.*

99N2 *Among many Coast Salish groups, tales abound*: These stories are anthologized in Ella E. Clark's *Indian Legends of the Pacific Northwest.*

101 *This was "the World-as-it-Should-Be"*: as Harvey recounted in "Something Lost Behind the Ranges," *The Wild Cascades* (May 1961).

104 *Not long afterward, an intense pain*: According to Harvey's son, Paul Manning, Harvey suffered from a heart ailment, but no one seems to recall the precise diagnosis.

## CHAPTER 9

107 *Japanese American classmates*: During World War II, the US government sent more than 110,000 Japanese Americans to internment camps. Many were from the Pacific Northwest. Later in life, Harvey developed a habit of creating collages. One of them, preserved by Paul, includes Harvey's typewritten memory: "In early 1942, on a dark (blacked-out, moonless) night, walking a beach on Puget Sound, I was arrested by the U.S. Army on suspicion of being Japanese. After a close flashlight examination of my face I was released." Below, Harvey had pasted in a haunting newspaper report: "In early 1942, Seattle fired all its employees of Japanese descent, and 9,600 Japanese Americans in King County were soon carted off to internment camps."

108 *In 1889, the prospector Joseph Pearsall*: This story is recounted in Philip R. Woodhouse's *Monte Cristo.*

109N1 *"Men can go where the clouds can go . . ."*: In "The Making of a Mountain Bum," Harvey attributed the lines to "some nameless alpine poetaster," but they appear to originate with Andreas Maurer.

109N2 *Betty had initially gone to Reed College*: For Betty Manning's college years and early climbs, see Paul's obituary of her in *The Wild Cascades,* Fall 2015.

111 *From here, as mountaineering historian Lowell Skoog*: See Skoog's essay in *Snow and Spire.*

## CHAPTER 11

120N1 *As journalist James Howard Kunstler*: See Kunstler's *A Geography of Nowhere.*

120N2 *"Junkspace," Dutch architect Rem Koolhaas mused*: As quoted in "Rem Koolhaas: Junkspace," *Icon* (March 6, 2014).

121: *"If wilderness could speak . . . "*: From Harvey's *Backpacking*: *One Step at a Time.*

122 *Diné mountaineer Len Necefer observes*: From Len Necefer's article in *Alpinist* 64, Winter 2018.

123: *"We grew into the name,"*: See Ted Beck and Pat Goldsworthy's "The Elderly Birdwatchers Hiking and Griping Society," *The Wild Cascades,* Winter 2006–2007.

124 *During a spring night*: As narrated in Dale Cole's memorial article about Harvey in *The Wild Cascades,* Winter 2006–2007.

## CHAPTER 12

129 *to "what had been determined . . ."*: This quotation from Harvey and the one that follows, "Gerry Cunningham was as energetic..." appear in *Backpacking*: *One Step at a Time.*

132 *The ubiquitous Fred Beckey*: Beckey's account of Mox Peaks/Twin Spires appears in *Challenge of the North Cascades.*

## CHAPTER 13

137 *"It's not like the murder mystery . . . "*: As quoted in Samantha Sacks's "The Revision of History," *Alpinist* 14, Winter 2005–2006. Paula LaRochelle also discussed this topic in "Litigating the Mountains?" *Alpinist* 73, Spring 2021.

## CHAPTER 14

144N1 *Maybe it was something about the combination of roiling clouds*: Mike Graber and mountaineering historian Andy Selters both expressed similar ideas to me about Beckey's thought process.

144N2 *Canadian climber Glenn Woodsworth*: Glenn Woodsworth, a longtime fellow seeker of imaginary mountains, shared multiple sources for this chapter from his own writing and research files. In addition, Dick Culbert's description about the history missing from alpine journals appears in "Freight Christmas" reprinted in *The Canadian Mountaineering Anthology.* Quotations about the firefly-like sparks and about Arthur Clore come from Woodsworth's "Glimpses of Different Worlds" in *Lived Experience,* Vol 15. (2015).

148N1 *Indigenous people had long been aware*: Raymond L. Collins's book *Dichinanek' Hwt'ana* and the Indigenous atlas *Shem Pete's Alaska* (James Kari, James A. Fall, Shem Pete) provide invaluable sources for the Indigenous cartographic history of the area that became known as the Kichatnas. Scholars James Kari, James A. Fall, and Gerad Smith and Denali National Park historian Erik K. Johnson also corresponded with me. The suggestions that Stepan and Slinkta might be Dena'ina Susitnuht'ana and that Stephen and Evan might be Dena'ina Susitnuht'ana come from Fall. (Any errors are my own.)

148N2 *Miska Deaphon, a storyteller*: This story is included in *Dichinanek' Hwt'ana.*

150 *Spurr contemplated "magnificent precipitous . . . "*: From Josiah Edward Spurr's *The Log of the Kuskokwim*, as quoted in his grandson Stephen J. Spurr's book, *In Search of the Kuskokwim.*

152 *Perhaps the guides were also concerned*: Gerad Smith included this theory in our correspondence.

153 *Decades afterward, Carl Seseui*: See *Dichinanek' Hwt'ana.*

## CHAPTER 15

**154N1** *Born in 1865, Frederick Cook*: Robert M. Bryce's book *Cook & Peary: The Polar Controversy, Resolved*—1,122 pages, including bibliography and endnotes—and his subsequent volume, *The Lost Polar Notebook of Dr. Frederick A. Cook*, provide the most comprehensive examinations of the controversies surrounding Frederick Cook and Robert E. Peary.

**154N2** *Like others of his era,*: See Frederick A. Cook's *To the Top of the Continent* for "the life-sapping conditions" and "the maddening pace of this material age."

**154N3** *And he'd sought refuge*: Bryce discusses Cook's childhood and young adulthood in depth in *Cook & Peary*.

**154N4** *a "yearning for something . . . "*: See Cook's *My Attainment of the Pole* for this quotation and for the one that follows on page 155: "It was as if a door to a prison cell...."

**155N1** *The resulting stories*: Beau Riffenburgh's *The Myth of the Explorer* analyzes the role of the media in mythologizing exploration.

**155N2** *In his account of the journey*: See Robert E. Peary's *Northward over the Great Ice*.

**155N3** *Cook, in turn, extolled Peary's "sublime courage."*: from Cook's manuscript, "Hell Is a Cold Place," as cited in *Frederick A. Cook: A Digital Exhibition*. The Ohio State University Libraries (http://go.osu.edu/frederickcook).

**156** *As Cook and his teammates*: Cook's version of the 1903 expedition appears in *To the Top of the Continent* and Robert Dunn's contrasting one in *The Shameless Diary of an Explorer*.

**157N1** *By then, Browne realized failure*: Belmore Browne's quotations and perspectives in this chapter come from *The Conquest of Mount McKinley*.

**157N2** *Many people initially believed*: In *Cook & Peary*, Bryce argued that Belmore Browne might have initially thought that Cook's account was real—and that Browne might have subsequently revised his own history in *The Conquest of Mount McKinley* to suggest earlier doubts.

**157N3** *Yet when Cook began to describe*: In *The Ascent of Denali*, Hudson Stuck famously declared, "The writer well remembers the eagerness with which his copy [of Cook's *To the Top of the Continent*] . . . was perused by man after man from the Kantishna diggings, and the acute way in which they detected the place where vague 'fine writing' began to be substitute for definite description."

**158** *a group of local miners*: Both Jon Waterman's examination of the Sourdough expedition in *Chasing Denali* and Bryce's "The Strange Saga of the Sourdoughs" in volume 23 of *DIO: The International Journal of Scientific History* provide recent examples of efforts to determine the truth of the Sourdough story.

**160** *In another twist*: See Bryce's *Cook & Peary*, Edwin Balch's *Mount McKinley and Mountain Climbers' Proofs*, and E.C. Rost's *Mount McKinley, Its Bearing on the Polar Controversy*.

**162** *"The world has important use for dreamers . . . "*: As cited in *Cook & Peary*.

**163N1** *"From the earliest days of poleward . . . "*: From pages 2–3 of Cook's unpublished manuscript, "Incorporate into Chapter 2, etc." in "Hell Is a Cold Place," Frederick A. Cook Society Records, Including Papers of Dr. Frederick Albert Cook, SPEC.PA.56.0017, Box 9 Folder 38, Byrd Polar and Climate Research Center Archival Program, The Ohio State University Libraries—generously scanned for me by Polar Curator Laura Kissel.

**163N2** *Peary had his own history*: David Welky's *A Wretched and Precarious Situation* and Bryce's *The Lost Polar Notebook of Dr. Frederick A. Cook* present careful reexaminations of the Crocker Land story in light of new research.

164N1 "*. . . Our judgment, then as now . . .*": In *The Last Polar Notebook* Bryce, after examining MacMillan's original field notebook, suggested the detailed description of the mirage might have been a later addition "to help bolster the theory that Peary was innocently deceived."

164N2 *"Peary had written simply*: See Welky's *A Wretched and Precarious Situation,* among other history books, for this quotation from Peary's diary.

165 *He was also pleased that Harper*: See the 1977 edition of Stuck's *The Ascent of Denali,* which also contains Walter Harper's expedition journal, as well as Patrick Dean's *A Window to Heaven* and Jan Harper-Haines's article "Denali, A Universe" in *Alpinist* 67, Autumn 2019.

## CHAPTER 16

166 *And when the air was crystalline*: David Roberts recalled seeing the Kichatnas from the top floor of the Westward Hotel in *On the Ridge Between Life and Death* and in his correspondence with me.

168 *Don was clearly interested*: The letters between Don Jensen and David Roberts come from the Henry S. Hall Jr., American Alpine Club Library. Other Jensen letters are from the collection of his widow, Joan, who kindly sent copies to me.

169 *For decades afterward, David would remember*: David Roberts's memories of this moment and of others in this section appear in *On the Ridge Between Life and Death.* For additional information, I relied on Roberts's *The Mountain of My Fear* and *Deborah: A Wilderness Narrative,* as well as his and Don Jensen's diaries and letters, and interviews with Roberts, Lin Jensen, and Joan Jensen.

172 *"See the whole thing . . .* ": Maurice Isserman's *Continental Divide* and Joseph Taylor's *Pilgrims of the Vertical* explore the influence of Beat culture on 1960s American climbing.

176 Life *magazine heralded the two men*: See Charles Champlin's "Magnificent Rescue on McKinley" in *Life* (June 6, 1960).

177 *"He had a strong will. . .*": See Jack Turner's memoir *Teewinot.*

178 *It wasn't there, however*: Brownell Bergen's account of his solving of the hoax comes from his interviews with me. Some details differ from second-hand information found in other sources.

## CHAPTER 17

186 *bushwhacked to the unclimbed east face*: For the Mount Chephren ascent, see Art Gran's report in the 1966 *American Alpine Journal.*

## CHAPTER 18

189 *David sat in a bar listening to Art Davidson*: David Roberts's accounts of the 1966 Kichatnas expedition appear in *On the Ridge Between Life and Death* and the 1967 *American Alpine Journal.* Other details come from interviews with participants.

192 *"One way or another . . .* ": See Rick Millikan's account in the 1967 *American Alpine Journal.*

194 *He thought of how ice age human wanderers*: Around 1968, David Roberts wrote a poem about this moment, later published in the *South Dakota Review.*

195 *For a short while*: For David Roberts's report of the 1970 expedition, and for Al DeMaria's story of the 1972 expedition, see the *American Alpine Journal* 1971 and 1973 respectively.

198 *"significant rocks, creek bends . . .* ": As Paul Ongtooguk said in a 2011 interview with me.

## CHAPTER 19

201 *". . . the 'Reisensteins' [sic] disgrace . . .*": Harvey's misspelling of his own imaginary range seems to be a deliberate allusion to the *Summit* editors' misspelling in the caption for the original 1962 hoax article.

204 *In a description of Golden Horn*: From *100 Classic Hikes in Washington.*

205N1 *In one of his many imaginary*: See "Gods, Devils, and Wilderness Pedestrians."

205N2 *He penned an impassioned letter*: As preserved in The Mountaineers Archive, along with Harvey's note to Don Graydon that follows.

207 "*The Pole was the excuse, not the reason,*": From *Walking the Beach to Bellingham.*

208 *During the last decade of Harvey's life*: The last chapter of *Wilderness Alps*, Harvey's history of the North Cascades conservation movement, published in 2007, after his death, contains some of his thoughts on the impacts of climate change.

## CHAPTER 20

214 *The Revelation Mountains*: See *On the Ridge Between Life and Death* and David Roberts's 1968 *American Alpine Journal* article.

216 *Fellow guide Doug Robinson recalled a recipe box*: Doug Robinson's account of the recipe box, along with some of his other memories of Don Jensen, can be read in his "Mountain Profile of the Palisades" in *Alpinist* 48, Autumn–Winter 2014. For other details about Jensen's final years, I am indebted to his widow, Joan, as well as the letters between her and Jensen.

217 "*The Englishmen looked dour and hard,*": See Roman Laba's article in the 1970 *American Alpine Journal* for the last expedition of John Hudson.

221 *He'd compare crystals of surface hoar*: In *Field Guide to Snow Crystals.*

224N1 *Austin referred to the hypothetical glacier*: Other reports of the quest for Eacas Glacier appear on John Roper's website, Rhinoclimbs.com, and in John Scurlock's profile of Austin Post for the *Northwest Mountaineering Journal*, no. 4 (2007).

224N2 *After other marriages*: The account of Austin Post's marriages, the fiction story about the dream world, and the reference to "doctoring" come from some of Austin's unpublished writings—"Social Life" and "The Dutch Miller's Cabin"—and from a letter that Austin composed for his friends after receiving his honorary doctorate, all sent to me by Richard Hubley Post.

225 *In our 2011 correspondence*: Some people still use the term "Cathedral Spires" for a section of the Kichatnas. In the *Dictionary of Alaska Place Names*, Donald J. Orth referred to the Cathedral Spires as "peaks in the center of Kichatna Mts."

## CHAPTER 21

228 *Washington climber Michael Layton*: Information about Michael Layton and Erik Wolfe's Mox adventures comes from Layton's interviews with me, as well as from his article in the 2006 *Northwest Mountaineering Journal.*

230 *pro-democracy activists have also*: Brad Rassler alerted me to the *Journal of American Folklore*'s special issue on "fake news" (Fall 2018), in which articles by Timothy H. Evans and other modern folklorists confront the Trump era.

232 *Their quest ended*: See Bradford Washburn's autobiography and Shiwei Chen's account in *Modern Asian Studies* 37, no. 3 (July 2003).

236 *In 2018, Fenn explained that he, too*: See Forrest Fenn's foreword to Jenny Kile's *Armchair Treasure Hunts.* Fenn's 2020 announcement about the location "under a canopy of stars" appeared on his website.

## CHAPTER 22

237 *a Tibetan visionary named Sera Khandro*: Sara Jacoby narrated the story of Sera Khandro, along with extensive translated source material, in *Love and Liberation.*

238 *In a guidebook for the journey*: The quotations from Tulshuk Lingpa appear in Thomas K. Shor's book *A Step Away from Paradise.* See also Ian Baker's *The Heart of the World* and Frances Garrett's "Kangchenjunga & Beyul," *Alpinist* 54, Summer 2016.

239 *In 2007, one villager told visiting scholar*: See Scheid's 2014 article for the *Journal of the Irish Society for the Academic Study of Religion.*

240 *From 1993 to 1998*: *The Heart of the World* details Baker's own search for Pemako and also the history of quests for paradises on Earth across many cultures.

## CHAPTER 23

243N1 *phantom roads still haunt*: For a 2017 conference paper, "Understanding 'Death by GPS,'" researchers looked at 158 news reports of disasters connected to the use of personal GPS devices, including people lost on dirt tracks in the Australian outback and drivers whose devices instructed them to take the wrong on-ramp to a highway. "It is tempting," the researchers noted, "to blame these incidents on users and users alone." But, they concluded, GPS couldn't keep up with all the changes in road conditions, closures, and detours, nor could it always determine the difference between a paved road, a dirt lane, a railroad track, or a footpath.

243N2 *In December 2020*: see Freddie Wilkerson's "How do you measure Everest? It's complicated by frostbite—and politics" in NationalGeographic.com, September 28, 2020.

244N1 *"an electronic tether to the world . . ."*: Damien Gildea's account of the history of GPS appears in *Alpinist* 69, Spring 2020.

244N2 *Back in 1972, a historian*: See Raymond H. Ramsay's *No Longer on the Map.*

246 *French chronicler Rodolphe Popier*: Rodolphe Popier's ideas are quoted from his notes for a 2019 presentation at the Université Savoie Mont Blanc as well as from our ongoing correspondence. Eberhard Jurgalski, Damien Gildea, John Hessler, Steve Swenson, Harish Kapadia, and Bob A. Schelfhout Aubertijn shared thoughts from many years of researching Himalayan geography and/or ascents. The 2019 reports on 8000-meter topography can be found on 8000ers.com.

249 *Hawley once told her biographer*: See McDonald's *Keeper of the Mountains: The Elizabeth Hawley Story* (Calgary, Alberta: Rocky Mountain Books, 2010).

255N1 *a "seagull's eye perspective"*: As quoted in Brian Dillon's "An Interview with Tim Robinson." *Field Day Review* 3 (2007).

255N2 *"Continually being mapped and unmapped,"*: From Richard Phillips's *Mapping Men and Empire: Geographies of Adventure.*

256 *But current writers, artists, activists*: Stories about Jim Enote's extensive work to create "counter maps" of A:shiwi (Zuni) territories can be found in the film *Counter Mapping* and in *Emergence Magazine.*

257N1 *Similarly, an interactive digital atlas*: A number of other atlases of Indigenous territories exist online, including native-land.ca, which covers much of the world.

257N2 *"all over the hills and mountains,"* As cited in *Shem Pete's Alaska.*

## CHAPTER 24

263 *"Sherpas need the money to support their families,"*: Expedition work and the mountain tourist industry still provide one of the few opportunities for economic advancement in Khumbu, Nepal. In recent years, there has also been a rise of professional Sherpa mountaineers who climb peaks for their own sake, including the Sherpa team who made the first winter ascent of K2 in 2021.

265N1 *Among all the tales of imaginary ranges*: I first read Michael Ende's book in 2019, after learning it was the favorite childhood story of one of my late writers, Japanese alpinist Kei Taniguchi. Akihiro Oishi's profile of Kei in *Alpinist* 68, Winter 2019–2020, describes the impact of the book on her.

265N2 *Daumal's notes make it clear*: See Véra Daumal's afterword to *Mount Analogue.*

268 *As Arctic explorer Robert E. Peary*: Peary uttered these words during a speech before the Eighth International Geographic Congress.

271N1 *Rebecca Solnit provides*: See *A Field Guide to Getting Lost*, in which she explains she was influenced by Socrates.

271N2 *I've met many other seekers*: One of the delights of researching imaginary mountains has been hearing from readers who have their own stories. For one example, see Stuart Parker's letter to the editor in *Alpinist* 71, Autumn 2020. Another reader, David Burgess, has urged me to recommend Mark Helprin's story of the Schreuderspitze (in the collection *Ellis Island and Other Stories*), about a hero who gives up a planned ascent in waking life after realizing that the peak he has already climbed in his dreams—"hundreds of times higher than the mountains represented on the map"—surpasses any real one.

# SELECTED BIBLIOGRAPHY

IN THE COURSE OF THE book research, I read more than a thousand books, articles, letters, unpublished manuscripts, field notebooks, and diaries. Because of space limitations, I am including only a selection of some of the major sources.

## BOOKS


Allen, John Logan. *Passage through the Garden*. Champaign, IL: University of Illinois Press, 1974.

Alter, J. Cecil. *Jim Bridger*. Norman, Oklahoma: University of Oklahoma Press, 1979.

Anderson, Darran. *Imaginary Cities: A Tour of Dream Cities, Nightmare Cities, and Everywhere in Between*. Chicago: University of Chicago Press, 2017.

Arnold, Daniel. *Early Days in the Range of Light: Encounters with Legendary Mountaineers*. Berkeley: Counterpoint, 2011.

Arthur, Paul Longley. *Virtual Voyages: Travel Writing and the Antipodes, 1605–1837*. London: Anthem Press, 2010.

Auden, W. H., and Christopher Isherwood. *The Ascent of F6: A Tragedy in Two Acts*. New York: Random House, 1937.

Auld, Jerry. *Hooker & Brown: A Novel*. Victoria, BC: Brindle & Glass, 2010.

*The Australia Directory*. London: The Hydrographic Office, Admiralty, 1879.

Baker, Ian. *The Heart of the World: A Journey to Tibet's Lost Paradise*. New York: Penguin Books, 2006.

Balch, Edwin *Mount McKinley and Mountain Climbers' Proofs*, Anchorage: Alaska eBooks, 2011.

Battutah, Ibn, and Tim Mackintosh-Smith ed. *The Travels of Ibn Battutah*. London: Picador, 2003.

Beckey, Fred. *Challenge of the North Cascades*. Seattle: Mountaineers Books, 1996.

———. *Climber's Guide to the Cascade and Olympic Mountains of Washington*. New York: American Alpine Club, 1949.

Benjamin, Walter. *Reflections: Essays, Aphorisms, Autobiographical Writings*. Translated by Edmund Jephcott. Edited by Peter Demetz. New York: Schocken, 1986.

Berg, Thomas Reinertsen. *Theater of the World: The Maps that Made History*. New York: Little, Brown, 2018.

Bishop, Peter. *The Myth of Shangri-La: Tibet, Travel Writing and the Western Creation of Sacred Landscape*. Berkeley: University of California Press, 1989.

Bonnett, Alastair. *Unruly Places: Lost Spaces, Secret Cities, and Other Inscrutable Geographies*. Boston: Houghton Mifflin Harcourt, 2014.

Borges, Jorge Luis. *Collected Fictions*. Translated by Andrew Hurley. New York: Penguin Books, 1999.

Bowman, W. E. *The Ascent of Rum Doodle*. New York: Vintage Classics, 2010.

Brandt, Anthony. *The Man Who Ate His Boots: The Tragic History of the Search for the Northwest Passage*. New York: Anchor Books, 2011.

Brewer, Keagan. *Prester John: The Legend and Its Sources*. London: Routledge, 2015.

Brooke-Hitching, Edward. *The Phantom Atlas: The Greatest Myths, Lies and Blunders on Maps*. San Francisco: Chronicle Books, 2018.

Brower, David. *Let the Mountains Talk, Let the Rivers Run*. New York: HarperCollins, 1995.

Browne, Belmore. *The Conquest of Mount McKinley*. New York: G. P. Putnam's Sons, 1913.

Bryce, Robert M. *Cook & Peary: The Polar Controversy, Resolved*. Mechanicsburg, PA: Stackpole Books, 1997.

———. *The Lost Polar Notebook of Dr. Frederick A. Cook*. 2nd ed. Monrovia, MD: Openlead Books, 2018.

Burdsall, Richard Lloyd, Arthur B. Emmons, Terris Moore, and Jack Theodore Young. *Men Against the Clouds*. Rev. ed. Seattle: Mountaineers Books, 1980.

Burke, Edmund. *A Philosophical Enquiry into the Origin of Our Ideas of the Sublime and Beautiful*. Oxford: Oxford University Press, 2015.

Caesar, Ed. *The Moth and the Mountain*. New York: Simon & Schuster, 2020.

Capello, Ernesto. *Mapping Mountains*. Leiden and Boston: Koninklijke Brill NV, 2020.

Carlson, Keith Thor, ed. *A Stó:lō-Coast Salish Historical Atlas*. With an introduction by Xwelixweltel. Vancouver, BC: Douglas & McIntyre, 2006.

Carr, Nicholas. *The Shallows: What the Internet Is Doing to Our Brains*. 2nd ed. New York: W. W. Norton, 2020.

Carroll, Siobhan. *An Empire of Air and Water: Uncolonizable Space in the British Imagination, 1750–1850*. Philadelphia: University of Pennsylvania Press, 2015.

*A Chinese Bestiary: Strange Creatures from the Guideways Through Mountains and Seas*. Translated by Richard E. Strassberg. Berkeley and Los Angeles: University of California Press, 2002.

Clark, Leonard. *The Marching Wind*. New York: Funk & Wagnalls, 1954.

Coleman, Arthur P. *The Canadian Rockies: New and Old Trails*. Calgary, AB: Rocky Mountain Books, 2006.

Collins, Raymond L. *Dichinanek' Hwt'ana: A History of the People of the Upper Kuskokwim Who Live in Nikolai and Telida, Alaska*. McGrath, AK: Raymond L. Collins, 2004.

Columbus, Christopher. *Select Letters of Christopher Columbus: With Other Original Documents, Relating to His Four Voyages*. Sydney: Wentworth Press, 2019.

Cook, Frederick Albert. *My Attainment of the Pole*. New York and London: Mitchell Kennerley, 1913.

———. *To the Top of the Continent*. New York: Doubleday, Page, 1908.

Coolidge, W. A. B., author and ed. *Josias Simler et les Origines de l'Alpinisme jusqu'en 1600*. Grenoble: Imprimerie Allier Frères, 1904.

Cordes, Kelly. *The Tower: A Chronicle of Climbing and Controversy on Cerro Torre*. Ventura: Patagonia, 2014.

Culbert, Dick. *A Climber's Guide to the Coastal Ranges of British Columbia*. Canmore, AB: Alpine Club of Canada, 1965.
———. *The Coast Mountains Trilogy: Mountain Poems, 1957–1971*. Vancouver, BC: Tricouni Press, 2009.
Custer, Henry. *Report of Henry Custer, Assistance of Reconnaissance Made in 1859 over the Routes in the Cascade Mountains in the Vicinity of the 49th Parallel*. Washington, DC: BiblioGov, 2012.
d'Allais, Denis Vairasse. *The History of the Sevarites or Sevarambi*. London: Henry Brome, 1675.
Danner, Lauren. *Crown Jewel Wilderness: Creating North Cascades National Park*. Pullman: Washington State University Press, 2017.
d'Anville, Jean Baptiste Bourguignon. *A Geographical Illustration of the Map of India*. Farmington Hills, MI: Gale ECCO, Print Editions, 2010.
Daumal, René. *Mount Analogue: A Tale of Non-Euclidean and Symbolically Authentic Mountaineering Adventures*. Translated by Carol Cosman. New York: Harry N. Abrams, 2004.
Davidson, Art. *Minus 148°*. 3rd ed. Seattle: Mountaineers Books, 1999.
Debarbieux, Bernard, and Gilles Rudaz. *The Mountain: A Political History from the Enlightenment to the Present*. Translated by Jane Marie Todd. Chicago: University of Chicago Press, 2015.
de la Fosse, Eustache. *Voyage à la Côte Accidentale d'Afrique en Portugal et en Espagne, 1479–1480*. Whitefish, MT: Kessinger Publishing, 2010.
della Dora, Veronica. *Mountain: Nature and Culture*. London: Reaktion Books, 2016.
Douglas, David. *Journal Kept by David Douglas during His Travels in North America, 1823–1827*. Cambridge, UK: Cambridge University Press, 2011.
Douglas, Ed. *Himalaya: A Human History*. New York: W. W. Norton, 2021.
du Maurier, Daphne. *The Birds and Other Stories*. London: Virago Press, 2003.
Dunn, Robert. *The Shameless Diary of an Explorer*. New York: The Outing Publishing Company, 1907.
Eco, Umberto. *The Book of Legendary Lands*. New York: Rizzoli Ex Libris, 2013.
———. *Serendipities: Language and Lunacy*. Boston: Houghton Mifflin Harcourt, 1999.
Elsner, Jaś, and Joan-Pau Rubiés, eds. *Voyages and Visions: Towards a Cultural History of Travel*. London: Reaktion Books, 1999.
Ende, Michael. *The Neverending Story*. Translated by Ralph Manheim. London: Puffin Books, 1993.
Ephrem, St. *Hymns on Paradise*. Translated by Sebastian Brock. Crestwood, NY: St. Vladimir's Seminary Press, 1990.
*The Epic of Gilgamesh*. Translated by Maureen Gallery Kovacs. Stanford: Stanford University Press, 1989.
Etheria [Egeria]. *The Pilgrimage of Etheria*. Translated by M. L. McClure and C. L. Feltoe. London and New York: Macmillian, 1919.
Eucherius of Lyon, St. *Formulae*. https://ccel.org/ccel/eucherius/formulae.v.html.
Fairley, Bruce. *A Guide to Climbing & Hiking in Southwestern British Columbia*. West Vancouver, BC: Gordon Soules, 1986.
Fitzgerald, F. Scott. *The Diamond as Big as the Ritz and the Curious Case of Benjamin Button*. Orinda, CA: SeaWolf Press, 2020.
Flieger, Verlyn. *A Question of Time: J.R.R. Tolkien's Road to Faërie*. Kent, OH: The Kent State University Press, 2011.
Flint, Richard. *No Settlement, No Conquest: A History of the Coronado Entrada*. Albuquerque: University of New Mexico Press, 2013.

Flint, Richard, and Shirley Cushing Flint, eds. *Documents of the Coronado Expedition, 1539–1542: "They Were Not Familiar with His Majesty, nor Did They Wish to Be His Subjects."* Albuquerque: University of New Mexico Press, 2012.

Franchère, Gabriel. *Narrative of a Voyage to the Northwest Coast of America*. Frankfurt am Main, Germany: Outlook Verlag GmbH, 2020.

Garth, John. *Tolkien and the Great War: The Threshold of Middle-earth*. Boston: Mariner Books, 2005.

Gildea, Damien. *Mountaineering in Antarctica: Climbing in the Frozen South*. Brussels: Editions Nevicata, 2010.

Gross, Rachel. "From Buckskin to Gore-Tex: Consumption as a Path to Mastery in Twentieth Century American Wilderness Recreation," PhD Diss. Madison: University of Wisconsin, 2017.

Hansen, Peter H. *The Summits of Modern Man*. Cambridge, MA: Harvard University Press, 2013.

Hansen, Valerie. *The Year 1000: When Explorers Connected the World—and Globalization Began*. New York: Scribner, 2020.

Harley, J. B. *The New Nature of Maps: Essays in the History of Cartography*. Baltimore: Johns Hopkins University Press, 2002.

Harpending, Asbury. *The Great Diamond Hoax and Other Stirring Incidents in the Life of Asbury Harpending*. Edited by James H. Wilkins. San Francisco: James H. Barry Co., 1913.

Herron, Joseph S. *Explorations in Alaska, 1899, for an All-American Overland Route from Cook Inlet, Pacific Ocean, to the Yukon*. Washington, DC: Government Printing Office, 1901.

Hesse, Hermann. *The Journey to the East*. Translated by Hilda Rosner. New York: Bantam Books, 1972.

Higginson, Thomas Wentworth. *Tales of the Enchanted Islands of the Atlantic*. New York: Macmillan, 1898.

Hilton, James. *Lost Horizon*. New York: Harper Perennial, 1994.

Humboldt, Alexander von. *Cosmos: A Sketch of a Physical Description of the Universe*, Vol. 1. Translated by E. C. Otté. London: Henry G. Bohn, 1849.

Hunt, Harrison J., and Ruth Hunt Thompson. *North to the Horizon: Searching for Peary's Crocker Land*. Camden, ME: Down East Books, 1980.

Isserman, Maurice. *Continental Divide: A History of American Mountaineering*. New York: W. W. Norton, 2016.

Ives, Jack D., and Bruno Messerli, eds. *Mountains of the World: A Global Priority*. New York: Parthenon, 1997.

Jacoby, Sarah H. *Love and Liberation: Autobiographical Writings of the Tibetan Buddhist Visionary Sera Khandro*. New York: Columbia University Press, 2014.

Kari, James, James A. Fall, and Shem Pete. *Shem Pete's Alaska: The Territory of the Upper Cook Inlet Dena'ina*. Fairbanks: University of Alaska Press, 2016.

Kelsey, Joe. *A Place in Which to Search: Summers in the Wind Rivers*. Wilson, WY: Black Canyon Books, 2016.

Kerouac, Jack. *The Dharma Bums*. New York: Penguin Books, 1976. First published 1958.

King, Clarence. *Mountaineering in the Sierra Nevada*. Kindle Edition. London: Lume Books, 2016.

Kunstler, James Howard. *The Geography of Nowhere*. New York: Free Press, 1994.

LaChapelle, David. *Navigating the Tides of Change: Stories from Science, the Sacred, and a Wise Planet*. Gabriola Island, BC: New Society Publishers, 2001.

LaChapelle, Dolores. *Deep Powder Snow*. Durango, CO: Kivaki Press, 1993.

LaChapelle, Dolores. *Deep Powder Snow*. Durango, CO: Kivaki Press, 1993.
LaChapelle, Edward. *Field Guide to Snow Crystals*. Seattle: University of Washington Press, 1969.
———. *Secrets of the Snow: Visual Clues to Avalanche and Ski Conditions*. Seattle: University of Washington Press, 2001.
Lane, Belden C. *Landscapes of the Sacred: Geography and Narrative in American Spirituality*. Baltimore: Johns Hopkins University Press, 2001.
Lewis, C. S. *The Chronicles of Narnia*. New York: HarperCollins, 2001.
Lewis, Meriwether, and William Clark. *Journals of the Lewis & Clark Expedition*. https://lewisandclarkjournals.unl.edu/journals.
Lewis-Jones, Huw, ed. *The Writer's Map: An Atlas of Imaginary Lands*. Chicago: University of Chicago Press, 2018.
Livy. *History of Rome*. Translated by Rev. Canon Roberts. New York: E. P. Dutton, 1912.
Lucian [of Samosata]. *A True Story*. Translated by A. M. Harmon. Cambridge: Harvard University Press, 1913.
Macfarlane, Robert. *Mountains of the Mind*. New York: Pantheon Books, 2003.
Machen, Arthur. *N*. London: Snuggly Books, 2018.
MacMillan, Donald Baxter. *Four Years in the White North*. New York and London: Harper & Brothers, 1918.
Mandeville, John. *The Travels of Sir John Mandeville*. Translated by C. W. R. D. Moseley. New York: Penguin Books, 2005.
Manning, Harvey. *Backpacking: One Step at a Time*. 4th ed. New York: Vintage Books, 1986.
———. *Cry Crisis! Rehearsal in Alaska*. Berkeley: Friends of the Earth, 1974.
———, ed. *Mountaineering: The Freedom of the Hills*. Seattle: The Mountaineers, 1960.
———. *Walking the Beach to Bellingham*. Corvallis: Oregon State University Press, 2002.
———. *The Wild Cascades: Forgotten Parkland*. San Francisco: Sierra Club, 1965.
———. *Wilderness Alps: Conservation and Conflict in Washington's North Cascades*. Bellingham, WA: Northwest Wild Books, 2007.
Manning, Harvey, Tom Miller, and Dee Molenaar. *The North Cascades*. Seattle: Mountaineers Books, 1964.
Manning, Harvey, Bob Spring, and Ira Spring. *Cool Clear Water: The Key to Our Environment*. Seattle: A Salisbury Press Book, 1970.
———. *High Worlds of the Mountain Climber*. Seattle: Superior Publishing Co., 1959.
Manning, Harvey, and Ira Spring. *Best Winter Walks & Hikes: Puget Sound*. 2nd ed. Seattle: Mountaineers Books, 2002.
———. *100 Classic Hikes in Washington*. Rev. and updated ed. Seattle: Mountaineers Books, 2013.
Mencken, H. L. *The Bathtub Hoax, and Other Blasts and Bravos from the "Chicago Tribune"*. London: Octagon Books, 1976.
Merton, Thomas. *Mystics and Zen Masters*. New York: Farrar, Straus and Giroux, 1999.
Merzbacher, Gottfried. *An Expedition into the Central Tian-Shan Mountains*. South Yarra, Australia: Leopold Classic Library, 2016.
Morris, Jan. *Coronation Everest*. London: Faber & Faber, 2003.
Muir, John. *The Mountains of California*. San Francisco: Sierra Club Books, 1989.
———. *Our National Parks*. Layton, UT: Gibbs Smith, 2018.
Munday, Don. *The Unknown Mountain*. London: Hodder & Stoughton, 1948.
Nash, Roderick Frazier. *Wilderness and the American Mind*. 4th ed. New Haven: Yale University Press, 2001.
Neale, Jonathan. *Tigers of the Snow*. London: Time Warner Books, 2003.

Norgay, Tenzing, and James Ramsey Ullman. *Tiger of the Snows: The Autobiography of Tenzing of Everest*. New York: G. P. Putnam's Sons, 1955.

Ortenburger, Leigh N., and Reynold G. Jackson. *A Climber's Guide to the Teton Range*. 3rd ed. Seattle: Mountaineers Books, 1996.

Papanikolas, Zeese. *American Silence*. Lincoln: University of Nebraska Press, 2007.

Peary, Robert E. *Nearest the Pole*. London: Hutchinson, 1907.

———. *Northward over the Great Ice*. Cambridge, UK: Cambridge University Press, 2012.

Peattie, Roderick. *Mountain Geography: A Critique and Field Study*. Cambridge, MA: Harvard University Press, 1936.

Perrin, Jim. *Shipton & Tilman: The Great Decade of Himalayan Exploration*. London: Hutchinson, 2013.

Phillips, Richard. *Mapping Men and Empire: A Geography of Adventure*. New York: Routledge, 1996.

Pirrit, John. *Across West Antarctica*. Glasgow: John Smith & Son, 1967.

Plato. *Dialogues of Plato*. Translated by Benjamin Jowett. New York: Simon & Schuster, 2010.

Pliny the Elder. *Natural History*. Translated by H. Rackham. Cambridge, MA: Harvard University Press, 1942.

Polo, Marco. *The Book of Ser Marco Polo: The Venetian*. Vol. 1. Edited and translated by Henry Yule. Cambridge: Cambridge University Press, 2012.

Post, Austin. *Pyramid Mountain: My Forest Service Days*. Self-published (posthumous), 2018. Kindle.

Post, Austin, and Edward LaChapelle. *Glacier Ice*. Rev. ed. Seattle: University of Washington Press, 2000.

Price, Martin F. *Mountains: A Very Short Introduction*. Oxford: Oxford University Press, 2015.

Ptolemy. *Geography*. Translated by Edward Luther Stevenson. New York: New York Public Library, 1932.

Qazwīnī, Hamd Allāh al-Mustawfī al-. *The Geographical Part of Nuzhat al-Qulūb*. Translated by Guy Le Strange. Leyden: E. J. Brill; London: Luzac, 1915.

Ramsay, Raymond H. *No Longer on the Map*. New York: Viking, 1972.

Raspe, Rudolph Erich. *The Surprising Adventures of Baron Munchausen*. Chapel Hill, NC: Project Gutenberg, 2006.

Riffenburgh, Beau. *The Myth of the Explorer: The Press, Sensationalism, and Geographical Discovery*. New York: Oxford University Press, 1994.

Robb, Graham. *The Discovery of France: A Historical Geography*. New York: W. W. Norton, 2008.

Robbins, Royal. *Fail Falling*. Vol. 2 of My Life: Royal Robbins. Giraffe PR, 2010.

Roberts, David. *Great Exploration Hoaxes*. San Francisco: Sierra Club Books, 1982.

———. *Limits of the Known*. New York: W.W. Norton, 2018.

———. *"The Mountain of My Fear" and "Deborah": Two Mountaineering Classics*. Seattle: Mountaineers Books, 2012.

———. *On the Ridge Between Life and Death: A Climbing Life Reexamined*. New York: Simon & Schuster, 2005.

Robinson, Tim. *Setting Foot on the Shores of Connemara and Other Writings*. Dublin: The Lilliput Press, 1996.

Rock, Joseph. *Seeking the Mountains of Mystery: An Expedition on the China-Tibet Frontier to the Unexplored Amnyi Machen Range*. Whitefish, MT: Literary Licensing, 2011.

Roosevelt, Kermit, and Theodore Roosevelt. *Trailing the Giant Panda*. Birmingham, AL: Palladium Press, 2000.

Rosen, Ruth. *The World Split Open: How the Modern Women's Movement Changed America*. Rev. and updated ed. New York: Penguin Books, 2006.
Ross, Sir John. *A Voyage of Discovery*. London: John Murray, 1819.
Rost, E.C. *Mount McKinley, Its Bearing on the Polar Controversy*. Sheridan, WY: Franklin Classics, 2018.
Safier, Neil. *Measuring the New World: Enlightenment Science and South America*. Chicago: University of Chicago Press, 2012.
Scafi, Alessandro. *Mapping Paradise: A History of Heaven on Earth*. Chicago: University of Chicago Press, 2006.
Schaumann, Caroline. *Peak Pursuits: The Emergence of Mountaineering in the Nineteenth Century*. New Haven: Yale University Press, 2020.
Scurlock, John. *Snow and Spire: Flights to Winter in the North Cascade Range*. New Castle, CO: Wolverine Publishing, 2011.
Seguin, Margaret, ed. *The Tsimshian: Images of the Past, Views for the Present*. Vancouver: University of British Columbia Press, 1993.
Selters, Andy. *Ways to the Sky: A Historical Guide to North American Mountaineering*. Golden, CO: American Alpine Club, 2004.
Shelley, Mary. *Frankenstein*. Mineola, NY: Dover Publications, 1994.
Shepherd, Nan. *The Living Mountain*. Edinburgh: Canongate Books, 2011.
Shippey, Tom. *The Road to Middle-Earth: How J.R.R. Tolkien Created a New Mythology*. Boston: Mariner Books, Houghton Mifflin Harcourt, 2003.
Shipton, Eric. *The Six Mountain-Travel Books*. Seattle: Mountaineers Books, 1985.
———. *That Untravelled World*. Seattle: Mountaineers Books, 2015.
Shor, Thomas K. *A Step Away from Paradise: The True Story of a Tibetan Lama's Journey to a Land of Immortality*. City Lion Press, 2017.
Snow, Chief John. *These Mountains Are Our Sacred Places*. Markham, ON: Fifth House Publishers, 2005.
Sobel, Dava. *Longitude: The True Story of a Lone Genius Who Solved the Greatest Scientific Problem of His Time*. New York: Walker, 1995.
Solnit, Rebecca. *A Field Guide to Getting Lost*. New York: Viking, 2005.
Spence, Mark David. *Dispossessing the Wilderness*. New York: Oxford University Press, 2000.
Spufford, Francis. *I May Be Some Time: Ice and the English Imagination*. New York: Picador, 1999.
Spurr, Stephen J. *In Search of the Kuskokwim: The Life and Times of J. Edward Spurr.* Fairbanks, Alaska: Epicenter Press, 2018.
Stephen, Leslie. *The Playground of Europe*. Cambridge, UK: Cambridge University Press, 2013.
Stewart, Mary. *Wildfire at Midnight*. Chicago: Chicago Review Press, 2012.
Strabo. *Geography*. Translated by H. C. Hamilton and W. Falconer. London: George Bell & Sons, 1892.
Stuck, Hudson. *The Ascent of Denali: First Complete Ascent of Mt. McKinley, Highest Peak in North America. Containing the Original Diary of Walter Harper, First Man to Achieve Denali's True Summit.* Seattle: Mountaineers Books, 1977.
Sullivan, Walter. *Assault on the Unknown: The International Geophysical Year*. New York: McGraw-Hill, 1961.
Tallack, Malachy. *The Un-Discovered Islands: An Archipelago of Myths and Mysteries, Phantoms and Fakes*. New York: Picador, 2017.
Taylor, Joseph E., III. *Pilgrims of the Vertical: Yosemite Rock Climbers and Nature at Risk*. Cambridge, MA: Harvard University Press, 2010.
Thomson, Hugh. *Nanda Devi: A Journey to the Last Sanctuary*. Gurugram, Haryana: Hachette India, 2017.

Thoreau, Henry David. *The Journal of Henry David Thoreau*. https://www.walden.org/collection/journals/.
———. *Walden*. Chapel Hill, NC: Project Gutenberg, 1995.
Thorington, James Monroe. *The Glittering Mountains of Canada*. Philadelphia: John W. Lea, 1925.
Thrush, Coll. *Native Seattle: Histories from the Crossing-Over Place*. 2nd ed. Seattle: University of Washington Press, 2017.
Tilman, H. W. *The Ascent of Nanda Devi*. London: Lodestar Books, 2015.
Tolkien, J. R. R. *The Letters of J.R.R Tolkien*. Boston: Mariner Books, 2000.
———. *The Lord of the Rings* trilogy. With an introduction by Peter S. Beagle. New York: Ballantine Books, 1973.
Tuan, Yi-Fu. *Topophilia: A Study of Environmental Perception, Attitudes, and Values*. Morningside Edition. New York: Columbia University Press, 1990.
Turner, Jack. *Teewinot: Climbing and Contemplating the Teton Range*. New York: St. Martin's Griffin, 2001.
Vancouver, George. *A Voyage of Discovery to the North Pacific Ocean, and Round the World*. London: G. G. and J. Robinson, Paternoster-Row, and J. Edwards, Pall-Mall, 1798.
Walls, Laura Dassow. *Seeing New Worlds: Henry David Thoreau and Nineteenth-Century Natural Science*. Madison: University of Wisconsin Press, 1995.
Washburn, Bradford, and Lew Freedman. *Bradford Washburn, An Extraordinary Life: The Autobiography of a Mountaineering Icon*. Portland, OR: WestWinds Press, 2005.
Waterman, Jon. *Chasing Denali: The Sourdoughs, Cheechakos, and Frauds behind the Most Unbelievable Feat in Mountaineering*. Guilford, CT: Lyons Press, 2018.
Waterman, Laura, Guy Waterman, and Michael Wejchert. *Yankee Rock & Ice: A History of Climbing in the Northeastern United States*. Mechanicsburg, PA: Stackpole Books, 2018.
Welky, David. *A Wretched and Precarious Situation*. New York: W. W. Norton, 2017.
Wilford, John Noble. *The Mapmakers*. Rev. ed. New York: Vintage Books, 2001.
Winthrop, John. *The Journal of John Winthrop, 1630–1649*. Edited by James Savage, Richard S. Dunn, and Laetitia Yeandle. Cambridge, MA: Belknap Press, 1996.
Woodard, Bruce A. *Diamonds in the Salt: The First Authentic Account of the Sensational Diamond Hoax Chicanery*. Boulder, CO: Pruett Press, 1967.
Woodhouse, Philip R. *Monte Cristo*. Seattle: Mountaineers Books, 1979.
Young, Geoffrey Winthrop. *On High Hills: Memories of the Alps*. 5th ed. London: Methuen, 1947.
Young, Kevin. *Bunk: The Rise of Hoaxes, Humbug, Plagiarists, Phonies, Post-Facts, and Fake News*. Minneapolis: Graywolf Press, 2017.

## ARTICLES, CHAPTERS, PRESENTATIONS

Aiken, Joan. "Wolves and Alternate Worlds." *Locus Magazine*, May 1998.
Auld, Jerry. "Hooker & Brown: The Shrinking Peaks." *Alpinist* 54, Summer 2016.
Ax, Anders. "Mountains of Kong: The Vanishing Range." *Alpinist* 54, Summer 2016.
Baindur, Meera. "Meru: The Axis of the World." *Alpinist* 54, Summer 2016.
Barbarisi, Daniel. "The Man Who Found Forrest Fenn's Treasure." *Outside* online, December 7, 2020. https://www.outsideonline.com/2419429/forrest-fenn-treasure-jack-stuef.
Bassett, Thomas J., and Philip W. Porter. "'From the Best Authorities': The Mountains of Kong in the Cartography of West Africa." *Journal of African History* 32, no. 3 (1991): 367–413.

Beattie, Judith Hudson. "Indian Maps in the Hudson's Bay Company Archives: A Comparison of Five Area Maps Recorded by Peter Fidler, 1801–1802." *Archivaria* 21 (Winter 1985–1986): 166–175.

Beck, Ted and Pat Goldsworthy, "The Elderly Birdwatchers Hiking and Griping Society," *The Wild Cascades,* Winter 2006–2007.

Bliss, Laura. "MapLab: The Power of Counter-Maps." *Bloomberg CityLab*, December 4, 2019. https://www.bloomberg.com/news/articles/2019-12-04/maplab-the-power-of-counter-maps.

Brower, David. "How to Kill a Wilderness." *Sierra Club Bulletin*, August 1945.

Bryce, Robert M. "The Strange Saga of Sourdoughs: Alaskan Mushers' Myths, Legends, & Lies?" *DIO: The International Journal of Scientific History* 23 (2020).

Cajori, Florian. "History of Determinations of the Heights of Mountains." *Isis*. Vol 12. No. 3 (December 1929).

Caldbick, John. "Manning, Harvey (1925–2006)." HistoryLink.org. June 26, 2010.

Champlin, Charles. "Magnificent Rescue on McKinley." *Life* (June 6, 1960).

Chen, Shiwei. "The Making of a Dream: The Sino-American Expedition to Mount Amne Machin in 1948." *Modern Asian Studies* 37, no. 3 (July 2003): 709–735.

Collie, J. Norman. "The Canadian Rocky Mountains a Quarter Century Ago." *Canadian Alpine Journal* 14 (1924).

———. "Exploration in the Canadian Rockies: A Search for Mount Hooker and Mount Brown." *The Geographical Journal* 13, no. 4 (April 1899): 337–355.

Culbert, Dick. "Freight Christmas." *The Canadian Mountaineering Anthology*. Bruce Fairley and Roland Lines, eds. Vancouver, BC: Lone Pine Publishing, 1994.

DeMaria, Alvin. "Middle Triple Peak." *American Alpine Journal*, 1973.

DeMaria, Alvin, and Peter Geiser. "Ascents in the Cathedral Spires." *American Alpine Journal*, 1966.

Dhar, Amrita. "Travel and Mountains." *The Cambridge History of Travel Writing*, Nandini Das and Tim Youngs, eds. (Cambridge, UK: Cambridge University Press, 2019).

Dillon, Brian. "An Interview with Tim Robinson." *Field Day Review* 3, 2007.

Edwards, John. "Harvey Manning Statue Dedication." *The Wild Cascades*, Summer/Fall 2009.

Evans, Timothy H. "The Bowling Green Massacre." *Journal of American Folklore* 131, no. 522 (Fall 2018): 460–470.

Falkeid, Unn. "Petrarch, Mont Ventoux and the Modern Self." *Forum Italicum*. Vol. 43. No. 1 (2009).

Fenn, Forrest. Foreword to *Armchair Treasure Hunts: The Quests for Hidden Treasures*, by Jenny Kile. Self-published, CreateSpace Independent Publishing Platform, 2018.

Garrett, Frances. "Kangchenjunga & Beyul: Hidden Paradises of the Himalaya." *Alpinist* 54, Summer 2016.

Gildea, Damien. "Citadel of Seekers: Sentinel Range, Antarctica." *Alpinist* 44, Autumn 2013.

———. "An 8,000-Meter Mess." *American Alpine Journal*, 2020.

———. "Tool Users: GPS." *Alpinist* 69, Spring 2020.

Graber, Mike. "Eighteen Years after the Riesenstein Hoax: A History of the Cathedral Spires." *Ascent*, 1980.

Gran, Art. "The East Face of Mount Chephren." *American Alpine Journal,* 1966.

Hansen, Eric. "The High Priestess of Posterity." *Outside* online, March 9, 2011. https://www.outsideonline.com/1825881/high-priestess-posterity.

Harris, Rollin A. "Some Indications of Land in the Vicinity of the North Pole." *National Geographic*, June 1904.

Hessler, John. "Mount Qāf: The Home of the Clouds." *Alpinist* 54, Summer 2016.

———. "Verticality: A Short History of the Other Blank on a Map." *Alpinist* 41, Winter 2012–2013.

Hubley, Richard. "Glacier Studies during the International Geophysical Year, 1957–58." *American Alpine Journal*, 1957.

Ijames, Curtis. "The *First* Ascent of Bonanza Peak." *Mazama*, December 1937.

Jenkins, Mark. "'Hero of the Earth,' in Brief." *Backpacker*, August 1996.

Jurgalski, Eberhard. "True Summits or Tolerance Zones?" With accompanying reports by Rodolphe Popier and Tobias Pantel. 8000ers.com, July 31, 2019. http://www.8000ers.com/cms/en/news-mainmenu-176/1-latest/348-true-summits-or-tolerance-zones.html.

Kapadia, Harish. "Asia, India, Eastern Garhwal, Nanda Devi, Ascent and Environmental Clean Up." *American Alpine Journal*, 2002.

———. "Pemako: Cartography of Prayers." *Alpinist* 54, Summer 2016.

"Know Your Mountains." *Summit*, June 1962.

Laba, Roman A. "Northeast Ridge of Huayna Potosí." *American Alpine Journal*, 1970.

LaChapelle, David. "There Was Always the Mountain: The Passing of Edward LaChapelle." *Avalanche Review* 25, no. 4 (April 2007): 18–19.

Layton, Mike. "Tamed by the Beast." *Northwest Mountaineering Journal*, no. 3 (2006).

Lin, Allen Yilun, Kate Kuehl, Johannes Schöning, and Brent Hecht. "Understanding 'Death by GPS': A Systematic Study of Catastrophic Incidents Associated with Personal Navigation Technologies." In *CHI 2017: Proceedings of the 2017 ACM SIGCHI Conference on Human Factors in Computing Systems*, 1154–1166. New York: Association for Computing Machinery, 2017.

Long, Jeff. "The Glass Mountain: A Fable." *Alpinist* 54, Summer 2016.

Manning, Harvey. "Solvitur Ambulando: It is Solved by Walking." The Mountaineer, vol. 82, no. 12 (1988).

———. "A Proposed Issaquah Alps National Urban Recreation Area." *The Mountaineer* vol. 76, no. 7 (1982).

———."Preserving Our Walking Trails," *The Wild Cascades* (Summer–Fall 2002).

———. "Things to Climb When Mountains Aren't Worth It." *The Mountaineer*, vol. 53, no. 4 (1960): 22–32.

———. "Wilderness Lite." *The Wild Cascades*. (Spring 2003).

Manning, H. Hawthorne [Harvey Manning]. "By the Numbers." *The Mountaineer*, vol. 57, no. 4 (1964): 117–122.

———. "Sleeping System Rather Than Sleeping Bag?" *Summit*, July 1959.

Manning, Paul. "In Memoriam: Betty Manning." *The Wild Cascades*, Fall 2015.

Mason, Robert W. "North America, United States, Alaska, First Ascents in the Romanzof Mountains, Eastern Brooks Range." *American Alpine Journal*, 1959.

McBrian, Forest. "Mountain Profile: The Picket Range," *Alpinist* 47, Summer 2014.

McCarthy, Jim. "The Last Mountain Men and the Last Frontier." *Summit*, November–December 1971.

"Memories of Ed." Karl Birkeland, Bob Ferguson, Bill Glude, Rick Grubin, Rich Marriott, Mark Moore, Rod Newcomb, Jerry Roberts, Bruce Tremper, and Knox Williams. *Avalanche Review* 25, no. 4 (April 2007): 24–27.

Mengüç, Murat Cem. "Why We Still Need Thomas More's 'Utopia' in 2016." *Hyperallergic*, December 23, 2016. https://hyperallergic.com/347275/why-we-still-need-thomas-mores-utopia-in-2016.

Mercator, Gerardus, and E. G. R. Taylor. "A Letter Dated 1577 from Mercator to John Dee." *Imago Mundo* 13, no. 1 (1956): 56–68.

Molenaar, Dee. "Letter Questions Location of 'No Name' Peak." *Summit*, June 1960.

Nakamura, Tamotsu. "Alpine Paradise—Western Sichuan Highlands 2010." *Japanese Alpine News* Vol. 12 (2011).
Necefer, Len. "Children of the Mountains." *Alpinist* 64, Winter 2018–2019.
no one [sic]. "Book Review: And Not to Yield." *Vulgarian Digest* (Autumn 1970).
Odier, Hubert, and Sylvain Jouty. "Mount Analogue: On the Other Side of the Door." *Alpinist* 54, Summer 2016.
Peary, Robert E. "Address of the President of the Congress." In *Report of the Eighth International Geographic Congress, Held in the United States, 1904*, 76–82. Washington, DC: Government Printing Office, 1905. https://archive.org/stream/reporteighthint00unkngoog/reporteighthint00unkngoog_djvu.txt.
Peluso, Nancy Lee. "Whose Woods Are These? Counter-mapping Forest Territories in Kalimantan, Indonesia." *Antipode* 27, no. 4 (1995): 383–406.
Petrarch, Francesco. "The Ascent of Mount Ventoux." In *Petrarch: The First Modern Scholar and Man of Letters*. Translated by James Harvey Robinson. New York: G. P. Putnam's Sons, 1898.
Popier, Rodolphe. "La Preuve en Alpinisme: Les Enjeux de la Validation dans une Pratique Non Instituée." Conference presentation at Université Savoie Mont Blanc, Chambéry, France, May 9, 2019.
Post, Austin. "Annual Aerial Photography of Glaciers in Northwest North America: How It All Began and Its Golden Age." *Physical Geography* Vol. 16 (1995).
Potterfield, Peter. "The Warrior Writer." *Backpacker*, August 1996.
Prior, Daniel G. "Travels of Mount Qāf: From Legend to 42° 0'N 79° 51'E," *Oriente Moderno Nuova Serie*, Anno 89, no. 2, *Studies on Islamic Legends*, 2009.
Rassler, Brad. "The Beckey Effect." *Alpinist* 61, Spring 2018.
Reidy, Michael. "Cosmic Emotion." *Alpinist* 39, Summer 2012.
"Rem Koolhaas: Junkspace." *Icon* (March 6, 2014).
"Remembering Harvey Manning 1925–2006," Ken Wilcox, Rick McGuire, Karl Forsgaard, Dale Cole, Brock Evans, Carolyn McConnell, Tom Miller, Tom Hammond and others. *The Wild Cascades*, Winter 2006–2007.
"Reviews and Notices: To the Top of the Continent." *Alpine Journal*, 1909.
Robbins, Royal. "Californians in Alaska." *American Alpine Journal*, 1970.
Roberts, David. "The Black Heart of That Monster." *Ascent*, 2016.
———. "Cathedral Spires." *American Alpine Journal*, 1971.
———. "Challenges in the Cathedral Spires." *Summit*, June 1968.
———. "First Ascents in the Revelation Mountains." *American Alpine Journal* 1968.
Roberts, David, and Richard C. Millikan. "Kichatna Spire." *American Alpine Journal*, 1967.
Roberts, Michael. "The Poetry and Humor of Mountaineering." *Alpine Journal*, 1940.
Robinson, Doug. "The Palisades: Wringing Light out of Stone." *Alpinist* 48, Autumn–Winter 2014.
Robinson, Zac, and Stephen Slemon. "Deception in High Places: The Making and Unmaking of Mounts Brown and Hooker." In *Sustaining the West: Cultural Responses to Canadian Environments*, edited by Liza Piper and Lisa Szabo-Jones. Waterloo, ON: Wilfrid Laurier University Press, 2015.
———. "The Shining Mountains." *Alpinist* 50, Summer 2015.
Roper, John. "Raven Ridge via 'Eacas Glacier.'" Rhinoclimbs.com, 2005. http://www.rhinoclimbs.com/usgsmartinpeak.htm.
Rowell, Galen. "On and Around Anyemaqen." *American Alpine Journal*, 1982.
Rusk, Claude E. "On the Trail of Dr. Cook, Part III." *Pacific Monthly*, January 1911.
Sacks, Samantha. "The Revision of History." *Alpinist* 14, Winter 2005–2006.
Schaumann, Caroline. "Tool Users: Barometer." *Alpinist* 71 (Autumn 2020).

Scheid, Claire S. "Hidden Land and Changing Landscape: Narratives about Mount Khangchendzonga among the Lepcha and the Lhopo." *Journal of the Irish Society for the Academic Study of Religions*. Vo1. 1 (2014).
Schunk, George. "Cathedral Spires Ascents." *American Alpine Journal*, 1981.
Scurlock, John. "Austin Post." *Northwest Mountaineering Journal*, no. 4 (2007).
Sims, Ken and Cole Messa. "Jim Bridger: Yellowstone's Spinner of Tall Tales," USGS.gov. June 15, 2020.
Skoog, Lowell. "Burglars in a Crystal Fortress." In *Snow and Spire: Flights to Winter in the North Cascade Range*, by John Scurlock. New Castle, CO: Wolverine Publishing, 2011.
Smith, Barry, and David M. Mark. "Do Mountains Exist?" *Environment and Planning B* 30, no. 3 (2003): 411–427.
Soule, Gardner. "Scientists Probe Glaciers for Tomorrow's Weather." *Popular Science*, November 1953.
Spurr, Josiah Edward. "A Reconnaissance from Resurrection Bay to the Tanana River, Alaska, in 1898." *Annual Reports of the Department of the Interior for the Fiscal Year Ended June 30, 1899*. Washington, DC: Government Printing Office, 1900.
Spurr, Josiah Edward, and W. S. Post. "Report of the Kuskokwim Expedition." In *Maps and Descriptions of Routes of Exploration in Alaska in 1898*. Washington, DC: United States Geological Survey, 1899.
Suhl, Claude. "Claude Suhl on Vulgarians." The Vulgarian Chronicles. http://www.vulgarianchronicles.net/vulgarianchronicles.net/Claude_on_Vulgarians.html.
Takeda, Pete. "Into the Sanctuary: Nanda Devi Mountain Profile, Part I." *Alpinist* 62, Summer 2018.
———. "The Beleagured Sanctuary: Nanda Devi Mountain Profile, Part II." *Alpinist* 63, Autumn 2018.
Tens, Isaac. "The Career of a Medicine-Man, according to Isaac Tens, a Gitksan." In *Medicine Men on the North Pacific Coast*, by Marius Barbeau. Ottawa, ON: Dept. of Northern Affairs and National Resources, 1958.
Tejada-Flores, Lito. "The Guidebook Problem." *Ascent*, 1974.
Thorington, J. Monroe. "The Centenary of David Douglas' Ascent of Mount Brown." *Canadian Alpine Journal*, 16 (1928).
Tolkien, J. R. R. "On Faërie Stories." In *The Tolkien Reader*. New York: Ballantine, 1966.
Town, John. "Amne Machin: A Closer Look." *Alpine Journal*, 1988.
Van Duzer, Chet. "The Mythic Geography of the Northern Polar Regions: Inventio Fortunata and Buddhist Cosmology." *Culturas Populares*. Revista Electrónica 2 (2006).
Warth, John. "Do the North Cascades Really Exist?" *The Wild Cascades*, May 1961.
Washburn, Bradford and H. Adams Carter and Ann Carter. "Doctor Cook and Mount McKinley." *American Alpine Journal*, 1958.
Wilkinson, Freddie. "How do you measure Everest? It's complicated by frostbite—and politics." NationalGeographic.com. September 28, 2020.
Williams, Paul [pseud.]. "An Unclimbed No Name Peak." *Summit*, May 1960.
Woodsworth, Glenn. "Glimpses of Different Worlds." *Lived Experience* 15, (2015).
Wright, Paula. "The Art of the Topo." *Alpinist* 68, Winter 2019–2020.
———. "Jeff Long: The Story Behind 'The Glass Mountain.'" Alpinist.com, January 27, 2017. http://www.alpinist.com/doc/web16f/wfeature-jeff-long-the-story-behind-the-glass-mountain.
Yongdan, Lobsang. "Tibet Charts the World: The Btsan po No mon han's *Detailed Description of the World*, an Early Major Scientific Work in Tibet." In *Mapping the Modern in Tibet*, edited by Gray Tuttle, 73–134. Halle (Saale), Germany: IITBS, 2011.
"Your Letters." *Summit*, August, October, and November 1959.

## ARCHIVAL SOURCES

Letters, diaries, and other unpublished manuscripts come from the University of Washington Libraries Special Collections, The Mountaineers Archives, the Post family collection, the Manning family collection, the Joan Jensen collection, the Henry S. Hall Jr. American Alpine Club Library archives, the Joe Kelsey collection, the David Roberts collection, the North Cascades Conservation Council online archives, and the Byrd Polar Climate Research Archival Program at the Ohio State University Libraries.

Cook, Frederick A. "Incorporate into Chapter 2, etc." in "Hell is a Cold Place," Frederick A. Cook Society Records, Including Papers of Dr. Frederick Albert Cook, SPEC. PA.56.0017, Box 9 Folder 38, Byrd Polar and Climate Research Center Archival Program, The Ohio State University Libraries.

Manning, Harvey. "Mount Everest and Me"; "The Making of a Mountain Bum"; "Gods, Devils, and Wilderness Pedestrians"; "On the Trail of the Milky Way"; "This Petty Place"; "Summary of the Mount Hornblower Hearings"; "The Fellow Whose Screen Went Blank"; and other unpublished manuscripts. North Cascades Conservation Council online archives, courtesy of the Manning family. http://www.northcascades.org/wordpress/in-memoriam/about-2.

Post, Austin. "An Autobiographical Sketch of a Career Devoted to Glaciology"; "Reminiscences of My Youth on a Chelan Apple Ranch"; "The Dutch Miller's Cabin"; "Navy Experiences"; "Social Life"; and other unpublished stories and memoirs, courtesy of the Post family.

## FILM

Devine, Bonnie. *Bonnie Devine's Woodlands*. Art Gallery of Ontario, December 11, 2015. https://www.youtube.com/watch?v=dbNbRh04fuQ.

## WEB EXHIBIT

*Frederick A. Cook: A Digital Exhibition.* The Ohio State University Libraries. http://www.library.osu.edu/site/frederickcook.